THE CENTURY BIBLE

General Editors

† H. H. ROWLEY

M.A., B.LITT., D.D., LL.D., F.B.A. (Old Testament)

MATTHEW BLACK

D.D., D.LITT., F.B.A. (New Testament)

Job

THE CENTURY BIBLE

NEW SERIES

(Based on the Revised Standard Version)

JOB

Edited by

H. H. ROWLEY

Late Professor Emeritus, Manchester University

NELSON

THOMAS NELSON AND SONS LTD
36 Park Street W1
P.O. Box 2187 Accra
P.O. Box 336 Apapa Lagos
P.O. Box 25012 Nairobi
P.O. Box 21149 Dar es Salaam
77 Coffee Street San Fernando Trinidad

THOMAS NELSON (AUSTRALIA) LTD
597 Little Collins Street Melbourne 3000

THOMAS NELSON & SONS (SOUTH AFRICA) (PROPRIETARY) LTD
P.O. Box 9881 Johannesburg

THOMAS NELSON AND SONS (CANADA) LTD
81 Curlew Drive Don Mills Ontario

© Thomas Nelson & Sons Ltd 1970

First published 1970

17 123131 7

Printed in Great Britain by
Hazell Watson & Viney Ltd, Aylesbury, Bucks

CONTENTS

ABBREVIATIONS

BIBLICAL

OLD TESTAMENT (*OT*)

Gen.	Jg.	1 Chr.	Ps.	Lam.	Ob.	Hag.
Exod.	Ru.	2 Chr.	Prov.	Ezek.	Jon.	Zech.
Lev.	1 Sam.	Ezr.	Ec.	Dan.	Mic.	Mal.
Num.	2 Sam.	Neh.	Ca.	Hos.	Nah.	
Dt.	1 Kg.	Est.	Isa.	Jl	Hab.	
Jos.	2 Kg.	Job	Jer.	Am.	Zeph.	

APOCRYPHA (*Apoc.*)

1 Esd.	Tob.	Ad. Est.	Sir.	S. 3 Ch.	Bel	1 Mac.
2 Esd.	Jdt.	Wis.	Bar.	Sus.	Man.	2 Mac.
		Ep. Jer.				

NEW TESTAMENT (*NT*)

Mt.	Ac.	Gal.	1 Th.	Tit.	1 Pet.	3 Jn
Mk	Rom.	Eph.	2 Th.	Phm.	2 Pet.	Jude
Lk.	1 C.	Phil.	1 Tim.	Heb.	1 Jn	Rev.
Jn	2 C.	Col.	2 Tim.	Jas	2 Jn	

VERSIONS, ETC.

Akk.	Akkadian
AV	Authorized Version
Aq.	Aquila
EVV	English Versions
LXX	Septuagint (LXX^B=Codex Vaticanus)
M.T.	Massoretic Text
RSV	Revised Standard Version

RV	Revised Version
Sam.	Samaritan
Sym.	Symmachus
Syr.	Syriac (Peshitta)
Targ.	Targum
Vulg.	Vulgate
Ḳr	Ḳᵉri
Kt	Kᵉt̲ib
Theod.	Theodotion

GENERAL

AfO	*Archiv für Orientforschung*
AJSL	*American Journal of Semitic Languages and Literatures*
ALUOS	*Annual of the Leeds University Oriental Society*
ANET	*Ancient Near Eastern Texts relating to the Old Testament*, ed. by J.B. Pritchard, 2nd ed., 1955
ARW	*Archiv für Religonswissenschaft*
ASTI	*Annual of the Swedish Theological Institute*
AThR	*Anglican Theological Review*
BA	*Biblical Archaeologist*
BASOR	*Bulletin of the American Schools of Oriental Research*
BDB	F. Brown, S.R. Driver, C.A. Briggs, *A Hebrew and English Lexicon of the Old Testament*, 1907
BZ	*Biblische Zeitschrift*
BZAW	Beihefte zur *Zeitschrift für die alttestamentliche Wissenschaft*
CBQ	*Catholic Biblical Quarterly*
DB	J. Hastings (ed.), *Dictionary of the Bible*, 5 vols., 1898–1904 (also, where indicated, one volume ed., 1909; revised ed., ed. by F.C. Grant and H.H. Rowley, 1963)
DThC	A. Vacant, E. Mangenot, and E. Amann (ed.), *Dictionnaire de Théologie Catholique*, 15 vols., 1899–1950
EB	T.K. Cheyne and J.S. Black (eds.), *Encyclopaedia Biblica*, 4 vols., 1899–1903
ET	*Expository Times*
EThL	*Ephemerides Theologicae Lovanienses*
Exp	*Expositor*
GB	Gesenius-Buhl, *Hebräisches and Aramäisches Handwörterbuch über das Alte Testament*, 17th ed., 1921

GGA	Göttingische gelehrte Anzeigen
GK	Gesenius-Kautzsch, *Hebrew Grammar*, Eng. Trans. by A.E. Cowley, 1910
GSAI	Giornale della Società Asiatica Italiana
HN	Pliny, *Historia Naturalis*
HSAT	Die Heilige Schrift des Alten Testaments, ed. by E. Kautzsch and A. Bertholet, 4th ed., 2 vols., 1922–23
HTR	Harvard Theological Review
HUCA	Hebrew Union College Annual
IB	Interpreter's Bible, vol. III, 1954
JAOS	Journal of the American Oriental Society
JBL	Journal of Biblical Literature
JDTh	Jahrbücher für deutsche Theologie
JJS	Journal of Jewish Studies
JMEOS	Journal of the Manchester University Egyptian and Oriental Society
JPTh	Jahrbücher für protestantische Theologie
JPh	Journal of Philosophy
JPOS	Journal of the Palestine Oriental Society
JQR	Jewish Quarterly Review
JR	Journal of Religion
JSS	Journal of Semitic Studies
JTS	Journal of Theological Studies
KB	Koehler-Baumgartner, *Lexicon in Veteris Testamenti Libros,* 1953
LOT	S.R. Driver, *Introduction to the Literature of the Old Testament*, 9th ed., 1913
MFO	Mélanges de la Faculté Orientale de l'Université St Joseph de Beyrouth
NTT	Norsk Teologisk Tidsskrift
OTMS	The Old Testament and Modern Study, ed. by H.H. Rowley, 1951
OTS	Oudtestamentische Studiën
PEFQS	Quarterly Statement of the Palestine Exploration Fund
PEQ	Palestine Exploration Quarterly
PRE	Herzog-Hauck, *Realencyklopädie für protestantische Theologie und Kirche*, 3rd ed., 24 vols., 1896–1913
RB	Revue Biblique
RHR	Revue de l'Histoire des Religions
RQ	Revue de Qumran
RR	Review of Religion
RThPh	Revue de Théologie et de Philosophie

SDB	*Supplément au Dictionnaire de la Bible*, ed. by L. Pirot, A. Robert, H. Cazelles, A. Feuillet, 7 vols. (vol. VIII in progress), 1928—
SVT	*Supplements to Vetus Testamentum*
ThLZ	*Theologische Literaturzeitung*
ThR	*Theologische Rundschau*
ThT	*Theologisch Tijdschrift*
ThZ	*Theologische Zeitschrift*
VT	*Vetus Testamentum*
WO	*Die Welt des Orients*
WZKM	*Wiener Zeitschrift für die Kunde des Morgenlandes*
ZAW	*Zeitschrift für die alttestamentliche Wissenschaft*

WORKS CITED BY AUTHOR'S NAME ONLY

Ball	C.J. Ball, *The Book of Job*, 1922.
Beer	G. Beer, *Der Text des Buches Hiob*, 2 parts, 1895–97; and Edition of *Job* in Kittel, *Biblia Hebraica*, 2nd ed., 1913; 3rd ed., 1932.
Ben Yehuda	E. Ben Yehuda, *Thesaurus Totius Hebraitatis*, 16 vols and Prolegomena, 1908–59.
Bickell	G. Bickell, 'Kritische Bearbeitung des Jobdialogs', *Vienna Oriental Journal*, VI, 1892, pp. 137ff., 241ff., 327ff., VII, 1893, pp. 1ff., 153ff.; also: *Carmina Veteris Testamenti metrice*, 1882; *Das Buch Job*, 1894.
Bleeker	L.H.K. Bleeker, *Job*, 1926.
Budde	K. Budde, *Das Buch Hiob*, 1913.
Buttenwieser	M. Buttenwieser, *The Book of Job*, 1922.
Calmet	A. Calmet, *Commentaire littéral sur le livre de Job*, in *Commentaire littéral sur tous les livres de l'Ancien et du Nouveau Testament*, III, 1724.
Cheyne	T.K. Cheyne, 'Job', *EB*, II, 1901, cols 2464ff.
Davidson	A.B. Davidson, *The Book of Job*, 1884; revised by H.C.O. Lanchester, 1918.
Delitzsch	F. Delitzsch, *Biblical Commentary on the Book of Job*, Eng. tr. by F. Bolton, 2 vols., 1866.
Dhorme	E. Dhorme, *Le livre de Job*, 1926; Eng. tr. by H. Knight, 1966 (page references are to the English edition).
Dillmann	A. Dillmann, *Hiob*, 4th ed., 1891.
Driver	S.R. Driver, *The Book of Job in the Revised Version*, 1906.
Duhm	B. Duhm, *Das Buch Hiob*, 1897.
Ehrlich	A.B. Ehrlich, *Randglossen zur hebräischen Bibel*, VI, 1913, pp. 180ff.

Eichhorn	J.G. Eichhorn, *Hiob*, 1800.
Ewald	G.H.A. von Ewald, *Commentary on the Book of Job*, Eng. tr. by J.F. Smith, 1882.
Fohrer	G. Fohrer, *Das Buch Hiob*, 1963.
Gibson	E.C.S. Gibson, *The Book of Job*, 1899.
Graetz	H. Graetz, 'Lehrinhalt der "Weisheit" in den biblischen Büchern,' *MGWJ*, xxxvi, 1887, pp. 402ff., 544ff.
Gray	S.R. Driver and G.B. Gray, *The Book of Job*, 1921.
Hahn	H.A. Hahn, *Commentar über das Buch Hiob*, 1850.
Hirzel	L. Hirzel, *Hiob*, 1839 (2nd ed. by Olshausen; see below).
Hitzig	F. Hitzig, *Das Buch Hiob*, 1874.
Hoffmann	G. Hoffmann, *Hiob*, 1891; and: 'Ergänzungen und Berichtigungen zu Hiob', *ZAW*, N.F., viii, 1931, pp. 141ff., 270f.
Hölscher	G. Hölscher, *Das Buch Hiob*, 1937.
Hontheim	J. Hontheim, *Das Buch Job*, 1904.
Horst	F. Horst, *Hiob*, Fasc. i-iv, 1960-2.
Houbigant	C.F. Houbigant, *Notae criticae in universos V.T. libros*, ii, 1777.
Hupfeld	H. Hupfeld, *Commentatio in quosdam Iobeidos locos*, 1853.
Ibn Ezra	Abraham Ibn Ezra, Hebrew commentary on *Job* in the Amsterdam Rabbinical Bible, iv, 1728.
Irwin	W.A. Irwin, *Job*, in *Peake's Commentary on the Bible*, revised ed. by M. Black and H.H. Rowley, 1962.
Jastrow	M. Jastrow, *The Book of Job*, 1920.
Junker	H. Junker, *Das Buch Job*, in *Echter Bibel*, ed. by F. Nötscher, iv, 1959.
Kamphausen	A. Kamphausen, *Die Schriften*, in *Bunsen's Bibelwerk*, iii, 1868.
Kissane	E.J. Kissane, *The Book of Job*, 1939.
Klostermann	A. Klostermann, 'Hiob', in *PRE*, viii, 1900, pp. 97ff.
Knabenbauer	J. Knabenbauer, *Commentarius in librum Iob*, 1886.
König	E. König, *Das Buch Hiob*, 1929.
Larcher	C. Larcher, *Le livre de Job*, 2nd ed., 1957.
Le Hir	A.M. Le Hir, *Le livre de Job*, 1873.
Ley	J. Ley, *Das Buch Hiob*, 1903.
Marshall	J.T. Marshall, *The Book of Job*, 1904.
Merx	A. Merx, *Das Gedicht von Hiob*, 1871.
Montet	E. Montet, *Job*, in *La Bible du Centenaire*, iii, 1947.
Olshausen	J. Olshausen, *Hiob*, 2nd ed., 1852 (4th ed. by Dillmann, see above).
Peake	A.S. Peake, *Job*, 1905.
Perles	F. Perles, *Analekten zur Textkritik des Alten Testaments*, 1895; Neue Folge, 1922.

Peters	N. Peters, *Das Buch Job*, 1928.
Pope	M.H. Pope, *Job*, 1965.
Rashi	Rabbi Solomon ben Isaac, Hebrew commentary on Job in the Amsterdam Rabbinical Bible, IV, 1728.
Reichert	V.E. Reichert, *Job*, 1946.
Reiske	J.J. Reiske, *Coniecturae in Iobum et Proverbia Salomonis*, 1779.
Reuss	E. Reuss, *Philosophie religieuse et morale des Hébreux*, 1878.
Richter	G. Richter, *Erläuterungen zu dunkeln Stellen im Buche Hiob*, 1912; and: *Textstudien zum Buche Hiob*, 1927.
Robin	E. Robin, *Job*, in *La Sainte Bible*, ed. by L. Pirot and A. Clamer, IV, 1949.
Rosenmüller	E. F. C. Rosenmüller, *Scholia in Vetus Testamentum*, V, 1806.
Schlottmann	K. Schlottmann, *Das Buch Hiob*, 1851.
Schultens	A. Schultens, *Liber Jobi*, 2 vols., 1737.
Siegfried	C. Siegfried, *The Book of Job*, 1893.
Steinmann	J. Steinmann, *Le livre de Job*, 1955.
Steuernagel	C. Steuernagel, *Das Buch Hiob*, in *HSAT*, II, 1923.
Stevenson	W.B. Stevenson, *The Poem of Job*, 1947; and: *Critical Notes on the Hebrew Text of Job*, 1951.
Stickel	J.G. Stickel, *Das Buch Hiob*, 1842.
Stier	F.Stier, *Das Buch Ijjob*, 1954.
Strahan	R.H. Strahan, *The Book of Job interpreted*, 1913.
Stuhlmann	M.H. Stuhlmann, *Hiob: ein religiöse Gedicht*, 1804.
Szczygiel	P. Szczygiel, *Das Buch Job*, 1931.
Terrien	S. Terrien, *The Book of Job*, in *IB*, III, 1954.
Tur-Sinai	N.H. Tur-Sinai, *The Book of Job*, 1957.
Voigt	C. Voigt, *Einige Stellen des Buches Hiob*, 1895.
Volck	W. Volck, *Das Buch Hiob*, in Volck and Oettli, *Die poetischen Hagiographen*, 1889.
Volz	P. Volz, *Hiob und Weisheit*, 1921.
Weiser	A. Weiser, *Das Buch Hiob*, 1956; 5th ed., 1968.
Wright	G.H.B. Wright, *The Book of Job*, 1883.
Zöckler	O. Zöckler, *The Book of Job*, Eng. tr. by L.J. Evans, 1875.

BIBLIOGRAPHY

*Many commentaries and other works referred to by the authors' names alone
will be found in the preceding list, and are not repeated here. In addition,
many textual notes cited in the commentary with full references are not listed
here. Neither are the standard Introductions to the Old Testament.*

Alt	A. Alt, 'Zur Vorgeschichte des Buches Hiob', *ZAW*, N.F., XIV, 1937, pp. 265ff.
Bardtke	H. Bardtke, 'Prophetische Züge im Buche Hiob'; in *Das Ferne und Nahe Wort* (Rost Festschrift), 1967, pp. 1ff.
Batten	L.W. Batten, 'The Epilogue to the Book of Job', *AThR*, XV, 1933, pp. 125ff.
Baumgärtel	F. Baumgärtel, *Der Hiobdialog*, 1933.
Bertie	P. Bertie, *Le poème de Job*, 1929.
Bottéro	J. Bottéro, 'Le "Dialogue pessimiste" et la transcendance', *RThPh*, XCIX, 1966, pp. 6ff.
Budde	K. Budde, *Beiträge zur Kritik des Buches Hiob*, 1876.
Buhl	F. Buhl, 'Zur Vorgeschichte des Buches Hiob', *BZAW*, No. XLI, 1925, pp. 52ff.
Burrows	M. Burrows, 'The Voice from the Whirlwind', *JBL*, XLVII, 1928, pp. 177ff.
Carstensen	R.N. Carstensen, 'The Persistence of the "Elihu" Tradition in the later Jewish Writings', *Lexington Theological Quarterly*, II, 1967, pp. 37ff.
Cheyne	T.K. Cheyne, *Job and Solomon*, 1887.
Crook	Margaret B. Crook, *The Cruel God*, 1959.
Dennefeld	L. Dennefeld, 'Les discours d'Elihou', *RB*, XLVIII, 1939, pp. 163ff.
Duesberg	H. Duesberg, *Les Scribes inspirés*, 2 vols, 1939.
Eerdmans	B.D. Eerdmans, *Studies in Job*, 1939.
Fine	H.A. Fine, 'The Tradition of a Patient Job', *JBL*, LXXIV, 1955, pp. 28ff.
Fohrer	G. Fohrer, *Studien zum Buche Hiob*, 1963.
	G. Fohrer, '4QOrNab, 11QTgJob und die Hioblegende', *ZAW*, N.F., XXXIV, 1963, pp. 93ff.
Freedman	D. N. Freedman, 'The Elihu Speeches in the Book of Job', *HTR*, LXI, 1968, pp. 51ff.
Fullerton	K. Fullerton, 'The Original Conclusion of the Book of Job', *ZAW*, N.F., I, 1924, pp. 116ff.
Galling	K. Galling, 'Die Grabinschrift Hiobs', *WO*, II, 1954–59, pp. 1ff.
Gerleman	G. Gerleman, *Studies in the Septuagint. I: The Book of Job*, 1946.
Gese	H. Gese, *Lehre und Wirklichkeit in der alten Weisheit*, 1958.

Glatzer   N.H. Glatzer, 'The Book of Job and its Interpreters'; in
               Biblical Motifs, ed. by A. Altmann, 1966, pp. 197ff. (on
               ancient and medieval Jewish interpretation).
Gordis   R. Gordis, 'Elihu the Intruder: A Study of the Authenticity
               of Job (chapters 32–33)', in *Biblical and Other Studies*, ed.
               by A. Altmann, 1963, pp. 60ff.
               R. Gordis, *The Book of God and Man*, 1965.
Guillaume   A. Guillaume, 'The Arabic Background of the Book of
               Job'; in *Promise and Fulfilment*, ed. by F.F. Bruce, 1963,
               pp. 106ff.
               A. Guillaume, 'The Unity of the Book of Job', *ALUOS*,
               IV, 1964, pp. 26ff.
               A. Guillaume, *Studies in the Book of Job* (*ALUOS* Sup-
               plement II), 1968.
Hanson   A. and M. Hanson, *The Book of Job*, 1953.
Hempel   J. Hempel, 'Das theologische Problem des Hiob', in
               Apoxysmata, 1961, pp. 114ff.
Hertzberg   H.W. Hertzberg, 'Der Aufbau des Buches Hiob'; in
               Festschrift Alfred Bertholet, 1950, pp. 233ff.
Humbert   P. Humbert, *Recherches sur les sources égyptiennes de la
               littérature sapientale d'Israël*, 1929.
               P. Humbert, 'Le modernisme de Job', *SVT*, III, 1955,
               pp. 150ff.
Irwin   W.A. Irwin, 'Job and Prometheus', *JR*, XXX, 1950,
               pp. 90ff.
               W.A. Irwin, 'Job's Redeemer', *JBL*, LXXXI, 1962, pp. 217ff.
Jepsen   A. Jepsen, *Das Buch Hiob und seine Deutung*, 1963.
Jones   E. Jones, *The Triumph of Job*, 1966.
Junker   H. Junker, *Jobs Leid, Streit und Sieg*, 1948.
Kautzsch   K. Kautzsch, *Das sogenannte Volksbuch von Hiob*, 1900.
Kellett   E. Kellett, ' "Job": an Allegory?', *ET*, LI, 1939–40,
               pp. 250f.
Kraeling   E.G. Kraeling, *The Book of the Ways of God*, 1938.
Kramer   S.N. Kramer, ' "Man and his God". A Sumerian variation
               on the "Job" motif', *SVT*, III, 1955, pp. 170ff.
Kroeze   J.H. Kroeze, 'Die Elihu-reden im Buche Hiob', *OTS*, II,
               1943, pp. 156ff.
Kuhl   C. Kuhl, 'Neuere Literarkritik des Buches Hiob', *ThR*,
               N.F., XXI, 1953, pp. 163ff., 257ff.
               C. Kuhl, 'Vom Hiobbuche und seinen Problemen', *ThR*,
               N.F., XXII, 1954, pp. 261ff.
Kuschke   A. Kuschke, 'Altbabylonische Texte zum Thema "Der
               leidende Gerechte",' *ThLZ*, LXXXI, 1956, cols. 69ff.

Lambert	W.G. Lambert, *Babylonian Wisdom Literature*, 1960.
Laue	L. Laue, *Die Composition des Buches Hiob*, 1895.
Lindblom	J. Lindblom, *Boken om Job och hans lidande*, 1940.
	J. Lindblom, *La composition du livre de Job*, 1945.
	J. Lindblom, 'Job and Prometheus'; in *Dragma* (Nilsson Festschrift), 1939, pp. 280ff.
	J. Lindblom, 'Ich weiss, dass mein Erlöser lebt'; *Studia Theologica* (Riga), II, 1940, pp. 65ff.
Löhr	M. Löhr, 'Die drei Bildadreden', *BZAW*, XXXIV, 1920, pp. 107ff.
MacKenzie	R.A.F. MacKenzie, 'The Purpose of the Yahweh Speeches in the Book of Job', *Biblica*, XL, 1959, pp. 435ff.
Maeso	D. Gonzalo Maeso, 'Sentido nacional en el libro de Job'; *Estudios Bíblicos*, IX, 1950, pp. 67ff.
Marcus	R. Marcus, 'Job and God', *RR*, XIV, 1949–50, pp. 5ff.
Marshall	J. T. Marshall, *Job and his Comforters*, 1905.
May	H.G. May, 'Prometheus and Job', *AThR*, XXXIV, 1952, pp. 240ff.
Möller	H. Möller, *Sinn und Aufbau des Buches Hiob*, 1955.
Naish	J.P. Naish, 'The Book of Job and the Early Persian Period', *Exp.*, 9th ser., III, 1925, pp. 34ff., 94ff.
Noth	M. Noth, 'Noah, Daniel und Hiob in Ezechiel XIV', *VT*, I, 1951, pp. 251ff.
Nougayrol	J. Nougayrol, 'Une version ancienne du "Juste souffrant",' *RB*, LIX, 1952, pp. 239ff.
Orlinsky	H.M. Orlinsky, 'Studies in the Septuagint of the Book of Job', *HUCA*, XXVIII, 1957, pp. 53ff.; XXIX, 1958, pp. 229ff.; XXX, 1959, pp. 153ff.; XXXII, 1961, pp. 239ff.; XXXIII, 1962, pp. 119ff.; XXXV, 1964, pp. 57ff.; XXXVI, 1965, pp. 37ff.
Paulus	J. Paulus, 'Le thème du Juste Souffrant dans la pensée grecque et hébraïque', *RHR*, CXXI, 1940, pp. 18ff.
Peake	A.S. Peake, *The Problem of Suffering in the Old Testament*, 1904.
Pfeiffer	R.H. Pfeiffer, 'The Priority of Job over Is. 40–55', *JBL*, XLVI, 1927, pp. 202ff.
van der Ploeg	J. van der Ploeg, *Le Targum de Job de la Grotte 11 de Qumran*, 1962.
Prado	J. Prado, 'La perspectiva eschatológica en Job 19, 25–27'; *Estudios Bíblicos*, XXV, 1966, pp. 5ff.
von Rad	G. von Rad, 'Hiob XXXVIII und die altägyptische Weisheit', *SVT*, III, 1955, pp. 293ff.

Rankin   O.S. Rankin, *Israel's Wisdom Literature*, 1936.

Ranston   H. Ranston, *The Old Testament Wisdom Books and their Teaching*, 1930.

Regnier   H. Regnier, 'La distribution des chapitres 25–28 du livre de Job', *RB*, XXXIII, 1924, pp. 186ff.

Richter   H. Richter, 'Die Naturwissenschaft des Alten Testaments im Buche Hiob', *ZAW*, N.F., XXIX, 1958, pp. 1ff.
H. Richter, *Studien zu Hiob*, 1958.

H. Wheeler Robinson   H. Wheeler Robinson, *The Cross of Job*, 1916 (reprinted in *The Cross in the Old Testament*, 1954, pp. 9ff.).

T. H. Robinson   T. H. Robinson, *Job and his Friends*, 1954.

Rowley   H.H. Rowley, *Submission in Suffering and other Essays*, 1951.
H.H. Rowley, 'The Book of Job and its Meaning'; in *From Moses to Qumran*, 1963, pp. 141ff.

Sarna   N.M. Sarna, 'Epic Substratum in the Prose of Job', *JBL*, LXXVI, 1957, pp. 13ff.
N.M. Sarna, 'The Mythological Background of Job 18', *JBL*, LXXXII, 1963, pp. 315ff.

Schmid   H.H. Schmid, *Wesen und Geschichte der Weisheit* (*BZAW* No. CI), 1966.

Sekine   M. Sekine, 'Schöpfung und Erlösung im Buche Hiob', in *Von Ugarit nach Qumran* (Eissfeldt Festschrift, *BZAW*, No. LXXVII), 1958, pp. 213ff.

Skehan   P.W. Skehan, 'Strophic Patterns in the Book of Job', *CBQ*, XXIII, 1961, pp. 125ff.
P.W. Skehan, 'Job's Final Plea (Job 29–31) and the Lord's Reply (Job 38–41)', *Biblica*, XLV, 1964, pp. 51ff.

Snaith   N.H. Snaith, *The Book of Job: Its Origin and Purpose*, 1968.

Spiegel   S. Spiegel, 'Noah, Danel, and Job'; in *Louis Ginzberg Jubilee Volume*, I, 1945, pp. 305ff.

Stamm   J.J. Stamm, *Das Leiden des Unschuldigen in Babylon und Israel*, 1946.

Staples   W.E. Staples, *The Speeches of Elihu*, 1925.

Stewart   J. Stewart, *The Message of Job*, 1959.

Studer   G.L. Studer, 'Über die Integrität des Buches Hiob', *JPTh*, I, 1875, pp. 688ff.

Sutcliffe   E.F. Sutcliffe, *Providence and Suffering in the Old and New Testaments*, 1955.

Terrien   S. Terrien, *Job: Poet of Existence*, 1957.
S. Terrien, *Job* (Commentaire de l'Ancien Testament, XIII), 1963.
S. Terrien, 'Quelques remarques sur les affinités de Job avec le Deutéro-Esaïe', *SVT*, XV, 1966, pp. 295ff.

Tsevat   M. Tsevat, 'The Meaning of the Book of Job', *HUCA*,
                  XXXVII, 1966, pp. 73ff.
Weber   J.J. Weber, *Le livre de Job. L'Ecclésiaste*, 1947.
Weiser   A. Weiser, 'Das Problem der sittlichen Weltordnung im
                  Buche Hiob', in *Glaube und Geschichte im Alten Testament*,
                  1961, pp. 9ff.
Wellhausen   J. Wellhausen, review of Dillmann's *Hiob*, *JDTh*, XVI,
                  1871, pp. 553ff.
Westermann   C. Westermann, *Der Aufbau des Buches Hiob*, 1956.
van der Woude   A.S. van der Woude, 'Das Hiobtargum aus Qumran
                  Höhle XI', *SVT*, IX, 1962, pp. 322ff.

*Only a limited use could be made of some of the above, which appeared
between the writing of this Commentary and its publication.*

GENERAL
INTRODUCTION

1. TITLE AND PLACE IN THE CANON

The book of Job, like the books of Joshua and Ruth, bears the name of its hero. The Hebrew form of the name 'Iyyôḇ, was represented in Greek by Iōb, and thence through Latin came the English form, *Job*. On the meaning of the name, see on 1:1.

In the Hebrew Canon the book belongs to the third division, the Kethubim, which contains also Psalms, Proverbs, Ruth, the Song of Songs, Ecclesiastes, Lamentations, Esther, Daniel, Ezra, Nehemiah, 1 and 2 Chronicles. In some MSS. Job follows Psalms and Proverbs, and in some it stands between them. In Syriac it stands between Deuteronomy and Joshua, doubtless owing to the fact that the scene of the book is set in the patriarchal age.

In Greek MSS. the prophetical books were transferred from the second division of the Hebrew Canon to follow the three 'poetical' books, Job, Psalms, and Proverbs (these three not always in the same order), and Daniel was placed among the prophetical books, while the other books of the Kethubim were distributed. Similarly the MSS. of Vulgate vary, while following the same general principle as the Greek, and the English order follows what had become the prevailing order of Vulgate.

The three 'poetical' books have a special system of accentuation in the Hebrew. It is a mistake to think of them as distinct from the rest of the Old Testament in being in poetry. Very much of the prophetical books is written in poetry, since normally the prophetic oracles were of precisely the same literary form as these three 'poetical' books. The book of Lamentations and the Song of Songs are also in poetic form.

2. CONTENTS

The book opens with a prose Prologue (chapters 1–2), in which Job is presented as a man of unblemished character and piety, richly blessed in his family and possessions. The scene moves swiftly to the heavenly court, where the Satan, whose function would appear to be to expose the sins of men, appears among the angels. Here God challenges him to find any flaw in the character of Job. Unable to point to any defect, the Satan sneers at Job's motives, and attributes his piety to self-interest. In reply God so stakes himself on Job's unwavering piety that he permits the Satan to strip Job of his family and possessions. With ruthless thoroughness and with blows that fall in stunningly swift succession, the Satan proceeds to his task, only to find that Job meets sorrow and loss with immovable trust in God. A second scene in heaven, in which God triumphantly twits the Satan with his failure, brings a more malicious charge against Job that he can take calmly blows that fall on others so long as his own person is spared. Permitted to carry the test further, the Satan smites Job with an intolerable and loathsome disease, but still in vain. Three friends of Job's travel from far to visit him in his affliction and to condole with him.

After the friends had sat with Job in silent sympathy for seven days and seven nights, Job opens the poetic section of the book, which runs from 3.1 to 42.6, with a soliloquy in which he bitterly laments his lot (chapter 3).

This is followed by three cycles of speeches (chapters 4–27). In the first two cycles (chapters 4–14; 15–21) the three friends speak in turn, each speech being followed by a speech of Job's. In the third cycle, as the text now stands (chapters 22–27), only two of the friends speak, and Job replies to both and then utters a further speech. Some writers have supposed that this was deliberate, to suggest that the friends had run out of arguments. This is very improbable, and it is more likely that the third cycle was once complete, save that Job may not have made a reply to the third speech of the cycle. The friends speak in the same order, Eliphaz, Bildad, Zophar, probably in order of age. Job's replies are not directed exclusively to the immediately preceding speech, but often take up points raised earlier in the discussion. The friends' speeches rest on the assumption that Job has brought his sufferings on himself, since merit and fortune are inexorably correlated. Each cycle becomes more outspokenly critical of Job, and within each cycle Eliphaz is the gentlest of the three and Zophar the sharpest. Bildad has been called a traditionalist (so H. Ranston, *The Old Testament Wisdom Books*, 1930, p. 140) and Zophar the philosopher of the three (so J. T. Marshall, *Job and his Comforters*, 1905, p. 67; cf. Peake, p. 125). He is rather the coarsest and the most dogmatic of the three. Job throughout maintains that his phenomenal sufferings are not due to phenomenal sin, and while he, no less than his friends, believes that he is directly afflicted by God, he protests with increasing vehemence against the injustice of God. For the wild things he says in the course of the debate he is rightly rebuked by the friends, while he for his part bitterly resents the harsh things they say to him. For they argue from his sufferings to his sin, while he argues from his integrity to his title to blessing. Within Job's mind there is a conflict between the God he has known in his past experience and the God he believes to be unjustly afflicting him now, and more than once he appeals from the God of the present to the God of the past experience.

The reason for supposing that the third cycle of speeches is in some disorder is that in the present text sentiments are expressed by Job which do not fit his lips, but which do accord with the ideas of Bildad and Zophar. While this is widely agreed, there is less agreement as to the reconstruction of the material. On this, cf. the commentary on chapters 24–27, and for a number of proposed reconstructions, cf. H. H. Rowley, *From Moses to Qumran*, 1963, p.163 n.

The three cycles of speeches are followed by a magnificent poem on the elusiveness and true source of wisdom (chapter 28). In the present form of the book this is attributed to Job.

Following this Job utters a final soliloquy (chapters 29–31), in which he appeals to God to answer him, as he has more than once appealed in his earlier speeches.

A new character now appears on the scene. This is Elihu, apparently a young man, who has been unmentioned hitherto, and of whose presence we are given no explanation. He makes four speeches one after the other (chapters 32–37), to none of which Job answers. He is verbose and self-opinionated, and in his speeches there are references to the discussion that has preceded them and the elaboration of ideas already put forward, now claimed for Elihu with much contempt for Job and his friends.

Next God speaks from the whirlwind to answer Job in two speeches (38.1–40:2; 40.6–41:34), with a brief word of submission from Job separating them (40.4f.), and a further speech of submission following the second (42.2–6). The first Divine speech is of supreme brilliance, though it in no way solves the intellectual question debated by Job and his friends. No explanation of Job's suffering is given, and no defence of the Divine ordering of the world offered. Instead, Job is reminded by a swift succession of examples of the inscrutable wonders of the universe and the innumerable things that are beyond his understanding. The second speech is less brilliant than the first, and it consists largely of two long descriptions of the monsters Behemoth and Leviathan, instead of the rapid movement of the first speech from one vivid description to another. With Job's second speech of submission the poetic part of the book closes.

There follows an Epilogue in prose (42.7–17). Here God condemns the three friends of Job, but makes no reference to Elihu. Job is declared to be in the right, and the three friends are bidden to offer a sacrifice and to ask Job to pray for them. Elihu is as completely ignored by God as he has been by Job. When Job prays for his friends he is accepted by God and his fortunes are restored and a second family born to him.

3. CHARACTER AND PARALLELS

It would be hard to find writers today who regard the book as literal history, as did some older writers (cf. F. Spanheim, *Opera*, II, 1703, pp. 1ff.; A. Schultens, I, Preface, p. 33; S. Lee, *The Book of the Patriarch Job*, 1837, pp. 6ff.). This does not mean that Job never lived (so Maimonides, *Guide of the Perplexed*, English translation by S. Pines, 1963, p. 486; cf. Babylonian Talmud, Baba Bathra 15a), but rather that the present book was created by its author on the basis of an ancient story of a historical person.

The literary *genre* of the book has been held to be an epic, comparable with the work of Homer, or a drama, comparable with the works of Aeschylus, Sophocles, and Euripides, or as a dialogue, comparable with the Dialogues of Plato (for references, cf. H. H. Rowley, *From Moses to Qumran*, pp. 141f.). None of these is appropriate, and it is wiser to recognize the uniqueness of this book and to consider it without relation to any of these literary categories. Its supreme literary merit has been widely recognized, and Carlyle declared 'there is nothing written, I think, in the Bible or out of it, of equal literary merit' (*On Heroes*, The New Universal Library edition, p. 67), while Froude described it as 'towering up alone, far away above all the poetry of the world' (*The Book of Job*, 1854, p. 3).

It is usually reckoned among the Wisdom literature of the Old Testament. The other Wisdom books are Proverbs and Ecclesiastes, together with two books of the Apocrypha, Wisdom and Ecclesiasticus. The Song of Songs is also often considered along with these books, though its real character is probably quite other (cf. H. H. Rowley, *The Servant of the Lord*, 2nd ed., 1965, pp. 197ff.). Yet the aim of the book is less didactic than the other Wisdom literature and, as will be shown, it is more profoundly religious than intellectual or moral, and its author is more deeply involved in the problem with which he deals. Through the vehicle of the Dialogue and the divine intervention which follows it, he is concerned to deliver a spiritual message to tortured men which is unsurpassed in the Bible. On this, see below, pp. 18ff.

The author of this book was not the first or the only person to be troubled by the problem of the righteous sufferer. Jeremiah was troubled by his own sufferings and by the triumph of wicked men in his day (Jer. 11.18–12.6), as also was Habakkuk (Hab. 1.13), and Psalmists frequently complain that their lot does not match their piety. Nor can we suppose that it was only in Israel that men perceived that the good often suffer and were perplexed by the problem. From many countries and from the literature of many religions there is abundant evidence that it exercised many (cf. H. H. Rowley, *Submission in Suffering and other Essays*, 1951).

Particularly from Egypt and Babylon have texts dealing with this subject been adduced. From Egypt comes a man's dialogue with his own soul as to the merits of suicide as a way of escape from the miseries of life (cf. J. A. Wilson in *ANET*, pp. 405ff.), and another which narrates a man's bold and persistent appeal against social injustice until his wrongs were righted (ibid., pp. 407ff.). Neither of these is on all fours with the book of Job. It is true that Job longs for death as the escape from his sufferings, but that is incidental to the Dialogue rather than its major theme. Still less is it relevant to the main message of the book of Job. Similarly, while Job complains of the injustice of his sufferings, it is a complaint against God rather than against man, and though in the end his prosperity is restored, it is not because God has yielded to his defence.

More commonly certain Babylonian texts have been cited, including one called 'A Pessimistic Dialogue between a Master and his Servant' (cf. R. H. Pfeiffer, in *ANET*, pp. 437f.; W. G. Lambert, *Babylonian Wisdom Literature*, 1960, pp. 139ff.; cf. J. Bottéro, *RThPh*, xcix, 1966, p. 7ff.), and another called 'The Babylonian Job' (cf. Pfeiffer, loc. cit., pp. 434ff.; Lambert, op. cit., pp. 21ff.). The former has little serious affinity with the book of Job, which is fundamentally far other than a pessimistic work. The latter has more superficial points of similarity. In it a pious king is stricken with disease and is mocked by his friends; he does not know what he can have done to deserve his misfortune, but he thinks he may have unconsciously, or in some way he does not remember, offended against God and brought it upon himself, and cries for relief and is ultimately restored. The contrast with Job is striking. Job never allows that his phenomenal sufferings can have been brought about by his sin. In the Prologue the reader is told beyond a peradventure that Job is not suffering for his sin and there is Divine testimony to his integrity. He never cries for mere release from his sufferings, save by death, but for the vindication of his righteousness. Buttenwieser (p. 10) rightly says the Babylonian story 'lacks all those essential points that give the Job story its distinct character'. It also lacks the profound religious message which infuses the book of Job (see below, pp. 18ff).

A Sumerian text of much earlier date with some affinities with the book of Job has been published by S. N. Kramer (*SVT*, iii, 1955, pp. 170ff.). Here a man complains that he is scorned by God and man, and pleads with his god to restore his fortunes. He confesses his sin and is ultimately restored. Here again the vital elements of the Job story are missing. The sufferer is concerned only with his release and not with vindication, and there is nothing of the passionate declaration of innocence which we find in Job. Nor is there any approach to the climax of the message of the book of Job.

Several writers have remarked on the similarity between the story of Prometheus and that of Job (cf. J. Lindblom, *Dragma* (Nilsson

Festschrift), 1939, pp. 280ff.; W. A. Irwin, *JR*, xxx, 1950, pp. 90ff.; H. G. May, *AThR*, xxxiv, 1952, pp. 240ff.). But Prometheus knew that he was chained to the rock by the command of Zeus because he brought men the gift of fire. He rejected all urging to cease his defiance of Zeus and to pray for mercy, but protested against the injustice he suffered. Prometheus suffered because he angered the god who was responsible for his suffering; Job's integrity was avowed by the God who permitted his. Prometheus knew only hate for the god who punished him; Job never regrets his pious devotion to God, but even in his complaints against God appeals to him for vindication. Prometheus finds no release from his sufferings; Job, even before the restoration of his fortunes, finds a deeper release. (For a further study of Greek and Hebrew thought on the problem debated in the book of Job, cf. J. Paulus, *RHR*, cxxi, 1940, pp. 18ff.)

4. INTEGRITY

There is wide disagreement among scholars as to how much of the present book is from the original author and how much is secondary, and it is necessary to consider the challenged sections.

(a) *Prologue and Epilogue*. Some scholars have thought the Prologue (cf. R. Simon, *Histoire critique du Vieux Testament*, 2nd ed., 1685, p. 30; E. König, pp. 462ff.) or the Epilogue (cf. Buttenwieser, pp. 67ff., who rejects 42:10, 12–17; K. Fullerton, *ZAW*, N.F., I, 1924, pp. 116ff.) or both (cf. Schultens, I, Preface, p. 34; G. Studer, *JPTh*, I, 1875, pp. 706ff.; W. B. Stevenson, *The Poem of Job*, 1947, pp. 21ff.) were later additions to the book. But without some Prologue the book is unintelligible, and if it be supposed that a different Prologue once stood here, its disappearance needs to be accounted for. If it was more relevant than the present Prologue, its replacement is hard to understand; if less relevant, the inability of the brilliant author of the Dialogue to compose a suitable introduction would be remarkable. On the other hand, without some Epilogue the book would be incomplete. If originally there were neither Prologue nor Epilogue, Job's sufferings would be unaccounted for and without beginning or ending. The reader would know that Job was suffering, but would be unaware that he was a man of great piety who had suddenly been overwhelmed by loss and disease, and would be as ignorant of the reason as Job and his friends. With the Prologue but without the Epilogue, the test that is staged in the former would be unconcluded, and the malice of the Satan left to continue to vent itself on Job.

A more common view has been that the Prologue and Epilogue are older than the Dialogue, and that the author replaced what originally stood between them by the present Dialogue (cf. J. Wellhausen, *JDTh*, xv, 1871, p. 555; K. Budde, pp. xiii f.; T. K. Cheyne, *Job and Solomon*, 1887, pp. 68f.; and a long succession of followers). Cheyne (*Jewish Religious Life after the Exile*, 1898, p. 161) supposed that what originally stood in place of the Dialogue was something like: 'And these three men, moved at the sight of Job's grief, broke out into lamentations, and withheld not passionate complaints of the injustice of God. They said, "Is there knowledge in the Most High? And does God judge righteous judgment?" But Job was sore displeased, and reproved them, saying, "Bitter is the pain which racks me, but more bitter still are the words which ye speak." . . . And at the end of a season, God came to Eliphaz in a dream and said, "My wrath is kindled against thee and thy two friends, because ye have not spoken of Me that which is right, as My servant Job has." ' Of this there is no evidence but the fertile brain of the modern author, and as E. G. Kraeling (*RR*, x, 1946, p. 427) says: 'It is intrinsically unlikely and unthinkable that a folk-tale should have introduced three visitors with no other function than to accuse the God of Job in a few words.'

It is scarcely open to doubt that Job was known in tradition before the book of Job was composed. For Ezekiel, who probably lived before the book of Job was written (see below, p. 22), refers to Job along with Noah and Daniel (Ezek. 14.14,20) as an ancient righteous man (cf. S. Spiegel, *Louis Ginzberg Memorial Volume*, i, 1945, pp. 305ff.; M. Noth, *VT*, i, 1951, pp. 251ff.). The tradition may well have recorded his sufferings as well as his righteousness, and so have provided the material on which the author based his work. But on the basis of the tradition the author most probably wrote Prologue, Dialogue, and Epilogue, and to him we owe this masterpiece as a whole (cf. Gray, p. xxxviii; Dhorme, p. lxxxv).

Those who attribute the Prologue and Epilogue to an earlier or later writer emphasise the differences and inconsistencies they find between these and the Dialogue. In the Dialogue there is no reference to the real cause of Job's sufferings. The friends trace his affliction to his sin, and neither he nor they suspect the hand of Satan. But since they had not been present at the heavenly court or read the Prologue, they had no means of knowing of his activity, and if they had made reference to it any intelligent reader would have pounced on this as evidence of the author's incompetence.

It is argued that whereas in the Prologue Job is presented as a man of exemplary patience, in the Dialogue he is quite other. It is true that in the Prologue when his wife urges him to curse God he refuses to do so. But in the Dialogue he does not do this, though he is driven by the attacks of his friends to complain against the God they present, who is, he believes, the Author of his troubles. In his opening soliloquy he curses the day of his birth and longs for death, but this is not inconsistent with his refusal to curse God. It has been noted that in Job's mind there is a conflict between the God of his past experience and the God of the present, as represented by the friends and increasingly accepted by Job under the pressure of their taunts, and he appeals from the God of the present to the God of the past. Nowhere does he come near to cursing the God of his past experience, and it is this God he refuses to curse in the Prologue.

It is said that in the Dialogue Job refers to his sons as living (Job 19.17), whereas in the Prologue they had been killed. It is improbable that the reference in 19.17 is to Job's children, and the rendering of *RSV* is to be preferred (see note there). Moreover, 8:4 and 29:5 would seem to recognize that Job's children were dead, so that if there is inconsistency it is within the Dialogue and not merely between Dialogue and Prologue.

Again, it is maintained that the conception of religion in the Dialogue is different from that in the Prologue and Epilogue. In the Prologue Job's piety expresses itself in sacrifice, and sacrifice figures again in the Epilogue, whereas in the Dialogue there is no reference to it. It is not surprising that when Job was reduced to penury on the dunghill and suffering from a loathsome and painful disease he did not offer in sacrifice the animals he no longer possessed. What is clear is that though in his prosperity Job expressed his religion in sacrifice it was in essence something deeper and richer, and in his suffering he still clung to that inner integrity of spirit and longing for God. In the Prologue the Divine testimony to Job's piety is not expressed in terms of his sacrifice, but in terms of his moral and spiritual quality of character.

Attention is drawn to the diversity in the use of Divine names in the Dialogue as against the Prologue and Epilogue. Yahweh (the LORD) is avoided in the Dialogue, where El, Eloah, and Shaddai are used (see below, p. 24), whereas in the Prologue and Epilogue Yahweh freely stands. It is not surprising that a Hebrew author should use the name Yahweh while not putting it in the mouth of Job's foreign friends, or in Job's mouth in debate with them. It is improbable that Job was a Jew (see on 1:1), though he is represented as a worshipper of Yahweh. We are told that he feared God (1:1), but Yahweh makes it plain in 1:8 that he accepts Job as his worshipper. On the lips of Job the name Yahweh is found in the Prologue only in the expression of resignation (1:21). Once in the Dialogue the name Yahweh is found (12:9), and here it is on the lips of Job. This is often regarded as a copyist's error or as a lapse on the part of the author, and this may be correct. But whether it is original here or not, we cannot posit two authors on the ground of the Divine names. For in the rubrics introducing the Divine speeches and Job's replies (38.1; 40.3, 4) we find the name Yahweh. If we attribute the Prologue and Epilogue to a different hand on the ground of this name, we must attribute these rubrics to the author of the Prologue and Epilogue—which would be absurd.

By many writers the Epilogue is held to be a virtual giving away of Job's case to the friends, and a blot on the book. For here Job's prosperity is restored, and it is thought that the nexus between righteousness and prosperity is blatantly recognized. Job had consistently declared that these two should go together and the friends had maintained that they always do go together. Here then, it is claimed, the Dialogue and the Epilogue are at stark variance. This is completely to misunderstand the book. Job's prosperity is restored, not because he is righteous, but because the test is ended. The

Epilogue is demanded by the artistry of the book. It began with a scene in heaven and a test of the disinterestedness of Job's piety. The test is ended with a verdict of acquittal by Yahweh on the issue that is being tested. It would be intolerable if the torture, which was the form the trial took, were continued after the verdict had been given. Job is prosperous at the end because he was prosperous at the beginning. In the course of the trial he had said many foolish things; but these were irrelevant to the issue on which he was being tested. If Yahweh had abandoned him on the dunghill to continue his sufferings after he had vindicated the confidence he had had in Job, every reader would have felt it to be intolerable.

(b) *The Elihu speeches.* It has been noted above that Elihu appears abruptly, makes his speeches one after the other with no reply from Job, and then disappears from the book. No reference is made to him by Yahweh, who completely ignores him though he refers to the three friends of Job. Elihu's speeches could be dropped from the book without being missed. Yet he frequently picks up points from the speeches of Job and his friends, showing that the author of these speeches was acquainted with the rest of the book. It is therefore not surprising that the view is widely held that the Elihu speeches are a later addition to the book (cf. J. G. Eichhorn, *Einleitung in das Alte Testament*, 3rd ed., III, 1803, pp. 597f.; W. M. L. de Wette, *Introduction to the Old Testament*, English translation by T. Parker, II, 1843, pp. 558ff.; and very many of the standard commentaries).

A few writers have thought they were added by the author of the book (cf. A. Kamphausen, p. 494; H. Junker, p. 7; J. Pedersen, *Israel I–II*, 1926, p. 531), but most find the style and the level of genius below that of the author of the rest of the book. A curious exception is J. T. Marshall, who finds the pomposity and repetitiousness of Elihu 'on an immeasurably higher plane than the Dialogue' (*Job and his Comforters*, 1905, p. 6). More widely shared is the view of S. R. Driver, that 'the power and brilliancy which are so conspicuous in the poem generally are sensibly missing' (*LOT*, 9th ed., 1913, p. 429).

Not all scholars reject these speeches, however, Their authenticity is maintained by Budde (pp. 24ff., and *Beiträge zur Kritik des Buches*

Hiob, 1876, pp. 65ff.) and Cornill (*Introduction to the Old Testament*, English translation by G. H. Box, 1907, pp. 426ff.), as well as by many older and more recent writers, including Rosenmüller (pp. 756ff.), J. G. Stickel (*Das Buch Hiob*, 1842, pp. 224ff.), Hontheim pp. 20ff.), Szczygiel (pp. 24ff.), L. Dennefeld (*RB*, XLVIII, 1939, pp. 163ff.), and J. H. Kroeze, *OTS*, II, 1943, pp. 156ff.). Rosenmüller even thought Elihu was the author of the book (p. 765). In favour of the authenticity of these speeches it is argued that it is only here that there is any attempt to grapple with the problem of suffering. But the solution offered is that suffering is disciplinary, and this is irrelevant to the book of Job. The reader is told why Job is suffering, and it is not for this purpose. He is suffering to vindicate God's trust in him. It is not to correct the faults which Job developed in the course of his argument with his friends, but to prove the falsity of the Satan's calumny. If the author of the book intended to offer a solution, it should surely have been relevant to the situation he had himself created. And if, as the defenders of these speeches suppose, they are the climax of the book, Elihu should surely have been commended in the Epilogue, and not treated with contemptuous silence. We may therefore with confidence reject these speeches as secondary.

D.N. Freedman (*HTR*, LXI, 1968, pp. 51ff.) has propounded the interesting view that the Elihu speeches were composed by the author of the book of Job as part of a general plan to reorganize the book, but that the plan, which would have involved further changes to introduce Elihu into the Prologue and Epilogue and to connect these speeches with their context, was abandoned in favour of the addition of the Divine speeches, which used some of the same material. The industry of a later editor is then held to have saved these speeches and to have introduced them into the book where they now stand.

(c) *Chapter 28.* This chapter is almost universally held to be an addition to the book. In the present form of the book it appears to be uttered by Job. If part of the previous chapter should be attributed to Zophar (see notes there), it would follow on his speech without introduction. Yet it fits neither the lips of Job nor Zophar's. It declares that wisdom is beyond man's unaided attainment, but is the gift of God, and that it consists in humble reverence towards God and obedience to his will. But in the Prologue God's testimony to the character of Job is precisely that he had attained this wisdom. In some respects the chapter is an anticipation of the Divine speeches, in that it recognizes that many things are beyond man's understanding, and if Job had already reached this point, the sarcasm with which Yahweh afterwards underlined it would have been uncalled for. If this chapter is omitted, the Divine speeches, recalling Job from his anguished doctrinaire assumptions to the simple piety he once knew, are understandable. A further reason for doubting whether the chapter belongs here is that if Job had already reached this point, the temper of the soliloquy that follows would be most surprising.

Junker's view (p. 54), that the chapter should be compared with a chorus in a Greek tragedy, may be noted. But whereas we have rubrics introducing all the other speeches and telling us who uttered them, this is without any introduction, and we are not told whether it was meant for the reader alone, or for Job and his friends.

Of the brilliance of the chapter there is no doubt, and that it is worthy of the genius of the author of the book of Job may be readily agreed. It may well have been composed by that author, and subsequently preserved by being inserted in his masterly work, as several writers have thought (so Dhorme, pp. xcviif.; R. H. Pfeiffer, *Introduction to the Old Testament*, 1941, p. 671; A. Lods, *Histoire de la littérature hébraïque et juive*, 1950, p. 680).

(d) *The Divine speeches*. Some writers have rejected both of these speeches (cf. W. E. Staples, *The Speeches of Elihu*, 1925, pp. 11f. O. S. Rankin, *Israel's Wisdom Literature*, 1936, p. 93; W. A. Irwin, *JR*, XVII, 1937, pp. 45f.), while Sellin (*Introduction to the Old Testament*, English translation by W. Montgomery, 1923, pp. 207ff.) and Dhorme (pp. xcviif.) held that they were added to the book by the author. It is hard to suppose that the book ever existed without any speech of Yahweh, for without some speech from him the structure of the book collapses. A. van Hoonacker (*RB*, XII, 1903, pp. 165f.) thought the book once ended with chapter 31, and that in a second edition the Elihu speeches were added, while in a third the Elihu speeches were replaced by the Divine speeches and the Epilogue, and in a fourth the Elihu speeches were restored and followed by these. It is hard to think that the book ever ended with chapter 31, after an inconclusive debate and with Job left on the dunghill and Satan's test still continuing. It is equally hard to think of the book ending with the irrelevant solution of Elihu. The Epilogue follows appropriately after Job's submission, and Job's submission is under-standable after Yahweh has spoken, but not after chapter 31 or chapter 37.

Whether there were originally two Divine speeches, separated by a few words of submission by Job, is more questionable, and the second has been widely rejected by scholars (cf. Ewald, pp. 319ff.; Dillmann, pp. 339f.; Cheyne, *Job and Solomon*, pp. 56, 94; Gray, pp. 348f.; O. Eissfeldt, *The Old Testament: an Introduction*, English translation by P. R. Ackroyd, 1965, p. 463; and many others). The grounds for this are that the second speech adds little to the first and falls below it in brilliance, and that after Job's submission it is both unnecessary and harsh. The first speech is of superb quality, and Peake says it is 'unsurpassed in the world's literature' (p. 43). J. L. McKenzie (*Interpretation*, xx, 1966, p. 471) says: 'If there is no literary difference between the first Yahweh speeches and the speeches about Behemoth and Leviathan, then I do not know how literary differences can be detected anywhere'.

It should be added that not all scholars reject either of the speeches and not a few retain both (so A. Lefèvre, in *SDB*, iv, 1949, col. 1081; H. W. Hertzberg, in *Festschrift Alfred Bertholet*, 1950, pp. 253ff.; Lods, op. cit., pp. 678f.; P. W. Skehan, *Biblica*, xlv, 1964, pp. 51ff.; R. Gordis, *The Book of God and Man*, 1965, pp. 122f.). Moreover, if the Behemoth and Leviathan sections of the second speech are rejected, the opening verses, 40.8–14, should perhaps be retained and transferred to the end of the first speech (so Bleeker, p. 225).

(e) *Further excisions.* Mention may be made of a few individual views which have secured little following, but which reject some further passages. F. Baumgärtel rejected much of the Dialogue, holding that there was originally a single cycle of speeches, followed by a soliloquy by Job, of which fragments have been incorporated in the speeches in the second and third cycles as we now have them (*Der Hiobdialog*, 1933). Baumgartner comments (*OTMS*, p. 219): 'He never really succeeds in justifying these numerous deletions; and the fact that it is just those sections that do not belong to the Wisdom category and those portions that do not treat of Job's individual case upon which the axe falls, betrays a *petitio principii*.'

N. H. Snaith (*The Book of Job*, 1945, p. 15) reduces the original book to the Prologue, Job's soliloquy (chapters 3, 29–31), the first Divine speech, Job's submission, and the Epilogue. From the Prologue and the Epilogue he eliminates all the verses referring to the three friends, whom he dismisses from the book together with all Job's speeches replying to them. This view has much in common with the view of P. Bertie (*Le poème de Job*, 1929). It has won no following, since without the Dialogue the Divine speech is not to be understood, and the style of the rejected Dialogue is the same as that of the retained speeches. More recently Snaith (*The Book of Job: its Origin and Purpose*, 1968) has renewed his view of the original extent of the book and postulated three editions by the author, the second adding the references to the friends and the debate, together with chapter 28, and the third adding the Elihu speeches. If the author had the wit to modify the Prologue and the Epilogue when he added the debate to accommodate the friends, it is odd that he should be unable to make modifications to accommodate Elihu.

Lindblom (*La Composition du livre de Job*, 1945) also holds that the three-cycle Dialogue is secondary, and that originally a simple conversation between Job and his friends stood in its place. He rejects the Elihu speeches, chapter 28, and the second Divine speech, in agreement with the view outlined above. In addition, he rejects 42:1–6. Job's submission is then reduced to 40.4f., which merely say that Job has nothing to add. The reasons for rejecting the Dialogue do not seem convincing, and the rejection of the verses which record that Job has found relief from his distress in the presence of God robs the book of its climax. In addition, Lindblom offers a theory of a very complicated history of the Prologue and Epilogue. He propounds the view that they existed first in an Edomite form, in which neither Job's wife nor the Satan figured (the Satan passages are also deleted by K. Kautzsch, *Das sogenannte Volksbuch von Hiob*, 1900,

p. 88; Jastrow, *The Book of Job*, 1920, pp. 52ff.; L. W. Batten, *AThR*, xv, 1933, p. 127; Pfeiffer, op. cit., p. 669). Lindblom holds that an Israelite author introduced Job's wife and the Satan into the Prologue and substituted a new Epilogue for the original one. Later still the Edomite Epilogue was restored in an amended form to stand beside the other. All this is needlessly complicated.

E. G. Kraeling (*The Book of the Ways of God*, 1938), in addition to rejecting the Elihu speeches (pp. 125ff.) and one Divine speech (pp. 143ff.), rejects Job's closing soliloquy in chapters 29–31 (pp. 111ff.) and eliminates all the Prologue except 2.11–13, and thinks 42:10–17 came from the same hand as the secondary 1.1–2:10 (pp. 167, 175). This is once more too complicated to be convincing, and the rejection of Job's closing soliloquy is hard to accept.

Some other scholars have put forward theories which split the short Epilogue into fragments. Jastrow (pp. 52ff.) finds four Epilogues: 42.10–17; 42.7–9; 40.1–14; 42.1–6. K. Fullerton (*ZAW*, N.F., 1, 1924, pp. 126ff.) thought 42.7–9 was the oldest part of the Epilogue and that it came from the hand of one who sympathized with the positions taken by the author in the Dialogue, and that it was placed in its present position by the author of 42.1–6, 10–17.

From this survey we conclude that the original structure of the book was as follows:

    Prologue
    Job's opening soliloquy
    Three cycles of speeches
    Job's closing soliloquy
    The first Divine speech
    Job's submission (the two parts being brought together)
    Epilogue

It should be added that some recent writers still maintain the view that the whole book, as it stands, is a unity (so L. Bigot, *DThC*, VIII, 1925, cols. 1479ff.; Höpfl-Miller-Metzinger, *Introductio specialis in Vetus Testamentum*, 5th ed., 1946, pp. 280f.; E. J. Young, *Introduction to the Old Testament*, 1949, p. 313; H. Möller, *Sinn und Aufbau des Buches Hiob*, 1955; cf. also P. Humbert, *SVT*, III, 1955, p. 151n.). The reasons for the rejection of chapter 28 (though probably composed by the author of Job), the Elihu speeches, and the second

Divine speech, have been given above, and with their removal the meaning and purpose of the book become clear.

5. PURPOSE

S. R. Driver suggested that the principal aim of the book was to controvert the theory that suffering is a sign of the Divine displeasure (*LOT*, p. 409). It is certain that the friends firmly cherished such a view, while Job equally firmly asserted that whereas merit and experience ought to be matched, in fact they are not. Not seldom has it been asserted that the view of the friends was the orthodox view of the Old Testament until the author of the book of Job challenged it (cf. I. G. Matthews, *The Religious Pilgrimage of Israel*, 1947, pp. 171f.). But it is hard to suppose that the reader of the Bible is expected to conclude that Abel, Uriah the Hittite, and Naboth were murdered because they deserved to be.

The Deuteronomic theory of history was that the nation always got what it deserved (cf. Dt. 28), and in the book of Judges religious defection is regularly given as the cause of foreign oppression. It would appear that in some contemporary circles in the time of the author of the book of Job this had been individualized and had led to the hard doctrine of the friends. Surprisingly enough, Jeremiah is frequently held to be responsible for this by his formulation of the doctrine that 'every one shall die for his own sin' (Jer. 31.30). It is forgotten that Jeremiah also asked 'Why does the way of the wicked prosper?' (Jer. 12.1). Jeremiah was well aware that life is more complex than a simple principle can express, and knew that while some suffering is self-entailed, some is not. So, too, in the New Testament we find 'Whatever a man sows, that will he also reap' (Gal. 6:7), but also 'Christ also died for sins . . . the righteous for the unrighteous' (1 Pet. 3.18), warning us that a simple doctrine of retribution does not cover all experience.

While, therefore, it is wrong to suppose that the author of the book of Job was the first to perceive that all suffering is not self-entailed, it is true that he protests against such a doctrine, which lies in the mouth of Job's friends. So far as Job is concerned, the reader is clearly told in the Prologue that this is not the explanation of his suffering. Yet we can hardly suppose that the principal aim of the book was realized in the Prologue.

It is equally wrong to think its purpose was to solve the problem of suffering. Cornill says the author 'surely must have had a solution to the problem to offer' (*Introduction to the Old Testament*, English translation, 1907, p. 426). Yet it is only in the Elihu speeches that this is to be found, and Cornill uses this argument to justify their retention. But Elihu's solution is irrelevant to the case of Job, and so cannot express the purpose of the book.

So far as Job is concerned, the reader is told the reason for his suffering. But Job and his friends cannot deduce it, and in the Divine speeches no hint of the reason is given. If it had been, the book would have been of little value to others, who must suffer in the dark. Clearly, therefore, the purpose of the writer cannot have been to offer an explanation of innocent suffering, or of all suffering, and his failure to provide a solution cannot be interpreted as a failure to attain his purpose. As Terrien says: 'The poet of Job did not attempt to solve the problem of evil, nor did he propose a vindication of God's justice. For him, any attempt of man to justify God would have been an act of arrogance' (*Job, Poet of Existence*, 1957, p. 21). The aim of the book of Job was something more fundamental than this.

For tortured spirits theology is less satisfying than religion, and religion is encounter, encounter with God. It is in the sphere of religion rather than in theology that the meaning of the book is to be found. Job's friends were persuaded that by sin Job had brought his sufferings upon himself, and that his troubles were the evidence that God had cast him off. Despite his consciousness of innocence, Job himself was persuaded that his sufferings were the evidence of his isolation from God. Though he could not understand God's enmity and often longed for the fellowship with God he had once known, he felt himself shut out from the presence of God. A false theology sapped the springs of religion, when religion was most needed. Job was sure in his own conscience that his suffering was innocent, but he did not realize the corollary of this until the end of the book. For if suffering is innocent, it is not the proof of isolation from God. For he who is 'of purer eyes than to behold evil'

(Hab. 1.13) is 'near to all who call upon him . . . in truth' (Ps. 145.18), and the upright dwell in his presence (Ps. 140.13 (M.T. 14)).

When God speaks to Job from the whirlwind, he does not reveal to him why he is suffering, and he does not enter into the debate of Job and his friends. He reminds Job that there are mysteries in nature beyond his solving, and leaves him to realize that the mystery of suffering is one of these. To Job the supremely important thing is that God has come to him in his suffering, showing him that he is not isolated from God by his suffering. He has cried for God again and again, and God has come to him, not to enter into debate with him on the issues he has thrashed out with his friends, but to show him that now, when he most needs God, God is with him. That is why the closing words of Job are the climax of the book, and should on no account be eliminated. Job says, 'I had heard of thee by the hearing of the ear, but now my eye sees thee; therefore I despise myself, and repent in dust and ashes.' He is not repenting of any sin that had brought his suffering upon him, for on that issue he is vindicated in the Epilogue, as he had been justified to the reader in the Prologue. He is repenting of the foolish things he had said in the debate, and of his folly in not realizing the corollary of his innocence. If he had found God only after his restoration, the book would have been spiritually far inferior. It is of the essence of its message that Job found God *in* his suffering, and so found relief not *from* his misfortunes, but *in* them. God was to him now far more precious than he had ever been. The past experience of God he had known, of which he often wistfully speaks in the debate, is transcended in the experience he now has. Compared with this it was as the knowledge of hearsay compared with first-hand experience. It is completely unperceptive to find the message of the book in the pompous and irrelevant ideas of Elihu, when here the far richer meaning is that though men must suffer in the dark, their very suffering may be an enrichment if in it they know the presence of God, who is ever ready to dwell with him who is of a crushed (a word from the same root as 'bruise' in Isa. 53:10) and humble spirit (Isa. 57.15). To Elihu the suffering may bring enrichment; to the author of the book of Job it is the presence of God that is enriching, and that presence is given to men of integrity and piety in prosperity and in adversity alike.

It is of interest to note that the New Testament gets no further than this. It is often suggested that in the richer doctrine of the Afterlife which we have in the New Testament we are carried beyond this point. The hope of a life beyond this, where the inequalities and injustices of this life are rectified, does not touch Job's problem. No reward to the innocent sufferer in a future life can offer any solution in terms of justice. It may bring comfort, but it cannot bring explanation. And even in terms of comfort it is inferior to the message of Job, which is that here and now in the fellowship of God the pious may find a peace and a satisfaction that transcends all the miseries of his lot.

Paul knew physical suffering that was sometimes unbearable, and cried with all the earnestness of his being to be delivered from it. And to him there was given the experience of Job, and the awareness of the Lord's presence in his suffering, so that he cried, 'I will all the more gladly boast of my weaknesses, that the power of Christ may rest upon me' (2 C. 12:9). To sufferers in all ages the book of Job declares that less important than fathoming the intellectual problem of the mystery of suffering is the appropriation of its spiritual enrichment through the fellowship of God.

6. DATE AND AUTHORSHIP

The book of Job has been attributed to the widest variety of dates (for a considerable selection with references, cf. H. H. Rowley, *From Moses to Qumran*, pp. 173f.n.), ranging from the patriarchal age—due to the fact that the scene is set in that age—to the second or first century B.C. Even within the present century dates from the time of Solomon to the Hasmonaean period have found advocates (ibid.), and the *Seventh Day Adventist Bible Commentary*, edited by F. D. Nichol (III, 1954, p. 493), clings to the traditional ascription to Moses. It is impossible here to traverse all these proposals and the arguments whereby they are sustained. Most recent writers are agreed that in its original form the book was of post-exilic origin, and the secondary parts of later composition.

Reference has been made above to the Deuteronomic doctrine of the rigid correlation of desert and fortune on the national scale. It is generally accepted that the Deuteronomic school flourished in the seventh century B.C. and that the Deuteronomic history embodied in the Former Prophets was composed in the seventh and sixth centuries. It was probably under the influence of the application of this principle to the individual that the hard doctrine of Job's friends became accepted in certain circles. This may have owed something to one element of the teaching of Jeremiah, noted above, which was repeated by Ezekiel (Ezek. 18.4), though it must be remembered that to single out this element is to distort the teaching of Jeremiah. If this is correct, the book of Job must be placed later than the middle of the sixth century B.C., and probably a good deal later, to allow for the development of this distortion and the need for a protest against it. It is therefore likely that the book of Job is not earlier than c. 500 B.C., and more probably quite a bit later. Beyond that it is not possible to go with any confidence, and the present writer would agree with Gray (pp. lxvff.), that it is best assigned to the fifth century (so Bleeker, p. 8). Not a few have thought of a date around the end of that century, c. 400 B.C. (so Budde, p. liii; Peake, p. 40; J. A. Bewer, *The Literature of the Old Testament*, 1922, p. 317; Buttenwieser, pp. 70ff.; Jastrow, op cit., p. 36; H. Junker, p. 7; A. Lods, op. cit., p. 688), and this may well be correct, though the evidence is insufficient to define the date with precision. The substantial Aramaic colouring of the language (see below) would favour a date not earlier than the fifth century.

It should perhaps be added that a few writers have argued that Job was prior to Deutero-Isaiah; so T. K. Cheyne (*The Prophecies of Isaiah*, II, 5th ed., 1889, p. 267), R. H. Pfeiffer (*JBL*, XLVI, 1927, pp. 202ff.), S. Terrien (*IB*, III, 1954, pp. 889f.) and M. H. Pope (p. xxxiii).

Of the author we know nothing apart from this book, and it is idle to speculate who he may have been. J. P. Naish (*Exp.*, 9th series, III, 1925, pp. 95ff.) thought he was a disciple of Deutero-Isaiah, but of this we can have no assurance. Humbert thought the book was composed in Egypt (cf. *Recherches sur les sources égyptiennes de la littérature sapientale d'Israël*, 1929, pp. 75ff.), and Dhorme stresses (pp. clxxi f.) the author's acquaintance with Egypt. F. H. Foster (*AJSL*, XLIX, 1932–33, pp. 21ff.) thought the book had been translated from an Arabic original, and Pfeiffer (op. cit., pp. 678ff.) thinks the author was an Edomite.

It is hard to think that he was not an Israelite. That there is no reference to the land or cultus of Israel is not surprising, since the scene is set in the patriarchal age and the persons who figure in the books do not appear to be themselves Jews. The original tradition on which the book is based was probably a non-Israelite story, which the author adapted for his purpose. He was certainly a monotheist and a worshipper of Yahweh, and if he was influenced by Deuteronomic and post-Deuteronomic theory, it is hard to think of him as anything but a Jew. He had doubtless travelled widely, but the profoundly spiritual message with which his book is charged can be more easily understood in the setting of Old Testament religion than in the setting of any other country of the ancient Near East of which we have knowledge. The parallels that have been adduced show no more than that the author may have been acquainted with non-Israelite literature and traditions, and in no case present anything approaching the profundity of this book. Very strong evidence would need to be presented before we could suppose that a work preserved in Hebrew among the sacred literature of the Jews was of other than Jewish authorship.

7. LANGUAGE AND STYLE

The language of the book is marked by the use of many words found only here in the Old Testament. Aramaisms are frequent, and there are not a few words which can be explained only from Arabic. Very frequently the author uses a word or root common in Aramaic as a parallel to a Hebrew word. This is consistent with the view that the book is of post-exilic origin, coming from the period when Aramaic was increasingly influencing Hebrew speech. There are some linguistic differences between the Elihu speeches and the rest of the book (cf. Gray, pp. xli ff.), and in particular the Aramaic element is rather more prominent in the Elihu speeches (ibid., p. xlvi).

T.C.B.: J.—2*

In the use of the Divine names there would appear to be no difference between the Elihu speeches and the rest of the poetic part of the book, but between the poetic sections and the prose sections there is a clear difference. The prose sections are represented as from the pen of the author of the book, and here he freely uses the Divine name Yahweh (the LORD) and sometimes Elohim (God). In his rubrics introducing the Divine speeches he again uses Yahweh. This name appears on the lips of Job once in the Prologue and once in the Dialogue (see above). In the Dialogue, which is represented as the utterance of the friends and Job in debate with one another, we find that the friends never use the name Yahweh, and Elohim is found but rarely. Three other Divine names are used, both by the friends and Job. These are El, which is used thirty-three times, Eloah, also used thirty-three times, and Shaddai, used twenty-four times (cf. Gray, p. xxxv). Dhorme has shown (pp. lxviff.) that the author shows great skill in his use of these names to avoid the repetition of any one, and that he does not use them indifferently. Shaddai is used twelve times by Job, seven times by Eliphaz, twice by Bildad, probably three times by Zophar (including 27.10, 13), and six times by Elihu. It rarely appears save in association with El or Eloah. On the other hand El and Eloah may be used independently and interchangeably, save that Eloah never stands on Bildad's lips, and El only three times on Zophar's (if 27.10, 13 are rightly assigned to him).

Something should be said about the poetic forms of the book. Hebrew poetry is marked by parallelism and rhythm. Variety in parallelism is secured by completeness or incompleteness, and where it is incomplete there may, or may not, be compensation for the term or terms not paralleled. Moreover, the parallels may be synonymous or antithetic or merely formal. Rhythm is reckoned in terms of accented syllables, and normally one word counts as one unit. But there is no rigid rule as to the number of syllables the unit could contain. Hence short words are commonly not separately reckoned, while long words may be counted as two units. (On all this, cf. Gray, *The Forms of Hebrew Poetry*, 1915.) Sometimes, by anacrusis, an additional word may stand at the beginning of a verse, especially an adversative particle, without being reckoned in the scheme, and in the book of Job there are many examples of this. At

other times, for special emphasis, a line may be short, and the out-
standing example of this in the book of Job is 4.16b (see note there).

In general the rhythm of the book of Job is more regular than
most Hebrew poetry in the Old Testament, and it normally follows
the pattern 3:3, i.e. each of the parallel members contains three units,
each having one accented syllable. Often in Hebrew poems having
this rhythm we find 3:3:3 verses, sometimes called tristichs or
tricola, where the three parts belong together instead of the usual
two. In the book of Job there are a number of such verses, though
they are so infrequent that some editors would eliminate them
altogether by emendation or rearrangement. It is doubtful whether
we should impose complete regularity on the book, though its
general regularity is very remarkable. In a 3:3 poem occasional
2:2:2 lines are found, and this variety is found a few times in Job.

Finally, the brilliance of the author's style, which comes out even
in translation but which is yet more remarkable in the original, may
be noted.

8. TEXT AND VERSIONS

The Hebrew text of Job has suffered much corruption in the course
of transmission, and editors have resorted to emendation on a
greater scale than anywhere else in the Old Testament. It has therefore been necessary to take account of many of these in this commentary. Often the change of a vowel—and the vowels were added
to the text centuries after the consonantal text was written—or the
substitution of one letter for another visually similar letter, or a
redivision of words, will yield a widely different meaning. The
transliteration of the Hebrew will give the English reader some idea
of the amount of change involved, and so give some explanation of
the extraordinary variations in the translations proposed. That
excessive resort to emendation has often been made would be
generally agreed today, and the changes commended in this commentary are far fewer than in some. Nevertheless, it must be frankly
recognized that the text is often corrupt.

Even where the text is not corrupt, the rendering is often uncertain. The same form may be derived from more than one root,

with consequent wide divergence of meaning, and our growing knowledge of the languages of the ancient Near East, especially since the discovery of the Ras Shamra texts and the ever-increasing number of texts brought to light from other neighbouring countries, and the increasing recognition that meanings found in cognate Arabic roots may have been known in ancient times, have greatly widened the range of possible interpretation. It is as necessary to preserve a critical judgment in the use of all these sources as it is to view the M.T. critically.

Every commentator must take account also of the ancient versions, and especially of the LXX. Unfortunately the text is here some 350 to 400 lines shorter than in M.T. Origen supplied the missing lines from the later Greek version of Theod., but copyists often omitted to mark the added lines and copied them as though they were in the original LXX version. It is to be noted that passages omitted in LXX are not marked by a different style from the rest, and that the omissions often destroy the parallelism of the Hebrew. No presumption of superiority for the shorter text is therefore justified. This version must always be used with caution, but nevertheless it probably preserves some readings superior to M.T.

Particularly is this so where the meaning is supported by one or more of the other versions made from the Hebrew, i.e. from the Syriac, Targum, or Vulgate. (The newly discovered Targum from Qumran has not yet been published; cf. J. van der Ploeg, *Le Targum de Job de la Grotte 11 de Qumran*, 1962, and A. S. van der Woude, *SVT* IX, 1962, pp. 322ff.) The fundamental text must always be the Hebrew, and no version can be thought to be superior to it as a whole. Yet is must be recognized that sometimes any one or more of them may preserve an original reading. Even where the versions give no help, the want of sense often betrays some corruption which the commentator must attempt to cure, either by a conjectural emendation or by resort to a different root for the interpretation. Two things, not always avoided, he must seek at all costs to avoid: the attempt to make the writer say what the interpreter would like him to have said, and the resort to emendation where the preserved text yields a relevant sense.

THE BOOK OF
JOB

THE BOOK OF
JOB

1 There was a man in the land of Uz, whose name was Job; and
that man was blameless and upright, one who feared God, and
turned away from evil. ² There were born to him seven sons and
three daughters. ³ He had seven thousand sheep, three thousand
camels, five hundred yoke of oxen, and five hundred she-asses, and
very many servants; so that this man was the greatest of all the
people of the east. ⁴ His sons used to go and hold a feast in the house
of each on his day; and they would send and invite their three sisters

---

PROLOGUE 1–2

The first two chapters are in prose and provide the setting for the poetic dialogue.
They describe Job's exemplary character and condition (1.1–5), two scenes in
heaven where Job's character is impugned by the Satan (1.6–11 and 2.1–6), each
with its sequel of misfortune for Job which he received with patient resignation
(1.13–22 and 2.7–10), and the coming of his friends to comfort him (2.11–13). On
the relation of the prologue to the dialogue, see pp. 8ff.

JOB'S CHARACTER AND CONDITION 1.1–5

1. **There was a man:** the book begins in the manner of a story, the Hebrew
idiom being similar to that of the opening of Nathan's parable (2 Sam. 12.1).
in the land of Uz: the location of Uz is unknown. In Lam. 4.21 'the daughter of
Edom' is said to dwell in the land of Uz, but in Jer. 25.20 the land of Uz is mentioned separately from Edom, but alongside the Philistines, and therefore apparently
in the S. The name Uz is found also in some genealogies. In Gen. 36.28 Uz is said
to be a son of Dishan and to belong to the land of Seir. In Gen. 10.23 Uz is a 'son'
of Aram, and Nahor's eldest son was named Uz (Gen. 22.21). This would suggest
a location N. of Palestine. In an appendix to the book of Job in LXX (42.17*b*),
which is said to be taken from 'the Syriac book', Job's home is located 'on the
borders of Idumea and Arabia', and this location is favoured by some modern
scholars. Others favour a location NE. of Palestine in the Hauran, and this is more
in harmony with the connection of Job with 'the people of the east' (1.3). Job is
presented as a foreigner, and not a Jew.
whose name was Job: the meaning of Job's name also eludes us. In Hebrew it is
'Iyyôḇ, which some have connected with the root 'yb, to yield the meaning 'the

28

hated one', or 'the persecuted one', or 'the hater', or even 'the aggressor'. Others have looked to the Arabic *'wb* for the meaning, and have suggested 'the penitent one'. It is improbable that we should seek a meaning appropriate to the story, and the name may have been taken over by the author from the tradition on which he based his book.

that man was blameless and upright: more important for the understanding of the book than the home or the name of Job is his character. This is stated in unequivocal terms, which are later repeated by God (1.8). It is essential that the reader should know from the start that Job's misfortunes are not the penalty of his misdeeds, as the friends assume.

blameless: this is better than *AV* 'perfect'. The meaning is not that Job is sinless, but the word stresses the moral integrity of his character. Job does not claim that he is sinless, but does maintain that he has not sinned so egregiously as to have brought his troubles on himself, and the reader is here assured that this is so.

one who feared God: not only was Job ethically upright; religiously also he was above reproach. In Biblical thought right relations with God are the true spring of right living. For right living is obedience to the will of God, and reverence for God is the first essential to obedience.

2. There were born to him: the Hebrew suggests 'and so there were born to him', his blessings in his family being the result of his moral and spiritual character (cf. Ps. 127.3; 128.3).

seven sons and three daughters: seven sons represented the acme of blessing (Ru. 4.15; cf. 1 Sam. 2.5). Sons were more valued than daughters; cf. Bab. Talmud, Baba Bathra 16b: 'Happy is he whose children are sons; woe to him whose children are daughters.' The total number of children is ten, and multiples of this figure, sometimes divided in the proportion of 7.3, recur in what follows.

3. five hundred yoke of oxen: the oxen were used in pairs for ploughing, and are so reckoned here.

five hundred she-asses: in contrast to human offspring, she-asses were more esteemed than he-asses. The she-asses were valued for their milk and their foals.

servants: *AV* has 'household', and so *RSV* in the only other passage where the word stands (Gen. 26.14). In form it is an abstract, meaning 'service', but it stands for the whole body of male and female servants (cf. Gen. 12.16).

the people of the east. A general term for the people living E. of Palestine; cf. Gen. 29.1; Jg. 6.33; Isa. 11.14.

4. in the house of each on his day: the meaning is apparently that the seven brothers took it in turn to entertain on the seven days of every week, so that every day was a feast day. This is more natural than the view that the reference is to birthdays, when there would be seven feasts a year. This is all part of the artistry of the story, to build up the picture of the ideal happiness of Job and his family.

invite their three sisters: commentators call attention to this as unusual, and suggest that either exceptional affection or impropriety is implied. It is improbable that there is any thought of impropriety, since the whole account is intended to show that the misfortunes that came upon Job had no cause within his family.

to eat and drink with them. ⁵ And when the days of the feast had run their course, Job would send and sanctify them, and he would rise early in the morning and offer burnt offerings according to the number of them all; for Job said, 'It may be that my sons have sinned, and cursed God in their hearts.' Thus Job did continually.

The mention of the sisters here seems merely to indicate that they were not left out of the felicity of the household.

5. when the days of the feast had run their course: this probably means that at the end of every week Job in his piety sought to expiate any sins his children might have committed thoughtlessly in their merriment. It is neither implied that they had, or had not, committed such sin. It is the scrupulousness of Job that is indicated.

sanctify them: we should probably understand this to mean that by washings and perhaps by a change of garments they were ritually purified for the religious ceremony.

burnt offerings: the term used is not that used for sin-offering in the Priestly Code, but the term for the whole burnt-offering, no part of which was eaten by the offerer. It is clear that it was offered to expiate any sins that might have been committed. It is to be noted that there is no mention of priests here, any more than in the patriarchal stories in Genesis, but the sacrifice was offered by Job himself as the head of the family. This is doubtless to make the story appropriate to the patriarchal age, which seems to be its general setting.

according to the number of them all: as Job says **It may be that my sons have sinned,** the meaning is probably that he offered seven burnt-offerings, and not ten.

cursed God: the Hebrew says 'blessed God'. This may be a euphemism, or, more probably, a scribal change to avoid bringing the word 'curse' into immediate juxtaposition with the word 'God' (cf. S. H. Blank, *HUCA*, XXIII, Part i, 1950–51, pp. 83ff.). More far-fetched ideas have been that from a basic meaning of 'kneel' the word came to mean 'bless' or 'curse', since the same attitude may have been assumed for either, or that since blessing was pronounced at meeting or parting the latter may have been in mind here and so the meaning be 'renounced God' (so *RV*). What is clearly in mind is that the sons might have entertained thoughts which were an offence to God, or such as to call down judgment on them.

in their hearts: it is to be noted that Job's scrupulosity was concerned not merely with his children's acts or words, but even with their thoughts. No possible loophole is to be left for the reader to suspect that Job's misfortunes were to be explained by any deficiency for which he was responsible. Davidson observes: 'It is curious that the sin which Job feared in his children as the consequence of

6 Now there was a day when the sons of God came to present themselves before the LORD, and Satan also came among them. ⁷ The LORD said to Satan, 'Whence have you come?' Satan answered the

---

drinking too deeply of the joys of life was the sin to which he himself was almost driven by the acuteness of his misery.'

THE FIRST SCENE IN HEAVEN 1.6–12

We are now transported to the heavenly court, where Satan is challenged to find any flaw in the character of Job and replies by impugning his motives. He is given permission to test Job, but not to touch his person. Of this scene the reader must be given knowledge, so that he may know the actual cause of Job's sufferings; but the characters of the book cannot know of it, or the debate would be meaningless.

6. a day: Targ. interprets this as New Year's Day.

sons of God: LXX renders by 'angels', and this is certainly the meaning. The expression 'sons of God' means superhuman or celestial beings, just as 'sons of men' means human beings and 'sons of the prophets' means men of the prophetic order. There is no suggestion of physical descent from God. Neither is there any suggestion that these beings are morally superior to men. In Gen. 6.1–4 we read of unions between the 'sons of God' and the 'daughters of men', where the passage clearly thinks of their conduct as evil, and from this passage the myth of the Fallen Angels developed. In 1 Kg. 22.19–23 we read of a lying spirit in the court of God. Here the meaning is that the heavenly court was assembled and the spirits belonging to that court were gathered around God. Each of these spirits was probably thought of as having his own particular duties. In the book of Daniel each nation was conceived of as having its own angel responsible for it (Dan. 10.13, 20, 21; 12.1).

to present themselves: lit. 'to stand over', in the manner of servants standing before a seated master. Yahweh is not merely one of the assembled company. He is the monarch in this court.

Satan: the Hebrew says 'the Satan', or 'the adversary'. The word is used sometimes of an ordinary human adversary. But here it indicates the function of one of the spirits at the court of God who was charged with the exposure of men's pretences. We find this superhuman adversary first in Zech. 3.1, where he stands at God's right hand as the accuser. Here in Job he resorts to insinuation when he is without evidence, while in 1 Chr. 21.1 (cf. 2 Sam. 24.1) Satan has become a proper name, without the article, and he acts as an *agent provocateur*, inciting men to evil. Cf. A. Lods, *Mélanges Syriens* (Dussaud Festschrift), II, 1939, pp. 649ff.

7. Whence have you come? Duhm thinks this implies that God did not know where Satan had been. To this Ehrlich replies by citing Exod. 4.2, where God asks Moses, 'What is that in your hand?' and where God's ignorance can scarcely be presumed. In fact the question is merely the signal for Satan to speak.

LORD, 'From going to and fro on the earth, and from walking up and down on it.' ⁸ And the LORD said to Satan, 'Have you considered my servant Job, that there is none like him on the earth, a blameless and upright man, who fears God and turns away from evil?' ⁹ Then Satan answered the LORD, 'Does Job fear God for naught? ¹⁰ Hast thou not put a hedge about him and his house and all that he has, on every side? Thou hast blessed the work of his hands, and his posses-sions have increased in the land. ¹¹ But put forth thy hand now, and touch all that he has, and he will curse thee to thy face.' ¹² And the LORD said to Satan, 'Behold, all that he has is in your power; only

---

From going to and fro: it is improbable that this means idle wandering, but rather purposeful and unresting service, eagerly seeking to uncover the failings of men. Satan takes his duty too seriously, until it poisons his own nature.

8. Have you considered my servant Job? Satan's eagerness to catch men in fault is known to God, who here asks if he has paid close attention to Job. It is to be noted that God here endorses the estimate of Job given in verse 1, and indeed goes beyond it in declaring that there is none to equal him. It is for this reason that Job presents Satan with his supreme test to discover any flaw in his character.

9. for nought: the Hebrew word can mean 'without cause', as in 2.8, or 'without recompense', as here. Satan is unable to point to any flaw in Job, but ascribes his integrity to mere selfishness by pointing to the prosperity with which he is rewarded. His apparent piety is thus represented as based on love of self, and not love of God. It is interesting to note that whereas it is here suggested that it is easy for the prosperous to be pious, elsewhere in the Bible we are warned of the snare of riches; cf. Dt. 32.15; Prov. 30.8f.; Ps. 73.3–9; Mk 10.23.

10. Hast thou not put a hedge? The word 'thou' is emphatic. Satan justifies his own failure to find any flaw in Job by saying that it is because God himself has surrounded Job with a thorn hedge, so that he cannot get at him. The thorn hedge is, as he goes on to say, Job's prosperity and possessions.
increased: the verb means 'break out', and it is used in Gen. 38.29; Mic. 2.13. Here it means that Job's prosperity is unbounded. While his prosperity is a barrier against any attack, it is without barrier against its own increase.

11. curse thee: the Hebrew again says 'bless'; cf. verse 5. The form of the sentence is that of the oath, and the meaning is 'I swear that he will curse thee'.

12. all that he has is in your power: God does not put forth his own hand against Job, as Satan had suggested, since he does not need to be convinced. But he permits Satan to satisfy himself of the reality and disinterestedness of Job's piety. The test is to be limited to the taking away of the hedge to which Satan had

upon himself do not put forth your hand.' So Satan went forth from
the presence of the LORD.

13 Now there was a day when his sons and daughters were eating
and drinking wine in their eldest brother's house; [14] and there came
a messenger to Job, and said, 'The oxen were ploughing and the
asses feeding beside them; [15] and the Sabe'ans fell upon them and

---

referred. Duhm comments on the speed and coldbloodedness with which God
accepts Satan's suggestion, as though suspicion had been sown in his own mind.
Rather is it the evidence of God's complete trust in Job that he is willing to stake
himself on the unwavering integrity and piety of his servant.

JOB'S FIRST TRIAL 1.13–22

With an efficiency which would have graced a better cause Satan proceeds to
carry through the permitted test, and a series of swift disasters rob Job of family
and fortune. The blows fall one after the other in rapid succession, and in each
case a single servant is spared to carry the news to Job.

13. Now there was a day: this formula belongs to the style of the author, and
it occurs in 1.6 and 2.1 as well as here. Some interval is presupposed between the
scene in heaven and the trial, but this is not to be attributed to any lack of zeal on
the part of Satan. It is rather to be attributed to the artistry of the author, who had
to eliminate any possibility that the series of disasters might have been entailed by
Job's own or his family's misconduct.

in their eldest brother's house: the day is therefore that on which a new series
of feasts began, when Job's sacrifice for any possible sin during the previous round
had been offered. If, as is probable, a continuous round of feasts is envisaged, Job
would have offered sacrifice on that very morning. The complete unexpectedness
of the disaster is thus emphasized, and Job is left with no opportunity of self-
reproach for it. The point of the test is to see Job's response to misfortune, not his
analysis of its cause, and he must therefore be left with no opportunity to seek its
cause in himself.

14. the oxen were ploughing: the season was therefore winter.

the asses: these were she-asses, as in verse 3. Everything is described as perfectly
normal on the day when the blows fell.

15. the Sabeans: the Hebrew says simply 'Sheba', in accordance with the
common Hebrew practice; cf. Amalek for the Amalekites, Ammon for the
Ammonites, etc. Sheba was a S. Arabian state more than 1,000 miles S. of Jerusalem,
from which the Queen of Sheba came to visit Solomon (1 Kg. 10.1–10). This
seems rather remote for a raid, and the people of Sheba are not elsewhere mentioned as robbers, but as merchants (Isa. 60.6; Jer. 6.20; Ezek. 27.22). In Gen. 10.7;
25.3; Ezek. 38.13, Sheba is associated with Dedan, and hence many scholars find

took them, and slew the servants with the edge of the sword; and I alone have escaped to tell you.' ¹⁶ While he was yet speaking, there came another, and said, 'The fire of God fell from heaven and burned up the sheep and the servants, and consumed them; and I alone have escaped to tell you.' ¹⁷ While he was yet speaking, there came another, and said, 'The Chalde'ans formed three companies, and made a raid upon the camels and took them, and slew the servants with the edge of the sword; and I alone have escaped to tell you.' ¹⁸ While he was yet speaking, there came another, and said, 'Your sons and daughters were eating and drinking wine in their eldest brother's house; ¹⁹ and behold, a great wind came across the wilderness, and struck the four corners of the house, and it fell upon the young people, and they are dead; and I alone have escaped to tell you.'

20 Then Job arose, and rent his robe, and shaved his head, and fell upon the ground, and worshipped. ²¹ And he said, 'Naked I came from my mother's womb, and naked shall I return; the LORD gave, and the LORD has taken away; blessed be the name of the LORD.'

22 In all this Job did not sin or charge God with wrong.

---

the reference here to be either to a different Sheba from that in S. Arabia, or to trading stations of the S. Arabian state in N. Arabia.

the edge of the sword: the Hebrew expression is 'the mouth of the sword', as the sword was thought of as devouring its victims.

16. While he was yet speaking: this emphasizes the swiftness with which the blows fell. Job scarcely had time to take in one misfortune before the next followed. **the fire of God:** the first disaster was at the hands of men; the second at the hand of nature. By 'the fire of God' lightning is generally understood. Here it is directed by Satan and it is very extraordinary lightning to destroy 7,000 sheep and the men who looked after them. All this is part of the artistry of the story, which required the complete destruction of all Job's prosperity.

17. The Chaldeans: the Chaldeans are frequently referred to in the Bible as the people who provided the rulers of the Neo-Babylonian empire of Nebuchadrezzar. Our story is set in a much earlier age, and here they are a marauding tribe. The Chaldeans had Aramean connections (cf. Gen. 22.22, where Chesed, their eponymous ancestor, is the uncle of Aram), whereas the Sabeans were of Arabian stock, and the previous attack was probably thought of as coming from the S. and this from the N.

formed three companies: this device was frequently employed; cf. Jg. 7.16; 9.43; 1 Sam. 11.11; 13.17.

19. a great wind: since it struck the four corners of the house, it must have been a whirlwind. It is to be noticed that the third disaster, like the first, was brought about by human agency, and the fourth, like the second, by natural forces. Men and nature are alike moved by Satan, to whom power to carry through the test must be assumed to have been given in the permission to make the test. This blow is the climax of the test, robbing Job at a stroke of all his children.

the young people: the word is the same as that rendered 'the servants' in the accounts of the previous disasters. Here it must include the children of Job as well as the servants. Though only the masculine word is expressed, it obviously included the daughters also, since only one servant escaped from the building. Again it is the artistry of the writer which dictated the use of the same word in all four cases. Cheyne unkindly says: 'His wife . . . is spared; she seems to be recognized by the Satan as an unconscious ally.' It is doubtful if this was in the mind of the author. It would have been difficult to include Job's wife in the fourth disaster, since if she had been represented as attending the feast, Job's own absence from it would have been strange. Moreover, it is to be observed that at this stage she was not an ally of Satan, but seems to have accepted the terrible blows of the day with no more complaint than Job.

20. arose: Job had received the messengers seated.

rent his robe: this was a sign of grief; cf. Gen. 37.29, 34; 2 Sam. 13.31. The 'robe' was the *me'îl*, or mantle worn over the tunic by men of rank (1 Sam. 15.27; 18.4; 28.14), or by the high priest (Exod. 28.31).

shaved his head: this again was a rite of mourning; cf. Isa. 15.2; 22.12; Jer. 7.29; 16.6; Am. 8.10; Mic. 1.16.

fell to the ground: this was not in despair but in reverence; cf. 2 Sam. 1.2; 9.6; 14.4; 2 Chr. 20.18. Job's piety triumphed over the first series of trials, and he bowed himself before God in humble submission.

21. naked shall I return: commentators bring singularly prosaic minds to this phrase, and point out that Job could not return to his mother's womb, or suggest that he means to the womb of Mother Earth. Budde suggests that the word 'thither', which is unrepresented in *RSV*, is a euphemism for 'to Sheol', and against this it is argued that one does not 'return' to Sheol at death. Ricciotti (*ZAW*, LXVII, 1955, pp. 249ff.) proposes to find a reference to the custom of burying in the position of a foetus in the womb. But this is no more 'return' than going to Sheol. It is probable that the author did not intend to be precise and literal, and meant no more than 'Naked I came into life and naked I shall die' (cf. Ec. 5.15). This verse is in poetry, and is not addressed to prosaic minds.

blessed be the name of the LORD: in the Hebrew the word for 'bless' is the same as that used in verses 5,11, but whereas there it really stands for 'curse', here it clearly means 'bless'. So far from Satan's oath being justified, it is God's faith in Job which is triumphantly vindicated. On the use of the Tetragrammaton here, cf. Introduction, p. 11.

22. wrong: the *AV* has 'nor charged God foolishly', but the point is not to

2 Again there was a day when the sons of God came to present themselves before the LORD, and Satan also came among them to present himself before the LORD. ²And the LORD said to Satan, 'Whence have you come?' Satan answered the LORD, 'From going to and fro on the earth, and from walking up and down on it.' ³And the LORD said to Satan, 'Have you considered my servant Job, that there is none like him on the earth, a blameless and upright man, who fears God and turns away from evil? He still holds fast his integrity, although you moved me against him, to destroy him

---

express the writer's judgment on Job, but Job's attitude to God. The Hebrew word means 'tastelessness' (cf. the cognate word in 6.6). Here it is used metaphorically in a moral sense, to ascribe to God what is unseemly (so Horst) or unworthy (so Gray). *RV* has 'charged God with foolishness', which goes back to the LXX. For the development of meaning Dhorme compares the Latin *fatuus*, which meant both 'insipid' and 'foolish'. Tur-Sinai finds Arabic justification for the meaning 'spittle', and renders 'he did not throw spittle at God', or 'he did not lay reproach on God'. The former of these would more naturally become 'insult' than 'reproach'. The verb is more naturally rendered 'ascribe to', and the verse is best taken to mean that Job did not ascribe to God some quality which is morally reprehensible. His piety came through the test unscathed. Ehrlich proposed to emend the word from *tiplah* to *tᵉpillāh*, which normally means 'prayer', but to give it the unwarranted sense of 'protest'.

THE SECOND SCENE IN HEAVEN 2.1–5

The scene returns to heaven, where Satan is confronted by God with his failure. He refuses to recognize this and maintains that the test has been too slight, and is given permission to make a greater test. This second scene is described as far as possible in the same words as the first.

1. **a day:** Targ. interprets as the Day of Atonement.
to present himself before the LORD: these words are absent from LXX. Some (e.g. Gray) think they are a dittograph in the Hebrew, and it is to be noticed that they do not stand in 1.6. Budde, however, thinks they were deliberately omitted from LXX for reasons of reverence. It is hard to see how this can be maintained, since the meaning is unchanged whether they are retained or omitted. If Satan was among those who presented themselves to the Lord he must have presented himself with them.

3. Satan's reply makes no allusion to Job or to his own failure. God renews his testimony to Job's integrity of character, and charges Satan with having made a baseless accusation against him. Satan's function is to accuse, not to accuse falsely.

without cause.' **4** Then Satan answered the LORD, 'Skin for skin!
All that a man has he will give for his life. **5** But put forth thy hand
now, and touch his bone and his flesh, and he will curse thee to thy

---

without cause: God picks up the very word that Satan had used in 1.9, but in a
different sense (see note there). Satan had said Job did not serve God *hinnām*; God
now says that Satan incited him against Job *hinnām*. Here it might be translated
either 'without cause', or 'to no purpose', i.e. without effect.

4. Skin for skin: this expression has been much discussed and many different
interpretations offered. Olshausen suggests it means 'So long as you leave his skin
alone, he will leave yours'; but this seems very unlikely. Many commentators
have thought it reflects the language of barter: 'One skin a man will give up for
another.' To this Tur-Sinai replies that barter does not involve the exchange of
one thing for another of the same kind. An ancient Jewish explanation is that it
means that one will give up one member of the body to save another, e.g. an arm
to save the head. But the skin is not a member of the body in the same sense as an
arm. More relevant is the view that it means that one is prepared to give up
someone else's skin to save one's own, and so Job had been ready to sacrifice the
skins of his family and servants and animals to save his own. But Job had never
been confronted with this choice, and can scarcely be said to have sacrificed his
children and possessions. The preposition which is here rendered 'for' often means
'behind', and this has suggested the interpretation 'one skin behind another'. Only
Job's outer skin had yet been touched. In 1.10 this preposition had been used in the
expression 'put a hedge about him', where the thought was that Job was protected
behind a hedge. Here Satan is maintaining that he is still protected, but instead of a
hedge he speaks of skin, since he is carrying the thought to Job's person. All that
Job had been bereft of was but an outer skin; behind that was another.

for his life: Job's life was not in question, since if he was killed the motive of his
piety could not thereby be determined. The word rendered 'for' is again the same
as in 'skin for skin', but here it means 'on behalf of'. It cannot here mean 'in
exchange for', since life was something Job already had and not something offered
to him. Moreover, 'his life' (Hebrew *napšō*) goes beyond the probable meaning
here. A single word in Hebrew may represent a variety of words in English. In
verse 6 it must mean 'his life'; but here it appears to mean 'himself'—a meaning it
quite commonly has. What Satan here says is that a man is ready to give up
everything he possesses so long as his own person is spared. He is therefore asking
permission to carry the test beyond the outer hedge to the person of Job, as the
following verse makes plain.

5. his bone and his flesh: here it is made clear that the inner skin is not the
covering of Job's body but his whole physical frame.

curse thee: cf. on 1.5, 11.

face." ⁶And the LORD said to Satan, 'Behold, he is in your power; only spare his life.'

7 So Satan went forth from the presence of the LORD, and afflicted Job with loathsome sores from the sole of his foot to the crown of his head. ⁸And he took a potsherd with which to scrape himself, and sat among the ashes.

9 Then his wife said to him, 'Do you still hold fast your integrity? Curse God, and die.' ¹⁰ But he said to her, 'You speak as one of the foolish women would speak. Shall we receive good at the hand of God, and shall we not receive evil?' In all this Job did not sin with his lips.

---

6. only spare his life: if what Satan had meant in verse 4 was that the only adequate test of Job's piety was an attack on his life, then God frustrated him. But since the limitation here imposed was essential to the test proposed, we should render *napšô* differently in the two verses.

JOB'S SECOND TRIAL 2.7–10

This time no interval of time is presupposed by such a formula as 'now there was a day' (1.13). There was no need to delay a moment, and the Satan went straight from God's presence to attack Job's person.

7. loathsome sores: Job's disease is commonly identified with the form of leprosy known as elephantiasis, a disease so named because the swollen limbs and blackened skin give the victim some resemblance to an elephant. Gray objects that 'elephantiasis develops slowly . . . ; but the narrative almost certainly intends us to understand that Job was immediately smitten with intensely painful and loathsome symptoms, attacking every part of his body'. It should be remembered, however, that there was something phenomenal about every misfortune that struck Job. Macalister (*DB*, III, 1900, pp. 329f.) argued for identification with the Oriental sore, or Biskra button, but this was disputed by Masterman (*PEFQS*, L, 1918, p. 168), who maintained that it was 'a very extensive erythema'. Koehler (*KB*, *s.v.*) calls it smallpox, and S. L. Terrien suggests the skin disorder known as *pemphicus foliaceus*. G. N. Münch (*Die Zaraath der hebräischen Bibel*, 1893, p. 143) proposes the identification with chronic eczema. Dhorme thinks it is going too far to identify Job's disease with leprosy (and so Ball), but notes that Syriac and Greek tradition saw in the disease malignant ulcers (Syriac has the same expression as here in Rev. 16.2). It seems idle to try to give any precise identification of the disease. The symptoms mentioned in the book are: inflamed eruptions, 2.7; intolerable itching, 2.8, disfigured appearance, 2.12; maggots in the ulcers, 7.5; terrifying dreams, 7.14; running tears blinding the eyes, 16.16; fetid breath, 19.17;

emaciated body, 19.20; erosion of the bones, 30.17; blackening and peeling off of the skin, 30.30. It may be noted that in the Prayer of Nabonidus found among the Dead Sea Scrolls, Nabonidus is said to have been afflicted with *šhn' b'yš* for seven years (cf. R. Meyer, *Das Gebet des Nabonid*, 1962, p. 16, A 2f.), where the name for the disease corresponds to the name here.

8. to scrape himself: because of the intolerable itching.

sat among the ashes: Job may have been among the ashes in mourning for his children when the disease struck him, or he may have gone there when his loathsome disease came upon him. By 'the ashes' is meant the dunghill outside the town, vividly described by Wetzstein (in Delitzsch). Here dung and other rubbish were thrown, and it was the resort of children and outcasts. Here too came the dogs of the town. In course of time it often reached a considerable height and served as a watchtower. In time of public or individual calamity men came here to sit (Isa. 47.1; Jon. 3.6), or to roll in the ashes (Jer. 6.26, Mic. 1.10), or to throw dust on the head (Ezek. 27.30).

9. his wife said: in LXX a long speech is put into the mouth of Job's wife. Ball suggests that it may go back to a Hebrew original, but there is no reason to suppose it belonged to the authentic text. The author of Job shows great economy of words in setting the stage for the dialogue.

Curse God: cf. on 1.5, 11. The early Fathers compared the role of Job's wife with that of Eve in tempting Adam. It is all part of the artistry of the writer to emphasisze the unwavering piety of Job in not forsaking his resignation in adversity, when even the wife who was spared to him became, as Augustine called her, *diaboli adjutrix*, and added her voice to the misfortunes that had befallen him in trying his spirit. It is not clear whether she meant, 'Curse God and so call down on yourself the wrath of God which will kill you and end your misery,' or, 'Since death is imminent, curse God who has brought all this on you.'

10. one of the foolish women: this is less a reflection on the intelligence of Job's wife than a reflection on her moral and spiritual quality. The masculine form of this word provides the name of Nabal (1 Sam. 25.25), and it denotes one who is both mentally and morally obtuse. In Ps. 14.1 it is the man of this character who says 'There is no God', and *RV* marg. renders here 'the impious women'.

Shall we receive good? In this expression of resignation we have the clearest evidence of Satan's failure. Contrary to his prediction, Job no more now than formerly abandoned his piety. In the course of the dialogue Job sometimes approaches blasphemy, but it is the friends who come to 'comfort' him who drive him to this by their reproaches and misrepresentation of God more than his misfortunes.

Job did not sin with his lips: it is not implied that he sinned in any other way. It was sin with the lips that Satan had predicted, and the prediction is emphatically declared to have remained unfulfilled. Targ. cynically adds 'but in his mind he thought on words'.

11 Now when Job's three friends heard of all this evil that had come upon him, they came each from his own place, Eli'phaz the Te'manite, Bildad the Shuhite, and Zophar the Na'amathite. They made an appointment together to come to condole with him and comfort him. ¹²And when they saw him from afar, they did not recognize him; and they raised their voices and wept; and they rent their robes and sprinkled dust upon their heads toward heaven.

JOB'S FRIENDS COME TO COMFORT HIM 2.11–13

Some time must have elapsed for the news of Job's misfortunes to reach his friends and for them to journey to see him.

11. Eliphaz the Temanite: Eliphaz is an Edomite name (Gen. 36.4) and Teman is both an Edomite personal name (Gen. 36.11) and a local name frequently associated with Edom (Jer. 49.7, 20; Ezek. 25.13; Am. 1.12; Ob. 8). Albright (*AJSL*, XLIV, 1927–28, p. 36) suggests the possibility that 'Temanite' should be connected with Tema in Arabia.

Bildad the Shuhite: the name Bildad does not occur in the Bible outside the book of Job. It is found in the Nuzi tablets, however. Albright (loc. cit., p. 33) maintains that the name was proto-Aramean, meaning 'Dad brings forth'. On the other hand Speiser (*AfO*, VI, 1930–31, p. 23) finds it to mean 'son of Hadad' and to correspond to the name Benhadad. Shuhite is probably to be connected with Shuah, a son of Abraham by Keturah (Gen. 25.2), who was sent away to the E. (Gen. 25.6). Albright (in *Geschichte und Altes Testament*, 1953, p. 9) connects Shuah with Akkadian *Sûḫu* on the Middle Euphrates, and many scholars find a connection between *Sûḫu* and Shuhite (so Fohrer).

Zophar the Naamathite: there was a Naamah in Judah (Jos. 15.41), but this is unlikely to be the place referred to here. LXX makes Zophar the king of the Mineans, in the extreme S. of Arabia. This too is to be rejected. The location is unknown, and the name Zophar does not occur outside the book of Job.

made an appointment: it is all part of the artistry of the writer to make them arrive together to set the stage for the dialogue. It would have taken some time for them to communicate with one another to arrange a rendezvous.

to condole with him: the verb means lit. 'to move to and fro'. It then comes to mean 'to shake the head' or 'to rock the body to and fro', as mourners did as a sign of grief. It is used with the verb 'comfort', as here, in Job 42.11 (where *RSV* renders 'show sympathy'); Ps. 69.20 (where *RSV* renders 'pity'); Isa. 51.19; Nah. 3.7 (where *RSV* renders 'bemoan').

12. did not recognize him: he was so disfigured by his disease; cf. Isa. 52.14.
sprinkled dust upon their heads toward heaven: the verb is commonly used of liquids, but is used of coals in Ezek. 10.2, of ashes in Exod. 9.8, 10, and of

¹³ And they sat with him on the ground seven days and seven nights, and no one spoke a word to him, for they saw that his suffering was very great.

3 After this Job opened his mouth and cursed the day of his birth. ² And Job said:

---

cummin in Isa. 28.25. It means 'to toss in quantities'. The phrase is generally understood to mean 'they tossed dust into the air and it fell upon their heads', but this meaning is curiously expressed. Dhorme thinks 'upon their heads' and 'towards heaven' represent two alternative readings. The idea underlying the act is not clear. Duhm thinks it symbolizes the fact that Job's prosperity is laid waste, as duststorms lay waste fruitful land. Davidson suggests that it symbolizes the fact that they were laid in the dust by a calamity from heaven. Ball thinks the idea is to darken the air, since darkness is a natural symbol of sorrow.

13. sat with him on the ground: this was a customary posture for mourners; cf. Lam. 2.10.

seven days and seven nights: this is the usual time of mourning for the dead; cf. Gen. 50.10; 1 Sam. 31.13; Sir. 22.12. Job's friends mourn for him as one already dead. Ezekiel sat overwhelmed and in silence for seven days among the exiles (Ezek. 3.15).

JOB'S OPENING SOLILOQUY 3

After seven days of silent sympathy, Job utters his opening lament on his sufferings. He curses the day of his birth and the night of his conception (verses 1–10), wishes he had died at birth (verses 11–19), and asks why the wretched are forced to live (verses 20–26). Strahan observes: 'The faith which meets the first shock of disaster with noble fortitude may be unequal to the perpetual strain of the monotonous aftertime.' Job laments his misery, but does not complain of injustice, or lament his integrity. He does not complain of the suffering of the righteous, but raises the question why any man should suffer as he suffers.

JOB WISHES HE HAD NEVER BEEN BORN 3.1–10

With this passage Jer. 20.14–18 may be compared.

1. cursed the day of his birth: here the word 'cursed' is allowed to stand in the Hebrew (cf. on 1.5, 11). For 'the day of his birth', the Hebrew simply says 'his day'; but the context makes it clear that the reference is to the day on which he was born; cf. Jer. 20.14ff.

2. said: RV has 'answered and said'. But the Hebrew verb is often used where no previous speech has been mentioned, when it means speaking in response to a situation or occasion.

³ 'Let the day perish wherein I was born,
    and the night which said,
    "A man-child is conceived."
⁴ Let that day be darkness!

---

3. Let the day perish: Peake says, 'According to the thought underlying the expression, a day did not cease to be when it was succeeded by the following day. The same day would return in the following year.' To Job it was this inauspicious day which was responsible for his misery, and likely to bring misery to others. In Hebrew thought a curse was not the mere expression of a wish; it was charged with power to work for its own fulfilment, and once uttered it had passed beyond the power of its utterer, and gone forth on its evil errand. Cf. S. H. Blank, *HUCA*, XXIII, i 1950–51, p. 78.

and the night which said: the night in which Job was conceived is here personified and to it is ascribed knowledge even of the sex of the child then conceived. LXX has 'and the night in which they said: Behold a male'. This transfers the meaning from the night of conception to the time of Job's birth, so that we have only a more precise definition of the period of the day in which he was born. Ball prefers this reading, on the ground that the conception ought to have been mentioned before the birth if it was mentioned at all. Many other commentators favour the LXX reading (so Stevenson), which involves only a change of vocalization of a single word (*hªrēh* for *hōrāh*). On the other hand, Peake and Dhorme decidedly prefer the Hebrew, which seems far more vigorous and poetic (so also Horst and Fohrer). The prosaic and ultra-logical mind should avoid poetry. The *AV* rendering 'the night in which it was said' is grammatically possible, but inferior to the personification of the night, and leaves the speaker difficult to imagine, unless some angel is imported into the verse, since no human speaker could know the sex of the foetus at the time of conception. Tur-Sinai finds the meaning 'refuse' for the verb: 'Oh that the night had refused to let a male be conceived!'

4. that day: LXX^B has 'that night', but the reference is to the time of birth (see on verse 3), as in the Hebrew. Bickell, Cheyne, and Stevenson delete the first line of this verse, since the verse is a tristich, while Duhm transfers here the words 'let it hope for light, but have none' from verse 9, so as to make two distichs. But while tristichs are not common in Job, there are quite a number, and elsewhere in the *OT* it is by no means uncommon for a tristich to be found among distichs. Hebrew poetry was far more flexible than most of our English poetry, and it is unwise to try to put it in a strait-jacket. We should thus prefer the Hebrew, with Peake, Dhorme, and Horst, and this is supported by other LXX manuscripts. If it is desired to reduce the number of tristichs, the suggestion of Gray, that we should transpose verses 4*b* and 4*c*, is preferable.

> May God above not seek it,
>   nor light shine upon it.
> 5 Let gloom and deep darkness claim it.
>   Let clouds dwell upon it;
>   let the blackness of the day terrify it.
> 6 That night—let thick darkness seize it!

---

seek it: God is conceived of as summoning the days to take their place as their turn comes round.

nor light shine upon it: Job would have the day cursed by being totally without light. The word for 'light' (*nehārāh*) is found only here, but its meaning is not in doubt. Cheyne proposed to replace it by *lebānāh*, a poetic word for 'the moon', but this was to make it consistent with his interpretation of verse 4*a*.

5. deep darkness: AV and RV have 'the shadow of death', and the older view of the word *ṣalmāwet* was that it was a compound word, composed of *ṣal* = 'shadow' and *māwet* = 'death'. Most modern scholars prefer the view that the word should read *ṣalmût*, and that it is an abstract noun from the root *ṣlm* = 'be dark' (so KB and Dhorme). Nöldeke (*ZAW*, XVII, 1897, pp. 183ff.) defended the older view and he has been followed by Marti (*Das Buch Jesaja*, 1900, pp. 91f.), Budde, *BDB*, and Buttenwieser. Gray replied to Nöldeke's arguments and showed that they were inconclusive. The word is used in contexts where there is no thought of death (Am. 5.9; Job 28.3). More recently D. Winton Thomas has argued (*JSS*, VII, 1962, pp. 191ff.) that *ṣalmāwet* is the correct form and that it should perhaps be written as two words, and that *māwet* here, as in some other passages, has superlative force. Thus, without any change of the text he reaches the meaning 'deep darkness'.

claim it: RV has 'claim it for their own', and so *BDB* and *KB*. This connects it with the root *g'l*, from which the word for 'next of kin' or 'redeemer' is derived. Gray says: 'The word means properly to *claim effectively* property the possession of which has lapsed [i.e. to *redeem* it]; . . . hence the idea is, as soon as the day appears, let darkness, as its nearest relation, at once assert its rights, and take possession of it.' Tur-Sinai objects that darkness cannot be said to have next-of-kin rights in respect of the day, and Ehrlich says this is too artificial a view to be correct. AV 'stain it' connects the word with another root *g'l*, 'to pollute' (cf. Mal. 1.7, 12), and this is supported by Targ. and rabbinical commentators. Dhorme and Tur-Sinai follow this view. A. R. Johnson (*SVT*, I, 1953, p. 73) argues that the meaning is 'cover', and that this basic meaning can yield the two senses of 'protect' and 'defile'. He therefore renders here 'cover it' (so Jastrow, *Dictionary of the Targumim, s.v.*) On this root cf. also N. H. Snaith, *ALUOS*, III, 1963, pp. 60ff.

the blackness of the day: this is usually taken to mean the various things that cause darkness in the daytime and inspire terror, such as eclipses and storms.

let it not rejoice among the days of the year,
let it not come into the number of the months.
⁷ Yea, let that night be barren;
let no joyful cry be heard in it.
⁸ Let those curse it who curse the day,

Dhorme, however, takes it to mean thick mists and fogs. Less appropriate is the rendering of Targ, 'like the bitternesses of the day' (similarly Jerome and Aq.). These connect the word with a root *mrr*, whereas it should rather be connected with the root *kmr*='be black', which is found in Syriac. Cheyne emends the line to make it similar to verse 8*a* and then deletes it because it is similar!

terrify it: the verb which stands here is found eight times in Job, and eight times elsewhere in the OT. Stevenson renders 'overwhelm it', while Dillmann and Beer needlessly change the text to yield 'abhor it'.

6. let it not rejoice among: this meaning is favoured by Davidson, Peake, Gray. Targ. rendered 'be joined to' (similarly Sym.; Syr. and Vulg. 'be reckoned among'). This involves a slight change of vowels, and is followed by *AV* and many editors (so Ball, Dhorme, Hölscher, Stevenson, Tur-Sinai, Horst, Fohrer). It is also favoured by Gen. 49.6, where the same two verbs as in verses 6*b* and 6*c* here are used. Job would have the day blotted out on the calendar.

7. barren: this is not the usual word for 'barren'; it means 'stony', 'as unproductive as a rock'. Ball compares the Chinese *shih nü*='stony woman', 'barren woman'. Job desires that night never again to see offspring, so that no others may know the misery he experiences. Dhorme renders 'full of gloom' (cf. Buttenwieser), which is an extended meaning; the barren woman is sorrowful.

8. curse . . . curse: two different verbs are used in the Hebrew, both different from the verb of verse 1.

who curse the day: this is generally understood to mean those who are able to lay a spell on the day to make it unlucky or to produce eclipses. The verb is ordinarily translated 'curse', but E. A. Speiser (*JAOS*, LXXX, 1960, pp. 198ff.) maintains that it really means 'cast a spell on'. Dhorme takes the line to mean 'may it be execrated by those who curse their own birthday'. Gunkel (*Schopfung und Chaos*, 1895, p. 59) proposed to read *yām*='sea' instead of *yôm*='day', and this has been followed by Cheyne and Horst. The meaning then is that they are able to control the sea and its monster Leviathan (see note below). G. R. Driver (*SVT*, III, 1955, p. 72) cites an Aramaic incantation, 'I will cast spells upon you with the spell of the sea and the spell of the dragon Leviathan.' Budde, Duhm, Dhorme, Hölscher, Weiser, and Fohrer retain M.T. as more appropriate to the context. But 'let them curse that night who curse the day' is much flatter than the proposed reading. Albright (*JBL*, LVII, 1938, p. 227) reads *yām*, but identifies this with the sea-dragon Yam, who appears in the Ras Shamra texts as Yammu (cf. Pope).

who are skilled to rouse up Levi'athan.
9 Let the stars of its dawn be dark;
   let it hope for light, but have none,
   nor see the eyelids of the morning;
10 because it did not shut the doors of my mother's womb,
   nor hide trouble from my eyes.
11 'Why did I not die at birth,
   come forth from the womb and expire?

E. Ullendorff (*VT*, XI, 1961, pp. 350f.) derives the verb from *nākaḫ*='pierce', instead of *ḳabaḫ*='curse', and renders 'let the light-rays of day pierce it', finding the sense to be that as day is cursed by darkness, so night is cursed by light.
skilled: lit. 'ready'.

to rouse up: G. R. Driver (loc. cit.) proposes to find another root, meaning 'to revile', but this is less appropriate.

Leviathan: the name means something wreathed or coiled (cf. *liwyāh*='wreath', Prov. 1.9; 4.9). Leviathan is a sea monster (Ps. 104.26), and in the Bible (cf. H. Wallace, *BA*, XI, 1948, pp. 61ff.) it denotes a mythical, serpent-like creature (cf. Ps. 74.14; Isa. 27.1), who appears in the Ras Shamra texts as *ltn*, where it has seven heads (cf. R. de Vaux, *RB*, XLVI, 1937, p. 545). It is probable that eclipses were believed to be due to its swallowing the sun or the moon (cf. G. A. Smith, *Book of the Twelve Prophets*, II, 1928 ed., p. 512). *AV* 'their mourning' goes back to the Targum.

9. the stars of its dawn: may the harbingers of the day never announce the issue of that night into day! Dhorme transfers this verse to follow verse 6, to yield a more logical order. But the transfer is unnecessary.

the eyelids of the morning: dawn is thought of as a person, from whose opening eyelids rays of light proceed. Cf. Milton: 'the opening eyelids of the morn' (*Lycidas*, 26). The figure is repeated in 41.18. It is possible that this is a verbal reminiscence of a lost myth, but it could equally be just poetic metaphor. Cf. Homer's 'rosy-fingered Dawn' (*Odyssey*, II:1, etc.).

10. my mother's womb: the Hebrew says simply 'my womb', which here means 'the womb from which I emerged'. Here Job states the reason for the curse he had pronounced: because the night had not prevented his conception. The shutting of the womb is elsewhere a figure for the preventing of conception; cf. 1 Sam. 1.6. Similarly, the opening of the womb permits conception (Gen. 29.31).
trouble: properly 'work', 'toil', and then 'sorrow', 'suffering'.

JOB WISHES HE HAD DIED AT BIRTH 3.11–19

If his conception had not been prevented, he would at least have been better off

12 Why did the knees receive me?
   Or why the breasts, that I should suck?
13 For then I should have lain down and been quiet;
   I should have slept; then I should have been at rest,
14 with kings and counsellors of the earth
   who rebuilt ruins for themselves,

---

if he had perished at birth. He would have been in Sheol, which was to be preferred to his present condition.

11. at birth: *AV* and *RV* render literally, 'from the womb'. The same expression is found in Jer. 20.17, where *RSV* has 'in the womb', but where the meaning is probably, as here, 'at birth'. LXX has 'in the womb' here.

12. the knees: many editors find the reference here to be to the father's knees, taking the child in acknowledgement that it is his; cf. Gen. 50.23. But Dhorme interprets of the mother's knees, receiving the child to suckle it (so Buttenwieser). Beer and Duhm delete this verse and transfer verse 16 to follow verse 11. But verse 12 follows naturally on verse 11. On the other hand verse 16 does not follow naturally on verse 15. Hence Dhorme transfers verse 16 to follow verse 12, and this may be right.

13. been quiet: the measure of Job's misery is to be seen in his thinking of death as desirable compared with it. The Hebrews had no conception of a worthwhile Afterlife. Sheol was a land of darkness and gloom (10.12f.), where great and small were gathered together (3.19) behind bars (17.16), conscious of nothing but their misery (14.22), unconscious of the fortunes of their family (14.21), and with no hope of deliverance (7.9; 14.10ff.). Yet even this looked attractive to Job.

14. rebuilt ruins: the Hebrew could carry this meaning, but it does not seem very appropriate. But there is no necessary idea of rebuilding. Moreover, kings do not become famous by rebuilding ruined sites. Tur-Sinai renders 'built among ruins', but this is no better. Many emendations of the text have been proposed, as 'arāmôṯ='palaces' (Dillmann), hêḵālôṯ='palaces' (Beer), ḳiḇrôṯ 'ôlām='everlasting tombs' (Cheyne, *ET*, x, 1898–99, p. 380, and Peake). S. Daiches (*JQR*, xx, 1908, pp. 637ff.) connects the Hebrew word here, ḥorāḇôṯ, with the Arabic miḥrāb, and renders 'fortified cities' (cf. G. R Driver, *EThL*, xxvi, 1950, p. 349). Ewald proposed to emend to ḥarāmôṯ and to render 'pyramids', and this has been accepted by Budde, Duhm, Gray, Stevenson, Weiser, and Fohrer, and is pronounced attractive by Gibson, but is rejected as precarious by Ball and Horst. Dhorme secures the same meaning without change of text by rendering 'built in desert places' and observing that the pyramids and other tombs of the Pharoahs were built in desert places. Hölscher retains the text, but renders 'pyramids' by arguing that the Arabic word for 'pyramid' comes from a root meaning 'be decrepit with age' and reading the same into the Hebrew root used here. But the element of

¹⁵ or with princes who had gold,
    who filled their houses with silver.
¹⁶ Or why was I not as a hidden untimely birth,
    as infants that never see the light?
¹⁷ There the wicked cease from troubling,
    and there the weary are at rest.
¹⁸ There the prisoners are at ease together;
    they hear not the voice of the taskmaster.
¹⁹ The small and the great are there,
    and the slave is free from his master.

---

age does not belong to this root, and it is doubtful if the pyramids are relevant to this context at all. We may render 'who built for themselves the ruins', i.e. the places which today are ruins. Had Job died at birth he would have been in the same state as the mighty of past ages, whose building achievements, now lying in ruins, excited wonder.

15. filled their houses: Duhm took this to mean their tombs, and thought of treasures buried in the graves of the mighty. More naturally it refers to their palaces and the wealth they enjoyed in life.

16. Cf. on verse 12. If Job had to be conceived, why could he not have been killed at birth, or have been still-born? His present misery blots out all the memory of the years of happiness.

17. There: i.e. in Sheol, connecting with verse 15.
troubling: the meaning is probably 'cease from agitating themselves', not 'cease from troubling others'. The word is rendered 'rage' in 39.24 of the excitement of the horse, and 'rumbling' (of the thunder) in 37.2.

18. prisoners: not persons in confinement, but captives set to forced labour and brutally ill-treated.
taskmaster: the term used in Exod. 3.7; 5.6 of the Egyptian taskmasters, whose harshness left such enduring memories in Israel. It is also used of the oppressive exactor of tribute (Dan. 11.20), or of the oppressive foreign ruler (Isa. 14.4).

19. are there: many editors (Budde, Peake, Strahan, Dhorme, Horst, Fohrer) render 'are there alike'. Gray disputes this; but cf. Ps. 102.27 (M.T. 28). The meaning almost certainly is that death levels all; cf. Ec. 9.2, 10.
free: I. Mendelsohn (*BASOR*, no. 83, October, 1941, pp. 36-9; and no. 139, October, 1955, pp. 9-11) argues from Assyrian, Ugaritic, and Alalakh texts, that the fundamental meaning of this word, *ḥopšī*, is 'free proletarian' or 'tenant farmer', and E. R. Lacheman (*BASOR*, no. 86, April, 1942, pp. 36f.) that in Nuzi texts it means 'semi-free man'. In Ps. 88.5 *RSV* renders 'one forsaken' (*AV* 'free'; *RV* 'cast off'), in a context where it appears to mean 'set apart' from God or friends.

²⁰ 'Why is light given to him that is in misery,
    and life to the bitter in soul,
²¹ who long for death, but it comes not,
    and dig for it more than for hid treasures;
²² who rejoice exceedingly,
    and are glad, when they find the grave?

In 2 Kg. 15.5 Azariah, after he became a leper, dwelt in a *bêṯ haḥopšîṯ*, which *RSV* renders 'a separate house'. Hence R. Gordis (*JQR*, N.S., xxvii, 1936–37, pp. 43f.) thinks this root had contrasted meanings, 'freedom' or 'confinement'. R. de Vaux (*RB*, xlvi, 1937, p. 533) thinks Azariah was confined in a cave. Here the context indicates that it must mean 'free'.

3.20–26 Job returns from the thought of what might have been to his present misery, and asks why those in such anguish as his are compelled to live.

20. Why is light given? This rendering follows the ancient versions. The Hebrew says 'Why does he, or one, give', and many editors prefer the rendering 'he', with a covert reference to God, though Job hesitates to specify him. 'Light' is the light of life.

him that is in misery: the Hebrew word is the adjective from the same root as the noun rendered 'trouble' in verse 10.

the bitter in soul: 'the bitter' is plural. Job is thinking not only of himself, but of others who suffer.

21. who long for death: in Hos. 6.9 the verb is used for 'lying in ambush'. It is therefore an effective expression of their eagerness for death.

dig for it: the verb may have the more general meaning of 'search' (39.29, *RSV* 'spies out'). Here the context shows that it has the more literal meaning.

more than for hid treasures: Gibson and Peake quote Thomson (*The Land and the Book*, p. 135): 'There is not another comparison within the whole compass of human actions so vivid as this. I have heard of diggers actually fainting when they have come upon even a single coin. They become positively frantic, dig all night with desperate earnestness, and continue to work till utterly exhausted. There are, at this hour, hundreds of persons thus engaged all over the country. Not a few spend their last farthing in these ruinous efforts.'

22. exceedingly: lit. 'to the point of exultation' (Buttenwieser 'beyond measure'). The same expression is found in Hos. 9.1, where, however, it is probably not original and *RSV* has 'exult not'. Houbigant proposed to read *gal* for *gîl* and to render 'who rejoice over the grave heap', and this has been followed by many editors. Ball rejects this, but finds the same meaning by reading *gāḏiš*='tomb' (cf. 21.32). An alternative preferred by Hölscher is the reading *gôlēl*, which in post-biblical Hebrew means 'the stone used for closing a grave'. The parallelism

not in Hebrew text

²³ (Why is light given) to a man whose way is hid,
    whom God has hedged in?
²⁴ For my sighing comes as my bread,
    and my groanings are poured out like water.
²⁵ For the thing that I fear comes upon me,
    and what I dread befalls me.
²⁶ I am not at ease, nor am I quiet;
    I have no rest; but trouble comes.'

---

favours *gal* or *gôlēl* (so Steinmann, Weiser, and Larcher). Guillaume (*Promise and Fulfilment*, ed. by F. F. Bruce, 1963, p. 110) adduces Arabic *jāl*, 'the interior side of the grave'.

23. Why is light given: these words do not stand in the Hebrew here, but *EVV* rightly link this verse to verse 20.

to a man: Job here returns to his own condition.

whose way is hid: Job is bewildered because he cannot see his way. He finds himself suddenly hedged in and no path is visible before him.

whom God has hedged in: in 1.10 Satan had used the same verb when he said that God had put a hedge about Job. But there it was a protective hedge, whereas here it is restrictive.

24. as my bread: *AV* and *RV* 'before I eat' yields little sense. *BDB* gives 'like' for this passage, and many editors render so, or 'instead of'. The meaning for the word is rare and dubious, but may be found in 1 Sam. 1.16 (cf. G. R. Driver, *JQR*, N.S., XXVIII, 1937–38, pp. 121f.). The various emendations that have been proposed have won little following and bring no improvement of the sense, whereas Ps. 42.3 shows that the thought of *RSV* rendering is not unnatural. Duhm and Hölscher needlessly omit the verse.

my groanings: the word is used of the roaring of the lion, and here denotes the loud groans of Job.

25. Job in his anguish is tortured also by fear that he has only to think of some new evil and it is sure to come upon him.

26. trouble: again the same word as in verse 10; cf. on verse 20. It is misery and anguish that he endures. Throughout his soliloquy Job has complained bitterly of his lot, and his mood is far removed from the patient submission he had shown in the Prologue. But he has not cursed God. He has cursed the day of his birth and longed for the grave, as many another who has suffered a less sudden reversal of fortune than Job has done. The author knows how wearing long-continued pain can be. But Job has not forsaken God. He feels that God has forsaken him, and, as Gibson says, 'wild as his words are, there is beneath them the truth that in the case of the man who is really, and not only in appearance, cast off by God "it were good for that man if he had not been born" (Mt. 26.24).'

4 Then Eli'phaz the Te'manite answered:
2 'If one ventures a word with you, will you be offended?
Yet who can keep from speaking?

THE DIALOGUE 4–27

Job's friends had so far sat in silence. Now his unrestrained cry of anguish stirred them to speak and in turn they address him in three cycles of speeches in tones of growing sharpness, Job replying to each speech. If Job's outcry can only be understood in the setting of the magnitude of his suffering and the innocence of any provocation on his part, which the reader knows but the friends did not, their speeches can only be understood in the setting of the presuppositions of their theology. They were shocked by Job's words because from the start they took it for granted that he must deserve all he was getting. The first cycle consists of chapters 4–14, the second of chapters 15–21, and the third of chapters 22–27. In each cycle the order of the speakers is the same, the three friends probably speaking in order of seniority.

THE FIRST SPEECH OF ELIPHAZ 4–5

Eliphaz opens with a speech which Davidson describes as 'one of the masterpieces of the book', marked by 'great delicacy and consideration' and 'very wise and considerate as well as profoundly reverential'. Ranston (*The O.T. Wisdom Books*, 1930, p. 139) says he had 'something of the prophet about him' and was 'intense in religious conviction, a mystic recipient of heavenly visions'. Nevertheless, as Davidson observes, his speech failed for two reasons. 'If his religious tone was not too lofty, it was at least too cold, and too little tempered with compassion for the sufferings of men. . . . This error was due to another, his theory of suffering. . . . However true his theory might be as a general principle of moral government, it was not universal and did not include Job's case.' His theology has dried the springs of true sympathy. The speech falls into three parts: introduction and theory of retribution (4.2–11), Eliphaz's vision and its message (4.12–5.7), his counsel to Job (5.8–27).

INTRODUCTION AND THEORY OF RETRIBUTION 4.2–11

Eliphaz expresses wonder that Job, who had often counselled others, should so fall into despair and forget that the innocent are never cut off, but that the anger of God is reserved for the wicked.

2. If one ventures a word: Eliphaz opens on a note of apology, as one hesitant to speak to one in such anguish, yet wishing to offer advice and help.

offended: the same verb is rendered 'impatient' in verse 5. Davidson well renders 'will it be too much for thee?' i.e., 'can you bear it?' Dhorme does not understand the sentence as a conditional one, but takes the second part to express

³ Behold, you have instructed many,
    and you have strengthened the weak hands.
⁴ Your words have upheld him who was stumbling,
    and you have made firm the feeble knees.
⁵ But now it has come to you, and you are impatient;
    it touches you, and you are dismayed.
⁶ Is not your fear of God your confidence,
    and the integrity of your ways your hope?
⁷ 'Think now, who that was innocent ever perished?
    Or where were the upright cut off?

---

the response to the first: 'Shall we address you? You are dejected' (and so Steinmann). This seems less satisfactory. Ball renders: 'Should one try to speak to the
wearied (impatient)'; similarly Kissane.

3. you have instructed many: Eliphaz reproaches Job with forgetting advice
he has given to others. Peake observes: 'What Eliphaz fails to understand is that
Job's disease needs not an irritant but an emollient'. Cf. Job's remark in 6.14.

instructed: here instructed by word. The root can also mean 'discipline', and in
5.17 the noun from this root means 'discipline by suffering'.

weak hands: hands hanging down in helplessness and despair. Cf. Isa. 35.3;
Heb. 12.12.

4. stumbling: under the weight of his affliction.

feeble knees: cf. Isa. 35.3; Heb. 12.12.

5. impatient: see on verse 2. Ball renders 'despondent', Dhorme 'dejected'.
Davidson points out that there is no sarcasm in the words of Eliphaz. He is reminding Job of the wisdom he had shown in ministering to others, and urging him to
apply it now to himself. Buttenwieser, however, thinks Eliphaz is hypocritical.

6. fear of God: Eliphaz says simply 'your fear'. On his lips (cf. 15.4; 22.4)
the word is equivalent to the more usual 'fear of God', and almost comes to
mean 'your religion'. Cf. Moffatt's rendering: 'Let your religion reassure you.'
It is to be observed that Eliphaz recognizes that Job is a God-fearing man. He
believes that he must have erred, but of his fundamental character he has no
doubt.

confidence: LXX renders 'grounded in folly'. This is because polarized meanings
belong to this root. The word *kesel*='confidence' in 8.14 and 'folly' in Ec. 7.25.
Here we have the form *kislāh*. But the parallelism with 'hope' shows that the
meaning 'confidence' is intended.

integrity: this is the noun from the same root as the word rendered 'blameless'
in 1.1.

7. perished: Eliphaz reminds Job that the sufferings of the righteous are for

⁸ As I have seen, those who plough iniquity
   and sow trouble reap the same.
⁹ By the breath of God they perish,
   and by the blast of his anger they are consumed.
¹⁰ The roar of the lion, the voice of the fierce lion,
   the teeth of the young lions, are broken.
¹¹ The strong lion perishes for lack of prey,
   and the whelps of the lioness are scattered.

---

discipline and not for destruction. Job may therefore hope for a happy issue from his misfortunes. Cf. Ps. 37.24.

8. those who plough iniquity: those who are fundamentally wicked, who not merely fall into sin, but deliberately cultivate sin, or sin of set purpose.
reap the same: cf. Hos. 10.13; Gal. 6.7.

9. perish: cf. Ps. 37.20. This doctrine means that when one perishes in misfortune divine retribution for his wickedness has fallen upon him. In *NT* Jesus repudiates such a conclusion (Lk. 13.1–5).
by the blast of his anger: divine retribution is likened to a hot wind from the desert, which withers all the herbage.

10, 11. Strahan regards these verses as the addition of an inferior artist, and Ball also rejects them as a marginal note. Duhm goes farther and rejects as spurious verses 8–11. The relevance of verses 10f. is not very obvious, but the style is that of the author. In these verses we have five words for lion. With this cf. the piling up of synonyms for darkness in 10.21f. Peake relates verse 10f. to their context by suggesting that Eliphaz is here contrasting Job's case with that of the wicked. Similarly Davidson finds resemblances between the wicked and the lion: their power and their violence. There is the further resemblance of their calamitous end. Terrien sees no reason to eliminate these verses.
roar: the same word in Hebrew as that rendered 'groanings' in 3.24.
fierce lion: this rendering rests on the derivation of the word from a root meaning 'roar', cognate with the Arabic *sahala*='bray' (of the ass). *KB* derives it by metathesis from a root cognate with the Arabic *hisl*='young one', and so renders 'young lion' (so also Horst and Fohrer). Dhorme thinks it is the leopard which is referred to here (so Steinmann), but the context suggests rather some term for lion. It is used in Hebrew only as a poetic term.
are broken: this verb strictly belongs only to the teeth, but is used by zeugma of the three subjects. When the teeth are broken the lion is powerless and can no longer seize the prey. He therefore perishes of hunger and his cubs are left to fend for themselves and are scattered. Davidson comments on the graphic picture of the breaking up of the lion's home.

11. strong lion: the term is found only here and in Prov. 30.30; Isa. 30.6.

¹² 'Now a word was brought to me stealthily,
    my ear received the whisper of it.
¹³ Amid thoughts from visions of the night,
    when deep sleep falls on men,

THE VISION OF ELIPHAZ AND ITS MESSAGE **4.12–5.7**

Eliphaz now reinforces his warning to Job of the folly of his attitude by narrating a numinous experience which came to him in a night vision. Of this passage Cheyne (*Job and Solomon*, 1887, p. 19) says: 'There is no such weird passage in the rest of the Old Testament.' Peake says it ranks with the most wonderful triumphs of genius in the world's literature. Strahan observes that this vision is more like those of the patriarchs in Genesis than those of the prophets. The purport of the message that came to Eliphaz was that God alone is holy, and that man in his impurity and folly can expect only destruction at his hand. Eliphaz then reminds Job that there is none to whom he can appeal against God, and that misfortune is never accidental.

12. was brought to me stealthily: lit. 'was stolen to me'. For the metaphor, cf. 2 Sam. 19.3. In English we can say 'a feeling stole over me'. Note the skill with which the author produces the sense of the eeriness of the experience with great economy of words.

whisper: this word, *šēmeṣ*, is found in *OT* only here and in 26.14. The form *šimṣāh* is found in Exod. 32.25 only, where it is thought to mean 'derisory whisper'. *šēmeṣ* stands also in the Hebrew text of Sir. 10.10; 18.32, where Lévi (*L'Ecclésiastique*, II, 1901, pp. 64, 121) renders 'a little' in the first case and 'a lot' in the second, suggesting that it had polarized meanings (cf. *RSV*). In the Talmud it means 'a little' and this stands in *AV* here and in 26.14, in agreement with Syr. Dhorme agrees with this (so Robin), but most render 'whisper'. It is not easy to decide between the two meanings, but on the whole the sense of *AV* seems preferable. In that awesome moment, half-paralysed with terror, Eliphaz caught but a fragment of what was said. Yet that little was significant, and is recounted to Job.

13. thoughts: the word *śe‘ippîm* is found only here and in 20.2. The form *śar‘appîm* stands in Ps. 94.19 (*RSV* 'cares'); 139.23. In 1 Kg. 18.21 we find *se‘ippîm* ='divided opinions', and this connects with *se‘appāh*, *sar‘appāh*, ='bough' and *se‘ipîm* ='boughs'. Just as the boughs branch off from the trees, so thoughts and opinions can branch off in more than one direction, leading to bewilderment and indecision. Eliphaz is here thinking of the confused medley of thoughts that come to one in sleep. It was in his night vision that the awesome experience came upon him driving away his confused thoughts in a moment of arresting horror. Some editors think Eliphaz was awake when he saw the apparition, while others think it came to him in his sleep. The latter is the more natural view.

deep sleep: this is the word used of the sleep that fell on Adam at the creation of Eve (Gen. 2.21).

¹⁴ dread came upon me, and trembling,
    which made all my bones shake.
¹⁵ A spirit glided past my face;
    the hair of my flesh stood up.

---

14. my bones: Gray observes: 'The bones, as the supporting framework of the body, are often in Hebrew poetry taken as representing it; and affections, and even emotions, pervading or affecting strongly a man's being, are poetically attributed to them, or conceived as operating in them.' G. R. Driver (*WO*, I, 1947–52, p. 411) suggested that for 'bones' we should render 'calamities', from a different root, yielding 'the great number of my calamities made (me) afraid'. But there is no hint of any calamity suffered by Eliphaz, and more recently Driver has proposed (*SVT*, III, 1955, p.73) to leave 'bones' unchanged, and to read 'quaking' (*rîḇ*, Akkadian *rîbu*) instead of *rôḇ*='multitude'. The meaning would then be 'and quaking shook my bones'. This is supported by 33.19, where Kt has *rîḇ* with 'bones' and where Dhorme finds the same word 'quaking'. Tur-Sinai finds the same word, *rîḇ*, but renders 'terror'.

shake: the verb used here, *pḥd*, is that from which the word 'dread', *paḥaḏ*, is derived. It means 'tremble with fear'. Gray renders 'filled with dread'. Ball well renders 'my whole frame was convulsed with fear'.

15. spirit: the word could be rendered by 'wind' or 'breath', and Dhorme so takes it (so also Hölscher, Weiser, Horst, Fohrer). Nowhere else in OT is this word used of disembodied spirits. The shades in Sheol are called *rᵉpā'îm*, and Samuel, when raised by the witch of Endor, is called *'elōhîm*. Moreover, the verb rendered 'glided' is used elsewhere of the wind rushing by (Isa. 21.1; Hab. 1.11), though it is also used of the invisible passing of God (9.11; 11.10). We should therefore here take it to mean that a cold breath of air came upon him.

glided: Eliphaz here uses the imperfect form, equivalent to our historic present, vividly describing his experience as though he is passing through it again.

the hair of my flesh: Ball would read 'of my head' as in Ps. 40.12; 69.4, where, however, the meaning is not quite the same. The word *śaʿᵃraṯ* means 'a single hair', for which we should perhaps read the plural. Beer proposed *śᵉʿārāh* (not found elsewhere)='horror', while Merx (followed by Tur-Sinai) read *śᵉʿārāh*= 'tempest' (9.17; Nah. 1.3; elsewhere spelt *sᵉʿārāh*, cf. Job 38.1). Dahood, *Biblica*, XLVIII, 1967, pp. 544f.) adopts this view, but reads the form *śᵉʿārāṯ*: 'A storm made my body to bristle.' These are not to be preferred. The verb 'stood up' is used only here and in Ps. 119.120, where it is used of the flesh 'creeping'. The form used here is intensive. This experience was something that affected not only the hair of the head, but the whole body. Dhorme cites an Akkadian phrase: 'which makes the hair of my body to rise and of my skull to stand on end'.

16 It stood still,
    but I could not discern its appearance.
A form was before my eyes;
    there was silence, then I heard a voice:
17 'Can mortal man be righteous before God?
    Can a man be pure before his Maker?
18 Even in his servants he puts no trust,

---

16. It stood still: the subject is the mysterious unnamed object. Peake observes that a far more powerful impression is created than if Eliphaz had named it. The vagueness heightens the terror. The line is short, consisting of but a single word in the Hebrew, instead of the usual three. Many editors supply words to make up the line. It is, however, probable that it is quite deliberately that the author has this short line (so Duhm and Stevenson). The breaking off of the line suggests the sudden catch of the breath, as the horror of that moment returns to Eliphaz.
silence . . . a voice. Some editors find here a hendiadys and render 'a still low voice'; cf. 1 Kg. 19.12, where the same two words as here are found, but in the reverse order and with no copula between. Peake thinks the sense of *RSV* is finer. There was silence and then a voice. In the case of Elijah the 'voice of silence', or 'still small voice', is contrasted with the crash of thunder which preceded it. Here the voice is contrasted with the awe-inspiring silence which preceded it.
17. righteous before God: *AV* and *RV* have 'more just than God'. This is grammatically possible, but Job has never suggested this. *RSV* is therefore to be preferred. Alternatively it could be taken to mean 'righteous as against God' (so *GK*, § 133b N). This is less suitable here, however, as the vision is represented as having come to Eliphaz at some time in the past and not as connected with Job's complaint, and Job has not yet spoken of his case against God. In the presence of the awful holiness of God no man can be pure. Eliphaz leaves Job to reflect that his impurity in the sight of God is the justification of his sufferings. But this leaves out of account the question why Job's sufferings should be so phenomenal. Job nowhere affirms his absolute righteousness, but does maintain that he had not been so exceptionally wicked as to deserve what he endured.
18. servants: these are the angels as in the next line. Commentators note that the angelology of the OT does not recognize the distinction between good and evil angels. Satan appeared among the angels in 1.6. But the meaning here does not seem to be that because all angels are not good, God does not trust any of them. It is rather that even the purest angels are still impure in the presence of God. Eliphaz wishes to bring out the gulf that separates man in his impurity from God in his perfection, and this he does in a way that will always be impressive. The tragedy of the debate is not that all that the friends said was untrue or unworthy, but that it was so irrelevant. They applied to Job's case false conclusions which

and his angels he charges with error;
¹⁹ how much more those who dwell in houses of clay,
whose foundation is in the dust,
who are crushed before the moth.
²⁰ Between morning and evening they are destroyed;
they perish for ever without any regarding it.

---

they drew from unexceptionable principles.

error: this word (*toh°lāh*) is found only here. It is probably to be connected with Eth. *tahala*, a by-form of *tahala*='err'. *AV* and *RV* have 'folly', and some editors secure this meaning by reading *tiplāh* (cf. 1.22; 24.12 M.T.); so Hupfeld, Siegfried, Peake and Gray. In that case it is to be noted that God charges the angels with that quality which Job steadfastly refused to ascribe to God (1.21). Dhorme, following Jewish interpreters, derives the word from the root *hll*, and secures the sense 'madness' or 'folly', but this derivation had already been rejected by Delitzsch. Other proposed emendations are: *hattālāh*='deception' (Beer and Stevenson), *t°hillāh*='praise' (Ehrlich, Ball).

19. how much more: the Hebrew can mean 'how much more!', or 'how much less!' (*AV*). In the latter case it must be taken with verse 18*a*.

houses of clay: man was formed of the dust of the earth (Gen. 2.7; 3.19; cf. Job 10.9; 33.6; 2 C. 5.1). 'Eliphaz has a deep sense of the inherent corruption of all human beings, and of their consequent liability to be punished by the Creator' (Strahan).

foundation: this continues the metaphor of the houses. 'The accumulation of terms enhances the material nature of man in opposition to the spirits on high' (Davidson).

before the moth: this could mean 'sooner than the moth', but this hyperbole is improbable. Some take it to mean 'before the attack of a moth', meaning that the attack of the feeblest insects is fatal. But while it is true that the attack of a tiny insect may be fatal, the moth is not such an insect. In 3.24 we had the preposition *lip°nê* used in the sense 'like', and it seems best to take it so here (so Davidson, Budde, Gibson, Peake, Dhorme, Weiser, and Pope). Man is crushed by God as easily as one crushes a moth. G. R. Driver (*JQR*, N.S., xxviii, 1937–38, p. 121) renders 'they crush them like a bird's nest', which does not seem very probable. The whole line is deleted by Bickell, Hölscher, and Fohrer.

20. Between morning and evening: man is ephemeral, and his life is swiftly done. Cf. H. F. Lyte: 'Swift to its close ebbs out life's little day.' Cf. also Ps. 90.5f.

without any regarding it: this rendering implies the addition of the word *lēb*='heart', 'attention'. The ellipsis in the expression *mēśîm lēb* is very violent. Moreover, the verbal form is surprising. Further, men do not die unnoticed. If the meaning were that men are so unimportant in the eyes of God that he destroys

21 If their tent-cord is plucked up within them,
    do they not die, and that without wisdom?'

5 'Call now; is there any one who will answer you?
    To which of the holy ones will you turn?

---

them without even noticing it, it could be understood. But that is not what Eliphaz is saying. Merx suggested reading *môšia'* for *mēśîm*, yielding the meaning 'without a saviour', i.e. there is none who can protect man from death. This has been accepted by Dhorme, but is rejected by Stevenson and Horst. Kissane follows Ehrlich in reading *mēśîb* and renders 'and none can restore them', while Ball suggests *tūšiyyāh* and renders 'without insight'. M. Dahood (*The Bible in Current Catholic Thought*, edited by J. L. McKenzie, 1962, p. 55) for *mibbelî mēśîm* read *mibbelî-m šēm*='without a name', regarding -*m* as an enclitic ending, to be explained by Ugaritic. Hölscher omits the whole verse, while Steinmann omits verses 19*c*–21. The most satisfactory view seems to be that adopted by Dhorme.

21. If their tent-cord is plucked up within them: only here does the word *yeter* mean 'tent-cord'. Hence some editors read *yātēd*='tent-peg'. *AV* renders 'excellency', a meaning which *yeter* has in Gen. 49.3, but which is not appropriate to the verb here (though Kissane follows this). The verb is used of pulling up a tent-peg, or striking camp. Ball and Stevenson delete the verse as a marginal intrusion. Dhorme interprets *yeter* as 'what remains', a meaning it has in Exod. 23.11; Ps. 17.14; Isa. 44.19. He then renders 'Has not their excess of wealth been snatched from them?' This is not appropriate to the context here, and Dhorme accordingly transfers the line to follow 5.5*b* (so also Robin). This is the most satisfactory treatment of the line; verse 19*c* is parallel to verse 20*a*, and verse 20*b* is parallel to verse 21*b*. G. R. Driver (*ThZ*, XII, 1956, p. 486) reads *bemôtārām* for *yitrām bām* and renders 'are they not uprooted amid their plenty', and transfers to precede 5.5*a*. Pope retains 'tent-cord', but silently omits 'within them'.

On verses 17–21 Davidson comments: 'There is something very wise and considerate as well as profoundly reverential in these words of the aged speaker. . . . Eliphaz makes Job cease to be an exception, and renders it more easy for him to reconcile himself to his history and acknowledge the true cause of it. He is but one where all are the same.'

5.1. the holy ones: the angels. 'The heavenly beings are so termed, not on account of moral perfection (cf. 4.18), but of their proximity to God' (Gray). Hence Budde renders 'the heavenly ones'. Eliphaz here warns Job that it is futile to appeal to the angels against God. Siegfried and Duhm delete the verse, but Peake thinks it is too striking for a glossator. In 33.23 we have the thought of the angels as mediators. Eliphaz therefore supposes Job might think of appealing to them for help. Job has not suggested this, but Eliphaz warns him before he does that this can only draw the wrath of God upon himself.

² Surely vexation kills the fool,
    and jealousy slays the simple. /
³ I have seen the fool taking root,
    but suddenly I cursed his dwelling.

---

2. vexation: this is 'the feeling of chagrin aroused by treatment regarded as unmerited' (Gray). *Stuhow completely disagrees CBQ 1961*

the fool: Eliphaz here suggests that if Job appeals to the angels he will be a fool and may die of disappointment or of the fresh disaster he will provoke.

jealousy: the word can mean 'jealousy' or 'zeal' or 'strong passion'. Here *RV* marg. 'indignation' seems best to catch the meaning. Dhorme transposes this verse to precede verse 1, but it seems to connect well with verse 3.

3. taking root: instead of *mašrîš* Duhm read *mᵉšōrāš*, giving the meaning 'uprooted', and this is followed by Ball, Hölscher, and Stevenson, but rejected by Gray, Dhorme, and Fohrer. Eliphaz is giving an illustration from his own experience of one who by his own folly brought down ruin on himself.

I cursed: the same verb as in 3.8. The meaning of this verse is not clear. Does Eliphaz mean that he pronounced a curse which was then fulfilled? If so, the disaster that befell the fool was not self-entailed, but was brought about by Eliphaz. Dhorme retains this text and says that Eliphaz was simply reflecting current ethics in being incensed at the prosperity of the fool. Davidson thinks the meaning is that the judgment of God fell on him, and then Eliphaz cursed him. But this is not naturally expressed in the verse. Cheyne (*Exp*, 5th series, v, 1897, p. 407) proposed *wayyûkab* instead of *wā'ekkôb*, giving 'and it was suddenly cursed', and this is followed by Gray, Buttenwieser and Pope (cf. Stevenson). This involves little change and yields the most satisfactory meaning. The fool by his folly brought swift judgment upon himself. Of the many other emendations proposed, a few may be noted: *wayyippāqeḏ* (Budde)='was missed', 'was empty' (1 Sam. 20.18); *wayyōʾbaḏ* (Ball)='perished'; *wᵉʾābāk* (J. H. J., *AThR.*, xxii, 1940, pp. 47f.)= 'became dust'; *wᵉʾakkô* (Slotki, *ET*, xliii, 1931–32, p. 288)='a wild goat' (in his dwelling); *wayyikkôb* (I. Eitan, *HUCA*, xiv, 1939, pp. 12f.)='was uprooted'. All these give evidence of ingenuity, but have won no following. More acceptable have been Beer's *wᵉrākab* or Duhm's *wayyirkab*='became rotten' (or worm-eaten), which has been followed in one or the other form by Peake, Strahan, Hölscher, and Weiser. Gray suggested *wattēšam* (Ezek. 19.7)='was desolate', and Horst *wayyēʿāqēr*='was uprooted', while Gaster (*JBL*, lx, 1941, p. 300) read, *wᵉrākab* but changed the following word to *nôhô*, to yield 'but his shoot withered', and Cheyne (*ET*, x, 1898–99, p. 381) proposed to read *wayyirkab* and to change the following word to *'ᵃnāpô*, giving 'his branch became rotten'. His earlier proposal, which makes the least change of all the suggestions, is greatly to be preferred.

⁴ His sons are far from safety,
    they are crushed in the gate,
    and there is no one to deliver them.
⁵ His harvest the hungry eat,
    and he takes it even out of thorns;

---

4. His sons are far from safety: when misfortune falls upon the head of the family, the whole family is involved. When the father is destroyed his children are defenceless.

in the gate: this is where business was transacted and where law was administered. Too often judgment went to the powerful and the weak were helpless (cf. Prov. 22.22). The prophets constantly denounced the maladministration of justice, which is not here presented as the form of divine retribution on the father, but as the inevitable consequence of it. Sin is never simply an individual matter, because no one is only an individual, but is set in society. Sometimes a man's sin injures the victims of his act; but always it reacts upon himself and upon those most closely bound to him. It is inevitable that when a man disgraces himself his family must share his digrace, and when he involves himself in ruin, his family must share its consequences.

5. His harvest: lit. 'whose harvest', where the pronoun must go back to verse 3. LXX reads 'what they have reaped', and so most editors. The reference is then to the sons, who have lost their case in the courts and are deprived of their property, and even of the corn they have reaped. They are so helpless that the poor and the hungry can help themselves to it.

he takes it even out of thorns: this line is very difficult. Lit. it means 'unto from thorns he takes it'. The word for 'thorns' (ṣinnîm) is found here and Prov. 22.5 only. The line is commonly held to mean that the hungry take the corn from the enclosed field, which was protected by a thorn hedge. This is very improbable. Peake cites the suggestion of Thomson (*The Land and the Book*, p. 348), that the meaning is that they did not even leave the grain which grew among thorns, or that the grain was covered with thorns to protect it from animals. None of this is convincing, and many editors delete the line in despair (so Duhm, Hölscher, Stevenson, Weiser, Horst, and Fohrer). Others try to make sense by emendation, but no convincing proposal has been made. Budde (cf. Gray) secured the meaning 'and their sheaf, the poor takes it'; Bevan (*JPh*, XXVI, 1899, p. 305), 'and their strength (i.e. wealth), the barbs take it'; Ball 'and all their sustenance he taketh'. G. R. Driver (*ThZ*, XII, 1956, pp. 485f.) connects ṣinnîm with Aramaic ṣinnā= 'basket'. This had been suggested earlier by Delitzsch, but rejected by Dhorme on the ground that one carries *in* baskets and not *to* them. For 'el='to' Driver reads 'ēl='a strong man', and renders 'a strong man snatches it from the baskets' and interprets this of the baskets in which the grain is being taken from the field to

and the thirsty pant after his wealth.
6 For affliction does not come from the dust,
   nor does trouble sprout from the ground;
7 but man is born to trouble
   as the sparks fly upward.
8 'As for me, I would seek God,
   and to God would I commit my cause;

---

the threshing-floor. Voigt proposed *we'ayil-miṣṣōnām* for *we'el miṣṣinním* and rendered '(and he takes) even the ram from their flock' (cf. Gen. 31.38). A more attractive, though scarcely convincing, proposal is that adopted by Dhorme, which reads *'el-maṣpūním* for *'el-miṣṣinním* (a change of one consonant), to yield the meaning 'and unto hiding places he carries it'. Following this line Dhorme transfers here 4.21*a* (see note there). Guillaume (*Promise and Fulfilment*, ed. by F. F. Bruce, 1963, p. 111) reads *moṣním* for *miṣṣinním* and renders '(takes it) to the famished', adducing Arabic for the meaning.

and the thirsty pant after his wealth: RV renders 'and the snare gapeth for their substance'. This is not lucid. The word *ṣammím*='snare' is found only here and in 18.9. It offers a poor parallel to 'the hungry' in the first line. Some of the ancient versions connected the word with the verb 'to thirst', and many editors accordingly read *ṣemē'ím*='the thirsty', yielding the sense of RSV. For 'pant' Dhorme renders 'suck up', 'engulf' without change of text. Others make more violent changes: 'and the thirsty draweth from their well' (Duhm; cf. Gray); 'and the thirsty drink their milk' (Beer); 'and the thirsty gather their fruitage' (Ball); 'and thirst swallowed their wealth' (Tur-Sinai). AV 'and the robber swalloweth up their substance' rests on Targ. and is without justification. Guillaume (loc. cit.) reads *ṣāmím* for *ṣammím*, and renders 'the starving.' Despite the difficulties of the text the general sense is reasonably clear. It presents a picture of the helplessness of the sons of the once prosperous fool, who find all their substance slipping from them, crushed and robbed on every side.

6. Eliphaz now formulates the principle which he deduces from what he has said. Misfortune is not something that comes of itself, as weeds come up from the soil. It is self-entailed. Eliphaz falls into the logical fallacy of arguing that because the fool meets disaster, all who meet disaster must be fools. He therefore seeks to impress upon Job that he must himself be responsible for all his troubles. This is a philosophy which can satisfy the prosperous and sap the springs of their sympathy.

7. man is born to trouble: this appears to contradict verse 6. For here it would seem that Eliphaz says trouble comes naturally and inevitably to man, whereas verse 6 says the opposite. Beer and Duhm delete verses 6f. to get rid of the difficulty. But this is no solution and does not explain why a glossator should have placed the verses here. Peake conforms verse 6 to verse 7 by turning verse 6 into a question: 'Does not affliction come from the dust?' But this is still contrary to the thesis of Eliphaz. Davidson gives an unnatural interpretation to verse 7: it is man's nature through his sin to bring trouble upon himself. The verb rendered 'is born' may be vocalized in several ways and many editors vocalize *yôlēd*='begetteth'. The meaning then is that so far from trouble being natural and inevitable a man is responsible for his own ills. This view is followed by Duhm, Budde, Buttenwieser, Dhorme, Hölscher, Weiser, and seems most satisfactory, though Gray, Ball, Stevenson, Horst and Fohrer all prefer the other. It seems to agree most closely with the theological presupposition of Eliphaz that suffering is always the fruit of the sufferer's sin to find him here to say that trouble does not spring up out of the ground, but a man begets his own troubles. M. Dahood (*Biblica*, XLVI, 1965, p. 318) renders 'it is man who engenders mischief itself'.

as the sparks fly upward: endless discussion has gathered round this line. The expression rendered 'sparks' is *benê rešep*, which is held to mean 'sons of the flame', and hence 'sparks'. *Rešep*='flame' in some passages (e.g. Ca. 8.6). In Dt. 32.24 Targ. renders it by '*ôp*, which normally means 'birds' (cf. also Sir. 43.17). Hence Dhorme holds that it means some sort of bird here. He renders 'sons of the lightning', and then identifies with the eagle (so Horst; Kissane with the vulture). The words that follow could equally well be rendered 'fly high', 'soar aloft', and this would suit the eagle. But the explanation seems far-fetched. Siegfried and Ball substitute the common word for 'vulture' or 'eagle' for the word *rešep*, but it is improbable that a rare expression would be substituted for a common one. Hölscher (so also Pope) identifies *rešep* with Resheph the Phoenician god of the lightning (on Resheph cf. Alt, *ThLZ*, LXXV, 1950, cols. 513ff., and A. Caquot, *Semitica*, VI, 1956, pp. 53ff.). Buttenwieser understands *rešep* metaphorically to mean the fire of passion and so renders 'impetuous spirits soar high'. Peake (following Rashi, Schlottmann and Hoffmann) thinks the 'sons of the flame' were the angels (Targ. 'demons'), taking the meaning to be that whereas trouble is the common lot of man the angels escape (so also Strahan and Reichert). None of these suggestions seems to be preferable to the rendering of *RSV* which is accepted by Gray, Stevenson, Weiser and Fohrer. The meaning is that as surely as sparks fly upward man falls into sin and engenders trouble for himself. He is alone responsible for his misfortunes.

ELIPHAZ COUNSELS JOB 5.8-27

In Job's place Eliphaz would take refuge in God, who is mighty and wonderful. If only Job will recognize that he has offended against God and will accept his chastisement with submission he will find deliverance and renewed blessing. At the end of the book Job bows in submission before God and his prosperity is restored, but not on the terms which Eliphaz suggests. Job is not prepared to agree that his miseries are God's judgment on his sins, and in this he is right as the reader knows. It is just here that the heart of the discussion lies.

8. As for me: this is preceded in Hebrew by a strong adversative (*RSV* 'But'),

⁹ who does great things and unsearchable,
    marvellous things without number:
¹⁰ he gives rain upon the earth
    and sends waters upon the fields;
¹¹ he sets on high those who are lowly,
    and those who mourn are lifted to safety.
¹² He frustrates the devices of the crafty,
    so that their hands achieve no success.
¹³ He takes the wise in their own craftiness;

---

contrasting what is now to be said with what precedes. In verse 1 Eliphaz had warned Job against appealing to the angels for mediation. What he should do is to go straight to God and cast himself at his feet in penitence. Orlinsky (*JQR*, N.S., xxv, 1934–35, pp. 271ff.) argues on the basis of LXX for the substitution of 'Shaddai' for the second 'God'.

9. Job knows this as well as Eliphaz; cf. 9.10. Kissane omits it here as a gloss. But it is characteristic of Eliphaz that he has much perception of the truth, but draws the wrong conclusions from it. He is a sincere and pious man, who is bound by his own rigid, but defective, logic.

10. fields: the word so rendered is often rendered 'streets'. It means 'what is outside'—i.e. 'streets' when outside houses, or 'fields' when outside villages or towns. Duhm and Ball needlessly delete this verse on the ground that its metre is different from that of the rest of the poem. But Hebrew poetry commonly shows more flexibility than most of our own, and while that of the book of Job is unusually regular, it is unwise to try to make it uniformly so.

11. Cf. 1 Sam. 2.7*b*, 8; Lk. 1.52*b*.

those who mourn: the meaning of the root is 'be dark', 'be dirty'. The reference is therefore to the ash-sprinkled head of the mourner.

are lifted: lit. 'are set on high', with the flavour of the strength of the position. The word rendered 'stronghold' in Ps. 9.9 is from this root.

12. success: the word so rendered is a technical term of the Wisdom Literature, found, with two exceptions (Isa. 28.29; Mic. 6.9), only in Job and Proverbs. It means 'sound wisdom' or the 'abiding success' which wisdom achieves. It is a common thought of Scripture that the humble pious, who put their trust in God, are wiser than those who trust their own cleverness.

13. in their own craftiness: cf. Ps. 7.15; 57.6 (M.T. 7); Prov. 26.27; 28.10. This text is quoted in 1 C. 3.19 (the only quotation from Job in *NT*, though Rom. 11.35 may be an allusion to Job 41.11).

wily: lit. the 'tortuous' or 'twisted'. The root is found in Gen. 30.8; Ps. 18.26 (M.T. 27); Prov. 8.8.

and the schemes of the wily are brought to a quick end.
¹⁴ They meet with darkness in the daytime,
    and grope at noonday as in the night.
¹⁵ But he saves the fatherless from their mouth,
    the needy from the hand of the mighty.
¹⁶ So the poor have hope,
    and injustice shuts her mouth.

---

brought to a quick end: the sense of the word is that they are hurried on, i.e.
precipitated before they are ripe and so brought to nought. There is no need to
change the text, with Ball, to give the sense 'he maketh vain'.

14. Cf. Dt. 28.29; Isa. 59.10 (where the word for 'grope' is slightly different
from that used here; it is needless to make them the same, as some editors do).
For the groping of blind men, cf. Gen. 19.11; Ac. 13.11 (also cf. 2 Kg. 6.18f.).

15. **he saves:** by his frustrating the evil designs of the crafty, the poor, who
were to be their victims, are saved.

from their mouth: M.T. has 'from the sword, from their mouth', and lacks 'the
fatherless'. *RSV* follows Budde in reading *mippîhem yāt̲ōm* instead of *mēḥereb̲
mippîhem*, thus giving a term to balance 'the needy' in the next line. Siegfried
(followed by Duhm, Strahan, and Hölscher) reads *mēḥereb̲ ᶜānî* = 'the poor from
the sword' (so Ball, with 'the fatherless' as an alternative to 'the poor'); while
Peake does not decide between Budde and Siegfried. An alternative proposal of
Budde's, to read *mēḥarb̲ām yāt̲ōm* = 'the fatherless from their sword', is adopted by
Gray. Ewald proposed *moḥᵉrāb̲ mippîhem* (i.e. simply a change of vowels), and this
is followed by Dhorme, to yield 'from their mouth the desolated (or ruined) man'
(so also J. Reider (*HUCA*, III, 1926, p. 112), and Szczygiel). Syr., Vulg., and Targ.
read *pîhem* ('their mouth') instead of *mippîhem*, and this is followed by Weiser
and Fohrer, though it leaves 'the needy' of the following line without a parallel.
Other suggestions yield the following: 'the guileless from their sword' (Kissane
and Pope); 'the condemned from their mouth' (Stevenson); 'the snared from their
sword' (Horst); 'from the weapon into which they have converted their crafty
mouths' (without change of the Hebrew text: Buttenwieser; cf. Reichert). The
chief difference between most of these suggestions is as to whether deliverance is
from the sword or the mouth. The latter yields a closer parallel to 'the hand' of
the following line, and the meaning is that they sought to swallow up their
intended victim or to get him into their power. The reading of Ewald and Dhorme
involves no change of the Hebrew consonantal text, and is on that account to be
preferred.

16. This verse sums up the result of God's intervention in human affairs,
according to the preconceived idea of Eliphaz that even-handed justice always
triumphs. For verse 16b, cf. Ps. 107.42.

17 'Behold, happy is the man whom God reproves;
   therefore despise not the chastening of the Almighty.
18 For he wounds, but he binds up;
   he smites, but his hands heal.
19 He will deliver you from six troubles;
   in seven there shall no evil touch you.
20 In famine he will redeem you from death,
   and in war from the power of the sword.
21 You shall be hid from the scourge of the tongue,

---

17. Cf. Ps. 94.12; Prov. 3.11f.; Heb. 12.5f. Eliphaz now describes to Job the fair prospect which lies before him, if he will but accept the advice offered him. The unexceptionable generality of this verse is marred only by its inapplicability to the case of Job, who is not being disciplined. Hence what is intended to be comfort is only an irritant.

chastening: cf. on 4.3.

the Almighty: the name Shaddai, which stands thirty-one times in the book, occurs here for the first time; see p. 24.

18. Strahan comments: 'The "Celestial Surgeon"—to use Stevenson's phrase—who employs the lancet will next dress the wound. The language is as exquisite in simple beauty, but, in this context, also as lacking in moral depth, as the poetry which Hosea (6.1) puts into the mouths of the shallow optimists of Northern Israel'. Cf. Isa. 30.26.

19. six . . . seven: there are many examples of 'ascending enumeration' in OT. A number which would be regarded as sufficient is increased by one; cf. 40.4; 33.29; Sir. 50.25; Am. 1.3ff.; Prov. 30.18; Isa. 17.6; 2 Kg. 13.19; Prov. 6.16; Mic. 5.5; Sir. 25.7 (on similar 'ascending enumeration' in Ugaritic, cf. A. Bea, *Biblica*, XXI, 1940, pp. 196ff.). In the following verses we have specified famine, war, scourge of the tongue, destruction, destruction and famine, beasts. But 'destruction' is duplicated, and the two different words used for 'famine' are synonymous. But we should not attempt to find precisely seven calamities; Eliphaz simply means 'in all troubles'. Peake observes that 'the description that follows reminds one rather strikingly of the exquisite ninety-first Psalm'.

20. from the power of the sword: Hebrew 'from the hands of the sword'. This phrase recurs in Ps. 63.10. More commonly we find the expression 'from the mouth of the sword'.

21. the scourge of the tongue: cf. Sir. 26.6; 51.2. The reference is to slander or backbiting, and Dhorme thinks it is significantly placed after war, since it leads to strife. Other editors note that all of the other evils named are physical. Duhm therefore proposes *rešep* instead of *lāšôn* ('tongue'), and interprets of the scourge of

and shall not fear destruction when it comes.
22 At destruction and famine you shall laugh,
    and shall not fear the beasts of the earth.
23 For you shall be in league with the stones of the field,
    and the beasts of the field shall be at peace with you.
24 You shall know that your tent is safe,

---

pestilence (cf. Dt. 32.24; Hab. 3.5). Ball follows, save that he reads *beš̌ûṭ* for *beš̌ôṭ* and secures the meaning 'when pestilence is abroad'. It is then observed that we have in the list here the four judgments of Ezek. 14.21: sword, famine, evil beasts, pestilence. But there is no reason why the author of Job should follow Ezekiel exactly.

destruction: it is surprising to find this term repeated in the following line, and hence Gray proposes to read *š̌ô'āh*— 'desolation' for *š̌ôḏ* here. Hoffmann proposed to read *š̌ēḏ*— 'demon', and so Stevenson and Pope, while R. Gordis (*JTS*, XLI, 1940, pp. 40-2) with change of reading renders 'torrent' or 'tempest'.

22. The repetition of 'destruction' and 'famine' here is dealt with by the deletion of the whole verse by Beer, Budde, Duhm, Hölscher, Horst, and Fohrer. Ball emends the first line vigorously to yield 'At the lion and the cobra you will laugh', while Szczygiel proposes 'At blasting (cf. Dt. 28.22) and stones you will laugh'. Neither is convincing.

famine: this is not the word used in verse 20, but is an Aramaism found again in 30.3. There are many Aramaisms in the book of Job, especially when the author wants an alternative term to a Hebrew word already used in the context.

23. the stones of the field: Peake says: 'There runs through much of the OT a deep sense of the sympathy between man and nature, which often finds expression in the prophetic descriptions of the happy future.' The line has been very variously interpreted (cf. Knabenbauer, who lists a number). Peake and Gray think it means that the stones will not accumulate to mar the fertility of the field (for the contrary suggestion that the stones are a blessing, cf. Peake, *ET*, XXXIV, 1922–23, pp. 42f.). Other suggestions include the idea that the boundaries will no more be violated by enemies. Rashi records a reading *'aḏōnê* for *'abnê* ('stones'), giving 'the lords of the field'. This is then held to mean 'satyrs' or 'gnomes' (so Köhler, *ARW*, XIII, 1910, pp. 75ff.), Beer, *ZAW*, XXXV, 1915, pp. 63f.; Perles, *Analekten*, N.F., 1922, p. 29; Buttenwieser; cf. Reichert). Some secure the same meaning by reading *benê*='sons' (so J. Reider, *HUCA*, XXIV, 1952–53, p. 102;cf.Pope).Against this it is objected that *ba'alê* would be expected. Ball adopts the reading *benê* but takes 'the sons of the field' to be a synonym of 'the beasts of the field' of the parallel line.

shall be at peace: cf. Isa. 11.6-9.

and you shall inspect your fold and miss nothing.
²⁵ You shall know also that your descendants shall be many,
    and your offspring as the grass of the earth.
²⁶ You shall come to your grave in ripe old age,
    as a shock of grain comes up to the threshing floor in its
    season.
²⁷ Lo, this we have searched out; it is true.
    Hear, and know it for your good.'

---

24. fold: this is the same word as is rendered 'dwelling' in verse 3. *AV* here has 'habitation'. *RSV* is to be preferred.

miss: the verb normally means 'sin' (so *AV*; cf. *RV* marg.). But its primary meaning was to miss the mark (cf. Jg. 20.16) or to fail to find something (cf. Prov. 8.36; 19.2). Here it has its primary meaning. F. D. Coggan (*JMEOS*, XVII, 1932, pp. 53–6) reads the feminine form *neʷāṭeḵā* for the masculine *nāweḵa*='thy fold', and then renders 'it shall not be missing'. Not only Job's tent, but his property will be safe.

25. offspring: the word found here is used in Isa. 34.1; 42.5, of the produce of the earth. Elsewhere, as here, it is used of human offspring, save in 31.8 (see note there). Peake notes that Eliphaz forgets that Job's children had all been destroyed. He does not think the author meant him to predict what we read in 42.13, and so sees here the evidence that he was intended to offer conventional consolation. This is characteristic of Eliphaz, whose conventional theology is untouched by human feeling.

26. ripe old age: the Hebrew word is found only here and in 30.2. Its precise meaning is uncertain, but the meaning 'firm strength' is conjectured for it. Editors have proposed to emend it to yield 'in thy strength', or 'in thy sap' (cf. Dt. 34.7, *RSV* 'natural force'). But we should not emend away a rare word, which is found twice in Job. Peake says: 'Eliphaz can hold out no hope beyond the grave, but promises all that is possible, a long life and death without the failure of powers that usually attends old age.'

27. Eliphaz ends with a somewhat pontifical observation, sure that he has apprehended the whole truth—a common mark of the closed mind. Strahan describes him as a pedantic theorist, and adds: 'No wonder that, as a physician, Eliphaz only irritated the wounds he intended to heal; as a preacher, he offered "empty chaff well meant for grain".'

JOB ANSWERS ELIPHAZ 6–7

Job's irritation at the tone of Eliphaz's speech is to be understood, and he bursts out with a passionate defence. Eliphaz had not yet charged Job openly with sin, though he had implied that Job was suffering because he deserved to. But he had talked of Job's impatience and to this Job directs his reply, with but a passing

6 Then Job answered:
² 'O that my vexation were weighed,
   and all my calamity laid in the balances!
³ For then it would be heavier than the sand of the sea;
   therefore my words have been rash.
⁴ For the arrows of the Almighty are in me;
   my spirit drinks their poison;

---

repudiation of the implication that sin was the cause of his misfortunes. The speech falls into three parts: defence of his bitterness (6.2–13); his disappointment in his friends (6.14–30); renewed complaint at his lot and more open appeal against God's treatment of him (7.1–21).

JOB'S DEFENCE OF HIS BITTERNESS 6.2–13

Job admits that his words have been wild, but complains that his circumstances have not been sufficiently understood. His cries have been wrung from him by the greatness of his agony, which Eliphaz has ignored. To rebuke his words without understanding their cause is of no avail, and Job in his misery cries out anew for death and release from it all.

2. **vexation**: cf. on 5.2. Job picks up this word from the speech of Eliphaz, and says that if it could be weighed against what he has had to endure its moderation would be manifest. For his calamity would be shown to be heavier than all the sand of the seashore (verse 3).

3. **therefore**: Job admits that his words have been wild, but he insists that they have been justifiably so.

rash: *AV* 'swallowed up' derives the word from the root *lûaʿ*; but it should rather be derived from the root *lāʿaʿ* = 'speak wildly, rashly' (Prov. 20.25), or from *lāʿāh*, with the same meaning. Dhorme renders 'my words are but stammered out'. This is not very appropriate to Job's outburst. Sutcliffe (*Biblica*, XXXI, 1950, pp. 367f.) renders 'charged with grief'.

4. **of the Almighty**: Job now openly names God as the author of his distresses. He, no less than Eliphaz, believed that they came from God, but whereas Eliphaz concluded that they must have been provoked by Job, Job is bewildered and finds his pains the harder to bear just because he believed they were from God. The God he had known and the God he now experiences seemed irreconcilable. For he could not know that he was vindicating God's trust in him.

their poison: Dhorme notes that the ancient world was familiar with the custom of putting poison on the point of arrows, and quotes from Virgil and Ovid.

the terrors of God are arrayed against me.
⁵ Does the wild ass bray when he has grass,
   or the ox low over his fodder?
⁶ Can that which is tasteless be eaten without salt,
   or is there any taste in the slime of the purslane?

---

terrors: this word is found only here and in Ps. 88.16 (M.T. 17; *RSV* 'dread assaults'). G. R. Driver (*SVT*, III, 1955, p. 73) notes that the idea of suddenness is always present in this root, and renders 'sudden assaults'. Tur-Sinai takes the meaning to be 'dream demons', but this is far-fetched and improbable.

are arranged: Dillmann, Budde, Duhm, Hölscher, and Kissane (cf. also Stier) transpose two consonants and render 'trouble me' (the verb used in 1 Kg. 18.18), while Merx and Siegfried change one consonant (*ḳ* for *k*) and secure the meaning 'gnaw me'. G. R. Driver (*SVT*, III, 1955, p. 73), without change of text, finds the meaning 'wear me down', by connecting the word with a different Arabic root (so Saydon, *CBQ*, XXIII, 1961, p. 252). This seems to be the most appropriate meaning. Szczygiel secured a closely similar meaning by a metathesis of the consonants. There is little to be said for Tur-Sinai's treatment of the line. He notes that the verb can be used of preparing a table, as well as of setting an army in array, and then renders the line 'the demons of Shaddai are feeding me'.

5. Job again justifies his utterance by the intensity of his sufferings, and suggests that it is wiser to seek the cause than to complain of the cry. For the distress of the wild ass when it lacks food, cf. Jer. 14.6.

bray: this verb is found only here and 30.7, where it is used of the cries of destitute outcasts.

low: this verb is used only here and in 1 Sam. 6.12, where it is used of milch cows deprived of their calves.

6. that which is tasteless: cf. note on 1.22. Duhm comments that what Job finds savourless is the consolations of Eliphaz, which lack the salt of human sympathy. Ball desiderates the name of some succulent vegetable, but has no suggestion to offer. He connects the root with something slimy or sticky, but it is far more natural to suppose that what is insipid requires salt than what is slimy or sticky.

the slime of purslane: the purslane is a leguminous plant which exudes mucilage. The rendering rests on Syr. and the Arabic version of Sa'adia. The plant is identified with the bugloss (Dillmann), or the mallow (Hölscher, Szczygiel, Reichert, Stier, Horst, Fohrer), or the milkweed (Buttenwieser), or the purslane (*RV* marg., Gray, Ball, Stevenson). The rendering of *AV*, *RV* 'white of an egg' is still maintained by Davidson, Duhm, Budde, Dhorme, Kissane, Robin, Larcher, Steinmann, and Weiser. This rests on the Rabbinic interpretation as 'the slime of the yolk', i.e. the white of an egg. Tur-Sinai differently vocalises the second word

⁷ My appetite refuses to touch them;
  they are as food that is loathsome to me.
⁸ 'O that I might have my request,
  and that God would grant my desire;

---

and renders 'the saliva of dreams', while Klostermann, basing himself on LXX
rendering 'in empty words', proposed 'in dream words' and Peake seems to
incline to this. Pope, following Yahuda, renders 'slimy cream cheese'. It seems
more likely that some insipid edible object was named, though its precise
identification cannot be established.

7. **my appetite:** *AV* and *RV* 'my soul'. The word also means 'my throat', and
it probably has that meaning here. The line then means that Job cannot swallow
them.

to touch them: LXX has 'to rest', and this is followed by Duhm and others. We
should then have to translate: 'my soul refuses to be quiet'.

they are as food that is loathsome to me: lit. 'they are like the sickness (only
here and Ps. 41.3 (M.T. 4)) of my bread'. This is not very lucid. The ancient
versions could only guess at the meaning. LXX has 'for I perceive my food as the
smell of a lion', on the basis of which Merx and Beer reconstructed the line to
yield 'They are as the smell of a lion to me'. The first word *ḥēmmēh*='they' has
no clear antecedent in the Hebrew and a widely accepted reading is *zihámāh* or
zihēm='loathes'. The second word is variously read *ḥikkî*='my palate' (McNeile,
quoted in Gray), *ḥayyātî*='my life' (Ball), or *keḇôḏî*='my heart' (Dhorme). The
line is then very similar to 33.20. Duhm sees in the words an Aramaic gloss on
the last word of the previous verse, and renders 'that now is called the yolk' and
then deletes. This is more ingenious than probable, and we should probably accept
one of the three previously noted suggestions, of which the best seems to be
McNeile's: 'my palate loathes my food'. Eitan (*JBL*, LIII, 1934, p. 271), with the
change of two consonants, gets the meaning: 'my bowels resound with suffering'.
Pope retains the text but takes the word for 'bread' in the Arabic sense of 'meat',
which he then takes to mean human flesh here, and so renders 'They are putrid as
my flesh'. Steinmann transfers verses 6f. to follow verse 30. But they seem relevant
to the present context if Job is referring to the consolations of Eliphaz, which are
tasteless and nauseating to him.

8. Job now returns to his cry for release from his sufferings by death, as in
chapter 3.

my desire: *AV* and *RV* 'the thing that I long for'. Gray objects that this is not a
legitimate rendering. M.T. has 'my hope', for which Duhm and others read with
the change of one consonant, 'my desire'. But Dhorme defends the retention of
'hope'. Job is hoping that by his outcry he will provoke God to smite him and so
release him from his misery.

⁹ that it would please God to crush me,
   that he would let loose his hand and cut me off!
¹⁰ This would be my consolation;
    I would even exult in pain unsparing;
    for I have not denied the words of the Holy One.
¹¹ What is my strength, that I should wait?
    And what is my end, that I should be patient?

---

9. it would please: lit. 'he would be willing'.

let loose his hand: the verb is used of loosening the thongs of a yoke (Isa. 58.6), or of setting prisoners free (Ps. 105.20; 146.7). So far God's hand has been restrained, in that Job's life has been spared. Now Job would have it given free play to take his life.

10. Ball deletes this verse as a doctrinal gloss based upon Ps. 119.49f. But it is thoroughly relevant to this context. Job would welcome death, since it would bring him release.

exult: the verb is found only here, and Graetz, Gray, and Ball substitute other verbs meaning 'exult'. For the Hebrew verb here, *BDB* and *KB* give the meaning 'jump for joy', which would be most appropriate, but which is not quite certain.

for I have not denied the words of the Holy One: Siegfried, Duhm, Peake, and many other editors delete this line as inappropriate here. It is said to have no meaning, except on the assumption of vindication after death, and therefore attributed to a pious interpolator, who wished to give a more edifying turn to Job's words. This is not convincing. While Job never firmly grasps the hope of a worth-while Afterlife, in 19.24–27 he comes to the verge of it (see notes there), and he might well have had a first half hope of it here. But even without that the words have meaning here, and Dhorme defends their retention. Even in the agony of death he would still console himself (the word 'still' in the Hebrew of the first line has been omitted by *RSV*), as he does now, with the consciousness of his innocence. Eliphaz thought his present misfortune was the result of his sin, though he did not think it was a mortal sin. Job declares that even though death came to him he would still protest his innocence.

denied: the verb has this meaning in Ethiopic, but not in the *OT*, where it normally means 'hide', and Dhorme so renders it here. Gray gives it the nuance 'disowned'.

11. What is my strength? Job feels that he can endure no more. He has borne all that he is capable of bearing.

that I should wait: for the return of blessing that Eliphaz had promised him.

what is my end? What hope is there for release from his sufferings? What future is there for him?

¹² Is my strength the strength of stones,
    or is my flesh bronze?
¹³ In truth I have no help in me,
    and any resource is driven from me.
¹⁴ 'He who withholds kindness from a friend
    forsakes the fear of the Almighty.

---

12. stones . . . bronze: these are insensitive materials, incapable of feeling pain. But Job is a man of flesh and blood, from whom the cry of agony can be wrung, and whose power of resistance to circumstances is limited by his frailty.

13. In truth: the Hebrew word occurs elsewhere only in Num. 17.13 (M.T. 28), where it is translated as a simple interrogative. The meaning 'verily' or 'in truth' is doubtful. Syr. and Vulg. render 'Behold, there is no . . .', and some editors, with a slight change of reading or by a redivision of the first two words, secure this meaning. Others understand the first word to mean 'Is there not?', or change it (so Dhorme) to make it so mean. Sutcliffe (*Biblica*, XXXI, 1950, pp. 368ff.) transfers the first letter to the end of the previous verse (without change of meaning there) and omits the second letter, securing the meaning: 'What source of help have I within myself?' M. Dahood (*Biblica et Orientalia*, XVII, 1965, p. 13) combines the first two words and renders: 'should I increase a hundredfold.' The general sense of the line, in agreement with the context, is to emphasize that Job is at the end of his powers of endurance.

resource: this is the word rendered 'success' in 5.12 (see note there). Here it is given the most varied meanings: 'abiding success' (*BDB*); 'resource' (Strahan); 'effectual counsel' (Gray); 'support' (Stevenson); 'counsel' (Tur-Sinai). Sutcliffe (*Biblica*, loc cit.) thinks it has the meaning 'prudence', 'prevision', 'provision', and so here renders 'care for the morrow'. Many editors emend the text to yield 'deliverance' or 'salvation' (so Beer, Ball, Buttenwieser, Hölscher, Weiser), but Job is not here thinking of rescue from his troubles, but of strength to bear them.

JOB'S DISAPPOINTMENT IN HIS FRIENDS 6.14–30

Job now reproaches his friends for their lack of sympathy. They had failed him as a wady that dries up when it is most needed fails the caravans. Waxing sarcastic he reminds them that sympathy costs nothing, and then challenges them to tell him what sin of his could have merited his troubles, and asks whether he would dare to look them in the eye and asseverate his innocence if he were not innocent.

14. The Hebrew of this verse is very difficult. *RV* has 'To him that is ready to faint kindness should be shewed from his friend; even to him that forsaketh the fear of the Almighty'. This is very improbable, since Job has nowhere suggested that he is giving up religion. Moreover, Ball rightly objects that the sentiment of *RV* is alien to the spirit of *OT*. A verb is expected where 'to him that is ready to

15 My brethren are treacherous as a torrent-bed.
    as freshets that pass away,
16 which are dark with ice,
    and where the snow hides itself.
17 In time of heat they disappear;

---

faint' stands. In the rendering of *RSV* this is supplied by reading *mōnēaʿ* = 'he who withholds', instead of *lammās*. This rests on Syr., Vulg., and Targ., and is adopted by Merx, Graetz, and Gray. Instead Duhm reads *māna*ʿ = 'he withholds' instead of *mērēʿēhû* = 'from his friend', and so secures 'he who withholds kindness from the despairing forsaketh . . .'. Kissane by a further change gets 'When his friend faileth him who is in despair, he forsaketh . . .'. This is less appropriate than *RSV*, and lacks its support in the versions. Dhorme reads *māʾas* for *lammās*, giving 'his friend has scorned compassion and forsaken . . .', and then rejects the whole verse as a gloss. Other editors who delete the verse as a gloss are Strahan, Hölscher, Stevenson, and Fohrer. In *RSV* it is not Job but Eliphaz who has become the apostate. His unsympathetic spirit outweighs his theological rectitude, and the verse is not a confession but an accusation.

    15. a torrent-bed: a wady—a rushing torrent after rain and a dry bed in the dry weather; cf. Jer. 15.18.

freshets: M.T. 'as a stream bed of torrents', with repetition of the word of the first line. Budde avoided the repetition by reading 'as stream beds of water' (cf. Ps. 42.1 (M.T. 2): 'flowing streams').

pass away: this is a possible translation; but equally possible is the meaning 'overflow'. The latter seems more appropriate to the context. In the rainy season they are deep and sometimes impassable, and the following verse describes them at that time. Then, when summer comes, they are dry (verse 17). So are Job's friends. In his prosperity, when he did not need them, they were overflowing with friendship; but now in his need they are wanting.

    16. dark: a reference to the turbid waters, swirling down with broken ice and melting snow; or else to the frozen surface of the water in the winter.

hides itself: this is not a very suitable word for the snow, and Ball by the change of a letter gets the meaning 'piles itself'. Dhorme maintains that the Hebrew text can carry the meaning 'piles itself'.

    17. In time of heat: in Hebrew we have a verbal expression; cf. *RV* 'What time they wax warm'. The verb is found only here, and is regarded as a by-form of a verb found only in Ezek. 20.47 (M.T. 21.3), meaning 'be scorched'. Dhorme argues for the meaning 'flow', i.e. 'melt'. We then have the meaning 'When the snow and ice melt they (the torrents) disappear'. G. R. Driver (*ZAW*, N.S., XXIV, 1953, pp. 216f.) from the same meaning 'flow' gets the sense 'when they (i.e. the streams) pour down in torrents, they (straightway) die down'.

when it is hot, they vanish from their place.
¹⁸ The caravans turn aside from their course;
      they go up into the waste, and perish.
¹⁹ The caravans of Tema look,
      the travellers of Sheba hope.
²⁰ They are disappointed because they were confident;
      they come thither and are confounded.
²¹ Such you have now become to me;
      you see my calamity, and are afraid.

---

disappear: the word appears to mean 'are made silent' and thus 'are put an end to'.
vanish: lit. 'are extinguished'. The verb is used of a light in 18.5, 6; 21.17.

  18. **caravans:** *AV* 'paths'. The meaning then would be that the courses of the
streams wind about the stones in their beds and finally disappear in the ground.
This is the view of Budde and some other editors. Sutcliffe (*Biblica*, xxx, 1949,
pp. 68ff.) defends this view, but renders 'enter' instead of 'go up' in line *b*. But in
the next verse the same word must be rendered 'caravans' and it is probably so
here. So Duhm and most editors. The caravans come to where the streams have
been, seeking water but finding none. They turn aside to seek some other source,
but find none and perish. Just as the torrent beds disappoint the travellers who trust
them, so Job's friends fail him.

  19. **Tema:** this is an oasis SE. of the head of the Gulf of 'Aqaba; cf. Isa. 21.14;
Jer. 25.23.
Sheba: this is in South Arabia; see note on 1.15. There the Sabeans are raiders;
here they are merchants.

  20. **disappointed:** Hebrew 'ashamed', but often used in a wider sense than
'ashamed'.

  21. **such you have now become to me:** *AV* and *RV* have 'For now ye are
nothing'. There is variation in M.T. between *Kt* 'not' and *Kr* 'to him'. The former
is unusual Hebrew for 'nothing', and Dillmann emends to secure the usual
Hebrew. LXX and Syr. have 'to me', and this is followed by many editors, who
also change 'for' to 'thus', giving the sense of *RSV*. Stevenson prefers to reconstruct the line on the basis of LXX and Syr. to yield 'you too have turned against
me'. Reider (*VT*, iv, 1954, p. 288) proposes *lĕ'îm* instead of *lô* = 'not', and renders
'for now you are become hesitating'.
you see my calamity: *RV* 'Ye see a terror', i.e. something that fills you with
terror, or Job's calamity.
and are afraid: Bickell and Duhm excise this verse on the ground that Job's
friends were not afraid. But this is not convincing. Job charges them with
cowardice in withholding their sympathy from him, afraid lest they should become

²² Have I said, "Make me a gift"?
    Or, "From your wealth offer a bribe for me"?
²³ Or, "Deliver me from the adversary's hand"?
    Or, "Ransom me from the hand of oppressors"?
²⁴ 'Teach me, and I will be silent;
    make me understand how I have erred.
²⁵ How forceful are honest words!
    But what does reproof from you reprove?
²⁶ Do you think that you can reprove words,

---

sharers of the calamity if they provoked God by showing sympathy with one whom they judged to have offended God.

22–23. Here Job lashes out in sarcasm. If he had asked them for charity or to expend their wealth on his behalf, he could have understood their coldness. But he has looked for no more than understanding and sympathy from them.

24. Teach me: Job is willing to listen in silence if they will tell him wherein he has erred. The generalities of Eliphaz were but deductions from his sufferings that he must have committed some sin. Job asks for evidence before he is condemned.

erred: Job here deliberately uses a word implying sins of inadvertence (Lev. 4.13; Num. 15.22).

25. forceful: the root here occurs again only in Job 16.3 (*RSV* 'provokes'), 1 Kg. 2.8 (*RSV* 'grievous'), and Mic. 2.10 (*RSV* 'grievous'). Many editors prefer the sense of Targ. 'How sweet!', and secure this by changing one letter (*r* to *l*) and using the verb found in Ps. 119.103. Dhorme claims that this meaning can be found without changing the text as *l* and *r* are elsewhere interchanged, especially to produce some assonance (cf. Pope). G. R. Driver (*JTS*, xxix, 1927–28, pp. 394f.) argues that the verb means 'be bitter', but by rendering as a question instead of an exclamation ('How are honest words bitter?') gets the equivalent of the meaning 'How sweet!' Ball finds no reason to alter the text, but justifies from Akkadian the sense 'intolerable' or 'painful', while *KB* gives 'offending' (better 'offensive' or 'injurious'). Peake renders 'How irritating!' A satisfactory meaning can therefore be found in the text as it stands, and there is no reason to suppose that Job is renewing his sarcasm here. He is complaining of the harshness and cruelty of the words of Eliphaz, spoken in self-righteous rectitude.

what does reproof from you reprove? Job here repeats his demand to know what sin of his Eliphaz is reproaching him with. The bland generalities are meaningless, and fail to bring home to Job's conscience the sin that could have provoked his misfortunes. For *mikkem*='from you' some editors read *ḥākām*, and get the sense 'What does the reproof of the wise prove?'

26. reprove words: the meaning seems to be that the friends, as represented

when the speech of a despairing man is wind?
²⁷ You would even cast lots over the fatherless,
   and bargain over your friend.
²⁸ 'But now, be pleased to look at me;

---

by Eliphaz, have been concerned only to rebuke Job for the form of his expression
of his grief, instead of penetrating to the cause of his utterance. Buttenwieser
renders the phrase 'juggle with words', in which case the reference would be to
the debating skill of Eliphaz rather than to his lack of penetration.
a despairing man: this word is found elsewhere in Isa. 57.10; Jer. 2.25 (*RSV*
'hopeless'); and Jer. 18.12 (*RSV* 'in vain'). Finite verbal forms stand in 1 Sam. 27.1;
Ec. 2.20 (*RSV* 'despair').
is wind: M.T. 'for the wind'. The meaning is that they are soon blown away,
and so should not be taken too seriously. Many editors are not satisfied with this
sense, and want a word parallel to 'reprove', instead of 'for the wind', making
'the speech' the object. Among the suggestions are words meaning 'correct' or
'pursue', or 'wash away', or 'still', or 'relieve'. But the text yields a satisfactory
meaning as it is.
  27. cast lots: the word 'lots' is not expressed in the Hebrew. It is similarly
omitted in 1 Sam. 14.42. Bickell, Duhm, Beer, Strahan, Ball, and Stevenson
revocalize this word (following LXX and Vulg.) and redivide the two words that
follow, to give the sense 'will you even fall upon the blameless one?' But Gray
thinks M.T. to be preferred for its more caustic reproach. The verse does not seem
to agree with its context very well, and Fohrer rejects it as a gloss. Peake would
transfer it to follow verse 23, where it would fit excellently, and carry on the
sarcasm of verses 22f. Job has not asked them to make any sacrifice on his behalf,
since he knows it would be useless. They are the sort of people who want to
exploit every situation to their own advantage rather than to help others. Stevenson
regards this as an unfounded attack on their character or a piece of vulgar abuse.
But it agrees well with the stinging words of verses 14–23.
bargain over: the phrase is found again in 41.6 (M.T. 40.30). LXX here has
'rush against', whence Beer revocalizes the Hebrew to secure this sense (using a
verb elsewhere used in OT only in 2 Sam. 6.14, 16, of David dancing, and not
very appropriate to this context), while Duhm emends and reads the verb used in
Ps. 59.2 (M.T. 4; *RSV* 'band themselves'). Ball goes much farther from M.T.
and creates the meaning 'join words together against'. All this is quite unnecessary, and Gray and Dhorme retain the text, which is supported by 41.6.
Stevenson reverses the whole meaning of the verse and renders 'Or even to take
sides with the innocent and gently treat your friend', but this is far from Job's
reproachful words.
  28. The second line is cast in the form of an oath: 'I swear I will not lie.' In the
strongest possible way he asseverates his innocence.

for I will not lie to your face.
²⁹ Turn, I pray, let no wrong be done.
Turn now, my vindication is at stake.
³⁰ Is there any wrong on my tongue?
Cannot my taste discern calamity?

---

29. Turn: *AV* and *RV* have 'return'. This does not mean, as some have supposed, that Job's friends were departing from him, and he appeals to them not to do so. He is rather pleading with them to change their attitude to him, and to cease to adjudge him guilty. Gordis (*JBL*, LII, 1933, p. 160) renders the verb 'be silent'.
my vindication is at stake: the Hebrew says 'my righteousness is in it'. Many editors change the text to read 'my righteousness is still in me'. Dhorme retains the text but takes the word '*ôd* (*AV* and *RV* 'again') with what follows: 'my righteousness is still intact'. Ball, as so often, is content with nothing short of a complete rewriting of the line and secures 'and hear my righteous words'. The sense of *RSV* is superior to all of these. The word 'righteousness' is often used in a forensic sense and can mean 'vindication' and the neuter 'in it' can mean here 'in question'. Job is too deeply involved to be willing to let the matter rest where it is, and he appeals to his friends to treat the issues more seriously.

30. wrong on my tongue: as the parallel line shows, Job does not mean 'Am I saying wrong things?' but 'Have I lost the taste of things?' When he asks **Cannot my taste** (lit. palate) **discern calamity**? he means 'Am I unable to discern the true flavour of my misfortune?' i.e. to know whether it is deserved or not. Pope renders 'Can my palate not discriminate words?', giving a sense found in Ugaritic to the word rendered 'calamity' in *RSV*.

JOB'S RENEWED COMPLAINT AND APPEAL 7.1–21

Job's consciousness that he can discern the true flavour of his misfortunes leads him to lament afresh on the bitterness of his experience, and to make a more open complaint against God, whom he, no less than Eliphaz, believes to be the author of his troubles. He asks why God should so torment him until his supreme desire was for death. Whatever sin he might have committed could not have injured God, to whom he appeals to pardon him before it was too late.

1. hard service: *RV* has 'a warfare'. The word can be used of military service (so Dhorme here) or of any hard service. It is sometimes used of the service of the Levites. It is to be observed that Job is not so obsessed with his own sorrow as to forget others. He realizes that the common lot of man is a hard one. Toil and misery are experienced widely, and his experience, while exceptional in the intensity of his sufferings, is typical in the fact of suffering.
hireling: this is the man who works for wages. He may be a hired labourer, or he may be a mercenary soldier (Jer. 46.21).

2. The **slave,** who is compelled to work through the heat of the day, eagerly looks forward to the evening, when he may get rest; and the hired labourer, who

7 'Has not man a hard service upon earth,
       and are not his days like the days of a hireling?
 ² Like a slave who longs for the shadow,
       and like a hireling who looks for his wages,
 ³ so I am allotted months of emptiness,
       and nights of misery are apportioned to me.
 ⁴ When I lie down I say, "When shall I arise?"
       But the night is long, and I am full of tossing till the dawn.

---

works through the day through pressure of economic need, longs for the end of
the day, when he will receive his wages. The wages were paid daily, as in the
parable of the vineyard (Mt. 20.1ff.). This verse connects with what follows, so
that Job is here returning to his own experience.

3. I am allotted: lit. 'I am made to inherit'.

months . . . nights: the months indicate the duration of his sufferings, and the
nights the intensity, since they were harder to bear in the night when sleep was
denied (cf. 30.17).

emptiness: the word denotes what is materially or morally hollow, groundless,
and unsubstantial. Job's life is devoid of any satisfaction, empty and meaningless.

4. the night is long: the verb normally means 'measure', but here it has to be
given the meaning 'extend'. Ball objects that the first word means 'evening' and
not 'night', so that the only meaning could be 'and evening measure', which is
nonsense. He would either delete these words (so Bickell, Beer, Kissane, Tur-Sinai)
or reconstruct a tetrastich instead of a tristich. Ibn Ezra understood 'my heart',
to secure 'my heart measures the evening'—which is not very lucid. J. Reider
(*JBL*, xxxix, 1920, pp. 60ff.) renders 'from the breast of the evening', i.e. from
early evening. Gray, with the change of *middaḏ* to *middê* secured the meaning 'as
often as evening comes' (so also Fohrer). LXX read a different text, which
resembles Dt. 28.67, and on the basis of this Dhorme adds the word 'day' after
'when' and replaces *middaḏ* by another *māṯay*='when', to get 'If I lie down, I say:
"When comes the morning?" If I rise up, I say: "How long till evening?" '
Duhm supplied additional words and so obtained: 'If I lie down, I say: "When
will it be day that I may arise?" And if I rise: "When will it be evening?", '
making a tetrastich of the whole verse (so also Hölscher and Weiser; Ball's
reconstructed tetrastich is somewhat different). Of these proposals Gray's makes
the least change in the Hebrew and is to be preferred. LXX could just as easily
be due to a reminiscence of Dt. 28.67 as the original Hebrew be based on that
passage.

tossing: Dhorme thinks the meaning here is 'the rambling fancies of the mind',
but it is more likely that it refers to the physical restlessness of the sufferer in the
night. Despite the uncertainty of detail in the verse, the general sense is clear. Job

⁵ My flesh is clothed with worms and dirt;
  my skin hardens, then breaks out afresh.
⁶ My days are swifter than a weaver's shuttle,
  and come to their end without hope.
⁷ 'Remember that my life is a breath;

---

is describing the ceaseless pain and torture his malady imposes on him, so that
neither by night nor by day can he find any relief. Peake observes: 'The full
meaning can be understood only by those who have suffered through a night from
violent pain; time literally seems to stand still.'

dawn: lit. 'twilight', here the morning twilight. Szczygiel retains the more usual
sense of evening twilight by extending the text to read 'from twilight to dawn'.

5. Job's ulcers had worms and formed hard crusts, which then broke out again.
The dirt (lit. 'clods of dust') is the dirty scabs which covered his body. The verb
rendered 'hardens' is held to be from a root found only here in *OT*, the meaning
of which finds support in Ethiopic, though *KB* connects it with a verb spelt the
same, meaning 'rest': 'comes to rest' developing the sense 'forms a crust'. Dhorme
finds yet another meaning here and in 26.12 (*RSV* 'stilled'), and in both passages
renders 'split' (cf. *AV* 'is broken' here), and thinks the previous line described the
forming of scabs and this line their breaking and running with pus. G. R. Driver
(*SVT*, III, 1955, pp. 73ff.) says 'clods of dust' is nonsense (many editors omit 'of
dust'), and the second line makes sense only by the addition of 'afresh'. Instead of
'āpār='dust' he reads 'āpar='covers', and renders 'my flesh is clothed with
worms, and scab covers my skin', deleting the rest of the verse as a gloss. It should
be noted that while some of the wide varieties of translation depend on the
ingenuity of editors to rewrite the text, others reflect different possible renderings
of a single Hebrew word.

6. Job is sometimes charged with inconsistency in complaining that life is brief
immediately after complaining that time is inexpressibly slow. In the previous
verses he has been complaining about the sufferings of life, and now he complains
of its brevity. At its best it is short. Why should it also be filled with misery?

shuttle: in Jg. 16.14 the word appears to mean the 'loom', but here the 'shuttle'.
Ball emends the text to bring it into closer accord with 9.25 and renders 'a royal
post'. But it is unnecessary to make Job say the same thing twice. Still more improbable is Cheyne's emendation to 'crane'. Tur-Sinai renders 'smoke' for 'a
weaver's shuttle', adducing an Arabic root meaning 'smell'. But this is no
improvement.

without hope: i.e. of recovery. Marshall gives to the word rendered 'hope' the
meaning 'thread', which it has in Jos. 2.18 (*RSV* 'cord') and renders 'for lack of
thread' (so also Dhorme). This is so relevant to the context that it is to be
preferred.

7. a breath: Dhorme sees here an allusion to Gen. 2.7. This verse is addressed

my eye will never again see good.

⁸ The eye of him who sees me will behold me no more;
   while thy eyes are upon me, I shall be gone.

⁹ As the cloud fades and vanishes,
   so he who goes down to Sheol does not come up;

¹⁰ he returns no more to his house,
   nor does his place know him any more.

¹¹ 'Therefore I will not restrain my mouth;
   I will speak in the anguish of my spirit;
   I will complain in the bitterness of my soul.

---

to God. Peake says: 'The pathos of this pitiful appeal to God, just before the bitter reproaches he is about to fling at Him, is very fine and moving. It is like an echo of the old familiar relations between them.'

never again see good: Rashi observes that Job denies the resurrection. He does not assert it, but in 19.24–27 he reaches the verge of faith in something better than Sheol. Elsewhere, as here, he reflects current views on the finality of death.

8. This verse is absent from LXX and is omitted by Dillmann, Budde and Gray. Other editors find no reason to omit it, and Dhorme notes that the verb rendered 'behold' is characteristic of the book of Job, being found in it ten times, as against six occurrences in the rest of OT. Dillmann observes that the meaning is not that God will look upon him with hostile eye, but in friendliness. The thought is very bold, that God will relent when it is too late. J. Weingreen (VT, IV, 1954, pp. 56f.) holds that the first line should be rendered 'no seeing eye shall behold me'. This avoids the necessity of supplying 'no more', where the Hebrew has the simple negative.

9. fades: Beer proposed to read for this 'goes up', but, as Ball says, this produces a false antithesis to 'does not come up' at the end, where the same verb would then be repeated. Dhorme declares Beer's reading 'pure fantasy'. The Hebrew word means 'comes to an end'.

Sheol: in the book of Job Sheol is described as a land from which there is no return (here and 10.21); as a land of darkness and gloom (10.21f.); as deep down (11.8); as a place where the dead lie hidden (14.13); as the place appointed for all (30.23), whether great or small (3.19). The Babylonians spoke of 'the land of no return', and it is clear that Job is here denying the possibility of any resurrection after death to share again the life of those living on earth.

10. For the second line, cf. Ps. 103.16b.

11. Here Job resumes his complaint, but now addressed to God rather than to his friends. He goes far beyond what he had said in his earlier speech, and openly charges God with being his tormentor. Peake observes that he comes perilously near to fulfilling Satan's prediction that he would curse God to his face. He

¹² Am I the sea, or a sea monster,
   that thou settest a guard over me?
¹³ When I say, "My bed will comfort me,
   my couch will ease my complaint,"
¹⁴ then thou dost scare me with dreams
   and terrify me with visions,
¹⁵ so that I would choose strangling
   and death rather than my bones.

---

certainly casts off all restraint, feeling that he has nothing to lose by his boldness. The verse is a tristich and Bickell and Duhm reduce to a distich by deleting 'in the anguish of my spirit I will complain', while Ball supplies conjecturally a fourth line. But while tristichs are uncommon in Job, there are enough of them to make it unwise to iron them all out of the text, and the second and third lines are so excellently parallel that they should not be questioned.

12. Here we have an allusion to the figures of Babylonian mythology, which told how Marduk, after his conflict with Tiamat, divided her body to form heaven and earth, and then drew bolts and set a guard, to prevent her waters from issuing forth. But M. Dahood (*JBL*, LXXX, 1961, pp. 270f.) argues on the basis of Ugaritic evidence that we should render 'muzzle' rather than 'guard'. In the thought of OT creation was the work of God, who was supreme over all powers and over all the elements. He controls the sea (38.8ff.) and all the monsters of mythology. Here 'the dragon' may be Leviathan (3.8) or Rahab (26.12). An alternative view finds a reference to the Ugaritic myth of the conflict of Baal and Yam. Job reminds God that he is no monster, able to threaten God or to defeat his purposes.

13. **my bed will comfort me:** the weary sufferer always hopes that the night will bring him rest and sleep, even though his experience has been of restless tossings (verse 4).
my complaint: not my sickness, but my complaining or my sorrows. 'Sleep is the resource of the unhappy' (Dhorme).

14. **thou dost scare:** Job attributes the nightmares which arise from his fevered state to the direct hand of God.
terrify: this is one of the characteristic words of the book of Job, where it occurs in the intensive form eight times, out of a total of thirteen in OT.

15. **strangling:** the noun is found only here in OT; the verb stands in 2 Sam. 17.23. A sense of choking is often experienced by the leper, and Job wishes one might prove fatal.
bones: this reads oddly (though it is retained by Johnson, *The Vitality of the Individual*, 1949, p. 70n.), and is sometimes taken to imply that Job had wasted away until he was a mere bag of bones. But very many editors slightly change

¹⁶ I loathe my life; I would not live for ever.
    Let me alone, for my days are a breath.
¹⁷ What is man, that thou dost make so much of him,
    and that thou dost set thy mind upon him,
¹⁸ dost visit him every morning,
    and test him every moment?

---

one letter to yield 'sufferings'. This gives a more natural sense. But G. R. Driver
(*ET*, LVII, 1945–46, p. 193) secures this sense without emendation by resort to an
Arabic word, meaning 'great', and then by rendering 'great misfortunes' or
'sufferings'. But here the vital word 'misfortunes' or 'sufferings' has to be supplied
and does not belong to the word. In Isa. 41.21 we have the adjective from this
root used for 'strong arguments' and J. Reider (*VT*, II, 1952, p. 126) revocalises the
word 'bones' here to agree with that and renders 'defensive arguments'. The slight
change of one letter seems preferable to this forced interpretation.

16. **I loathe my life:** 'my life' is not in the Hebrew. Merx, Duhm and others
attach the verb to the previous verse and render 'I despise death more than my
pains', but Gray objects that the verb means 'despise so as to reject'. Fohrer deletes
the verb here as a gloss, while Bickell and Kissane read *massôṭî* instead of *mā'astî*
and render 'I melt away'. But in verse 5 the verb *mā'as* occurs as a by-form of
māsas (*RSV* 'breaks out afresh', lit. 'melts'), and so without emending the text
Dhorme renders 'I am pining away', and so Hölscher. This yields a perfectly
appropriate meaning. Job asks God to realize that he is nearing death and to give
him a last moment of comfort.
I would not live: Ball renders 'I cannot always live', and so it is not worth God's
while to persecute so ephemeral a creature.
a breath: a puff of wind, a figure of what is transient. This is the word rendered
'vanity' in 'vanity of vanities' in Ec. 1.2.

17f. These verses are almost certainly a parody of Ps. 8.4f. (though Duhm
thinks Ps. 8 is later than Job). Whereas the Psalmist asks what is man that God
should so honour him, Job asks what is man that God should so torment him.
make so much of: this is clearly ironical. Job says that God exaggerates the
importance of man by devoting so much unfriendly attention to him.
set thy mind: *AV* and *RV* 'set thine heart' gives a wrong impression. The phrase
is a common one for 'pay attention to'.

18. **visit:** the term is used of inspecting, and the related noun means 'overseer',
'inspector'. Job thinks of God as an unfriendly inspector who comes round dealing
out penalties.
test him: the verb is used of testing gold in 23.10; Zech. 13.3. It means 'to pass
through the crucible in order to discover the degree of purity of a metal' (Dhorme).
The verbs 'visit' and 'test' are used in parallel again in Ps. 17.3.

¹⁹ How long wilt thou not look away from me,
    nor let me alone till I swallow my spittle?
²⁰ If I sin, what do I do to thee, thou watcher of men?
    Why hast thou made me thy mark?
    Why have I become a burden to thee?
²¹ Why dost thou not pardon my transgression
    and take away my iniquity?

---

19. look away: take your eyes off me for a moment. Job feels that he cannot get away from the hostile eye of God. How far removed is Job's experience from that of the Psalmist in Ps. 33.18, where the thought is of the comfort that the sense of God's gracious eye brings (cf. Ps. 34.15 (M.T. 16)).

till I swallow my spittle: this is a proverbial expression, still found in Arabic, meaning 'for a moment'.

20. The rhythm of the first half of the verse is unusual and Bickell, Beer, Hölscher, and Fohrer omit, while Merx cuts out **thou watcher of men.** Dhorme thinks this line is deliberately reduced to two beats instead of three (cf. 4.16, where we have a line reduced to one beat) for emphasis. In that case there would be some scorn in this description of God, who ought to find something better to do. But LXX has an additional term, which in verse 17 is used to render $l\bar{e}\underline{b}$='heart', 'mind'. Ball therefore suggests here 'watcher of the hearts of men'. God is too exalted to be affected by Job's actions. Why should he spend his time concerning himself with what Job is doing? Even if he has sinned (Job does not admit that he has brought on his troubles by his sin), he has not injured God. God is often spoken of in *OT* as watching over men to guard them from danger. But here his watch is depicted as hostile.

mark: this is not a target at which one aims, but something which one strikes. The word is found only here in *OT*. The cognate verb stands in 1 Kg. 2.25 (*RSV* 'struck down').

to thee: the Hebrew text reads 'to myself' (so *AV* and *RV*). But this is one of the eighteen 'scribal corrections' of the text for reasons of religious reverence. The original text is said to have been as in *RSV* and this is supported by LXX. 'The thought is one of amazing boldness, that Job is a burden on the Almighty! but not too bold for the poet' (Peake). Many editors favour this reading, including Duhm, Peake, Dhorme, Szczygiel, Hölscher, Kissane, Weiser, Horst, and Fohrer. On the other hand, Budde and Gray retain the reading 'to myself', holding that the other reading would be an anticlimax. With the reading 'to myself' the meaning is that Job is so weary of being buffeted about by God that his life has become an intolerable burden. Bickell assumes the meaning 'butt' instead of 'burden' and Beer and Ball emend to get the meaning 'target'.

21. If Job has committed some inadvertent sin, why does not God forgive it

For now I shall lie in the earth;
thou wilt seek me, but I shall not be.'

8 Then Bildad the Shuhite answered:
   ² 'How long will you say these things,
   and the words of your mouth be a great wind?

---

before it is too late, since it cannot injure him anyway? For the second line, cf.
verse 8.

seek me: this is a poetic word, derived from the noun meaning 'dawn'. It means
'seek early', and then, since if one gets up early to seek one must be eager to find,
'seek diligently' (cf. Prov. 8.17). Jeremiah frequently speaks with fine poetic
anthropomorphism of God 'rising up early' to send the prophets to Israel (7.25;
25.4) or to plead with Israel (7.13; 25.3) to express the eagerness of God's yearning
over his people (*RSV* here rubs all the poetry out by rendering 'persistently'). It
is to be noted that Job is confident that God will in the end realize his mistake,
but it will be too late. Job still retains the belief in the God of justice and love,
even though he is declaiming against his cruelty and injustice. Two views of God
are struggling in his mind, and he appeals to the God of one view against the God
of the other.

THE FIRST SPEECH OF BILDAD 8.1-22

Bildad now takes up the debate in a speech which ignores Job's cry of anguish
and attack upon his friends, and fastens on his impugnment of God's justice. It is
unthinkable to him that God should be unjust. He therefore concludes that Job's
children must have drawn on themselves punishment by their sin, and that Job's
deliverance depends on his humbly making supplication to God. Whereas Eliphaz
had appealed to the divine revelation granted to him, Bildad appeals to the wisdom
of the ancients, from whom he quotes maxims, making clear that his theology is
unashamedly traditional. Strahan says: 'It Bildad is neither a seer nor an original
thinker, he may at least claim to be an erudite man who cherishes a profound
respect for the wisdom of the ancients.' His speech falls into three parts: affirmation
of the justice of God (verses 2–7); appeal to the wisdom of the ancients (verses
8–19); summary conclusion (verses 20–22).

BILDAD'S AFFIRMATION OF THE JUSTICE OF GOD 8.2-7

After rebuking Job for uttering mere wind, he enunciates the principle of justice
in God's rule. Misfortune is the evidence of sin, and the only hope of escape from
it now it has struck Job is by turning to God.

2. say: the verb is an Aramaism (cf. comment on 5.22).
a great wind: full of sound and empty of content.

³ Does God pervert justice?
   Or does the Almighty pervert the right?
⁴ If your children have sinned against him,
   he has delivered them into the power of their transgression.
⁵ If you will seek God
   and make supplication to the Almighty,
⁶ If you are pure and upright,
   surely then he will rouse himself for you
   and reward you with a rightful habitation.
⁷ And though your beginning was small,
   your latter days will be very great.
⁸ 'For inquire, I pray you, of bygone ages,
   and consider what the fathers have found;

---

3. Great emphasis is placed in the Hebrew on 'God' and 'Shaddai'. Bildad is shocked that Job seems not to realize that it is God against whom he is making charges. God and injustice are mutually incompatible terms. Job and his friends are agreed that rigid justice should be dealt out by God in all the affairs of men, but whereas the friends go on to say that what ought to be is, Job complains that it is not. Neither side will examine the basic assumption of both, for neither will recognize any other principle in life than retribution. Life is even more complex than theorists will allow, and Job was as much a theorist as his friends.

pervert . . . pervert. It is unusual for the same word to stand in two parallel members, though Gray, Ball and Fohrer think the repetition here may have been deliberate, for emphasis, to bring home to Job the enormity of his charge. But LXX and Targ. seem to have read two different verbs, and many editors substitute a synonym for one of the verbs.

4. he has delivered: this rendering makes verse 4 complete in itself. *AV* and *RV* carry the protasis down to the middle of verse 6. Duhm, following LXX, changes the 'if' at the beginning of verse 5 to 'then' and makes that verse the apodosis (so Hölscher). The meaning is then that Job should take warning from what has happened to his sons. Gray, Dhorme, Weiser, Horst, and Fohrer all understand the passage as *RSV*.

into the power of: lit. 'into the hand of', with the implication that sin carries its own punishment. Svi Rin (*BZ*, N.F., VII, 1963, pp. 32f.) adduces Ugaritic evidence for rendering 'because of'. The cruelty of the suggestion that Job's children had brought their death on themselves, even though it is expressed in a conditional sentence, illustrates the lack of human feeling that doctrinaire theology can lead to.

5. seek: Bildad picks up Job's word (7.21; cf. note there). But whereas Job had spoken of God's seeking him, Bildad says it would be more fitting if Job would seek God.

make supplication: implore mercy. The sin of Job's sons had been mortal, but there was still time for Job to save himself from death. But there was only one way to do this. Without delay he should turn in penitence and surrender to God.

6. if you are pure and upright: some editors (so Merx, Siegfried, Duhm) delete the following line to reduce this verse to a distich. But Dhorme deletes this line on the ground that in Bildad's view if Job were righteous he would not be suffering (so Ball, Hölscher, Horst, Fohrer).

he will rouse himself for you: note the anthropomorphism here. LXX has 'he will answer your prayer', which some editors restore, and which Peake thinks more befitting Bildad's reverence. It may be, however, that it was the reverence of the LXX translator which dictated the change. Dhorme retains the Hebrew, but renders 'watch over you' (so H. L. Ginsberg (*BASOR*, no. 72, Dec. 1938, p. 19) and H. N. Richardson (*JBL*, LXVI, 1947, p. 322) on the basis of Ugaritic evidence), while Reider (*VT*, II, 1952, p. 126) renders 'will bestow wealth on you', claiming Arabic support.

reward you with a righteous habitation: lit. 'and restore the habitation of thy righteousness'. Bildad promises Job the restoration of his fortunes if he will follow his advice. Ball proposes emendations to yield 'he will make good according to your righteousness', which Dhorme declares prosaic, or the more radical change 'you shall pay him your vows', which has not the merit of any obvious appropriateness to the context.

7. Note Bildad's unconscious prophecy, which was fulfilled through quite other means.

BILDAD'S APPEAL TO THE WISDOM OF THE ANCIENTS **8.8–19**

Bildad now claims that his principles are supported by the accumulated wisdom and experience of the ages.

8. of bygone ages: lit. 'of the first (or former) age (or generation)'. Ball thinks the reference is to the patriarchal age. But the scene is laid in that age. Gray thinks the entire past of mankind is viewed as a single generation, so that the phrase is equivalent to 'of former generations'. Dhorme, on the other hand, thinks the reference is to the immediately past generations. Peake observes that it is not clear on what principle Bildad considers the wisdom of the ancients to be superior. Dillmann thinks the idea is that one generation is too short to attain wisdom, and that Bildad thinks of the accumulated stock of experience.

consider: the Hebrew says 'fix'. Dhorme understands *lēb*='heart', 'mind', 'attention', and finds the meaning 'pay attention to'. Many editors change one consonant of the text, to secure a more ordinary word for 'consider'. כֹּונֵן

what the fathers have found: the Hebrew says 'search of their fathers' but it must here mean the fruit of the research of the fathers. LXX and Vulg. have 'the fathers' for the somewhat surprising 'their fathers' of the Hebrew, and many

⁹ for we are but of yesterday, and know nothing,
    for our days on earth are a shadow.
¹⁰ Will they not teach you, and tell you,
    and utter words out of their understanding?
¹¹ 'Can papyrus grow where there is no marsh?
    Can reeds flourish where there is no water?
¹² While yet in flower and not cut down,
    they wither before any other plant.
¹³ Such are the paths of all who forget God;
    the hope of the godless man shall perish.

---

editors follow this. J. A. Fitzmyer (in W. F. Albright, *Yahweh and the Gods of Canaan*, 1968, p. 124) reads *'ōḇôṯām* for *'aḇōṯām*, and renders 'set about to examine their ghosts'.

9. of yesterday: the longest life is but brief; hence the need to take account of the extended experience of mankind.
our days . . . a shadow: cf. 1 Chr. 29.15.
10. they: emphatic. Duhm deletes the verse on the ground that the sentiment is too empty even for a Bildad. But Strahan observes that it is impossible not to feel that the author is sometimes smiling at his solemn traditionalist.
from their heart: Dhorme comments that Bildad means that their words do not come from their lips alone, but from the depths of their heart and understanding.
11. Bildad now cites proverbial sayings which embody the wisdom of the ancients.
papyrus . . . reeds. The words used both have Egyptian connections, and it has been suggested that the author may have known Egypt, or perhaps regarded Egypt at the home of wisdom. The papyrus usually grew to a height of six feet, and hence the word for 'grow' means 'grow high'. From its stem skiffs (Isa. 18.2) and writing materials were made. The word for 'reed' is found in Gen. 41.2, 18 (*RSV* 'reed grass') of the Nile grass on which the fat cows fed.
marsh: the word recurs in 40.21 (cf. Jer. 38.22, where another form from the same root is found—*RSV* 'mire').
12. in flower: *AV* and *RV* 'in its greenness'. The word is found again in OT Hebrew only in Ca. 6.11 (*RSV* 'blossoms'). In Biblical Aramaic it means 'fruit'. From the same root comes *'āḇîḇ* = 'fresh, young ears of barley'.
and not cut down: probably means 'not ripe for cutting'.
13. paths: LXX has 'latter end', with the transposition of two consonants and a slight change of another, and very many editors follow this reading. But Dhorme retains M.T., adducing in its support Prov. 1.19, where 'paths' comes to mean 'fate'.
godless: this is a characteristic word of the vocabulary of Job. It occurs eight times

14 His confidence breaks in sunder,
   and his trust is a spider's web.
15 He leans against his house, but it does not stand;
   he lays hold of it, but it does not endure.
16 He thrives before the sun,
   and his shoots spread over his garden.

---

in the book. The verb means 'to be profane', and it is used especially of profaning by bloodshed or idolatry. The term used here is used of the irreligious man. The corresponding word in Syriac is used as the epithet to describe Julian 'the Apostate'. Ball renders 'the worldling'.

14. confidence: see on 4.6.

breaks in sunder: the Hebrew word *yāḵôṭ* is otherwise unknown, and the parallel line suggests that we should have a noun here. Sa'adia's Arabic translation has 'sun cords' or 'gossamer'. Beer, Duhm, Gray, and Hölscher read *ḵûrîm* (used in Isa. 59.5 'spider threads', i.e. 'spider's web'). Others reconstruct in various ways 'summer threads', while Ball suggests *kaḥûṭ*='like a thread' (Ca. 4.3), and Dhorme *yalḵûṭ*='wallet' (1 Sam. 17.40), i.e. an empty bag is their confidence! Reider (*VT*, IV, 1954, pp. 288f.) conjectures that *yāḵôṭ* is a noun connected with the Aramaic *ḵayiṭ*='summer', and that it meant 'gossamer', and Tur-Sinai that it meant 'a water-hole'. The meaning 'gossamer' excellently suits the context, but it is impossible to establish how this was originally expressed.

spider: only mentioned here and in Isa. 59.5.

web: lit. 'house', picked up in verse 15.

15. Budde deletes this verse as a gloss, but on insufficient grounds. The confidence of the wicked is no more substantial than a spider's web, which is proverbial in the east for flimsiness. Cf. Qur'an 29.40: 'Verily, frailest of all houses is the house of the spider.'

16. The figure changes and we now have the description of a flourishing tree suddenly cut off. Irwin (*ZAW*, N.F., x, 1933, pp. 205ff. and in *Peake's Commentary*, revised edition, 1962) holds that the description of the godless man ended with verse 13, and that verses 14–19 'described in some sort of metaphor corresponding to the figure in verse 11f. the vicissitudes of an upright man'. This involves some very radical conjectural emendations. He denies that Bildad assumes sin to be the cause of misfortune, and holds that what he argues is that suffering is the common lot of good and bad. It is hard to see how he can base this on the justice of God (verse 2).

thrives: lit. 'is moist' or 'sappy'', a word found only here. The verb stands in 24.8 only (*RSV* 'they are wet').

before the sun: under the sun's warmth. Dhorme takes it to mean 'before the sun rises', but this is improbable as the meaning.

over his garden: some editors find this inappropriate and Budde slightly emended

17 His roots twine about the stoneheap;
     he lives among the rocks.
18 If he is destroyed from his place,
     then it will deny him, saying, "I have never seen you."
19 Behold, this is the joy of his way;

---

to yield 'over the roofs', which sounds much less appropriate for suckers. But 'his garden', as Dhorme says, is the garden in which he is rooted, carrying on the figure of the plant. LXX has 'out of his corruption', which arose, as Orlinsky (*JQR*, N.S., xxvi, 1935–36, pp. 134f.) cleverly shows, by an inner-Greek corruption, *saprias* having replaced *prasias*='garden'.

17. Some editors suppose that the meaning is that the tree stands in stony soil in which it can find no nourishment and so dies, representing the fate that befalls the ungodly. But it is more likely that the stones around which the roots twine themselves promise strength to the tree, and protection against the uprooting, which nevertheless comes in verse 18. So the wicked may appear to be flourishing and secure, yet are swiftly destroyed.

stone-heap: Merx and Cheyne render 'spring', since the word has that meaning in Ca. 4.12. But the parallel with 'house of stones' is against this. Hence they go on to emend this to secure 'he looks with delight on a luxuriance of fresh growths.' But M.T. is clear and intelligible in the first line.

he lives: M.T. has 'he beholds the house of stones' (cf. *AV*, *RV*). LXX has 'he lives in the midst of stones'. This involves reading *yihyeh* instead of *yeḥᵉzeh*, and rendering *bêṭ*, which normally means 'house', by 'between', which is normally written *bên*. Buttenwieser argues that *bêṭ* is a correct Hebrew form for 'between', while others change to *bên*. The sense of LXX is represented in *RSV* and is accepted by Siegfried, Duhm, Peake, Strahan, Dhorme, and Kissane. Others emend to secure 'they (i.e. the roots, or he) grasp(s) (it)' (so Hoffmann, Bickell, Budde, Hölscher, Szczygiel, Fohrer, Pope), or 'they (or he) pierce(s)' (so Davidson, Budde, Gray). Without change of text Ball strains the meaning of the Hebrew to render 'he chooses', and Stevenson to render 'he comes to'. It seems best to follow LXX with *RSV*. The sense then accords with the context and the line speaks of the strengthening of the hold of the tree on the earth.

18. If he is destroyed: the Hebrew says 'if one destroy him' with indefinite subject. Ball reads 'God (*'ēl* instead of *'im*) will destroy him', perhaps rightly. Since no vestige of the tree is left, it must be completely uprooted, despite its hold on the stones.

deny: or 'disown'. The word stands again in 31.28 (*RSV* 'be false to'). Cf. Ps. 103.16.

19. the joy of his way: this can only be ironic, if the text is in order, and the meaning be that his joy is short-lived. Dhorme transforms the meaning by taking

and out of the earth others will spring.
²⁰ 'Behold, God will not reject a blameless man,
     nor take the hand of evildoers.
²¹ He will yet fill your mouth with laughter,
     and your lips with shouting.
²² Those who hate you will be clothed with shame,
     and the tent of the wicked will be no more.'

9 Then Job answered:
     ² 'Truly I know that it is so:

$m^e\hat{s}\hat{o}\hat{s}$='joy' to be for $m^e\hat{s}\hat{o}\hat{s}$='rotting' (there are other cases in Job of interchange of $\hat{s}$ and s), and so renders 'Behold him rotting on a path'. Others make more radical changes.
others will spring: his place is soon taken and he will not be missed. In the Hebrew the subject is singular and the verb plural.

SUMMARY 8.20–22
Bildad repeats his affirmation of God's justice and his promise of restoration to Job, the implied condition being that his advice should be followed.
   20. blameless: Bildad here uses the term which describes Job (1.1) and which God had used of him (1.8).
take the hand: cf. Isa. 42.6; 51.18.
   21. yet: almost all editors follow this reading, which represents a revocalizing of the Hebrew: '$\hat{o}\underline{d}$='yet' instead of '$a\underline{d}$='until' (cf. AV).
He will fill: Syr. and Vulg. have '(your mouth) will be filled', and so Dhorme.
shouting: this is the shout of jubilation. It can also mean 'war-cry' (39.25). On this word, cf. P. Humbert, La 'Terou'a', 1946.
   22. will be clothed with shame: cf. Ps. 35.26, 132.18 (also 109.29). Shame is thought of as a garment which the wicked wear, for all to see.

JOB ANSWERS BILDAD 9–10
Job's reply to Bildad seems to concern itself more with things said by Eliphaz than with what Bildad has said. He begins with a sarcastic recognition of the principle enunciated by the friends, that man cannot be righteous in the eyes of God, because God overwhelms him with his power and refuses to appear with man at the bar of justice. He will therefore boldly proclaim his challenge to God's justice and calls on God to cease to torment him. His speech ends with a renewed complaint and longing for death. The speech falls into the following sections, though they are not very sharply marked off: his recognition of the

But how can a man be just before God?
³ If one wished to contend with him,
 one could not answer him once in a thousand times.
⁴ He is wise in heart, and mighty in strength
 —who has hardened himself against him, and succeeded?—
⁵ he who removes mountains, and they know it not,

---

inscrutability and power of God (9.2-13); the impossibility of facing God in court (9.14-21); God's indiscriminate flouting of justice (9.22-24); Job's renewed complaint (9.25-35); his review of God's dealings with him and longing for death (10.1-22).

JOB'S RECOGNITION OF THE INSCRUTABILITY AND POWER OF GOD 9.2-13

Man cannot be justified as against God, because God is too clever and too powerful for him. He commands all the forces of the universe, and no one can face him in argument.

2. Many of Job's speeches open with sarcasm or irony. Eliphaz had asked in 4.17 how a man could be righteous before God and Bildad argued in 8.3 that God is invariably just. Of course, says Job. God sets the standard of justice. There is no higher court to which appeal can be made against his decisions. 'Job here touches on the problem whether a thing is right because God declares it to be so, or whether He declares it is right because it is so' (Peake). The second part of the verse is repeated in 25.4.

3. If one wished: *RV* takes God to be the subject of the verb. So Ball, who then takes the next line to mean God would refuse to answer man's questions. He notes that Job's constant complaint is that he cannot extract any response from God. But most take as *RSV* and understand the verse to mean that God would overwhelm man by posing questions he could not answer. Peake notes that when God speaks from the tempest, this is just what he does.

contend: with a forensic reference, 'go to law'.

once in a thousand times: lit. 'one (fem.) from a thousand'. E. E. Kellett (*ET*, XLIV, 1932-33, pp. 283f.) reads 'one (masc.)' and interprets in the light of 33.23, the 'one of a thousand' then being one of the thousand angelic mediators between God and man. It is then necessary to render 'will answer for him', i.e. will act as his advocate. This is very forced.

4. heart: here, as frequently, 'heart' stands for 'intelligence'.

hardened: the object is unexpressed. It may be the neck (2 Kg. 17.14) or the heart (Ps. 95.8). No one can resist or challenge God with impunity. God always comes off best. Many editors think there may be some allusion to Pharaoh in this line.

5. they know it not: against this reading it is prosaically argued that the moun-

> when he overturns them in his anger;
> **6** who shakes the earth out of its place,
>   and its pillars tremble;
> **7** who commands the sun, and it does not rise;
>   who seals up the stars;
> **8** who alone stretched out the heavens,

---

tains would not know it whoever moved them. Syr. reads 'and he does not know it', i.e. the moving of mountains is such a trifling thing to God that he could do it without noticing it (so Beer, Duhm, Peake, Strahan). Most, however, prefer M.T., and take the meaning to be 'suddenly', i.e. before they know anything about it (so Budde, Gray, Dhorme, Hölscher, Buttenwieser, Weiser, Horst, Fohrer). Ball emends to secure 'he is not perceived' (and so Stevenson), i.e. God acts, but does not let himself be found doing it. D. Winton Thomas (*JTS*, N.S., xv, 1964, pp. 54f.) renders M.T. 'so that they are no longer still', connecting the verb with the Arabic root *wadaʿa*.

when: this might equally be rendered 'who' or 'that', and there are advocates of each of these views. If it is rendered 'who' it could be taken as a parallel statement to the first line (so Gray), or a relative sentence: 'they do not know who overturns them' (so Dillmann, Dhorme).

6. pillars: note the conception of the earth as standing upon pillars (cf. Ps. 75.3 (M.T. 4)), and the earthquakes as caused by the shaking of the pillars.

tremble: this verb is found only here, but three nouns from this root are found once each. The root idea is 'to shudder with horror'.

7. sun: the word used here is rare and poetic, but it forms an element in some proper names. Ball suggests that it may be derived from the name Horus. If so, there is no more reference to the Egyptian god here than there is to Jupiter in our thought when we call someone 'jovial'.

it does not rise: Dhorme thinks the reference may be to the piling up of the clouds or the oncoming of a mysterious darkness, while others think of eclipses. The word rendered 'rise' is usually used of the rising of the sun, but it may be used more generally here, meaning 'shine'. None of the suggested causes of darkness is limited to the early morning. A poet's thought is not to be understood in a literal way, and the meaning is probably no more than that God controls the sunshine and the starlight.

8–10. Beer, Duhm, Budde, and Hölscher delete these verses on the ground that the mention of God's creative work is not in place here. Other editors do not feel the reasons alleged are cogent. Fohrer regards verses 5–10 as a hymn proclaiming the power of God over nature. Job wishes to show that he is no whit behind the friends in recognizing the mighty works of God in nature.

8. For the first line, cf. Isa. 44.24.

and trampled the waves of the sea;
⁹ who made the Bear and Ori'on,
   the Plei'ades and the chambers of the south;

---

the waves of the sea: lit. 'the heights of the sea'. Three MSS. have 'clouds' instead of 'sea', and this is followed by Fohrer. *RSV* marg. 'the back of the sea dragon' reflects the view of Albright (*JBL*, LVII, 1938, p. 227), who sees in 'the sea' (Hebrew *yām*) the Ugaritic Yammu, the primordial sea dragon, and who connects *bāmºtê=* 'heights' with Ugaritic *bmt=*'back' (cf. in H. H. Rowley (ed.), *Studies in Old Testament Prophecy*, 1950, p. 18). On the Ugaritic myth of the conflict of Baal and Yam, cf. O. Kaiser, *Die mythische Bedeutung des Meeres*, 1959, pp. 44ff.

9. the Bear: the Hebrew here has '*āš*, but in 38.31f., where the same three constellations are mentioned in the reverse order, we find '*ayiš*, which is a more accurate form. Syr. has the phonetically equivalent '*îyûṯā*', which Bar-Hebraeus identifies with Aldebaran (so Hoffmann, *ZAW*, III, 1883, p. 107), a star in Taurus. In Am. 5.8 the same Syriac word is used to render the term here rendered Orion in *RSV*. In 38.32 Targ. interprets '*ayiš* as 'the Hen'. Vulg. here has Arcturus, which in 38.31 renders the term rendered Orion here. It is thus clear that there is no firm tradition for the identification of the names. Modern scholars are also not agreed. *BDB* gives the Bear, and so Budde, Dhorme and Weiser. Schiaparelli (*Astronomy in the Old Testament*, 1905, pp. 54ff.) identified with Aldebaran ('her children' of 38.32 being the Hyades, stars in Taurus associated with Aldebaran), and this view is followed by Mowinckel (*Die Sternnamen im A.T.*, 1928, pp. 52ff.), G. R. Driver (*JTS*, N.S., VII, 1956, p. 1f.), and Horst. *KB* gives Leo, and so Fohrer. **Orion:** there is a much stronger tradition for the identification with Orion, despite Syr. in Am. 5.8 and Vulg. in 38.31 (see preceding note), and there is general agreement among modern scholars here. The name means 'fool', and behind it there may be the myth of a giant who was chained to the sky (cf. 38.32, 'the cords of Orion').

the Pleiades: this identification is also generally accepted, though Vulg. has Hyades here, and in Am. 5.8 Arcturus (so also Aq.). In classical mythology the seven Pleiades were sisters of the Hyades, who were pursued by Orion, until they and their pursuer were changed by Zeus into stars. The myth was probably derived from an older Oriental myth, which is reflected in bringing together the names in this verse, and this is an added reason for finding Aldebaran and the Hyades in '*ayiš* and her sons.

the chambers of the south: Driver (loc. cit., pp. 9f.) proposes to revocalize the word rendered 'chambers', and then renders 'the encirclers of the south' and interprets as the *circulus austrinus* of Martianus Capella, in the fourth century A.D., and of other classical writers (cf. Schiaparelli, op. cit., pp. 63ff.).

¹⁰ who does great things beyond understanding,
   and marvellous things without number.
¹¹ Lo, he passes by me, and I see him not;
   he moves on, but I do not perceive him.
¹² Behold, he snatches away; who can hinder him?
   Who will say to him, "What doest thou?"
¹³ 'God will not turn back his anger;
   beneath him bowed the helpers of Rahab.

---

10. Cf. 5.9. Dhorme thinks there was a touch of irony in repeating this verse from Eliphaz. Ball thinks it was a marginal gloss. Davidson finds a different nuance in the words on Job's lips: 'while to Eliphaz all God's operations have an ethical meaning and subserve one great purpose of goodness, to Job they seem the mere un-moral play of an immeasurable force'.

11. Gray comments: 'Job, like the mountains (verse 5), lay in the path of God as He passed along in His anger; and though He passed invisibly, Job knows that He has passed by the effect of His passage; like mountains overturned by the same cause, Job's life lies in ruins.'

12. snatches away: the verb here (*ḥātap*) is found nowhere else in *OT* (also Sir. 15.14; 32.21; a noun from it stands in Prov. 23.28 (*RSV* 'robber'); Sir. 50.4), but a root *ḥātap* = 'seize' is found in Jg. 21.21; Ps. 10.9, and some MSS. have that verb here. Some editors follow that reading here, but Dhorme finds no reason to emend, since the two roots are synonymous. Gard (*JBL*, LXXII, 1953, p. 183) thinks LXX translator for reasons of reverence avoided ascribing destructive action to God, and renders the Greek 'If he set free'. But the Greek can equally be rendered 'If he removes' or 'If he destroys', and the former of these meanings is usually found here.

What doest thou? Cf. Dan. 4.35; Sir. 36.8 (Hebrew). God's power is irresistible, and he is responsible to none, save himself.

13. Not only can no other stay God's hand; he will not stay it himself, but lets his wrath vent itself on any he pleases.

the helpers of Rahab: Rahab is usually identified with Tiamat of the Babylonian Creation Epic, and with Leviathan (see on 7.12). It is used in parallel to the sea (26.12; cf. on 3.8), sometimes with reference to the crossing of the Red Sea (Ps. 74.13), and hence it becomes a symbol for Egypt (Isa. 30.7). In Isa. 51.9 it is associated with 'the dragon', while in Ps. 74.13 it is Leviathan who is associated with 'the dragon'. In the Creation Epic there is a reference to the helpers of Tiamat, and this will explain the reference here. Allusions to ancient mythology no more imply its acceptance by the sacred writers than Milton's allusions to classical mythology imply his acceptance of it. H. L. Ginsberg (*JBL*, LVII, 1938, p. 210) finds Ugaritic evidence for the meaning 'be strong' for the root *'āzar*, and suggests

14 How then can I answer him,
  choosing my words with him?
15 Though I am innocent, I cannot answer him;
  I must appeal for mercy to my accuser.
16 If I summoned him and he answered me,
  I would not believe that he was listening to my voice.
17 For he crushes me with a tempest,

---

that this meaning should be found here instead of 'help'. But the usual meaning makes excellent sense.

THE IMPOSSIBILITY OF FACING GOD IN COURT 9.14–21

If Job were to summon God and he were to appear in court, he would refuse to answer Job's charges, but would simply overwhelm him with his power.

14. How then? The Hebrew uses an expression which can mean 'How much more!' or 'How much less!' (cf. 4.19). Here it must mean the latter. If monsters like Rahab are powerless against him, how can Job expect to face him?
answer him: rebut his charges against me.
choosing my words with him: Job would be so overwhelmed that he would be unable to choose words with which to argue with God.

15. innocent: *AV* and *RV* have 'righteous'. The term is here forensic, meaning 'in the right', 'innocent'.
I cannot answer him: LXX, Theod., Syr. have the passive 'I am not answered' and many editors follow this reading, to avoid the repetition of the same word as in verse 14 (so Siegfried, Beer, Budde, Dhorme, Hölscher, Fohrer). But Gray rejects as unnecessary. At this point Job is only concerned with his inability to answer God's charges against him, since he would be overawed by his presence. It is not until the next verse that he turns to the question of his citing God.
my accuser: *AV* has 'judge'; but the meaning is 'my adversary at law'. Since Job cannot force his accuser, he has no resource but to cast himself on his mercy.

16. and he answered me: here the meaning is 'answered my summons', i.e. appeared in court, not 'replied to my charges'. Beer and Duhm follow the reading of LXX^B, 'then he would not answer me'. But the Hebrew yields a clear meaning and is followed by Gray, Ball, Dhorme, and others.
listening to my voice: God is deaf to the summons, and no court can compel his attendance.

17. crushes me: the verb used here is that used in Gen. 3.15 (*RSV* 'bruise'). G. R. Driver (*JTS*, xxx, 1928–29, pp. 375ff.) disputes the meaning 'bruise', and renders here 'swept close over'.
with a tempest: Syr. and Targ. with a difference of vocalization read 'with (or for) a hair', and this reading is followed by Dhorme, who understands it to mean

and multiplies my wounds without cause;
18 he will not let me get my breath,
   but fills me with bitterness.
19 If it is a contest of strength, behold him!
   If it is a matter of justice, who can summon him?
20 Though I am innocent, my own mouth would condemn me;
   though I am blameless, he would prove me perverse.
21 I am blameless; I regard not myself;

'for a trifle', parallel to 'without cause' in the next line (so Kissane, Robin, Larcher, Steinmann). Most editors see no reason for change, but 'a tempest' does not seem relevant to this context, and elsewhere in Job 'tempest' is written with s and not ś, as here.

without cause: the same word as in 2.3.

   18. **get my breath:** cf. 7.19.
filleth me with bitterness: cf. Lam. 3.15.

   19. The first line is cryptic in the Hebrew. The literal meaning is: 'If of the strength of the strong, behold!' We should either read 'behold him!' or change *hinnēh*='behold!' to *hū'*='he', and render 'If it is a question of strength, he is the mighty one'. Those who retain M.T. have to supply words: 'he is there' (*RV*) or 'I am here, saith he' (Gray). In the second line M.T. has 'who will appoint me a time?', but LXX and Syr. render 'appoint him a time' instead of 'appoint me a time'. The verb used here is that used in 2.11 of the fixing of a rendezvous for the friends. Whether it be a trial of strength or an appeal to justice, Job is helpless against God.

   20. **innocent:** cf. verse 15.
my mouth: some editors read 'his mouth' (so Olshausen, Siegfried, Hölscher, Fohrer), and Dahood (*Biblica*, XLVIII, 1967, p. 543), without changing the reading, so renders. But most prefer M.T. (so Budde, Duhm, Gray, Ball, Dhorme, Horst, Pope). Job is afraid he will be overawed and confused by God's presence and will argue against himself.

he would prove me perverse: Dhorme takes the verb as declarative: 'declare me perverse'. Others find the meaning to be: 'would twist me', or 'would twist my words'. The subject is uncertain. It could be 'he' as *RSV* or 'it', i.e. my mouth (so *AV*, *RV*, Dhorme, Kissane). The parallelism favours the latter.

   21. Job here 'speaks in impassioned recoil from the terrible possibility, to which he feels he may be driven, that he may renounce the honour that is more to him than life' (Peake). He protests his innocence recklessly, though it should cost him his life. The rhythm is irregular, and Budde suggests that this was intentional, to give the impression of the intense emotional strain under which Job was speaking (cf. on 4.16).

I loathe my life.
²² It is all one; therefore I say,
  he destroys both the blameless and the wicked.
²³ When disaster brings sudden death,
  he mocks at the calamity of the innocent.
²⁴ The earth is given into the hand of the wicked;

I regard not myself: lit. 'I do not know myself'. The meaning is 'I do not care' (cf. Gen. 39.6).

I loathe my life: *RV* 'I despise my life', rendering the verb as in 19.18. It means 'despise so as to reject'. Job means that he is ready to throw his life away, rather than disavow his innocence.

GOD FLOUTS JUSTICE INDISCRIMINATELY 9.22–24

He destroys good and bad alike and mocks at the misfortunes of the good. The world is handed over by him to the wicked, and injustice is triumphant.

22. It is all one: LXX omits these words. In their present position, they appear to mean that it does not matter whether Job lives or dies. Ball inverts the two halves of this line, and so Dhorme and Robin: 'Therefore I say: "It is all one".' The meaning then is that Job is prepared to risk his life by denouncing God's indifference to moral considerations. He thus contradicts what Bildad said in 8.20.

23. disaster: the word means 'scourge' or 'whip'. Here it appears to mean plague or natural disaster (Fohrer thinks of a sudden flood), which carries off good and bad indiscriminately, while God but mocks at their sufferings. Dhorme finds here a rejection of the argument of Eliphaz in 4.7.

he mocks: Eliphaz had said (5.22) that if Job patiently bore the discipline of God, he would laugh at destruction and famine. Job retorts that it is God who mocks when disasters come.

calamity: the meaning is uncertain. *AV* and *RV* 'trial' connects it with the verb *nāsāh*='test' (so Hitzig, Gray, Kissane). Most connect it with the verb *māsās* ='melt', and render 'despair' or the like (so Dillmann, Dhorme, Hölscher, Tur-Sinai, Weiser, Horst, Fohrer, Pope). This is to be preferred, since Job is not saying that God tests men by disaster, but destroys them. There is no need to change the text, to read 'slaughter', with Graetz, Cheyne, and Ball.

24. The miscarriage of justice in human courts, from which God fails to protect the righteous, is advanced by Job as a further refutation of the view that desert and reward are invariably matched.

The earth: Dhorme thinks Job's thought is limited to the land, but it seems more natural to think he is enunciating a universal principle.

he covers the faces of its judges—
if it is not he, who then is it?
²⁵ 'My days are swifter than a runner;
they flee away, they see no good.
²⁶ They go by like skiffs of reed,

---

covers the face of its judges: in Exod. 23.8 bribery is condemned because it covers the eyes of officials so that they cannot see where justice lies. Job here says it is God who blinds the judges to the truth. All the injustice that prevails in the world is laid at his door. That Job's words are wild is undeniable. But he is only exposing the implications of the friends' arguments. They maintained that a man's fortunes reflected his merits, since God invariably dispenses justice in the world. But Job sees injustice rampant, and if God is responsible for everything, he must be responsible for this, and be incapable of discriminating between justice and injustice. The conclusion is wrong because the premises are wrong.

If it is not he, who then is it? The Hebrew is cryptic, and Gray renders: 'If not, then who is it?' *AV* has: 'If not, where, and who is he?' It is one of the scribal conjectures that the words 'then' and 'he' should be transposed, yielding the sense of *RSV*, and most editors follow this. Szczygiel reads *'appô* = 'his wrath' for *'ēpô* = 'then', giving 'If it is not his wrath, who is it?' This is not to be preferred. Job is challenging his friends to say who is responsible for these things, if God is not.

JOB'S RENEWED COMPLAINT 9.25–35

Job now returns to lament his miserable condition, and his inability to establish his innocence, and cries to God to cease to torment him.

25. Job once more soliloquizes, and laments the shortness of life (cf. 7.6, where the shuttle takes the place of the royal post here). The runner is the swift messenger conveying a despatch or tidings (cf. 2 Sam. 18.19ff.).

they see no good: Dhorme comments: 'Life passes away so swiftly that the happy moments are swallowed up without trace.'

26. skiffs of reed: the word rendered 'reed' means 'papyrus', but is different from that used in 8.11. What is meant is the Nile boat with a wooden keel and papyrus sides, light and very swift. The author's metaphors are well chosen. The eagle is proverbial for its swiftness in flight. He has used the shuttle, the runner, the speedboat of ancient Egypt, and the swiftest of birds to describe the swiftness of the days of his brief life. Strahan says: 'The poet displays a wonderful insight into the psychology of moods, making Job's fear of God and his longing for Him, his contempt of life and his yearning for it, alternate throughout the whole book with a perfect fitness which, as Duhm remarks, is in itself a sufficient proof that the writer was a born dramatist.'

like an eagle swooping on the prey.
27 If I say, "I will forget my complaint,
    I will put off my sad countenance, and be of good cheer,"
28 I become afraid of all my suffering,
    for I know thou wilt not hold me innocent.
29 I shall be condemned;
    why then do I labour in vain?
30 If I wash myself with snow,
    and cleanse my hands with lye,
31 yet thou wilt plunge me into a pit,
    and my own clothes will abhor me.
32 For he is not a man, as I am, that I might answer him,
    that we should come to trial together.
33 There is no umpire between us,
    who might lay his hand upon us both.
34 Let him take his rod away from me,
    and let not dread of him terrify me.
35 Then I would speak without fear of him,
    for I am not so in myself.

---

eagle: this word indicates both the eagle and the vulture. But since the latter with us has only ignoble associations, while the eagle has noble associations also, often 'eagle' is the appropriate term to use in English.

27. I will put off my sad countenance: lit. 'I will abandon my face', i.e. I will change my countenance. M. Dahood (*JBL*, LXXVIII, 1959, p. 304) derives the verb from another root, exemplified in Ugaritic, and renders 'I shall arrange my face'. G. R. Driver (*SVT*, III, 1955, p. 76) renders 'I will make pleasant my countenance', adducing an Arabic cognate.
be of good cheer: lit. 'brighten (my face)'.

28. become afraid of: the word rendered 'dread' in 3.25. Whenever Job resolves to cheer up he is haunted by dread that this will only bring some new agony. God is so determined to treat him as a criminal that he will not suffer him a moment's ease. Perles (*JQR*, XVIII, 1905–06, p. 387), on the basis of post-biblical Hebrew, renders 'I shudder in every nerve'.

29. I shall be condemned: this line is short, and some editors add 'if' at the beginning to lengthen it, since all the versions except Targ. so render. But without any addition it could be so rendered. Job here says that since it is so certain that he will be pronounced guilty, it is of little use to present his defence. Duhm and Hölscher delete the verse as a gloss.

labour: i.e. in clearing himself.

30. **with snow:** So *Kt. Ķr* has 'with snow water', and so *AV* and *RV* in agreement with Syr., Vulg. and Targ. Snow water is not likely to have appeared specially cleansing, though it can be understood that snow might. Merx and Ball read 'like snow' (cf. then Ps. 51.7 (M.T. 9); Isa. 1.18). Peters notes that in later Hebrew the word *šeleḡ* means 'soap' as well as 'snow' (cf. Ben Yehuda, *s.v.*), and this is favoured by the parallel (so Fohrer; cf. Pope 'soapwort').

with lye: i.e. with a vegetable alkali, made from the ashes of plants, and used for cleansing. *AV* and *RV* follow Syr. in taking the word to mean 'cleanness' and so render 'make my hands never so clean'. In 22.30 and Ps. 18.20, 24 (M.T. 21, 25) the word means 'cleanness', and in Isa. 1.25 'lye'.

31. **a pit:** *AV* and *RV* have 'ditch', but Ball notes that this meaning for *šaḥaṭ* is without parallel, and thinks the meaning is a cesspool. Hoffmann, Dhorme, Hölscher, Horst, and Fohrer make this meaning clearer by reading *šūḥōt*, and Beer and Duhm similarly by reading *sūḥāh* (cf. Isa. 5.25, *RSV* 'refuse'), while Hoffmann (*ZAW*, N.F., VIII, 1931, p. 142) proposes *seḥî*='offscouring' (Lam. 3.45). Pope (*JBL*, LXXXIII, 1964, pp. 269ff.) argues that the word rendered 'pit' here has the meaning 'filth', rendering emendation unnecessary.

my own clothes: the meaning is that if Job washes his body, God will at once befoul it to such a degree that his very clothes would refuse to cover him. By slight changes Duhm and Lagarde (*Prophetae Chaldaice*, 1872, p. L) secured the meaning 'my friends', but M.T. is much more forcible.

32. Job returns to the thought of the impossibility of meeting God on equal terms before a fair court.

come to trial: that we should go to law with one another (cf. Ps. 143.2).

33. **there is no:** some MSS. and LXX, Syr. read 'Would that there were!' and so some editors. It is not necessary to make any change.

umpire: an arbiter, or a mediator. Strahan observes that while Job is ostensibly pleading for justice, deep down he is seeking for reconciliation, and finds here an unconscious prophecy of incarnation and atonement. This is denied by Davidson, who continues: 'That the cry is uttered under a misconception of God and of the meaning of His providence does not make the expression of man's need any the less real or touching, for in our great darkness here misconceptions of God prevail so much over true conceptions of Him.'

might lay his hand upon us: symbolizing that he is taking both parties under his authority and protection. For the phrase, cf. Ps. 139.5.

34. **Let him take his rod away:** Dhorme thinks the appeal is to the arbiter to remove God's rod from him, but Davidson thinks the appeal is to God to withdraw his hand. The meaning is then in close agreement with 13.21.

rod: this is the word so rendered in Ps. 23.4. To the Psalmist it is a comfort because it is for his defence against his enemies; for Job it is no comfort because it is wielded against him.

35. This verse is not very clear, the last line being very cryptic. Dhorme transposes the two halves of the verse and finds the sense to be: 'Since it is not so',

10 'I loathe my life;
     I will give free utterance to my complaint;
     I will speak in the bitterness of my soul.
² I will say to God, Do not condemn me;
     let me know why thou dost contend against me.
³ Does it seem good to thee to oppress,
     to despise the work of thy hands
     and favour the designs of the wicked?

---

i.e. since I cannot come face to face with God on equal terms, or in the presence of an arbiter, 'I with myself will speak and will not fear him', i.e. I will make my defence to myself. Others take the last line to mean 'for in my own conscience I am not such as he thinks' (so Hölscher; cf. F. Field, *Exp*, 6th series, IV, 1901, p. 397). Kissane, with less probability, emends the line to yield 'not thus doth he argue with me'.

JOB'S REVIEW OF GOD'S DEALINGS WITH HIM AND LONGING FOR DEATH 10.1–22

Job appeals to God to acquit him, and then recalls all the loving care God has bestowed upon him, and concludes that all his suffering was designed from the start and all the kindness was but intended to make his present suffering the more acute. Finally he asks why he was ever born, and cries for a brief respite before he dies.

   1. Cf. 7.11. Job once more decides to abandon all restraint and speak out.
my complaint: the Hebrew says 'my complaint upon myself'. Some editors, with a slight change, read 'my complaint against him', but Fohrer rejects this as needless. Similarly Dhorme, who observes that Job is going to commune with himself. Dahood (*JBL*, LXXVIII, 1959, p. 305) understands the verb differently, and renders 'I shall prepare on my own behalf my complaint'.
   2. **Do not condemn me:** Job as much as his friends concludes from his afflictions that God holds him guilty.
   3. **Does it seem good to thee?** This interpretation is not certain. The words could equally be understood to mean 'Is it profitable to thee?' (so Dhorme, Hölscher, Fohrer), or 'Is it fitting for thee?' (so Ewald).
and favour the designs of the wicked: lit. 'and shine upon the counsel of the wicked' (so *AV*, *RV*). The same verb is used in 3.4. Duhm, Gray, Ball, Hölscher and Fohrer reject this line as a gloss unsuited to the context, but Dhorme thinks it is too picturesque to lose. Kissane retains this line, but transfers verse 3*ab* to precede verse 8. G. R. Driver (*WO*, I, 1947–52, p. 411) finds a different meaning for the word 'counsel' and renders 'and shinest upon the disobedience of the wicked'. But the normal meaning yields a good sense. R. Bergmeier (*ZAW*,

⁴ Hast thou eyes of flesh?
  Dost thou see as man sees?
⁵ Are thy days as the days of man
  or thy years as man's years,
⁶ that thou dost seek out my iniquity
  and search for my sin,
⁷ although thou knowest that I am not guilty,
  and there is none to deliver out of thy hand?
⁸ Thy hands fashioned and made me;
  and now thou dost turn about and destroy me.

LXXIX, 1967, pp. 229ff.) renders 'fellowship (or circle) of the wicked' (so also in
21.16, 22.18).

4. The meaning is 'Art Thou liable to errors of judgment? Hast Thou no more
insight than my friends?' (Ball).

5. as man's years: the Hebrew says 'as man's days', but Gray thinks this is an
accidental replacement of 'as man's years'. Duhm and Hölscher delete this verse,
as separating verse 4 from verse 6; but Dhorme and most editors retain. Job asks
if God is afraid that he will die before he can deal with Job, that he should be in
such a hurry to torment him, even before Job has done wrong.

6. Note that Job is sure that God has not found iniquity in him, but is eagerly
seeking it and torturing him to extract a confession, and so justify himself.

7. The two halves of the verse seem unrelated. Ehrlich emends the first line to
yield 'since thou knowest that I cannot save myself'. Beer and Duhm emend the
second to give 'there is no iniquity (or perfidy) in my hand'. Peake defends M.T.
God knows Job to be innocent, yet seeks to drive him to the confession of guilt;
he knows that no one can deliver Job from his hand, yet crushes him with
suffering, as though he is about to slip through his fingers. This finds a good
meaning in both halves of the verse, but does not relate them to one another, and
indeed Peake admits a lack of parallelism in the verse. Dhorme protests that we
should not press too rigid a parallelism on the text.

8. fashioned: BDB and GB connect the verb with an Arabic root, meaning
'cut off'. But Ball and KB connect it with another Arabic root, meaning 'bind' or
'tie', giving 'Thy hands have tied me together' (cf. verse 11). In either case the
general sense is clear, and the text asserts that man is God's creature.

now thou dost turn: the Hebrew says 'together round about' (AV, RV). Almost
all editors read with LXX and Syr. 'afterward' for 'together', and many substitute
for the adverb 'round about' a finite verbal form from the same root, to yield
the sense of RSV. Dhorme, however, retains M.T. here and understands the
adverb as in 19.10 (RSV 'on every side'). 'Thou dost destroy me on every side'

⁹ Remember that thou hast made me of clay;
  and wilt thou turn me to dust again?
¹⁰ Didst thou not pour me out like milk
   and curdle me like cheese?
¹¹ Thou didst clothe me with skin and flesh,
   and knit me together with bones and sinews.
¹² Thou hast granted me life and steadfast love;

---

then means, 'Thou dost destroy me utterly.' Reider (*HUCA*, III, 1926, p. 113)
needlessly emends to get, 'Thy anger kindleth against me.'

9. of clay: the Hebrew says 'as clay', which could equally be translated 'as
with clay' (cf. Isa. 9.4 (M.T. 3), where Hebrew has 'as the day of Midian' for
RSV 'as on the day of Midian'). 'The figure is that of a potter who has lavished
infinite care upon his vessel, and now reduces his work of elaborate skill and
exquisite ornament into dust again' (Davidson). Cf. Isa. 34.9, Jer. 18.5ff.;
Rom. 9.20ff.

10. This and the following verses describe the processes of generation and
growth in the womb.

11. knit me together: this verb is found only here and in Ps. 139.13. But
nouns from this root are common, meaning 'thicket' or 'booth'.

12. Thou hast granted me: the English conceals the difficulty of the Hebrew,
which says 'thou hast made (or done) with me'. This would be idiomatic Hebrew
with the second word meaning 'show kindness to', but does not go naturally with
the first word. We have here, therefore, a somewhat extreme case of zeugma.

life and steadfast love: some editors find this a strange combination. Ehrlich
deletes the first word, while Beer substitutes 'favour' for it (so Gray and Ball).
For 'steadfast love' Duhm and Hölscher read 'duration of life' (change of *s* to *l*)
and render 'life and strength', but Gray disputes the rendering, and others the
relevance. Dhorme and Buttenwieser defend M.T., which Dhorme renders 'the
favour of life' (the word 'life' specifying the nature of the grace), and Buttenwieser
'life and love'. The word for 'life' also carries the meaning of 'happiness' or
'prosperity' (cf. Baudissin, *Adonis und Esmun*, 1911, pp. 396f., and *KB*) and with
this meaning the text is left unchanged by Stevenson, Horst and Fohrer.

steadfast love: this word, *ḥeseḏ*, is without precise equivalent in English. In *AV*
it is frequently represented by 'lovingkindness'. Snaith (*Distinctive Ideas*, 1944,
p. 95) calls it 'covenant love' and G. A. Smith (*Jeremiah*, 3rd ed., 1924, p. 104)
'troth', neither of which is relevant here. A. R. Johnson (*NTT*, LVI, 1955, pp. 100ff.)
finds the root meaning to be 'devotion'. Lods (*The Prophets and the Rise of Judaism*,
Eng. trans., 1937, p. 89) says '*Ḥèsèḏ*, a very comprehensive word, which, for want of
an adequate equivalent, we are obliged to translate, now by piety, now by mercy,
love or grace'. Sometimes it indicates the initiative in kindness and sometimes the

and thy care has preserved my spirit.
13 Yet these things thou didst hide in thy heart;
    I know that this was thy purpose.
14 If I sin, thou dost mark me,
    and dost not acquit me of my iniquity.
15 If I am wicked, woe to me!
    If I am righteous, I cannot lift up my head,
    for I am filled with disgrace
    and look upon my affliction.

---

response to the constraint that kindness lays on one. Here it stands for the marks of the divine favour.

care: lit. 'visitation'. Sometimes it stands for 'punishment' (Hos. 9.7), but here it means 'gracious visitation'. Job emphasizes the extraordinary care God has taken of him as the prelude to turning on him.

13. these things . . . this: to be described in the following verses.

thy purpose: God's very kindness, says Job, was part of his calculated cruelty. The deepest agony that Job suffered was in the belief that all his afflictions were the direct act of the God who had been so gracious to him and were the proof that he had suddenly turned against him for no reason that Job could discover.

14. If I sin, thou dost: better, 'If I sinned, then thou wouldst.' This expresses what Job believed to have been God's purpose from the start. By sin, Job is here thinking of the more trifling sins, into which one slipped, rather than the more grievous sins one committed of set purpose. God was determined to deal sternly with Job's every slip.

mark: this is the same verb as 'preserved' in verse 12. It means 'guard' or 'watch', in a friendly or protective way or in a hostile way. Job uses the same word deliberately. The friendly watch had become hostile. His protector had become his warder.

15. Job here declares that it was God's intention that he should suffer either way. Whether wicked or righteous, he was destined to suffer. Cf. 9.22.

woe to me! This expression is found here and in Mic. 7.1 only.

I cannot lift up my head: the lifting up of the head is the symbol of pride and self-respect (cf. Jg. 8.28). Elsewhere in Job we find 'lift up the face' in the sense of being in fellowship with God, with a clear conscience (11.15; 22.26).

and look upon my affliction: Beer, Duhm, Ball, Hölscher, and Fohrer needlessly delete the second half of the verse and the beginning of verse 16. 'Look upon' is curious and inappropriate. Geiger (*Jüdische Zeitschrift*, IV, 1866, p. 283) suggested reading $r^e w\bar{e}h$ = 'saturated' instead of $r\bar{e}'\bar{e}h$, giving the meaning 'steeped in affliction', which is a good parallel to 'sated with ignominy'. Most editors follow this reading. But G. R. Driver (*EThL*, XXVI, 1950, p. 351) secures this meaning without change

16 And if I lift myself up, thou dost hunt me like a lion,
   and again work wonders against me;
17 Thou dost renew thy witnesses against me,
   and increase thy vexation toward me;
   thou dost bring fresh hosts against me.
18 'Why didst thou bring me forth from the womb?
   Would that I had died before any eye had seen me,
19 and were as though I had not been,
   carried from the womb to the grave.
20 Are not the days of my life few?

---

of text, finding instances elsewhere in *OT* of a verb *rā'āh=rāwāh*, distinct from *rā'āh*='see' (cf. also de Vaux, *RB*, XLVIII, 1939, p. 594). Horst transfers 'for I am filled . . . affliction' to follow 'woe to me'. But it is better to leave this where it is. What Job says is that either way he gets nothing but trouble.

16. If I lift myself up: the Hebrew has 'and he lifts himself up' (cf. RV 'if (my head) lifts itself up'; *AV* 'it increaseth'). *RSV* follows Syr. (so Gray, Ball, Weiser). Kissane reads 'And thou exaltest thyself', while Pope secures this meaning by reading the adjective *gē'eh*='proud', instead of the verb *yig'eh*. Dhorme reads *weyāḡēa*'='and faint' instead of *weyig'eh*='he lifts himself up', and thinks it continues the previous verse 'and exhausted' (so Steinmann). But this is very unlikely. The sense of *RSV* is to be preferred. Job has said that even if he is righteous he dare not raise his head. He now says that if he should raise it he would be immediately attacked by God.

like a lion: it is not certain whether Job likens himself to a hunted lion, or God to a lion hunting its prey in cruel strength.

work wonders: commentators draw attention to the irony of the choice of this word. God's wonderful works in the creation of Job are now matched by his wonders in tormenting him.

17. thy witnesses: these are interpreted as Job's sufferings, which were held to testify his guilt. Ehrlich and Dhorme revocalize and secure the meaning 'thy hostility' which yields a good parallel to 'thy vexation' (so Stevenson, Steinmann and Pope).

thou dost bring fresh hosts against me: lit. 'changes and a host (probably hendiadys, "relieving troops") are with me'. This probably means 'relieving troops are brought against me'. Some editors change the first word to a verb and render 'Thou wouldest renew thine armies (or warfare) against me' (so Budde, Duhm, Gray, Hölscher, Steinmann), but this is unnecessary. Ball renders 'the relief of my service (cf. on 7.1) tarrieth', and then deletes as a gloss!

18f. Job returns to his lament that he was ever born (cf. 3.11ff.).

20. the days of my life: the Hebrew says 'my days; cease' (*AV*, *RV*). LXX and

Let me alone, that I may find a little comfort
21 before I go whence I shall not return,
    to the land of gloom and deep darkness,
22 the land of gloom and chaos,
    where light is as darkness.'

11 Then Zophar the Na'amathite answered:
2 'Should a multitude of words go unanswered,

Syr. render 'the days of my life' (reading *yᵉmê ḥeldî* instead of *yāmay waḥᵃḏāl*).
This is followed by *RSV* and many editors. Gordis (*JQR*, N.S., xxvii, 1936–37,
pp. 40f.) thinks the verb rendered 'cease' had contrasted meanings, 'cease' and
'continue', and renders 'but little will my days continue'. *RSV* is to be preferred.
Let me alone: many editors emend to get 'Look away from', claiming the
support of LXX (so Beer, Ball, Gray, Weiser, Fohrer; also Joüon, *Biblica*, viii,
1927, p. 60). But it is doubtful if LXX read this. The Hebrew here means simply
'put from me' and is found nowhere else. We must understand the ellipsis of
'thy hand' or 'thy attention'. Job is appealing to God to take his attention off him
and to give him a respite.
that I may find . . . comfort: the Hebrew is the same as that found in 9.27
(*RSV* 'be of good cheer').
   21. Cf. 7.9f.
deep darkness: cf. on 3.5.
   22. The verse is overloaded with synonyms for darkness. *RSV* omits 'as
darkness, deep darkness', both of which terms are repeated in verse 21 or here.
Job wishes to emphasize to the utmost the dreary prospect of Sheol, and achieves
this especially in the final clause 'and it shineth as darkness', i.e. the very shining
is but darkness. Job's speeches often end in some similar reference to the miserable
prospect of death (cf. 7.21; 14.20–22; 17.13–16; 21.32f.). Throughout this chapter
Job's thought oscillates between the God of his past experience and the God of
the present experience, and he is bewildered to reconcile them. His bewilderment
arises from the fact that he shares the friends' view that his sufferings prove that
God is against him, and the old fellowship with God no longer possible. It is
false theology which creates the problem.
and chaos: lit. 'without order'. G. R. Driver (*SVT*, iii, 1955, pp. 76f.) renders
'without ray of light', adducing Arabic evidence.

THE FIRST SPEECH OF ZOPHAR 11.1–20

Zophar is described by Strahan as 'a plain orthodox dogmatist'. He is incensed by
Job's protestation of his innocence, and roundly asserts that his punishment is less
than he deserves. Job may be unaware of his sins, but God knows them and

and a man full of talk be vindicated?
³ Should your babble silence men,
    and when you mock, shall no one shame you?
⁴ For you say, "My doctrine is pure,
    and I am clean in God's eyes".
⁵ But oh, that God would speak,
    and open his lips to you,

---

through his afflictions is awakening Job to repentance and amendment of life. The speech falls into three parts: Zophar's rebuke and wish that God would speak (verses 2–6); the unsearchable wisdom of God (verses 7–12); repentance is the way of restoration (verses 13–20).

ZOPHAR'S REBUKE OF JOB AND WISH THAT GOD WOULD SPEAK 11.2–6

With wounding words Zophar scornfully rejects Job's plea of innocence, and assures him that he is getting off lightly, as he would soon perceive if God would but speak to him.

2. a multitude of words. With the exception of Syr., the ancient versions render 'he who is a great talker' (a difference of vowel only), and most editors follow this. But Gray prefers M.T. for its variety. Zophar dismisses Job as a mere glib talker.

a man full of talk: Hebrew 'a man of lips'. There is perhaps here an insinuation that Job is speaking without thought or conviction.

be vindicated: be given the verdict.

3. your babble: your pratings, or boastings (Isa. 16.6; Jer. 48.30).

you mock: Job's 'mocking' was not at his friends, but a scoffing at religion by his rejection of the doctrine that suffering and sin were inevitably related. Zophar feared that such ideas were subversive of morality and religion alike.

4. you say: Job had not uttered these words, but Zophar is here summarizing what he has been saying.

My doctrine: many editors are dissatisfied with this on the grounds that Job has not claimed that his doctrine is pure, but only that his conduct is innocent and that conduct yields a better parallel to the next line. They therefore amend the text to yield this sense. But this is unnecessary. In rejecting the theology of the friends Job was implicitly claiming superior understanding.

in God's eyes: the Hebrew says 'in thine eyes'. Siegfried and Duhm arbitrarily change this to 'in my eyes'. Job has consistently asserted his innocence in God's eyes, and maintained that God was well aware of his innocence, and RSV rightly interprets the 'thine' as God's. Pope emends to secure, 'You are clean in your own eyes.'

5. Job had expressed his readiness to meet God and plead his cause with him.

⁶ and that he would tell you the secrets of wisdom!
  For he is manifold in understanding.
  Know then that God exacts of you
    less than your guilt deserves.
⁷ 'Can you find out the deep things of God?

Zophar wishes that God would take up the challenge. Job would soon learn how mistaken he was.

6. secrets: lit. the hidden things. The singular stands in 28.11 (*RSV* 'the thing that is hid'), and the plural in Ps. 44.21 (M.T. 22). Pope needlessly deletes 'of wisdom'.

manifold in understanding: the word rendered 'understanding' is rendered 'success' in 5.12 (see note there). The Hebrew here says 'it is double for effectual wisdom'. The meaning is obscure. Davidson explains as 'double what you think it is'. Dhorme offers the far-fetched interpretation 'double to the understanding', i.e. ambiguous. Several editors (including Duhm, Hölscher, Horst, Fohrer) for *kiplayim* read *kipelā'îm*='as wonders'. The meaning then is 'they (the secrets) are as wonders'. But God's secrets *are* wonders and not merely *like* wonders. Hence others read *pelā'îm* (deleting *k*='like' as a dittograph), and secure the meaning 'they are wonderful (or mysterious) to the understanding' (so Budde, Gray, Buttenwieser, Stevenson). What Zophar means is that the wisdom of God is inscrutable to the human mind.

God exacts of you less than your guilt deserves: the Hebrew means 'God causeth to be forgotten for you part of your iniquity'. Budde alters the text to read 'according to your iniquity'. But we should not weaken the cruel words of Zophar, who is the most ruthless of Job's friends. Tur-Sinai similarly weakens the words by rendering 'God makes you forget your sin'. A different weakening is represented by emending 'causeth to be forgotten for you' to make it mean 'will demand a reckoning from you (for your sin)' (so Ehrlich, Dhorme, Sutcliffe (*Biblica*, xxx, 1949, p. 67), Fohrer). Many editors delete the line as a gloss (so Duhm, Ball, Hölscher, Stevenson, Steinmann). But Gray objects that it is wanted to deny verse 4.

THE UNSEARCHABLE WISDOM OF GOD 11.7–12

Zophar enlarges on the inscrutable knowledge and wisdom of God and his irresistible might: he sees and knows all things, whereas man is devoid of understanding.

7. The rendering of *AV* and *RV* 'Canst thou by searching find out God?' is grammatically impossible, and the meaning is as *RSV*. Zophar is affirming that God is immeasurable and unfathomable, and far beyond the measure of our minds. The statements of Job's friends are often right, though they draw the

Can you find out the limit of the Almighty?
⁸ It is higher than heaven—what can you do?
Deeper than Sheol—what can you know?
⁹ Its measure is longer than the earth,
and broader than the sea.
¹⁰ If he passes through, and imprisons,
and calls to judgment, who can hinder him?
¹¹ For he knows worthless men;
when he sees iniquity, will he not consider it?
¹² But a stupid man will get understanding,

---

wrong conclusions from them, just as Job himself draws the wrong conclusions from his experience and his theology.

find out (2°): Gray and Dhorme think an Aramaic sense is given to the verb here: 'Can you reach?' Dahood (*The Bible in Current Catholic Thought*, edited by J. L. McKenzie, 1962, p. 57) justifies this meaning also from Ugaritic.

8. It is higher than heaven: the Hebrew says 'Heights of heaven', but most editors follow Vulg. (with the change of one consonant) and render as *RSV*. This is favoured by the parallelism. Less probably Dahood (loc. cit.) conforms the second line to the first.

9. In all dimensions God's wisdom is too vast for man to reach its limits.

10. passes through: many editors change one letter to get the verb used in 9.12, since Zophar here appears to have 9.11f. in mind. They then render 'If he seizes'. Dhorme retains M.T., but gives to the following words the sense 'keeps a matter secret, or divulges it'. But the sense of *RSV* is more probable. The whole verse is omitted as a gloss by some editors, on the ground of its links with 9.11f. But it is relevant here. Zophar has spoken of God's vastness, and now he speaks of his irresistible power.

calls to judgment: the word means 'summons an assembly', here for judgment. Dhorme presents no evidence for the unusual meaning he proposes, 'divulges', and it is not to be adopted. Tur-Sinai finds an Arabic meaning here, 'causes to ignore' or 'forget', and then instead of 'hinder him' (lit. 'turn him back') he has 'cause it to return'.

11. worthless men: lit. 'men of emptiness'. The same phrase is found in Ps. 26.4 (*RSV* 'false men'). God knows which men are false without any effort. Many editors for 'will he not consider it?' read 'he does consider it' (*lô* for *lō*'), but Gray objects that the position of 'it' would then be unnecessarily emphatic. The words need not be read as a question, but may be taken as a circumstantial clause, 'without considering it'. The meaning then is that God does not have to probe into men's conduct to know their wickedness; he immediately knows it.

12. Ball notes that the form of this verse suggests a proverb. Its meaning,

when a wild ass's colt is born a man.
13 'If you set your heart aright,
    you will stretch out your hands toward him.
14 If iniquity is in your hand, put it far away,

---

however, is not clear and is very variously understood. There is assonance between some of the words. The word rendered 'stupid' means 'hollowed out' (root *nābab*), while the word rendered 'will get understanding' chimes with it (root *lābab*). *RV* 'is void of understanding' gives an improbably privative sense to the verb. *BDB* takes the line as an interrogative: 'Will an empty man get a mind?' Several editors render the verse 'And so an empty man gets understanding, and a wild ass's colt is born a man' (so Duhm, Peake, Gray). The verse is then supposed to mean that by the chastening which may be understood to follow God's perception of iniquity understanding is knocked into a man. But it is hard to see what relevance there is in the wild ass being born a man. The verse could equally well be rendered as by *RSV*, where it is a sarcastic comparison. The stupid man will acquire sense when the ass's colt is born a man, i.e. never. Pope differently construes the verse and takes *'āḏām* (man) here to be for *'aḏāmāh*='ground', here taken to mean 'steppe' and renders 'when a wild ass is born an ass (i.e. a tame ass)'. Ball revocalizes one word and renders: 'A witless wight will get wit, when a wild ass's colt *begets* a man.' But 'colt' seems a little pointless here. Sutcliffe (*Biblica*, xxx, 1949, pp. 70f.) cleverly reads *pereḏ*='stallion' for *pere*'='wild ass', and renders 'a witless wight may get wit when a mule is born a stallion'. Budde deleted the word 'man' and changed one consonant to secure the meaning: 'A hollow man may get understanding, and a wild ass's colt may be *taught* (tamed).' The sense of *RSV*, which is obtained without emendation, seems the most likely.

REPENTANCE IS THE WAY OF RESTORATION 11.13-20

Zophar exhorts Job to turn from his evil ways and so secure a new happiness and prosperity and warns him that continuance in his wickedness will bring final disaster.

13. you: this is emphatic in the Hebrew, setting Job in contrast to the 'hollow man'.

you will stretch out: this could equally well be taken as a continuation of the protasis, as in *AV* and *RV*, and most editors so take it. Zophar then calls for (a) the setting right of Job's heart; (b) prayer; (c) the reform of his life; (d) the rectification of his home. The stretching out of the hands was the attitude of prayer (cf. Isa. 1.15).

14. put it far away: Dhorme follows Vulg. in reading 'If you put away the iniquity', making clear that this is a continuation of the protasis and not an

and let not wickedness dwell in your tents.
15 Surely then you will lift up your face without blemish;
   you will be secure, and will not fear.
16 You will forget your misery;
   you will remember it as waters that have passed away.
17 And your life will be brighter than the noonday;
   its darkness will be like the morning.
18 And you will have confidence, because there is hope;
   you will be protected and take your rest in safety.
19 You will lie down, and none will make you afraid;
   many will entreat your favour.
20 But the eyes of the wicked will fail;
   all way of escape will be lost to them,
   and their hope is to breathe their last.'

---

intrusion between verse 13 and verse 15. The change in reading is almost imperceptible.

15. without blemish: Job's face will no longer bear the marks of a guilty conscience. It is to be noted that Zophar treats Job's guilt as beyond question.
secure: the word means 'firmly established', like cast metal. It comes from a verb used of pouring out metals (cf. 28.2; 37.18).

16. waters that have passed away: in 6.15 a similar metaphor was used for treachery; here for oblivion. The author's skill in the selection of similes and metaphors should be noticed. Zophar here promises Job such a restoration of his fortunes that all his present misery will be swallowed up. The restoration that came to Job did not come by following Zophar's prescription.

17. your life: here there is the nuance of 'lasting life', so that the verse has in mind not merely the quality of Job's life, but its continuance.
be brighter than: the Hebrew says 'arise from' or 'more than', with the omission of the point of comparison, which is implied in the 'noonday'.
darkness: this rendering involves a slight revocalization of the Hebrew, which is adopted by *BDB*, Budde, Duhm, Peake, Dhorme and others, following Syr. and Targ. Gray prefers to retain the unusual Hebrew verbal form and to interpret as a hypothetical sentence: 'though it be dark, it will become as morning' (cf. *RV*). Again it should be observed how effectively the author uses his words. In 10.22 Job had described the darkness of Sheol by saying that its shining was but darkness. Here, with reference to that verse, Zophar says that Job will find that even darkness will be light.

18. you will have confidence: you will have a sense of security.
hope: in contrast to Job's present despair.

12 Then Job answered:
² 'No doubt you are the people,

---

you will be protected: the Hebrew verb ordinarily means 'search', or 'dig'. Targ. understands it here in the sense of digging a grave, which is inappropriate (*AV* has 'dig about thee'). *RV* has 'thou shalt search'. According to Davidson the meaning then is that before retiring at night, Job will go round and find all in order. But this is far-fetched. Ehrlich and Dhorme connect the verb with an Arabic root meaning 'protect', and this seems much to be preferred (so Hölscher, Steinmann). This involves a change of vocalization. With the same change of vocalization *KB* connects the word with another root common in Hebrew, and gets the meaning 'you will feel abashed' (so Fohrer). But this seems less appropriate.

19. none will make you afraid: the same phrase recurs in Mic. 4.4, to express confidence.
will entreat your favour: lit. 'will soften your face'. The expression is sometimes used of appeasing God; here of the fawning sycophants who will flock around Job in his prosperity.
20. Cf. 8.22, where Bildad had attached this prediction to Job's enemies. Here Zophar appears to mean that Job will share this fate if he does not amend his way. **to breathe their last:** lit. 'the breathing out of the soul', and hence the giving up of the ghost. The brightest hope of the wicked is death. This again is an effective way of describing their misery—a misery which Job, who was not wicked, had already experienced. It is by this subtle means that Zophar puts a final barb into Job.

JOB ANSWERS ZOPHAR 12–14

Stung by Zophar's cruel words, Job now lashes out at his friends. So far he has been engrossed with the thought of his own misery and the treatment God has meted out to him. Now he charges them with trying to curry favour with God, whose power and wisdom he recognizes no less than they. But Job protests that no moral purpose governs his exercise of his power and wisdom and that it is so often destructive in its working. He laments the brevity of life and wishes that he might be temporarily hidden in Sheol until God's anger is spent, instead of having nothing better to look forward to than the unrelieved misery there. The speech falls into three parts: Job's resentment of the assumed superiority of his friends and recognition of God's wisdom and power (12.2–25); his determination to reason with God and scorn for the hollow arguments of his friends (13.1–28); his lament at the brevity of life and the finality of death (14.1–22).

JOB'S RESENTMENT OF THE ASSUMED SUPERIORITY OF HIS FRIENDS AND RECOGNITION OF GOD'S WISDOM AND POWER **12.2–25**
With biting sarcasm Job exposes the real character of the professed friendship of

and wisdom will die with you.
3 But I have understanding as well as you;
   I am not inferior to you.
   Who does not know such things as these?
4 I am a laughingstock to my friends;
   I, who called upon God and he answered me,
   a just and blameless man, am a laughingstock.

---

his comforters, and then in a series of rapid sketches reviews the exercise of God's wisdom and power in the world of nature and in the affairs of men to show that it is inspired by no moral purpose.

2. you are the people: editors complain that the article is not expressed in the Hebrew. But in poetry nouns are frequently definite without the article, and there is no need to add it as Duhm does (so Weiser). Still less is it necessary to make larger changes, such as 'you are knowing ones' (Steinmann, Horst) or 'the knowing ones' (Klostermann (*PRE*, 3rd ed., VIII, 1900, p. 107), Peake, Gray, Ball, Hölscher, Stevenson), or 'the cunning ones' (Beer), or 'the people of heart (intelligence)' (Kissane). Dhorme, Tur-Sinai, and Fohrer retain the text, which means 'you are everybody', i.e. the only people who count. J. Reider (*VT*, IV, 1954, pp. 289f.) connects with an Arabic word, meaning 'complete', 'perfect' and renders 'ye are the perfect (or superior)'. But the root meaning of the Arabic word is 'to be universal' rather than 'to be superior', and it supports the interpretation 'you are everybody'. Pope renders 'you are the gentry'.

wisdom will die with you: Job sarcastically admits their claim to a monopoly of wisdom, only to go on to deny it in reality.

3. understanding: lit. 'a heart'. Job may be referring to what Zophar had said in 11.12 (see note there).

I am not inferior to you: this line is repeated in 13.2, and many editors omit it here.

4. a laughingstock: the word means 'laughter' (8.21) or 'an object of laughter' (Jer. 20.7).

I, who called upon God and he answered me: the Hebrew says 'one calling unto God and he answered him'. This could be rendered as *RSV*, but Job's complaint is that God has not answered him and will not do so. It is more probable, therefore, that these words are Job's representation of the derisive words of his friends, who think God has answered Job by his afflictions. To Job his afflictions are not God's answer, but his arbitrary action.

just and blameless: these epithets are applied to Noah in Gen. 6.9, and Dhorme notes that Job is associated with Noah in Ezek. 14.14, 20. A number of editors excise verses 4-6 on the ground that they interrupt the connection of verse 3 with verse 7. It is possible that they may be misplaced, but they should not be

⁵ In the thought of one who is at ease
    there is contempt for misfortune;
    it is ready for those whose feet slip.
⁶ The tents of robbers are at peace,
    and those who provoke God are secure,
    who bring their god in their hand.

---

rejected. They excellently fit the mouth of Job, and we ought not to try to impose the orderliness of a dissertation on one who is speaking under great emotion.

5. This is a difficult verse for which countless emendations have been proposed. The first word, *lappíd*, can mean 'a torch' (whence Ehrlich renders 'a torch of contempt', cf. *AV*) or 'for ruin' (so most editors). The word rendered 'thought' is found only here, but there is no reason to question it. The verb from which it comes stands in Jon. 1.6. Another noun from it occurs in Ps. 146.4 (*RSV* 'plans'), but there is no need to substitute this, with Gray. The general sense is unexceptionable. Job is observing that the theology of the friends is the theology of the prosperous, who can afford to look down on the unfortunate and excuse themselves from giving sympathy by the assumption that they have brought it upon themselves. This is precisely the attitude of the friends, and the line as interpreted is more suitable to the context than such a reconstruction as Bickell's 'the prosperous despises the times of Shaddai'.

it is ready for those whose feet slip: if this is correct the meaning is that contempt is ready for those who fall into trouble. But many editors think that a word parallel to 'contempt' is wanted instead of 'it is ready', and they understand the word so rendered as a noun from the verb meaning 'smite' and render 'a blow for those whose feet slip'. This means that they not only withhold sympathy; they add to the troubles of the unfortunate. This interpretation is followed by many editors, including Budde, Peake, Dhorme, Hölscher, Weiser, Horst, Fohrer, and it yields relevant sense.

6. Job bitterly comments that while the fortunate are kicking the unfortunate who are down and regarding them as the wicked, those who are really wicked live at ease.

who bring their god in their hand: this cryptic line is deleted by Fohrer as a gloss. But Dhorme interprets it in the light of the phrase *leʾēl yādí* found in Gen. 31.29 (cf. Mic. 2.1; Dt. 28.32), where *EVV* have 'in the power of my hand'; but while this sense is clear, the origin of the phrase is uncertain and *ʾēl* may be originally 'God'. Dhorme takes it to mean 'my hand serves me as God'. In the present phrase *ʾelôah* replaces *ʾēl*, and Dhorme understands it to mean the man who considers himself to be invested with the power of God. He can dispense with God because he believes he wields the power of God. While this interpretation is far from certain, it is as satisfactory as any yet proposed. It should, however, be noted

⁷ 'But ask the beasts, and they will teach you;
    the birds of the air, and they will tell you;
⁸ or the plants of the earth, and they will teach you;
    and the fish of the sea will declare to you.
⁹ Who among all these does not know
    that the hand of the LORD has done this?

---

that the line is in the singular, whereas we should expect the plural after the preceding lines.

7. So far from the friends being possessed of all wisdom, the very beasts could teach them.

and they will teach you: omitted by Budde, Dhorme, Hölscher, Steinmann, and Fohrer, since the same word stands in the following verse, and it is supposed to spoil the metre. But the first word 'But' is extra-metrical, by anacrusis, which is frequently found with such words as this. Hölscher and Steinmann delete the whole of verses 7–10 as a gloss, but on insufficient grounds.

8. the plants of the earth: AV and RV have 'speak to the earth', but this represents a strange use of the word normally understood as 'muse'. Many editors desiderate a word meaning reptiles, or wild beasts, and emend accordingly. RSV finds here the word rendered 'bush' in 30.4, 7; Gen. 21.15, and so Weiser. But Peake thinks it unlikely that plants would be mentioned here. It must be agreed that some word for creeping things would be more natural than plants among beasts, birds and fishes. Dahood (*The Bible in Current Catholic Thought*, edited by J. L. McKenzie, 1962, p. 58) retains 'speak to the earth' and understands 'earth' as the nether world. We then have reference to beasts, birds, nether world, fish. Tur-Sinai renders 'speak of the vermin', adducing Arabic evidence for this unusual meaning of a common word.

9. among all these: it is not clear whether this is the meaning, and 'all these' refers to the creatures mentioned in the preceding verses, or whether we should render 'by means of all these', and the sense be 'who is not instructed by nature?'

the LORD: the use of the Tetragrammaton here is surprising and is contrary to the author's usage in the dialogue (see Introduction, p. 11). Some MSS. read 'Eloah', which may be original or a copyist's correction to bring the passage into accord with the usage elsewhere. Dhorme thinks the reminiscence of Isa. 41.20*b* imported the word 'Yahweh' here and displaced 'Eloah', and this seems most likely.

this: the meaning here is very obscure. Some hold it to mean 'all that Zophar has said'. On this view all nature is credited with knowledge that God is all powerful and whatever happens is his doing. Kissane takes it to mean that all creation knows what Job has said in verses 4ff., that there is no moral sanction in the world.

¹⁰ In his hand is the life of every living thing
   and the breath of all mankind.
¹¹ Does not the ear try words
   as the palate tastes food?
¹² Wisdom is with the aged,
   and understanding in length of days.
¹³'With God are wisdom and might;
   he has counsel and understanding.

---

10. The issues of life and death for every living creature are in the hands of God alone. The words here rendered 'life' and 'breath' are the same as those rendered 'soul' and 'spirit' in 7.11. Hebrew *rûaḥ* means 'wind' or 'spirit', just as the Greek *pneuma* does. In Ec. 12.7 *RSV* uses 'spirit' when referring to what God withdraws from man at death, whereas here it uses 'breath', where the meaning is the same. M. Dahood (*Biblica*, xlvii, 1966, pp. 107f.) proposes to read *bāśār 'ōš* for *beśar 'îš* and to render 'and the spirit in all flesh is his gift', adducing Ugaritic evidence for the meaning of *'ōš*.

11. The point of this verse is apparently that just as the palate discriminates between foods and accepts only what commends itself to it, so the ear discriminates and receives only what commends itself. Hence Job asserts his right to the exercise of his own critical judgment and to question the testimony of the ancients. to which appeal has been made.

12. This is not the opinion of Job, but of the friends. Hence some delete as an intrusion. But surgery is not always the best way of dealing with textual problems. *RV* marg. has 'With the old men, ye say, is wisdom' (so Hitzig, Budde, Gray), making this Job's citation of what the friends had argued. Others regard the verse as interrogative, either without interrogative particle or with the addition of one, and secure the same sense (so Strahan, Hölscher, Weiser, Tur-Sinai). But if Job was really citing this opinion merely to reject it, we should expect this to be more clearly indicated. It is therefore better to transfer *lô* from the end of verse 11 (where it is not wanted and is left untranslated in *RSV*) to the beginning of verse 12 and to read *lō'* (the two words are often confused)='not', and to make the verse a clear denial by Job of the opinions of the friends (so Beer, Stevenson, Fohrer): 'Wisdom is not with the aged.' More radical changes of text are proposed by Duhm and Ball, but this simple change is to be preferred.
the aged: this word is found three times in Job and in Sir. 8.6. A related word stands in 2 Chr. 36.17.

13. Job here sharply contradicts the idea that wisdom is with the aged. It is with God alone. With him is wisdom (where God is understood). But Job shows in the following verses that by 'wisdom' he here means skill in doing what God wants to do. He knows how to cope with every situation and to get his way.
counsel: Budde proposed the addition of a letter to turn this into 'might', so as

¹⁴ If he tears down, none can rebuild;
  if he shuts a man in, none can open.
¹⁵ If he withholds the waters, they dry up;
  if he sends them out, they overwhelm the land.
¹⁶ With him are strength and wisdom;
  the deceived and the deceiver are his.
¹⁷ He leads counsellors away stripped,
  and judges he makes fools.

---

to get chiastic parallelism with the preceding line. Ball adds the further consideration that throughout the book 'counsel' is used for human, and not for divine,
wisdom. None of this is cogent. Outside the book of Job 'counsel' is used of God
(cf. Isa. 28.29), and there is no reason why Job should not so use it. An author
cannot be forbidden to say a thing unless he says it twice. Moreover, parallelism
is not so rigid and complete as to make a change necessary, though if the text had
read 'might' it would have been unexceptionable. G. R. Driver (*WO*, 1, 1947–52,
pp. 410f.) finds a homonym of the word for 'counsel' here, with the meaning
'hardness', 'endurance' or 'disobedience'. While it commonly has a bad sense, he
thinks it has a good sense here, and renders 'endurance'. But in Job's thought God
does not have to persist and struggle to get his way. There is no opposition to his
will that can hinder him.

  14. none can rebuild: lit. 'it is not rebuilt', the subject having to be supplied
from the unexpressed object of the previous verb. Peake thinks some definite
events were in the author's mind in this verse.
shuts a man in: probably in prison.

  15. withholds: the word rendered 'restrain' in 4.2 and 'refrain' in 29.9. Job is
here emphasizing the arbitrary and irresistible might of God, as shown in his
works in nature. Drought and flood are the work of his hands.
overwhelm: the word rendered 'overturn (mountains)' in 9.5. The root is
frequently used of the overthrow of Sodom and Gomorrah in OT.

  16. wisdom: cf. on 5.12. Ball would again change the word on the ground
that it is not elsewhere ascribed to God in Job. But there is no reason why it
could not be (cf. Isa. 28.29). Ball further complains that it is alien to the context,
which is concerned with God's might rather than his wisdom, and so he substitutes
a word with this meaning. But cf. verse 13, where wisdom is mentioned. In fact,
this word is very relevant to Job's thought here. It is the efficient wisdom that
leads to success in one's enterprises. Pope here renders 'victory'.
the deceived and the deceiver: an alliterative phrase in Hebrew, perhaps meant
to include everybody. A similar alliterative phrase to include everybody is 'bond
and free' (Dt. 32.36; 1 Kg. 14.10).

  17. stripped: this word is found in verse 19 and in Mic. 1.8, and means

¹⁸ He looses the bonds of kings,
    and binds a waistcloth on their loins.
¹⁹ He leads priests away stripped,
    and overthrows the mighty.
²⁰ He deprives of speech those who are trusted,

'stripped' or 'barefoot'. *AV* and *RV* take it from another root, meaning 'spoiled' (cf. LXX 'captives'; Aq. 'as prey'). G. R. Driver (*AJSL*, LIII, 1935–36, p. 160) derives it from yet another root, connected with an Arabic verb meaning 'be mad' or 'giddy' and renders 'crazy'. Others secure this sense by emendation, noting the similarity of verse 17a and verse 19a, and seeking to avoid it and provide a better parallel to 'makes fools'. Duhm reconstructs the line to yield 'he makes foolish the counsellors of the earth' (so Strahan, Ball, Stevenson, Fohrer, Pope, *KB*). In verse 19 the meaning 'crazy' is not very appropriate, and if it is retained it should be given the same sense here as there. LXX seems to have read the text of M.T. and despite the repetition and want of balance it seems best to retain it.

18. bonds: the Hebrew has 'discipline', which is not used elsewhere of royal authority. With different vocalization it means 'bond' and so *EVV* and most editors. It then means the bonds with which kings have bound others. God reverses human fortunes. He sets the prisoners free and he reduces kings to slavery. Dhorme thinks it means he looses the chains on kings who are in bondage, and fetters those who are free, making both halves refer to the kings themselves.
a waistcloth: many editors prefer to read '*ēsûr*='bond', on the ground that binding the loins with a girdle means to strengthen (so Duhm, Peake, Hölscher, Steinmann). But this is quite unnecessary. The binding the loins with a girdle or waistcloth would mean the degradation of kings to do menial service, and this is perfectly suited to the context. Strahan finds in this verse and its context evidence that the author lived in troubled times.

19. stripped. See on verse 17. Priests are mentioned only here in Job. They are mentioned here as persons of honour and influence, yet impotent against God.
the mighty: this word is often used of ever-flowing streams, as contrasted with the wadies. Here it is used of the enduring authority of the hereditary nobles, who seem firmly established in their positions of honour.

20. deprives of speech: lit. 'removes the lip'.
those who are trusted: some rabbinical commentators connected this word with the root *nā'am*='speak as a prophet' (Jer. 23.31), and then take it to mean those who talk much', or 'the eloquent'. This would yield an excellent sense, and would involve revocalizing. But it is rather fanciful, and any allusion to the prophets is unlikely here. It is rather the honoured leaders of the community who are in mind, who are dumbfounded and bewildered by a sudden turn of fortune.

and takes away the discernment of the elders.
21 He pours contempt on princes,
   and looses the belt of the strong.
22 He uncovers the deeps out of darkness,
   and brings deep darkness to light.
23 He makes nations great, and he destroys them:
   he enlarges nations, and leads them away.
24 He takes away understanding from the chiefs of the people of
     the earth,
   and makes them wander in a pathless waste.
25 They grope in the dark without light;
   and he makes them stagger like a drunken man.

---

discernment: lit. 'taste'.

21. belt: found only here, but a closely similar word is found in Ps. 109.19, where it is used for bracing or strengthening the body. Here the loosening of the belt signifies incapacitation. H. Geers (*AJSL*, XXXIV, 1917–18, pp. 131f.) proposes to connect the word with a root found in Sir. 8.11, where it means 'rise', and in post-biblical Hebrew where it means 'be overbearing'. He then renders the line 'the pride of the learned he brings down'. P. Joüon (*Biblica*, XI, 1930, p. 323) secures a similar sense by emending to read 'forehead' and renders 'he humbles the brow of the mighty', the brow being the seat of pride (Ezek. 3.7f.). Neither is convincing and no change is necessary to secure an excellent sense.

the strong: elsewhere this word means 'channels of waters', which is inappropriate here. But the verb means 'be strong', and there is no reason why the meaning here should not be 'strong' (so *KB*). There is thus no need to emend with many editors to secure one or other of the more ordinary words to express this meaning. Pope denies any connection of the word with the root 'be strong', and inclines to delete the verse.

22. Budde deletes this verse as out of its proper context (so Dhorme, Steinmann, Fohrer, Pope). Kissane transfers it to follow 11.9. The preceding verses and verse 23 deal with God's action in society, but this with his illumination of what is hidden. Duhm relates it to the context by the forced interpretation of 'the deeps' as the humble poor, who are raised to honour.

the deeps: the reference is not clear. It could mean the deep designs of men which God brings out to the light, or possibly his own deep purposes which are revealed as they are realized.

deep darkness: see on 3.5.

23. makes . . . great: the verb used here is an Aramaism. The rise and fall of nations, which does not seem to be governed by any moral principle, is adduced by Job as another instance of the arbitrary use of God's power. Instead of repeating

13 'Lo, my eye has seen all this,
my ear has heard and understood it.

---

the word 'nations', Syr. and Targ. read a different word. Hence many scholars substitute a word meaning 'peoples' for the second. In both cases Tur-Sinai, with different vocalization, renders 'waves', adducing Arabic evidence.

enlarges: lit. 'spreads abroad'. Ball notes that it is nowhere else used of the expansion of nations, but only of the literal spreading of things out. But must a metaphor be used twice before it is allowable? Tur-Sinai renders 'smootheth (the waves)'; cf. lit. meaning.

leads them away: the verb usually has a favourable meaning, 'guide', but if correct here it must mean 'leads them into captivity', the vital word 'away' or 'into captivity' having to be supplied. Wright and Gray revocalize and render 'abandons', while many editors change one consonant and render 'exterminates them' (so Ball, Dhorme, Hölscher, Steinmann, Kissane, Horst, Fohrer). Reider (*VT*, IV, 1954, pp. 290f.) renders the line 'he prostrates the nations and brings them to rest', making this line the antithesis of the preceding. This is not convincing. The slight emendation of Ball is to be preferred.

24. The first half of the verse seems too long, and LXX omits one word. Hence many editors omit either 'of the people' (so Duhm, Gray, Dhorme, and others), or 'of the earth' (so Ball). Probably M.T. is a conflation of two readings.

understanding: Hebrew 'heart', which may mean either 'intelligence' or 'courage'. For the second half of the verse, cf. Ps. 107.40*b*, where the Hebrew is exactly the same as here.

waste: this is the word rendered 'without form' in Gen. 1.2, of the primeval chaos.

25. grope: Gray notes that the picture is more vivid than this, and that it means 'they feel darkness'—darkness being conceived of as a concrete something over which their hands pass, as a blind man's pass over objects around him.

in the dark without light: i.e. in the unrelieved darkness.

stagger: this is the same word as that rendered 'wander' in verse 24. Hence many editors emend to read the verb used of the staggering of a drunken man in Isa. 19.14. Peake observes: 'When God deprives the leaders of understanding, they still keep on moving, but only in an aimless, witless way.'

JOB'S DETERMINATION TO REASON WITH GOD AND HIS SCORN FOR THE HOLLOW ARGUMENTS OF HIS FRIENDS. 13.1–28

Job charges his friends with unwillingness to face facts in their special pleading for God. But they will earn no thanks from him for their insincerity. From them Job turns to God to plead his cause face to face at whatever cost, affirming that only his consciousness of innocence could fortify him for this. He asks only that God will ease his sufferings and cease to terrify him, and he will appear as plaintiff or defendant.

² What you know, I also know;
  I am not inferior to you.
³ But I would speak to the Almighty,
  and I desire to argue my case with God.
⁴ As for you, you whitewash with lies;
  worthless physicians are you all.
⁵ Oh that you would keep silent,
  and it would be your wisdom!

---

2. Zophar had appealed to the inscrutability of God. Job knows all about this, and has argued that God's acts are inscrutably arbitrary and undirected by moral purpose. The second line is duplicated in 12.3*b* (cf. note there). Here it is required for the balance of the verse.

3. But: this word is repeated at the beginning of verse 4, and in both verses it stands by anacrusis outside the metrical scheme. The repetition is not impressive, and the repeated anacrusis is not natural. *RSV* does not translate it in verse 4, and many editors omit it there. Here it seems to be needed. It is a strong adversative, and Job is saying that despite the arbitrariness of God of which he has spoken he yet wishes to appeal to God rather than to his friends. He will appeal to God against God. Here we see how two conceptions of God are struggling in his thought.

argue my case: the verb means 'argue', 'convince', 'convict', 'reprove'. It is used in the reflexive in Isa. 1.18 (*RSV* 'reason together'). Job here wishes to appeal to God's reason.

4. Before Job can begin his appeal to God, he cannot forbear to attack his friends. He will not reason with them, but simply denounces them.

you whitewash with lies: lit. 'plasterers of lies' (cf. Ps. 119.69). A similar idiom is found in Akkadian for lying slanderers. LXX, under the influence of the next line, took it to refer to false surgical plasters, and rendered 'ye are false physicians' (so Kissane). What Job is saying is that the friends cover up the facts with their lies.

worthless physicians: lit. 'healers of worthlessness' (cf. Zech. 11.17). Ewald and Dillmann render 'patchers' instead of 'healers', resorting to a meaning of the root known in Arabic and Ethiopic, but not in Hebrew. This would yield a suitable sense here. The friends then are called mere botchers, who try to cover up the rents in the pattern of the universe which Job is exposing. If the meaning 'healers' is retained, we must suppose that Job means that these friends who came to minister comfort and healing to him are unable to do so.

5. The friends have talked about wisdom; if they would show it, they would keep silent. Dhorme cites the Latin proverb: *si tacuisses, philosophus mansisses.* Cf. Prov. 17.28.

6 Hear now my reasoning,
    and listen to the pleadings of my lips.
7 Will you speak falsely for God,
    and speak deceitfully for him?
8 Will you show partiality toward him,
    will you plead the case for God?
9 Will it be well with you when he searches you out?
    Or can you deceive him, as one deceives a man?
10 He will surely rebuke you
    if in secret you show partiality.

---

6. my reasoning: this noun is derived from the verb rendered 'argue my case' in verse 3 (see note there). Here some would render 'my reproof'. In that case we should have to render 'accusations' in the next line. These are both possible renderings (cf. Prov. 1.23; Job 31.35); but *RSV* is to be preferred. LXX renders 'the reasoning (or reproof) of my mouth', and many editors adopt this as yielding a better parallel and rhythm. The sense is unchanged.

7. speak falsely: lit. 'speak injustice'. The noun is rendered 'wrong' in 6.29f. It is used parallel to 'deceit' in 27.4.

for God: in the Hebrew this stands emphatically at the beginning, with the nuance: 'Do you think it is for God that you are speaking falsely?'

speak: some editors vary the word for 'speak' since LXX appears to have had two different words.

deceitfully: lit. 'treachery'. The word is usually employed, as here, of speech.

8. show partiality: lit. 'lift up his face'. It is used of judges showing favouritism, usually in return for a bribe. Here it is very sarcastic.

plead the case: i.e. 'take up cudgels'. Job is full of scorn for their servility towards God which then leads them to patronise him and take him under their protection. Both halves of the line are shorter than usual. Hence some editors supply words to fit the line to their Procrustean standards.

9. Job continues his sarcasm. God is too great to be deceived by their fawning sycophancy, and he will penetrate their shallow souls and see through their insincerity. It will go hard with them then!

searches: this is the word used by Eliphaz in 5.27. He claimed to have searched out the truth; but he and his friends will be searched out by God!

10. rebuke: this is the verb used in verse 3 (see note there). Here it clearly bears the sense 'reprove', or 'convict'.

show partiality: cf. on verse 8. Peake well observes: 'It is noteworthy as showing the conflict of feeling in Job, that while he attacks with the utmost boldness the unrighteousness of God's conduct he should have such deep-rooted confidence in

¹¹ Will not his majesty terrify you,
　　and the dread of him fall upon you?
¹² Your maxims are proverbs of ashes,
　　your defences are defences of clay.
¹³ 'Let me have silence, and I will speak,
　　and let come on me what may.
¹⁴ I will take my flesh in my teeth,
　　and put my life in my hand.
¹⁵ Behold, he will slay me; I have no hope;
　　yet I will defend my ways to his face.
¹⁶ This will be my salvation,
　　that a godless man shall not come before him.
¹⁷ Listen carefully to my words,
　　and let my declaration be in your ears.

---

his righteousness as to believe him incapable of tolerating a lying defence even of himself.'

11. his majesty: there is a play on words here in the Hebrew. The meaning of the word is literally 'lifting up', and the expression for 'show partiality' is 'lift up the face'. So Job is saying that, if the friends lift up the face of God, his lifting up will strike terror into them.

12. maxims: the word is derived from the verb 'remember', and it probably means 'memorable sayings', 'epigrams'. It is also possible that it means 'your memorised sayings', which you repeat parrot-like.

proverbs of ashes: Job is again biting and scornful. Ashes may once have served a useful purpose, but now they are dead, and their usefulness is at an end. Such is the wisdom of Job's friends. They have appealed to the past, and ashes belong to the past.

defences: the word *gaḇ* means the 'boss' of a shield. It may be a symbol for defence as in *RSV*, or it may stand for the shield itself. Dhorme connects the root *gāḇaḇ*, from which this word comes, with *gûḇ*, for which he advances an Arabic meaning, 'answer' (so also Beer, Hölscher, Steinmann, Weiser). He then renders 'your answers are answers of clay' (cf. I. Eitan, *AJSL*, XLV, 1928–29, p. 203). But this is not so satisfactory as the more usual translation.

of clay: an earthenware shield, or one with an earthenware boss, would be a poor defence. At the first blow of the enemy it would be shivered.

13. Let me have silence: M.T. has a pregnant construction 'Be silent from me', i.e. 'Stand away from me in silence'. But LXX does not render 'from me', and some editors delete it.

what may: the Hebrew says simply 'what'. LXX has 'that I may desist from anger', apparently reading *ḥēmāh* for *māh*. Ball accepts this reading and renders 'and let wrath pass over me'. But LXX is no authority for this, and M.T. is more vigorous. Job is determined to speak out fearlessly and to brave the consequences.

14. The verse begins with 'Why?', which spoils both sense and metre, and which is unrepresented in LXX. Most editors delete it as a dittograph of the last words of verse 13. M. Dahood (*Biblica et Orientalia*, XVII, 1965, p. 16) rejects this and renders 'till eternity'. A few editors transfer it to the end of verse 13, to yield 'what upon what' instead of simply 'what' (so Duhm, Klostermann, Hölscher). Gray pronounces the suggestion clever but hazardous.

I will take my flesh in my teeth: Ball thinks the metaphor is of a wild beast at bay, snatching its young in its teeth, and even so hampered facing its foes. Others think it refers to the ferociousness of a wild beast disturbed while it is devouring its prey. Neither of these seems a likely interpretation of 'my flesh'. In the second line 'my life' is Job's own life, and 'my flesh' must also mean Job's flesh. We can best approach the first line through the second. 'I will put my life in my hand' means 'I will risk my life' (cf. Jg. 12.3; 1 Sam. 19.5). The first line must have a similar meaning. An animal that fights with flesh in its mouth will risk having to lose it in the fight. Job says he will take his own flesh in his mouth and will therefore risk losing it. In his desperate state he will risk losing body and soul, the two constituents of man's being in Hebrew thought, in his encounter with God. The point is not the ferocity of the holder of the flesh but the holder's risk of the flesh. **my life:** the Hebrew word *nepeš* can also carry the meaning 'throat', and Pope so takes it here, understanding the reference to be to a symbolic gesture of asseveration accompanying an oath.

15. The first line has been most variously interpreted. *AV* 'Though he slay me, yet will I trust in him', despite the sublimity of its thought, is irrelevant to the context, which speaks of challenge, not trust. One of the difficulties arises from the fact that Kt reads *lō'*='not' while Ķr has *lô*='to him' (so the Versions). *RSV* renders Kt: 'Behold, he will slay me; I have no hope' (so Duhm, Gray, Hölscher, Weiser), while *RV* rendered Ķr: 'Though he slay me, yet will I wait for him' (so Horst, Fohrer). Against this Gray raised the objection that the verb is never used of waiting for anything evil. But Job does not regard death as an evil. He looks forward to it, and so is prepared to challenge God with the abandon of desperation. Ehrlich emended the text to give 'I will not tremble' (so Dhorme, Pope). The general sense is clear despite the uncertainty of details. Job is prepared to speak at the risk of his life.

yet: this is a strong adversative in Hebrew. Nothing shall make Job refrain from maintaining his righteousness before God. His conscience is clear, and he is certain his misfortunes were not self-entailed.

16. This: defined in the following line. The thought seems to be that the fact that Job comes voluntarily face to face with God itself argues his righteousness, since an evil man naturally and inevitably flees from the presence of God, as Adam hid himself in Paradise after his sin (Gen. 3.8).

17. my declaration: this word is an Aramaism. The verb has to be supplied.

¹⁸ Behold, I have prepared my case;
    I know that I shall be vindicated.
¹⁹ Who is there that will contend with me?
    For then I would be silent and die.
²⁰ Only grant two things to me,
    then I will not hide myself from thy face:
²¹ withdraw thy hand far from me,
    and let not dread of thee terrify me.
²² Then call, and I will answer;
    or let me speak, and do thou reply to me.
²³ How many are my iniquities and my sins?
    Make me know my transgression and my sin.

Some editors turn this noun into a verb 'I will show' and then have to supply an object 'my knowledge'. But this is no improvement.

18. prepared: the verb is sometimes used of marshalling an army in battle array. Job has marshalled his arguments and he is confident that he will win his case.

my case: the word has many meanings: court of law, process at law, sentence, execution of judgment, ordinance, right, custom. Here it means 'case' for presentation to the court (so 23.4; 1 Kg. 3.11, where *RSV* 'to discern what is right' means 'to hear cases').

shall be vindicated: shall win my case (cf. 11.2).

19. contend with me: plead against me. Job feels that his case is so strong that no one would dream of challenging it. But if one should appear, he would give up his case at once and resign himself to death. He has confidence that the God he has known will not dispute his case, but if he should, then Job is ready to die, but with the unshakable certainty of the rightness of his cause.

20. grant: the Hebrew says 'do not do' i.e. 'spare me'. This is in formal disagreement with what follows, since one request is positive and one negative. But the meaning is not in doubt. For the substance of Job's requests cf. 9.34. Peake notes that, when God does speak to Job from the tempest, he does not fulfil these requests. God gave to Job peace in his sufferings before he gave him relief from them. From here Job turns from his friends to address God.

21. The second line is repeated verbatim from 9.34.

22. The boldness of Job is without limits. He is equally ready to appear as plaintiff or as defendant. He can defend his case against God, but he also has a strong case to bring against God. Throughout Job finds himself in a dilemma created by a false theology against the background of his past experience of God.

23. Job first asks that the charges against him be specified, so that he may know

²⁴ Why dost thou hide thy face,
     and count me as thy enemy?
²⁵ Wilt thou frighten a driven leaf
     and pursue dry chaff?
²⁶ For thou writest bitter things against me,
     and makest me inherit the iniquities of my youth.
²⁷ Thou puttest my feet in the stocks, and watchest all my paths;

---

the number and the nature of the counts he has to face. Note that three words for
sin stand side by side here. The first comes from a root meaning 'err', the second
from one meaning 'miss the mark', and the third from one meaning 'rebel'. It is
improbable that these ideas are kept strictly in mind when the words are used,
and they are commonly almost, if not quite, synonymous. Here Job does probably
deliberately use them to indicate the various causes from which sin may arise, so
that he may be told precisely what he is held to have done. The second of the
words stands in both halves of the verse. But here few editors raise any complaint.
Ball, however, would mar the rhythm of the verse by removing it in the first half.

24. hide thy face: a sign of anger (Ps. 27.9; Isa. 54.8) or unfriendliness (Ps.
30.7 (M.T. 8); 104.29). Peake notes that some editors think a pause separated this
from the preceding verse, to give God a chance to answer. But the meaning is
more probably simply 'Why dost thou refuse to be friendly?'

25. frighten: a strong word, rendered 'terrify' in Isa. 2.19, 21.
a driven leaf . . . dry chaff: figures for what is so insignificant that it is blown
hither and thither by the slightest wind. Job regards himself as the sport of God's
every whim and fancy. In Lev. 26.26 the 'driven leaf' is mentioned as a trivial
cause of terror to those who disobey God. Here Job suggests that it is very unworthy of God to harass and persecute one so insignificant as himself.

26.writest bitter things: Hitzig took this to mean 'prescribest bitter medicines',
but this is highly improbable. The picture is of the judge recording sentence (cf.
Isa. 10.1). Ball suggested that it should be rendered 'writest upon me bitter things',
with reference to the marks of Job's disease. But this is more far-fetched. The
word rendered 'bitter things' means 'poison' in 20.14, and 'gall bladder' in 20.25.
Dahood (*The Bible in Current Catholic Thought*, 1962, pp. 59f.) suggests that the
meaning is 'writest acts of violence against my account'.

iniquities of my youth: Job does not claim that he is sinless. He only maintains
that he has committed no such heinous sins as could justify his exceptional sufferings. Here he sarcastically suggests that his misfortunes must be a belated requital
of the long-forgotten sins of his youth. By 'inherit' the sins of his youth, he means
'inherit the consequences' of them. By the use of this word Job skilfully suggests
that youth and manhood are two different persons.

27. in the stocks: the word is found only here and in 33.11. The same word

thou settest a bound to the soles of my feet.
28 Man wastes away like a rotten thing,
   like a garment that is moth-eaten.

---

in Syriac is used in Ac. 16.24. It was a wooden instrument in which the feet of prisoners were made fast. It may have been a heavy wooden clog, which the prisoner might drag about a little, or it may have had a transverse bar under which the feet were immovable. Some think the former is the more likely, since the next clause presupposes some liberty of movement. But the next clause may have nothing to do with this. Job is not writing history, but representing God's treatment of him under various figures.

watchest all my paths: God keeps him under close observation. This is an alternative figure to express God's determination not to let Job get away from him. Beer (also Ball, Hölscher, Stevenson, Fohrer) rejects this line to reduce the verse to a distich. On the other hand, Duhm transfers here 14.5c to make the verse into a tetrastich. This would give a good parallel to the last line of the verse, though some change would be necessary. Pope transposes this line and the next.

thou settest a bound to the soles of my feet: lit. 'thou inscribest upon (or against, or about) the roots of my feet'. This would seem to mean that God draws a ring around Job, out of which he is not allowed to step. If 14.5c is transferred here, we should need to alter to the plural 'Thou fixest their limits, that they cannot pass'. Duhm objects to the repetition of 'feet' in the verse, and changes the figure by reading 'my root'. The expression 'roots of the feet' is not found elsewhere, and is a strange one. *BDB* pronounces it arbitrary of Duhm to vary the figure to that of a tree with circumscribed roots. As the verse stands, while the figures change, all have to do with circumscribing the movements of a man. In Job's thought God is determined to restrict his freedom of movement or action, and so he uses these various figures. *AV* has 'Thou settest a print upon' and Pope follows this view, thinking that the reference is to the marking of slaves to make the tracking of a runaway slave easier.

28. Man wastes away: the Hebrew begins 'and he' or 'and it'. *RV* 'Though I am like a rotten thing' is not a translation. On Duhm's view the 'it' refers to the root of the tree. When the root has been circumscribed, it rots. But it would be strange to describe the tree as a moth-eaten garment! If the 'he' is interpreted as in *RSV*, the verse has no clear relevance to its context. Merx would remove it to follow 14.2a, while Siegfried and Dhorme would place it after 14.2b (so also Steinmann and Pope). Bickell would put it after 14.3, and Kissane after 14.6. Szczygiel removes it to follow 13.24. Budde takes the short way and simply deletes (so Hölscher). Of these suggestions, that of Siegfried seems the best.

like a rotten thing: LXX has 'like a wineskin', involving only a change of vowels (so Beer, Nestle (*ZAW*, xx, 1900, p. 172), Fohrer). But this is not appropriate. The word is used elsewhere of dry rot in a house or of rotting bones

14

'Man that is born of woman
   is of few days, and full of trouble.
2 He comes forth like a flower, and withers;
   he flees like a shadow, and continues not.
3 And dost thou open thy eyes upon such a one
   and bring him into judgment with thee?
4 Who can bring a clean thing out of an unclean?
   There is not one.

(caries). It is used parallel to 'moth', as here, in Hos. 5.12. For the second line cf. Isa. 50.9; Ps. 102.26; Sir. 14.17. As a curiosity of misplaced ingenuity, Cheyne's rewriting of the verse (with the exception of the first word) may be recorded. He secures the meaning 'such an one is like a blossom that fadeth, Like a vine which caterpillars have eaten'.

OB'S LAMENT ON THE BREVITY OF LIFE AND THE FINALITY OF DEATH 14.1–22

Job returns once more to bemoan his condition and indeed the condition of all mankind. Life is short and none are pure. Why, then, should God harass men instead of letting them enjoy their brief day in peace. A lopped tree may grow again, but for man death is final. He then wishes that God would give him temporary refuge in Sheol until his anger was overpast, but ends, as he has done before, by reflecting on the cheerlessness of the prospect of Sheol.

1. **born of woman:** of frail origin.
of few days: Job has already lamented the shortness of life (7.6ff.; 9.25f.), and the thought is common. Even the longest life is but brief; cf. Gen. 47.9.
trouble: cf. on 3.17.
2. 'Nothing is so ephemeral as the flower; nothing so fugitive as the shadow' (Dhorme). For the thought cf. Ps. 90.6; 103.15f.; Isa. 40.6f.; Jas 1.10f.; and Job 8.9; Ps. 144.4; Ec. 6.12.
comes forth: this verb is used of plants in 1 Kg. 4.33 (M.T. 5.13), Isa. 11.1. There is therefore no need to change it as do Beer and Ball.
3. Job is astonished that God should scrutinise one so ephemeral as man. To 'open the eye upon' is to pay attention to, and the meaning is as in 7.17.
him: M.T. has 'me', but most editors read 'him' with LXX, Syr., Vulg. In the Hebrew the word is placed in an emphatic position. Job has previously been clamouring to face God in court. Here he asks if God will really go to law with so insignificant a creature as man.
4. **Who can bring?** We should render 'Oh for!' Many editors delete this verse on the ground that the context speaks of the brevity of man's life and not his sinfulness. But this is not cogent. In Hebrew thought childbirth is regarded as unclean (cf. Ps. 51.5 (M.T. 7)), so that when Job refers to man as 'born of woman'

⁵ Since his days are determined,
 and the number of his months is with thee,
 and thou hast appointed his bounds that he cannot pass,
⁶ look away from him and desist,
 that he may enjoy, like a hireling, his day.
⁷ 'For there is hope for a tree,
 if it be cut down, that it will sprout again,
 and that its shoots will not cease.

---

he suggests that he is frail and unclean. The second line is abnormally short: 'not one'. Duhm, who retains the verse, would add '(is) without sin' to extend the line, without changing the thought. Dhorme, on the other hand, thinks the shortness is for studied effect.

5f. Since man's life is brief and he cannot overstep the divinely appointed limits, let God leave him alone for its brief course.

5. determined: lit. 'cut' (cf. Lev. 22.22 'mutilated'). Dhorme thinks rather of the extended meaning 'engrave', and of the custom of engraving decrees on stone, and hence renders 'decreed'. The line is short, and LXX adds 'upon earth'. Some editors reduce the verse to a distich by deleting the third line (so Ball, Fohrer), or by transferring it to 13.27 (see note there). Dhorme retains it where it is, while Hölscher rejects the whole of verses 4f. (so also Steinmann).

is with thee: under thy control.

his bounds. The word is often rendered 'statutes'. It means something cut or engraved, and then by extension anything prescribed or decreed. In Gen. 47.22 it means an allowance of food. If the line is retained here, it means a prescribed limit of time. But see on 13.27.

6. desist: the Hebrew says 'and let him desist', which *AV* and *RV* render 'that he may rest'. But this rendering is unjustified, and most editors make the slight change required to secure the sense of *RSV*. Ball would add 'from him', as in 7.16. This must in any case be understood. R. Gordis renders 'that he may survive' (cf. on 10.20).

enjoy: the poor pleasure of the hireling (cf. on 7.1) is confined to the short evening of his day, when he has received his wages and can rest. Job asks no more than that he might have a short season of similar poor pleasure ere life ends.

7. The figure now changes to a tree, and the thought of the finality of death. Trees can be cut down and they will sprout again. According to Wetzstein (in Delitzsch), in the region of Damascus trees are still renewed by being cut down with an axe. Why, Job asks by implication, should man be denied what is granted to a tree? In contrast to this suggestion that man is more hardly treated than nature, Peake cites the words of Jesus in Mt. 6.30.

cease: come to an end. The root is the same as that rendered 'desist' in verse 6.

⁸ Though its root grow old in the earth,
    and its stump die in the ground,
⁹ yet at the scent of water it will bud
    and put forth branches like a young plant.
¹⁰ But man dies, and is laid low;
    man breathes his last, and where is he?
¹¹ As waters fail from a lake,
    and a river wastes away and dries up,

---

8. Instead of being cut down the tree may fail because its root grows old, and its stump dies or decays. What Job is thinking of here is the failing of the tree through drought rather than its complete death, since the following verse speaks of its revival with the coming of water.

9. at the scent of water: the crediting of the tree with the sense of smell is a fine poetic figure.

it will bud: since the sprouting or blossoming of a tree is the sign of its flourishing, this verb may sometimes be rendered 'flourish' (Ps. 92.12f. (M.T. 13f.); Prov. 14.11).

10. man. The Hebrew uses two different words for man in this verse. The first is from a root meaning 'be strong'.

is laid low: *AV* and *RV* have 'wasteth away'. Gray says mordantly that if this verb has this meaning, any word may mean anything. The root meaning is 'be weak', and it provides a strong antithesis to the word here chosen for 'man'. Even a strong man dies and becomes powerless. The same two roots are brought into contrast again in Jl 3.10 (M.T. 4.10). Where words are so carefully chosen, it is gratuitous to substitute less expressive words as some editors do. I. Eitan (*JBL*, XLII, 1923, pp. 25ff.) without change of text renders 'is snatched away', but this is less good.

where is he? This terse question is far more effective than LXX 'and is no more', which Ball prefers. Here as elsewhere Job reflects the view that there is no worthwhile Afterlife.

11. from a lake: the Hebrew has 'from a sea' (cf. *AV*, *RV*), but the word has a wider use than our 'sea', and can stand for a lake; cf. Sea of Galilee. In Isa. 19.5 it is used for the Nile, and *RSV* renders it there by 'the Nile'. Davidson compares Arabic *baḥr*, which can mean sea, or any mass of water whether salt or fresh, or a river. Peake notes that the illustration is not very effective. For though lakes and rivers may become dry in drought, they fill up again when the rains come and therefore do not illustrate the permanence of death. Dhorme seeks to meet this by finding the meaning: even if, *per impossibile*, seas and rivers dried up, the time that would be needed would make no difference to the dead. But this is very forced. The second line of the verse is identical with Isa. 19.5b in the Hebrew.

¹² so a man lies down and rises not again;
   till the heavens are no more he will not awake,
   or be roused out of his sleep.
¹³ Oh that thou wouldest hide me in Sheol,
   that thou wouldest conceal me until thy wrath be past,
   that thou wouldest appoint me a set time, and remember me!
¹⁴ If a man die, shall he live again?
   All the days of my service I would wait,
   till my release should come.
¹⁵ Thou wouldest call, and I would answer thee;
   thou wouldest long for the work of thy hands.

---

12. till the heavens are no more: the Hebrew construction is unusual and is found only once elsewhere. Aq., Sym., Theod., Syr. and Vulg. all render 'till the heavens wear out' (cf. Ps. 102.26 (M.T. 27); Isa. 51.6), and this is followed by Bickell, Beer, Duhm, Ball, Dhorme, involving the omission of one consonant. But Gray thinks M.T. possible, and finds the very unusualness of the construction to be in its favour. H. M. Orlinsky (*JQR*, N.S., xxviii, 1937–38, pp. 57ff.) finds an Arabism in the word rendered 'will not awake', and translates 'so long as the heavens are not rent asunder'. He then deletes the last line as a mistaken gloss on this verb, which could only have come into existence after the meaning of the verb had been lost. Similarly G. R. Driver (*SVT*, iii, 1955, p. 77).

13. Note how Job continues to cherish the wish for resurrection. After emphatically denying the possibility of such a thing, he pauses to meditate on what it might mean and longs for its realisation, and utters the bold longing for God to give him temporary refuge in Sheol.
a set time: the same word as is rendered 'bounds' in verse 5 (see note there).

14. shall he live again? LXX omits the interrogative, and makes Job assert that man will live again (so Ball; cf. D. H. Gard, *JBL*, lxxiii, 1954, pp. 137f.). Budde and Duhm render 'If only a man might die and live again!' (so Peake). Most editors follow M.T. Some think this line is either misplaced or a gloss (so Gray, Hölscher). Dhorme transfers it to follow verse 19, while Fohrer suggests that it may belong to verse 13.
my service: cf. on 7.1.
my release: 'The word appears to embody a military figure of one soldier or troop being replaced or relieved by another; but obviously the figure is not to be pressed' (Gray).

15. Again we see how two views of God are struggling in Job's thoughts.
long for: as Job longs for the old fellowship with God, from which he feels cut off, since his sufferings are to him as to his friends the evidence that he is abandoned by God, so he believes that God will one day yearn for his fellowship.

¹⁶ For then thou wouldest number my steps,
   thou wouldest not keep watch over my sin;
¹⁷ my transgression would be sealed up in a bag,
   and thou wouldest cover over my iniquity.
¹⁸ 'But the mountain falls and crumbles away,
   and the rock is removed from its place;
¹⁹ the waters wear away the stones;
   the torrents wash away the soil of the earth;

---

16. then. *RSV* follows the view of Budde, that verses 16f. continue the previous verse, and describe God's gracious numbering of Job's steps and friendly watch over him, when he returns to desire his fellowship (so Hölscher, Weiser, Horst). *AV* and *RV* render 'now' and see God's present jealous watch over Job. In that case the second line must be taken, as by *AV/RV*, as a question (so Fohrer). Dhorme interprets the first line of the present and the second of what would be when God returned to friendliness. LXX renders 'thou dost not pass over my sin', and Ewald, Dillmann, Duhm, Gray and Ball emend to secure this sense. Pope thinks the first half of the verse refers to an unfriendly numbering, and so inserts a negative.

17. in a bag: Pope suggests the possibility that Job's sins were thought of as represented by tally stones kept in a bag (cf. A. L. Oppenheim, *JNES*, XVIII, 1959, pp. 121ff.). O. Eissfeldt had previously used the same idea to interpret 'the bundle of the living' (1 Sam. 25.29).

cover over: the verb used in 13.4, 'plasterers of lies'. The difference of interpretation extends to this verse. On Budde's view it means that God would tie up Job's sins in a bag and cover them from sight and memory. On the alternative view, the meaning is that God treasures up Job's sins and keeps them securely, so that they are not forgotten and full punishment is exacted.

18. Even the greatest mountain can be shaken and destroyed. How then can man escape destruction?

crumbles away. The verb usually describes the fading of a flower, and this reads strangely here. LXX and Syr. render 'will fall', and many editors read this, with revocalisation of the preceding word, and render 'will surely fall' (so Dhorme, Hölscher, Steinmann, Weiser, Horst, Fohrer). Duhm, on the other hand, assimilates the preceding word to this, and accepts the application of the metaphor of a flower to the mountain. The essential meaning of the verse is the same on either view. It is the impermanence of even the eternal hills.

19. Editors try to avoid the tristich by rearrangement. Budde would bring verse 12*a* to follow verse 19*c*, while Dhorme would bring verse 14*a* to precede verse 19*a*. The latter is very difficult to accept, and the former is not convincing. Hölscher and Fohrer think that a line has been lost from this verse.

the torrents: *RV* 'the overflowings thereof'. Budde proposed to read *seḥîpāh* for

so thou destroyest the hope of man.
20 Thou prevailest for ever against him, and he passes;
   thou changest his countenance, and sendest him away.
21 His sons come to honour, and he does not know it;
   they are brought low, and he perceives it not.
22 He feels only the pain of his own body,
   and he mourns only for himself.'

15 Then Eli'phaz the Te'manite answered:
   2 'Should a wise man answer with windy knowledge,

---

sᵉpîḥêhā and to render 'a cloudburst', from a root which is used in Prov. 28.3, and is followed by Ball, Dhorme, Hölscher, and Fohrer. The same meaning is given with the reading *sᵉpîḥāh* by Szczygiel and Horst, who assume a metathesised Hebrew form of the Arabic *saḥîfeh*='rainstorm'.

the hope of man: this can hardly be the hope of a return to life, or it would be irrelevant to its position. It must mean the hope of a continuance of life. Death shatters man's hopes, as destruction brings the mountains to an end, and the torrent sweeps away the soil.

20. Thou prevailest for ever against him: 'In his last struggle for life God worsts him, and his defeat is final' (Peake). D. Winton Thomas (*JSS*, I, 1956, p. 107) suggests that the word 'for ever' here and in a number of other passages is used as a superlative, translating 'Thou prevailest utterly against him'.

changest his countenance: 'a graphic and pathetic description of death' (Davidson).

21f. Knowledge does not survive death, but feeling does. Apparently the thought is that the mouldering of the flesh in the grave is accompanied by misery for the shade in Sheol. He is only conscious of his own intense misery.

are brought low: i.e. come to dishonour, the opposite of 'come to honour' in the previous line. The same verbs stand in antithesis in Jer. 30.19. The corresponding root is used in Syriac to render 'without honour' in Mt. 13.57 and 'dishonour' in 1 C. 18.43. F. Perles (*JQR*, N.S., II, 1911–12, p. 118) follows LXX in finding the sense 'be many' for 'come to honour' and 'be few' for 'be brought low', but this is inferior to the sense of *RSV*.

22. he mourns for himself: *RV* 'his soul mourneth'. G. R. Driver (*Gaster Anniversary Volume*, 1936, p. 75) found the meaning 'throat' for 'soul' here, and rendered the verb 'be dry': 'his throat is parched'. But this does not seem convincing here.

THE SECOND SPEECH OF ELIPHAZ 15.1–35

The second cycle of speeches now begins. In the first Eliphaz had emphasised the

and fill himself with the east wind?
3 Should he argue in unprofitable talk,
    or in words with which he can do no good?
4 But you are doing away with the fear of God,

---

moral perfection of God, Bildad his unwavering justice, and Zophar his omniscience. Job in reply had dwelt on his own unmerited sufferings and declared his
willingness to meet God face to face to argue his case. Having failed to stir his
conscience, the friends see in him a menace to all true religion, and in the second
cycle their rebukes are sharper than in the first, though their characters are still
carefully preserved. Eliphaz is still the most dignified of the three. After rebuking
Job for his irreligion and his arrogance, he depicts in impressive terms the fate
which the wicked bring down upon themselves. His speech falls into three parts:
rebuke of Job for his rashness and irreverence (verses 2–6); analysis of his presumption in his confidence in his own wisdom (verses 7–16); his own doctrine of the
fate of the wicked (verses 17–35).

REBUKE OF JOB FOR RASHNESS AND IRREVERENCE 15.2–6
Eliphaz declares that Job's words are ill-considered and irreverent, and that they
only demonstrate the rightness of the charges made against him.
   2. wise: in 12.3, 13.2 Job had claimed that he was not inferior in wisdom to
the friends. Against this Eliphaz picks up the thought of Bildad in 8.2, that
his speeches are mere blustering and not born of true reflection. Peake thinks it
possible, though unlikely, that Eliphaz thinks of himself as the wise man,
and asks whether he should answer Job. But the second half of the verse does not
favour this.
windy knowledge: empty knowledge, with no real content. The word *rûaḥ*
('wind' or 'spirit') is here equivalent to *heḇel* ('breath', 'emptiness', or 'vanity'),
so frequently used in Ec., and hence *AV* and *RV* have 'vain knowledge'.
himself: lit. 'his belly'. In 32.18 Elihu says that the wind of his belly (*RSV* 'the
spirit within me') constrains him.
the east wind. This is a dreaded wind, violent and hot. The term here indicates
the passion with which Job had spoken and the mischievous sentiments he had
expressed.
   3. argue: Eliphaz here picks up the word Job had used in 13.3, and declares
his argument profitless.
unprofitable: lit. 'which does not profit'. This verb, which is a synonym of that
found in the next line, is found five times in the book of Job in this sense, and
nowhere else.
   4. the fear of God: i.e. religion; cf. on 4.6. Eliphaz says simply 'fear', i.e.
reverence.

and hindering meditation before God.
5 For your iniquity teaches your mouth,
    and you choose the tongue of the crafty.
6 Your own mouth condemns you, and not I;
    your own lips testify against you.
7 'Are you the first man that was born?
    Or were you brought forth before the hills?
8 Have you listened in the council of God?

---

hindering: lit. 'diminishing'. It is in this verse that Eliphaz brands Job's dangerous ideas as a menace to society. Strahan observes: 'In thus accusing Job of irreverence, Eliphaz is only superficially right, and it is the purpose of the drama to exhibit a seeker after truth who never really ceases to be profoundly religious, however far he may shift from his old theological moorings, and however unconventional may be the language which his hard experiences sometimes wring from his lips.' Tur-Sinai's rendering of the second line, 'and stealest speech from a god's presence', has little to commend it.

meditation. Cf. Ps. 119.97, 99.

5. Here Job's blasphemous utterances are traced to nothing higher than a desire to conceal his own wickedness by an asseveration of his innocence.

crafty: like the serpent in the Garden of Eden, Job is declared to use his craftiness to misrepresent.

6. Cf. 9.20, where Job had complained that he would be overawed by God's presence and led to incriminate himself. Here Eliphaz argues that his protestation of innocence is itself his own condemnation. Bickell would needlessly delete the verse, while Duhm would transfer it to follow verse 12.

JOB'S PRESUMPTION 15.7–16

With biting scorn Eliphaz directs a series of questions to Job, anticipating something of the burden of the divine speeches, reminding him of the limits of his knowledge and experience.

7. the first man. This is taken to be an allusion to the myth of the primeval man, who existed before the creation of the world, and who learned the plans of God in the divine council. Here he is said to have existed before the hills were created, and to have listened in the council of God. Schlottmann quoted the Hindu ironical proverb: 'Yes, indeed, he is the first man; no wonder he is wise!'

before the hills: cf. Prov. 8.25.

8. Have you listened: i.e., before the creation of the world. Jeremiah conceived of the prophet as one who stood in the council of God (23.18), to learn his word for men in his own day.

And do you limit wisdom to yourself?
9 What do you know that we do not know?
What do you understand that is not clear to us?
10 Both the grey-haired and the aged are among us,
older than your father.
11 Are the consolations of God too small for you,
or the word that deals gently with you?
12 Why does your heart carry you away,
and why do your eyes flash,

---

limit: this is the same word as that translated 'hindering' in verse 4, but it here has a different sense. Here it means 'to draw, or reserve, for oneself', and hence 'to have a monopoly of'. On the basis of Syr., Beer suggested reading 'was wisdom revealed to you?' and Ball would read either this or 'did wisdom come to you?', claiming LXX support for the latter. Dhorme rejects this claim, and neither change is an improvement.

9f. Eliphaz echoes the claim of Job (12.3; 13.2) and his questions (12.3c, 9), and declares that so far from Job having unique antiquity he was junior to some of his present company. Davidson and others think Eliphaz was referring to himself as 'the grayhaired and the aged', both of which words are in the singular. In that case Eliphaz is making the same claim to wisdom by seniority which he rebuked in Job, though Job had denied that wisdom necessarily came with age (12.12; cf. note there); cf. Wis. 4.8f.

11. the consolations of God: Eliphaz claims that the consolations of the friends are divinely inspired. He is doubtless thinking primarily of his own speech in which he had referred to a revelation which he had received. In 16.2 Job dismissed the friends as 'miserable comforters'.

deals gently: again this is probably a reference to his own former speech, which Eliphaz regards as very considerate. AV and RV marg. 'is there any secret thing with thee?' connect the word with the root meaning 'wrap closely', yielding a noun meaning 'secrecy' found in Jg. 4.21; 1 Sam. 18.22. It is to be connected, however, with the word found in Isa. 8.6 and 2 Sam. 18.5.

12. carry you away: this is a very free rendering of a verb meaning simply 'take', but G. R. Driver (WO, I, 1947–52, p. 235) finds here a different root (=Ar. *wakiḥa*), and secures the meaning 'why has thy heart emboldened thee' (cf. Prov. 6.25, where he finds the same root). Pope renders 'What has taken from you your mind?' Eliphaz is asking Job why he allows himself to be swept away by his passion instead of calmly reflecting.

flash: the Hebrew word is found only here. Targ. and Syr. appear to have equated it with a verb found in Aramaic and in post-biblical Hebrew, with the same consonants metathesised, meaning 'wink' (AV, RV), or better, as RSV, 'flash'

¹³ that you turn your spirit against God,
  and let such words go out of your mouth?
¹⁴ What is man, that he can be clean?
  Or he that is born of a woman, that he can be righteous?
¹⁵ Behold, God puts no trust in his holy ones,
  and the heavens are not clean in his sight;
¹⁶ how much less one who is abominable and corrupt,
  a man who drinks iniquity like water!
¹⁷ 'I will show you, hear me;
  and what I have seen I will declare
¹⁸ (what wise men have told,
  and their fathers have not hidden,
¹⁹ to whom alone the land was given,

(in anger). Gray prefers another meaning of the root, 'What do thine eyes hint at?' But this seems less appropriate. Budde preferred the reading of LXX (almost indistinguishable from M.T.), 'Why are thine eyes so lofty?' (cf. Prov. 6.17; 30.13). It is improbable that an ordinary word would have been replaced by a rare one, and metathesis is not uncommon. Moreover a few Hebrew MSS. have the form reflected in Targ. and Syr. Tur-Sinai equates the Hebrew word with an Arabic root, meaning 'dwindle away', 'become weak', and finds the meaning 'why have thine eyes weakened?' and this is followed by Pope. But RSV is more appropriate to the context. Job is not being rebuked for his helplessness, but for his passion.

13. your spirit: i.e. your anger (cf. Jg. 8.3). Ehrlich interpreted in the light of Ec. 12.7 'return your spirit to God'. But this is not appropriate here. By a slight change of vocalisation Ball secures the meaning 'blow your breath against God'. But this is not very convincing.

such words: Duhm proposed to read 'revolt', but has found no following. The only reason advanced for the change is that the Hebrew is weak. Ball would strengthen the meaning by reading 'in his face' for 'out of your mouth'. The change is not great, and the meaning is then 'and speak in defiance of him'. The word 'such' is not in the Hebrew, but may be legitimately inferred from the previous line. The words for which Job is here rebuked are prompted by his anger against God, and so are directed against him.

14. cf. 4.17ff.

born of a woman: in 14.1 this expression is evocative of man's frailness; here of his impurity. The low oriental estimate of woman is here to be noted.

15. his holy ones: the angels. Eliphaz here returns to the thought of 4.18.

heavens are not clean: cf. 25.5. It is disputed whether the reference is to the

material heavens or to heavenly beings. For the former cf. Exod. 24.10 (where
the word rendered in *RSV*, 'clearness', means 'purity'). But the parallelism here
suggests that heavenly beings are meant, as Targ. understood the line.

16. one: it is improbable that Eliphaz is here referring specifically to Job,
though Job is of course included.

abominable: disgusting. On the significance and use in *OT* of this root and its
derivative noun, cf. P. Humbert, *ZAW*, N.F., xxxi, 1960, pp. 217ff. It is used of
what is physically revolting (Ps. 107.15, *RSV* 'loathed'), ritually forbidden
(Dt. 14.3), or ethically repulsive (Ps. 119.163, *RSV* 'abhor').

corrupt: this root is found in the *OT* only here and in Ps. 14.3 and its parallel
Ps. 53.3 (where *RSV* has 'depraved'). In Arabic the root is used of milk turning
sour. On Akkadian uses of this root, cf. G. R. Driver, *JTS*, xxix, 1927–28, pp. 391f.

drinks . . . like water: i.e. freely and in large draughts, as one would not drink
stronger liquids; cf. 34.7.

THE FATE OF THE WICKED 15.17–35

Eliphaz claims that his doctrine rests upon the accumulated wisdom of the ages,
and then unfolds the torments of the troubled conscience of the wicked and his
dread of retribution, the coarsening of his moral fibre, and the miserable end to
which he will come. Strahan says: 'His eloquence becomes like the roll and swell
of a great organ, ending in a resounding crash which typifies the doom of iniquity'.
The only trouble with this doctrinaire theory is that it does not fit all the facts of
experience. The author of Ps. 73 had a truer insight when he turned from such a
theory to recognize that the righteous man is more to be envied than the prosperous wicked, in that while the latter may have his prosperity the former has
God, both here and hereafter.

17. Eliphaz here as elsewhere draws on his personal observation, which he
claims accords with traditional teaching; cf. 4.8, 12; 5.3.

18. and their fathers have not hidden: this represents the text followed by
LXX, omitting one letter of M.T. Pope secures the same sense with the retention
of the letter by treating it as an enclitic *m*, a form which is found in Ugaritic.
M.T. would most naturally be rendered 'and did not conceal from their fathers'.
Most editors since Houbigant, including Beer, Budde, Peake, Strahan, Ball,
Hölscher, Fohrer, re-divide the Hebrew words and render 'which their fathers did
not conceal from them'. *AV* and *RV* take 'from their fathers', which stands at
the end of the second line, as belonging to the first line, and Gray defends this
by taking the two verbs together, and so Dhorme: 'What wise men declare,
hiding nothing, according to the tradition of their fathers'. Eliphaz is here
claiming that his observation merely confirms that of former generations
stretching far back into the past.

19. Some commentators have supposed that here a contrast is being made
between the past, when Israel possessed the land of Canaan alone, and the present,
when she shared it with strangers; and either the fall of Samaria or the fall of
Jerusalem is thought to mark the division of the two periods. But, apart from the

and no stranger passed among them).

²⁰ The wicked man writhes in pain all his days,
   through all the years that are laid up for the ruthless.
²¹ Terrifying sounds are in his ears;
   in prosperity the destroyer will come upon him.
²² He does not believe that he will return out of darkness,
   and he is destined for the sword.

---

fact that Israel did not possess the land alone after the conquest and that there was much contamination of Israelite religion by Canaanite, it is very improbable that Eliphaz would be represented as thinking in these terms. Edom was the proverbial home of wisdom (cf. Jer. 49.7), and doubtless Eliphaz the Temanite believed that the purest wisdom was the possession of his own people.

no stranger passed among them: cf. Jl 3.17 (M.T. 4.17).

20. Eliphaz now unfolds the contents of the wisdom handed down and confirmed by his own observation. He declares that the prosperity of the wicked is hollow, since he is tortured by his conscience and his dread of retribution.

writhes in pain: with the reading of *h* for *ḥ*, Theod. has 'is foolish' or 'is mad', and Sym., Vulg., Syr. 'boasts himself'. Margolis (*ZAW*, xxv, 1905, p. 200) adopts the former and Beer the latter. Both are inferior to M.T. The context speaks not of the conduct of the wicked, but of his apprehension.

all the years: Ball renders 'but few years', as some older editors had done. But this would have been expressed differently in Hebrew. The parallel 'all his days' favours the rendering of *RSV*.

ruthless: the same word as that rendered 'oppressors' in 6.23; 27.13. The root means 'to inspire awe' or 'to terrify' (cf. 13.25, *RSV* 'frighten'; 31.34, *RSV* 'stood in fear').

21. Imaginary terrors haunt the wicked, so that his outward condition is belied by his inner. It is not implied that the destroyer actually breaks in upon him, but that in his own imagination he already experiences this. Cf. Prov. 28.1.

destroyer: the same word is rendered 'robbers' in 12.6.

22. return: Dhorme renders 'escape'. The meaning may be that he dreads night, being always afraid that he will not wake up, or he dreads misfortune, being afraid that it will be final. In either case we have a vivid picture of the torments of conscience. Duhm needlessly proposes to read *yāsûr* for *yaʾamîn šûb*, to get 'he will not depart', and is followed by Peake. This makes the line identical with verse 30*a*.

destined: M.T. has 'he is watched (or waited for) by the sword'. G. R. Driver (*SVT*, iii, 1955, p. 78) renders 'he is marked down for the sword'. Ewald suggested reading *ṣāpûn* for *ṣāpûy*, giving 'he is laid up for the sword', and many editors follow this. Ball proposed *ṣōpeh*, yielding the meaning 'he looketh out for the

²³ He wanders abroad for bread, saying, "Where is it?"
  He knows that a day of darkness is ready at his hand;
²⁴ distress and anguish terrify him;

---

sword', and this seems to continue the thought better. It is the oppressor's constant dread of assassination that is then expressed.

23. If the text is right, we must understand it to mean that in his prosperity the wicked is haunted by fears of poverty. LXX has 'he hath been appointed for food to vultures', reading 'ayyāh for 'ayyeh. This carries on the thought of the previous verse. In his imagination he sees himself slain by the sword and devoured by vultures. Many editors follow this view, but with a variety of minor changes and of changes in the first word of the verse: nittān='is given' (Siegfried, Peake, Ball) for nōḏēḏ; mûʿāḏ (Beer) or nōʿāḏ (Duhm, Buttenwieser, Hölscher, Kissane) ='is appointed'; nōḏaḏ='is known' (Dhorme). The second of these can claim the support of LXX, while the third involves no change of M.T. consonants. Fohrer and Pope retain the first word unchanged: 'he wanders as food for vultures'; but this does not seem very appropriate. Gray finds no reason to change M.T., and so Weiser and Horst. While it does not link directly with the preceding verse as its sequel, it presents a graphic picture of the gnawing dread which Eliphaz attributes to the wicked.

a day of darkness . . . at his hand: some editors think this is a strange picture, and as LXX attaches 'a day of darkness' (in Hebrew at the end of the verse) to verse 24, they transfer these words to that verse. Duhm then proposed to read nēḵer='disaster' (cf. 31.3) instead of nāḵôn='ready'. Others prefer to change beyāḏô='at his hand'. Beer proposed leʿêḏ='(he is ready) for calamity'. Wright (followed by Peake, Ball, Dhorme, Hölscher, Kissane, Horst, Fohrer, Pope) read pîḏô, a much slighter change yielding a stronger word for 'disaster', found in 12.5 (RSV 'misfortune') and 31.29 (RSV 'ruin'). LXX here has the word which renders Beer's 'êḏ in 18.12 and Wright's pîḏ in 31.29. Of these proposals that of Wright seems the best, and it well brings out the constant fear of a crash that Eliphaz pictures the wicked as experiencing.

24. If the words 'a day of darkness' are transferred to this verse with LXX (see preceding note), we have 'A day of darkness terrifies him, Distress and anguish prevail against him'. This is followed by many editors. The last line of the verse 'like a king prepared for battle' is held by Duhm to be a gloss unsuited to this context (so Strahan, Ball, Stevenson, Fohrer). Others see no reason to delete it.

battle: this word is found nowhere else in OT. The rendering 'battle' rests on Syr. The cognate verb in Arabic means 'swoop down', and in Syriac a cognate noun means 'vulture', while in post-biblical Hebrew the word found here means 'attack', 'assault'. This meaning well suits here. He is afraid that misfortune will come swiftly upon him, like an enemy all prepared for the assault.

they prevail against him, like a king prepared for battle.
25 Because he has stretched forth his hand against God,
   and bids defiance to the Almighty,
26 running stubŏrnly against him
   with a thick-bossed shield;
27 because he has covered his face with his fat,
   and gathered fat upon his loins,

25-28. Siegfried, Duhm and Beer regard these verses as intrusive, save that Duhm retains the last line of verse 28 in an altered form. Most, however, retain them. Strahan observes: 'If Eliphaz is here painting a picture for Job's benefit, he lays his colours on somewhat recklessly.'

25. stretched forth his hand: in challenge. It is his impious challenge to God and rebellion against him which is the source of the uneasy conscience and the constant apprehension of the wicked. For the outstretched hand as the symbol of threat, cf. Isa. 5.25; 9.21 (M.T. 20); 10.4. In Prov. 1.24 it is a symbol of appeal. **the Almighty:** cf. p. 24.

26. This verse continues the picture of the foolish defiance of God by the wicked, whose vain trust in his own strength is described. **stubbornly:** the Hebrew says 'with a neck', which *RV* understands to mean 'with a stiff neck'. Kissane renders 'insolently', understanding 'neck' in the sense of Ps. 76.5 (M.T. 6), while Dhorme thinks it means an 'outstretched neck'. LXX has 'with insolence' (*hybris*). Tur-Sinai preferred here to find a concrete reference to the armour of the wicked, parallel to the following line, and renders by 'hauberk' (so Pope), while others have proposed changes of the text. Graetz suggested 'like a warrior' (cf. 16.14*b*); Beer 'like a ruthless man' (the word found in verse 20; see note there), but this seems quite inappropriate; Ehrlich 'like an adversary'. The general sense demanded by the context is the headstrong assault on God by the wicked. **with a thick-bossed shield:** lit. 'with the thickness of the bosses of his shields', i.e. the bosses of his shield are set closely together. Needless emendations have again been proposed.

27. This verse indicates that the wicked is not really in a condition to fight, and so emphasises the folly of his defiance. He is bloated with luxury and self-indulgence. Cf. the picture of the wicked man in Ps. 73.7; Jer. 5.28; also Dt. 32.15. **gathered:** lit. 'made'. I. Eitan (*HUCA*, XII-XIII, 1937-38, p. 74) connects the root here with an Arabic root meaning 'cover', 'conceal', getting the meaning 'and covered his loins with fat', giving a closer parallel with the preceding line. **fat** (2°): *RV* 'collops of fat'. The word is found only here, and is clearly some synonym of 'fat'. The versions render by 'lard', 'suet' and the like. Pope renders by 'blubber'.

²⁸ and has lived in desolate cities,
    in houses which no man should inhabit,
    which were destined to become heaps of ruins;
²⁹ he will not be rich, and his wealth will not endure,
    nor will he strike root in the earth;

---

28. Dhorme thinks the meaning is that the tyrant has ravaged the regions around him so that he can occupy the room of others. But Delitzsch rightly notes that these are not cities that he has himself laid waste. They are ruined sites, believed to be under a curse (cf. Jos. 6.26; 1 Kg. 16.34). They were thought to be haunted by demons and wild beasts (cf. Isa. 13.20ff.; 34.13f.). The wicked man, as conjured up in the mind of Eliphaz, is ready to risk the curse in his confidence in his own prosperity. It is to be noted that the thought has moved from the torments of conscience to the ostentatious luxury and brazen conduct of the wicked. But there is no attempt to link all this doctrinaire description to the behaviour of Job as the explanation of his sufferings.

desolate: lit. 'hidden' (with ruins), or 'effaced'.

destined: lit. 'made ready'.

29. Here we seem to be back to the fears of the godless, and it is on this account that some regard verses 25–28 as out of place. But it is unwise to impose on an oriental author the strictly logical development of his theme that a modern western writer would desire.

strike root in the earth: the meaning here is very uncertain. *AV* '(Neither shall he) prolong the perfection thereof upon the earth'; *RV* '(Neither shall) their produce bend to the earth'. The versions differ widely, and *RSV* is based on Vulg. Sa'adia understood the *hapax legomenon minlām* to mean 'their possessions', and this meaning is defended, with a change of vowels, by Dahood (*The Bible in Current Catholic Thought*, 1962, pp. 60f.), who then takes 'earth' to mean 'the netherworld', and renders 'his possessions will not go down to the netherworld'. Pope follows this, though it does not seem very relevant. Neither the righteous nor the wicked can take their property to the nether world (cf. Job 1.21). Innumerable suggestions for the improvement of the text have been offered: Hitzig proposed 'their ear of corn (will not bend to the ground)', and Gray and Peake incline to this (the meaning then being their crops produce no ripe ears); Dillmann preferred 'their ears of grain' (the word used in Gen. 41.5, different from Hitzig's); Buttenwieser 'his harvest'; G. Hoffmann (*ZAW*, N.F., VIII, 1931, p. 144) 'their night-lodge (will not be spread out (reading passive verb) in the earth)', with which cf. Kissane '(he shall not spread out) a night-lodge (in the land)'. LXX has 'he will not cast a shadow on the earth'. On the basis of this, Graetz read *ṣillām*='their shadow' for *minlām*, while Dhorme preferred *ṣilmô* ='his shadow', translating 'his shadow will not lengthen itself on the ground' (cf.

30 he will not escape from darkness;
   the flame will dry up his shoots,
   and his blossom will be swept away by the wind.
31 Let him not trust in emptiness, deceiving himself;
   for emptiness will be his recompense.

Montet *ṣelem*). This yields a relevant meaning. The stretching out of the shadow is a figure of the extent of his influence (cf. Ps. 80.8ff. (M.T. 9ff.)).

30. he will not escape from darkness: many editors omit these words as a misplaced variant of verse 22*a*. It interrupts the comparison of the wicked with a tree that fails to mature.

flame: this word is used in Ezek. 20.47 (M.T. 21.3) of a forest fire, and it is possible that the thought here is of such a fire which will swiftly burn up the tree. **his blossom will be swept away by the wind:** the Hebrew has 'he shall depart by the breath of his mouth' (cf. *AV*, *RV*). If this is read, we must understand the reference to be to God's mouth, though God has not been referred to since verse 26. LXX has 'flower' instead of 'his mouth' (*pirḥô* for M.T. *pîw*), and 'fall' instead of 'depart'. Many editors base on this the rendering of *RSV*, with minor variations, reading *yᵉsô'ar* or *yissā'ēr*, instead of M.T. *yāsûr*. LXX cannot be claimed in support of the rendering 'will be swept away', but it is close to the Hebrew consonants, and the thought recurs in Isa. 40.24. Ball prefers *yiššal* 'will drop off' (cf. Dt. 28.40) instead of 'will be swept away', and follows Duhm and others in reading *piryô* = 'his fruit' instead of 'his blossom'. The former is farther from the Hebrew consonants, and the latter cannot claim the support of LXX. The thought of the verse continues that of the preceding verse, describing the swift disaster that is laid up for the wicked, whose prosperity will vanish like a tree consumed by a forest fire or blasted by the wind.

31. emptiness: cf. on 7.3: note the repetition of this word, which Gray thinks is deliberate and forceful. For the first Dhorme reads *bᵉšî'ô* instead of *baššaw* and renders 'his stature' (so Larcher), while Kissane with the same reading translates 'his greatness'.

deceiving himself: here Dhorme needlessly reads 'we know that (it is vanity)'. This is much flatter than M.T.

his recompense: in 20.18 the same word, *tᵉmûrātô*, is rendered 'trading'. It means either the exchanging of goods or the profit gained thereby. The next verse begins in LXX with a word unrepresented in M.T., and many editors supply a word similar to the word rendered 'recompense' which could easily have fallen out after it. Houbigant, followed by others, supplied *tîmōrātô* = 'his palm tree'. Dhorme prefers *zᵉmōrātô* = 'his vine shoot', which he reads instead of 'his recompense', and transfers to verse 32. Very many editors delete the whole of verse 31, or all except the last word, and regard it as a gloss which interrupts the

³² It will be paid in full before his time,
 and his branch will not be green.
³³ He will shake off his unripe grape, like the vine,
 and cast off his blossom, like the olive tree.
³⁴ For the company of the godless is barren,
 and fire consumes the tents of bribery.

---

thought, or alternatively transfer it elsewhere. Kissane places it after verse 21*a*. But while trading seems alien to the context, unless the author is for a moment leaving the figure of the tree for the actual prosperity of the wicked, and declaring that it is illusory, if we render 'Let him not trust in his stature (of greatness), deceiving himself, for it is vanity', the figure of a tree is not abandoned. The tree which by its nature should be a great one will never reach its full height; it will be destroyed by fire or stripped of blossom by the wind, and all its promise be belied by experience.

32. it will be paid in full: M.T. *timmālē'*. LXX, Vulg. and Syr. seem to have read *timmāl*='it will be withered'. This is supported by the parallel line, which speaks of a tree and not of a trading profit. If we supply the subject 'his palm tree' or 'vine shoot' here (or transfer the word from verse 31), the verse is then a balanced whole. 'Palm tree' is nearer to the Hebrew, and is to be preferred. The figure of a tree is being continued, but now successively thought of as a palm, a vine, or an olive tree.

his branch: this word is used especially of the palm branch (cf. Isa. 9.13). This supports the view that 'palm tree' should be supplied in the preceding line.

33. shake off: lit. 'treat with violence'. Delitzsch observes that the vine does not cast its unripe grapes, but that the unripe grapes hold the more firmly to the tree. The thought is therefore that the tree will fail to bring to maturity its unripe grapes (so *BDB*).

his unripe grape: the word used in Jer. 31.29f.; Ezek. 18.2 (*RSV* 'sour grapes').

cast off his blossom: Wetzstein (in Delitzsch) says: 'In order to appreciate the point of the comparison, it is needful to know that the Syrian olive tree bears fruit plentifully the first, third, and fifth years, but rests during the second, fourth, and sixth. It blossoms in these years also, but the blossoms fall off almost entirely without any berries being formed.'

34. godless: cf. on 8.13.

barren: cf. on 3.7.

fire: there is perhaps a reference here to the fire of God which caused one of Job's calamities (1.16).

the tents of bribery: carrying the suggestion that the wealth the wicked man enjoys has been gained unjustly, by either the giving or the acceptance of bribes to pervert justice.

T.C.B.: J.—6

³⁵ They conceive mischief and bring forth evil
   and their heart prepares deceit.'

---

35. their heart: lit. 'their belly'. At the beginning of his speech Eliphaz reproaches Job with filling his belly with the east wind (cf. verse 1). Here he return to his thought. The rendering 'heart' conceals this, and is less relevant to the context. Strahan says: 'Eliphaz's contempt is surely allied with a certain deliberate coarseness, which does not miss the fitting term.' In the traditional doctrine which Eliphaz sets forth, wickedness leads to the undoing of the wicked, and from this he draws the conclusion that all misfortune is self-entailed.

JOB ANSWERS ELIPHAZ 16–17

Job now feels himself abandoned by God and man. Scornfully he rejects the irrelevant speeches of his friends, and in moving bitterness of soul complains that the isolation from God which his suffering proclaims is aggravated by the isolation from man, of which he is now so painfully aware. Yet he is but the more conscious of his innocence of any sin which could explain his suffering, and resolves to maintain his innocence to the death. With that unresolved tension between the God of his past experience and the God of his present experience he appeals to God against himself, and proclaims his faith that the God he has known is still his Witness in heaven against the God who so torments him. He ends his speech, as he has done before, by renewed longing for the grave. The speech falls into four parts: dismissal of the 'comforts' of his friends (verses 2–5); his abandonment by God and man (verses 6–17); his appeal to his Witness in heaven (16.18–17.9); his anticipation of death as the end of his troubles (verses 10–16).

JOB'S DISMISSAL OF THE 'COMFORTS' OF HIS FRIENDS 16.2–5

To Job all the bland generalities of the friends are without meaning, and a mere stringing of words together such as he himself could so easily imitate.

2. miserable comforters: lit. 'comforters of trouble', i.e. comforters who increase trouble instead of ministering comfort. Job picks up the word that Eliphaz had just used (15.35, *RV* 'mischief'). It is rendered 'trouble' in 3.10; 4.8. D. Winton Thomas (*ET*, XLIV, 1932–33, p. 192) renders 'breathers out of trouble', connecting the participle with a different Arabic root.

windy words: Job rebuts the rebuke of his friends (8.2; 15.2) by turning their words against themselves.

provokes: or 'irritates'; cf. on 6.25.

4. join words together: from the root from which 'an associate' comes. *GB* and *KB* connect the word used here with a different Arabic root, meaning 'beautify', 'make artistic', yielding 'I could make a polished speech' (so Weiser). But Gray thinks this was a late meaning of the Arabic root. J. J. Finkelstein (*JBL*, LXXV, 1956, pp. 329ff.) connects the word with an Akkadian root, meaning 'to

16

Then Job answered:
² 'I have heard many such things;
  miserable comforters are you all.
³ Shall windy words have an end?
  Or what provokes you that you answer?
⁴ I also could speak as you do,
  if you were in my place;
  I could join words together against you,
  and shake my head at you.
⁵ I could strengthen you with my mouth,
  and the solace of my lips would assuage your pain.
⁶ 'If I speak, my pain is not assuaged,

---

make a din', and renders 'harangue'. O. Loretz (*CBQ*, XXIII, 1961, pp. 293f.) connects with the same root and renders 'I could be noisy with words', i.e. speak with mere noise. Tur-Sinai invokes Ugaritic to support the meaning 'heap up words', while Dhorme secures almost the same meaning 'multiply words' by changing one letter of the Hebrew word, and compares 35.16. The general sense is clear. Job claims that he could moralise in a detached way as cleverly as the friends without getting anywhere.

shake my head: this is a sign of mockery (Ps. 22.7 (M.T. 8), *RSV* 'wag their heads'; Isa. 37.22; cf. Mt. 27.39).

5. Job is here very sarcastic and scornful. He could offer strength and comfort that lay in mere words and involved no genuine sympathy, i.e. suffering with them.

solace: here we have a noun from the root used in 2.11 (*RSV* 'condole with'). The original meaning of the verb was 'to be agitated', and *BDB* has 'quivering motion' for the noun. Job could go through the motions of comfort and utter all the time-honoured clichés.

would assuage your pain: 'your pain' is unexpressed in the Hebrew. The verb means 'restrain' or 'withhold'. LXX and Syr. read 'I would not withhold', and many editors follow this. It involves but a slight change, and avoids the necessity to supply 'your pain'. Ehrlich, however, renders M.T. 'compassion would restrain my lips' (cf. Prov. 10.19). G. R. Driver (*JTS*, XXXIV, 1933, p. 380) maintains that the verb is here intransitive and Fohrer follows this, but with the addition of the negative from LXX and Syr.: 'the solace of my lips would not be withheld'. It seems preferable to follow LXX and Syr. as above. If the roles were reversed Job could offer unlimited comforting words to his friends.

JOB'S ABANDONMENT BY GOD AND MAN **16.6–17**

God's attack on Job has made men turn against him, though he is innocent of any offence. The violence of God's assault is described under figures which are drawn

and if I forbear, how much of it leaves me?
7 Surely now God has worn me out;
  he has made desolate all my company.
8 And he has shrivelled me up,

---

from the behaviour of a wild animal and from that of a human foe. Behind him line up men who basely take advantage of Job's helplessness and strike him.

6. my pain is not assuaged: here the noun is expressed and the passive of the verb stands. The thought is of finding relief through giving vent to his feelings. Neither by speaking nor by silence can Job find relief. Since his friends can minister no comfort to him and God has forsaken him, he is without hope of any relief.

how much of it? the implication is that none of it leaves him. The Hebrew *māh*, which means 'what?' sometimes corresponds to Arabic *mâ*='not', and it is possible that it should be so understood here: 'it does not depart'.

7. God: this is unexpressed in the Hebrew. Vulg. thought the subject was 'my sorrow', and Merx that it was Eliphaz. Moreover in the next line for **he has made desolate** M.T. has 'thou hast made'. The change of person and reversion to third person in verse 8, together with the want of balance in verse 8, led Dhorme to redivide the verses. With slight changes (*haššimmôṯ* for *haśimmôṯā*, *'aḏāṯô* for *'aḏāṯî wa*, *keḥāśî* for *kaḥaśî*) he secures the meaning: 'For now the jealous man has wearied me, All his company take hold of me, He has become a witness and risen up against me, My slanderer gives evidence against me'. Duhm, followed by Strahan, Gray, and Hölscher, read *haśimmanî* for *haśimmôṯā*, and *rā'āṯî* for *'aḏāṯî wa*, to yield 'Only now hath he wearied me and appalled me, All my calamity hath seized hold on me'. This seems preferable to Dhorme's reconstruction, though it does not seem necessary to understand God to be the subject of the first line. It seems preferable to follow the view of Vulg. and make 'my pain' the subject and to bring the line into harmony with the rest of verses 7f.

has worn me out: the same verb is used in the intransitive form in 4.2 (*RSV* 'be offended'); 4.5 (*RSV* 'be impatient').

made desolate: the verb is used in the sense of 'devastate' and 'appal'. If 'my pain' is the subject (see above) the reference is to the ravages of disease.

my company: this is not very relevant to the context. Job has no company, since his friends are all against him and not with him. The reading 'my calamity' is to be preferred, and the change involved is very slight (*d* and *r* are frequently confused and almost indistinguishable, and the reversal of two consonants is not uncommon).

8. shrivelled me up: this is a meaning the root can have in Syriac, but it is not very appropriate here; cf. *AV* 'filled me with wrinkles'. In Syriac, too, the intransitive form can mean 'be drawn (with pain)'. In *OT* the root is found only

which is a witness against me;
and my leanness has risen up against me,
it testifies to my face.
⁹ He has torn me in his wrath, and hated me;
he has gnashed his teeth at me;
my adversary sharpens his eyes against me.

---

here and in 22.16, where it cannot have either of these meanings. In both of these passages the meaning 'seize', 'lay hold of', found also in Syriac and in post-biblical Hebrew, is more suitable. The subject (see above) is 'my calamity'.

which is a witness: this is not very lucid. It is better to render 'it (i.e. my calamity) is a witness'. In the eyes of men the fact of his sufferings was the evidence of his sin. The words 'and has risen against me' stand in M.T. immediately after this and should be taken here.

my leanness: in Ps. 109.24 the cognate verb has the meaning 'become gaunt', and hence the meaning 'leanness' can be justified here. On the rearrangement of the text of verses 7f. (see above) this word becomes the subject of 'testifies'. The fact that Job is shrunk to a skeleton is to men testimony to his guilt. Elsewhere the word rendered 'leanness' has the meaning 'lying' (cf. Ps. 59.12 (M.T. 13); Nah. 3.1; Hos. 7.3 (*RSV* 'treachery'); 10.13 (*RSV* 'lies'); 12.1 (*RSV* 'falsehood')). Dillmann preferred this meaning, but 'my lie testifies against me' is not convincing. Dhorme points the consonants as an adjective, 'my deceptive one' (i.e. a false witness), while Larcher makes a greater change to secure 'it testifies against me with lies'. These are not to be preferred to *RSV*.

9. The figure here is of a wild beast, with whom God is compared.

He hath torn me in his wrath: lit. 'his wrath has made (me) its prey'.

and hated me: the root means 'persecute' (so *RV* here, and *RSV* in 30.21; cf. Gen. 49.23 ('harassed'), or 'hate' (so *AV* here, and *RSV* in Gen. 27.41; 50.15; cf. Ps. 55.3 (M.T. 4, 'cherish enmity against'), and the noun 'hated' in Hos. 9.7f.). Tur-Sinai translates 'hunteth', and this is more relevant to the figure of a wild beast pursuing its prey than 'hate' or 'persecute'.

gnashed his teeth: cf. Ps. 37.12. The meaning is in anger; cf. Ac. 7.54. In Mt. 8.12 it is the expression of unspeakable misery.

sharpness: the verb is used of whetting a sword in Ps. 7.12 (M.T. 13); here of looking keenly, as an animal looks for its prey. The whole verse describes how with concentrated hostile attention God relentlessly pursues Job. Duhm deletes the last line of this verse and the whole of verses 10f. and is followed by Gray, Hölscher and Fohrer, while Siegfried deletes verses 10f. Others find no reason to reject these verses. The reason for the rejection is to conform the passage to our tidy ideas and finish the verses relating to God before coming to those relating to men. The poet should not be treated as an essayist.

¹⁰ Men have gaped at me with their mouth,
   they have struck me insolently upon the cheek,
   they mass themselves together against me.
¹¹ God gives me up to the ungodly,
   and casts me into the hands of the wicked.
¹² I was at ease, and he broke me asunder;
   he seized me by the neck and dashed me to pieces;
   he set me up as his target,
¹³   his archers surround me.
   He slashes open my kidneys, and does not spare;

---

10. Men have gaped: the subject has to be supplied. These are the people who like jackals follow God's attack on Job by their assaults. The figures used here are all of human actions. The verb is used of opening the mouth wide, either in eager desire (cf. 29.23), or in greed to swallow (cf. Isa. 5.14); cf. Ps. 22.13 (MT. 14), where the verb is different.

struck me: insulting me; cf. Ps. 3.7 (M.T. 8); Mic. 5.1 (M.T. 4.14); Lam. 3.30.

mass themselves: D. Winton Thomas (*JJS*, III, 1952, pp. 47ff.) has shown that this verb sometimes has a military connotation='mobilise'. Kissane renders 'They have their way against me', but this is less satisfactory.

11. ungodly: the Hebrew word *'awîl* means 'child' (cf. 19.18; 21.11). Either we must give it an unusual meaning here, deriving it from a different root, or we should read *'awwāl*, which means 'unrighteous' (27.7). The parallel makes it clear that this is the meaning. Some retain M.T. and render 'knavish child', but here the significant element has to be brought to the word.

12. Job here emphasises the suddenness and unexpectedness of God's onslaught. Driver (*SVT*, III, 1955, p. 78) thinks the picture intended is that of a beast of prey catching small game, in which case **broke me asunder** and **dashed me in pieces** are inappropriate. He adduces Arabic cognates to provide the meanings 'mangled' or 'worried' and 'dismembered' or 'mauled'. On this view the last line of the verse introduces a quite different figure. But all the verse may be a description of a human attack. Gray connects the first of these verbs with that found in Ps. 74.13 (*RSV* 'divide'); Isa. 24.19 (*RSV* 'rent asunder'), and renders 'cleft me asunder'. The second verb is found elsewhere only in Jer. 23.29, where it is used of a hammer shattering a rock.

the neck: cf. Gen. 49.8.

target: not the same word as in 7.25, but that found in 1 Sam. 20.20; Lam. 3.12.

13. archers: so Jer. 50.29. LXX, Syr., Targ. and Vulg. here have 'arrows', and many editors follow this as more appropriate. Job is the target at which God shoots.

slashes open: the verb means 'cleave' (cf. Ps. 141.7) or 'pierce' (cf. Prov. 7.23).

he pours out my gall on the ground.
14 He breaks me with breach upon breach;
   he runs upon me like a warrior.
15 I have sewed sackcloth upon my skin,
   and have laid my strength in the dust.
16 My face is red with weeping,
   and on my eyelids is deep darkness;
17 although there is no violence in my hands,
   and my prayer is pure.

For the thought, though the verb is different, cf. Lam. 3.12f.
my gall: the word is found only here; but a closely similar word stands in 13.26 (*RSV* 'bitter things'); 20.14, 25 (*RSV* 'gall'). For the thought, cf. Lam. 2.11.

   14. The figure now changes to the storming of a stronghold.
warrior: better than *AV* and *RV* 'giant'.

   15. sewed: the verb used of sewing fig leaves in Gen. 3.7.
sackcloth: the sign of mourning, which was worn next to the skin (2 Kg. 6.30). The sewing of it on may indicate, as Davidson suggests, that it was to be his permanent garment. But Strahan thinks the expression is a pregnant one, and that the meaning is that he sewed a garment of sackcloth which he wore next to his skin.
laid my strength: lit. 'I have caused my horn to enter'. The horn is a common symbol of strength or of pride. *AV* 'defiled my horn' follows Rashi. For this we should expect *gēʾaltî* instead of *ʿōlaltî*. Svi Rin (*BZ*, N.F., VII, 1963, p. 23) renders M.T. 'I shall lower, or dip my horn in the dust', adducing Ugaritic evidence.

   16. is red: better than *AV* and *RV* 'is foul', which follows Ḳimḥi. The verb, which is found only here, means 'is inflamed'. From the same root comes the word for 'ass' (from its reddish brown colour). Davidson notes that involuntary weeping is said to be a symptom of elephantiasis.
eyelids: *pars pro toto*: the eyelids stand for the eyes.
deep darkness: cf. on 3.5.

   17. Cf. Isa. 53.7. Ewald observes: 'If everything on earth is lost and all present things are destroyed, if even the ancient God of the outward world appears to fail and must be given up, nevertheless innocence, with its clear conscience, can neither give up itself nor the eternal, necessary God.' In his despair all that Job has to cling to is his consciousness of innocence, and to this he clings unwaveringly.
my prayer is pure: when the hands are not clean, prayer is unacceptable to God (Isa. 1.15), but when the hands are clean, it is acceptable (Job 11.13f.). In 31.7 Job affirms that his hands are clean, and here that his prayer is pure.

¹⁸ 'O earth, cover not my blood,
      and let my cry find no resting place.
¹⁹ Even now, behold, my witness is in heaven,
      and he that vouches for me is on high.
²⁰ My friends scorn me;
      my eye pours out tears to God,
²¹ that he would maintain the right of a man with God,
      like that of a man with his neighbour.
²² For when a few years have come

JOB'S APPEAL TO HIS WITNESS IN HEAVEN 16.18–17.9

Assured that death is imminent, Job calls on the earth not to cover his blood, so that it may cry to God (cf. Gen. 4.10) for vindication. Davidson says it is impossible to escape the conclusion that Job prays or hopes for vindication not before but after death (so also Peake). This passage is therefore an important stage in the development of his thought towards 19.24ff. In his consciousness of innocence he scorns the friends who had failed him and turns from the God in whom they believed and the God he himself feels to be the source of his misery to the God who alone is worthy to be God.

18. Cf. Isa. 26.21. The assault of God upon Job, described in the preceding verses, of which death is the only issue, is equivalent to murder. And Job, being thus murdered by God, would give God no rest until he is cleared.

my blood: here figurative, and not actual blood shed.

no resting place: the Hebrew says simply 'no place'. M. Dahood (*The Bible in Current Catholic Thought*, ed. McKenzie, pp. 61f.) adduces passages from the Hadad and Eshmunazar inscriptions where the corresponding word has the meaning 'burial place' or 'tomb', and this may be the meaning here.

19. my witness: most scholars identify the witness with God. But Mowinckel (*BZAW*, XLI, 1925, pp. 207ff.) contested this, and he has been followed by Irwin (in *Peake's Commentary*, 1962, p. 398), and Pope, who hold that the witness is to be identified with the Mediator (see below, on verse 20) and the Redeemer (or Vindicator) of 19.25 (cf. Terrien, in *IB*), who is other than God. But it is to God that shed blood cries, and the psychological penetration of the struggle between two conceptions of God in Job's mind is greater than trust in a second heavenly figure.

he that vouches for me: *AV* 'my record'. Here we have an Aramaic synonym of the word 'witness'. The abstract noun 'witness' stands in Gen. 31.47 as the equivalent of the Hebrew word for 'witness'.

20. my friends scorn me: lit. 'my scorners (*mᵉlîṣay*) are my friends'. The word *mēlîṣ* has the meaning 'mediator' in 33.23 (cf. Gen. 42.23, 'interpreter'; Isa. 43.27), and Irwin and Pope (see on verse 19) give it the same meaning here,

Irwin rendering 'my mediator (sing.) is my friend' (cf. also Lindblom, *Composition du livre de Job*, 1945, p. 62), and Pope 'mediator of my thoughts (to God)' (taking the second word as in Ps. 139.2). Kissane renders 'My cry' (taking the second word as in Mic. 4.9; Exod. 32.17) 'is my advocate' (reading singulars, and taking the first word as in Targ.), while P. Joüon (*MFO*, II, 1912, p. 442) renders 'my friends are my advocates', but Job's complaint is that his friends are his accusers, not his advocates. The normal meaning of the verb from which *mēlîṣ* comes is 'scorn' (cf. Ps. 119.51 (*RSV* 'deride'); 1.1 (*RSV* 'scoffers'); Prov. 3.34; Hos. 7.5 (*RSV* 'mockers'), and this is more probably the meaning here. The word rendered 'friends' is used for Eliphaz, Bildad and Zophar in 2.11, 32.3, and 42.10, and it is more natural to find the same reference here than to find Job calling a mediator at the heavenly court his companion. LXX renders the verse 'May my prayer come to the Lord, and before him may my eye shed tears', and Beer reconstructed the Hebrew to agree with this. This would yield a well-balanced verse, but it is not easy to see how this could have become *mᵉlîṣay rēʿāy*, and Peake pronounces it inferior to M.T. Various other conjectural reconstructions have been attempted, but none are convincing. As the text stands it is, as Peake says, 'deeply moving. Mocked and betrayed by his friends, he lifts his face, all bathed in tears, to God. . . . The native instinct, crushed by God's cruelty, still springs irrepressibly to seek its satisfaction in Him.'

21. that: Dhorme reads 'Would that!', with the addition of one letter.

maintain the right: this is the verb from which 'umpire' (9.33) comes. It means 'reprove', 'argue', 'reason' (Isa. 1.18). In 9.33 Job had lamented that there was none to whom he might appeal to stand between him and God. He now longs that God would himself take up his case and present it to himself!

a man (2°): M.T. has 'a son of man' (so *RV*), but we should probably read *bên*='between (a man and)', instead of *ben*='son (of man with)'. 'A son of man' simply means 'a man', i.e. Job.

neighbour: Duhm thought the parallelism showed that this means God. But that is very improbable. The word used is the same as that for 'friend' in verse 20, and it is probable that it has the same meaning here as there. It could not mean the mediator here, and so probably does not there (see on verse 20). There the plural is used of the three friends, and here the singular is used in a general sense, rather than of Eliphaz in particular. *RSV* is probably right in taking the line as a comparison. That God should take up the case of a man against his neighbour might be expected, but that he should take up a man's case against himself is a daring thought.

22. This verse seems to mean that the time is short for God to answer his plea before death comes, and since this is held to be inconsistent with verse 18, Bickell proposed to read 'mourning women' (*šōnôṯ mispēḏ*) for 'a few years' (*šᵉnôṯ mispār*), who would appear on the scene immediately after Job's expected imminent death. But it is not necessary to make this change, and the term for 'mourning women' in Jer. 9.16 is different. Job but relapses into the thought of the inevitability and the finality of death that has been expressed before (7.9f.; 10.21).

I shall go the way whence I shall not return.

17 My spirit is broken, my days are extinct,
the grave is ready for me.
² Surely there are mockers about me,
and my eye dwells on their provocation.

---

a few years: lit. 'years of number', i.e. that can easily be numbered. The same idiom is found in Gen. 34.30; Ps. 105.12; Ezek. 12.16 (lit. 'men of number').

17.1. In this verse we have three short lines instead of two longer ones. This is probably deliberate. Job is represented as speaking under great emotional strain, perhaps due to some spasm of pain. This would account for the thought that death is imminent, immediately after he has said that but few years were left to him.

is broken: the meaning is not the same as in Ps. 51.17 (M.T. 19). Job is here thinking that his life is finished. The verb used here means 'is ruined' or 'is destroyed' (cf. Mic. 2.10). In Arabic it is used of mental derangement, but the parallel does not favour that meaning here. LXX reads 'I am perishing, borne away by the wind, And I beg for the grave, and do not obtain it'. This is not an improvement on the Hebrew. The same is to be said of Duhm's 'His spirit has destroyed my days, The grave is left to me', and Ball's 'My spirit is too disordered for speech, Words are abhorrent to me.'

are extinct: the verb *zāʿak* is found only here. It is either a by-form of, or an error for, *dāʿak*, which is used of a lamp being snuffed out (18.5, 6; 21.17), or of wadies running dry (6.17). This latter verb is found in some MSS. Fohrer follows Beer in reading 'My spirit is destroyed in me (*immî* for *yāmay*, 'my days'), The grave is left (*neʿezebû*, for *nizʿākû* 'is extinct') for me'. This is less effective than the staccato utterance of M.T.

grave: the word is plural in Hebrew (cf. *AV*), probably plural of extension, or perhaps meaning 'the graveyard'. Coverdale has 'I am harde at deathes dore'.

2. Surely: the Hebrew has the formula introducing an oath='I swear that' (as in 31.36).

mockers are about me: the noun is abstract='mockery'. It comes from a by-form (cf. 1 Kg. 18.27) of the verb used in 13.9, meaning 'deceive', 'mock'. Dhorme takes the preposition to mean 'aimed at', and renders 'I am an object of derision'. I. Eitan (*HUCA*, XII–XIII, 1937–38, pp. 78f). rendered 'dotards', connecting the word with an Arabic root meaning 'disorder the mind'.

my eye dwells on their provocation: the meaning is here obscure, and the Versions give no help in any convincing emendation. Duhm proposed, on the basis of Vulg. and Syr. 'on bitter things' instead of 'their provocation', and Dhorme 'in bitterness (my eye passes the nights)'. Neither seems very suitable.

³ 'Lay down a pledge for me with thyself;
   who is there that will give surety for me?
⁴ Since thou hast closed their minds to understanding,
   therefore thou wilt not let them triumph.
⁵ He who informs against his friends to get a share
   of their property,
   the eyes of his children will fail.

Hölscher changed the verb, and secured 'my eye is weary of their contentious-ness', and is followed by Fohrer. G. R. Driver (*SVT*, III, 1955, p. 78) renders 'mine eyes are wearied by (i.e. I am tired of) your stream of peevish complaints' (adducing an Arabic root, meaning 'pour out (water, tears, words)'). For the thought of words and deeds provoking the eyes, cf. Isa. 3.8 (*AV* and *RV* 'to provoke the eyes of his glory').

3. Lay down a pledge for me: the Hebrew has 'Lay down, pledge me' (cf. *AV*). Instead of the second verb we should read a noun (*'ēreḇōnî* for *'ōreḇēnî*) with *RSV* and almost all modern editors, following Syr. Job here turns to address God, beseeching him to act as guarantor for Job to himself. Peake compares Heb. 6.13ff., where God, because he can find none greater than himself to swear by, swears by himself. So here, Job asks him to give surety to himself.

give surety for me: lit. 'strike himself into my hand'. The expression 'strike the hand' is used elsewhere for becoming surety (cf. Prov. 22.26; also 11.18, without 'hand'). Here the form is a little unusual, and some editors read 'strike his hand for me'.

4. This verse is omitted by Bickell, Duhm and Ball, following LXX, which omits verses 3*b*–5*a*. It offers the explanation of the previous line. The **their** refers to Job's friends, to whom he might be expected to turn for help. The **who?** of verse 3 appears to mean 'who else but God?' since the friends are deprived by him of insight. Dhorme would make this plainer by making the second line read 'Therefore their hand is not raised', and comments 'Job is explaining why it is that no one is prepared to strike his hand as his guarantor'. Others take the view represented by *RSV* that Job is confident that God will not allow the expectations of the friends to triumph.

5. This verse is very cryptic. *AV* 'He that speaketh flattery to his friends' rests on the Jewish commentators, and connects the word rendered 'flattery' with the root meaning 'be smooth'. *RV* 'He that denounceth his friends for a prey' connects it with the root meaning 'divide' or 'share', and takes the verb as in Jer. 20.10. *RSV* varies the words, but secures the same essential meaning. On this view Job's friends are represented as turning on him for no higher motive than to secure the informer's share of the sequestrated property of the one they denounce. The verse then promises that their children will suffer for their heartlessness. Budde

⁶ 'He has made me a byword of the peoples,
    and I am one before whom men spit.
⁷ My eye has grown dim from grief,
    and all my members are like a shadow.

---

understood the sharing to be in a meal, and vocalized the noun as a verb, obtaining 'One invites his friends to share his table (while his own children's eyes fail (from starvation))'. Peake follows this (cf. also Dhorme and Buttenwieser), observing 'The friends have no understanding, but they invite Job to partake of their wisdom, while they have not enough wisdom to supply their own needs at home'; but Gray disputes the justification for the rendering 'invites'. Kissane, who also follows the view of Budde, holds that the verse is not directed against Job's friends, but against God, who is here likened to a man who let his children starve while he entertained others. On this view Job is the child allowed to starve by the failure to answer his plea. Ehrlich understood the sharing to be in the inheritance a man left, and found here a picture of a man bequeathing all his property to his friends and leaving his own children penniless. On the whole, the view of *RSV* seems to be the most satisfactory. In the previous verse Job had said that God would not suffer his friends to triumph, and here he says that their treachery will recoil upon their children too.

6. He has made me: God is here referred to in the third person. LXX has 'Thou hast made me', and many editors follow this. Ibn Ezra thought that it was Job's sufferings that had made him a byword, but noted that others had thought the reference was to Eliphaz. The verb could be indefinite third person singular, equivalent to a passive in English, 'I have been made' (so Dhorme).

one before whom men spit: M.T. 'a spitting to the face'. The word *tōpet* = 'spitting', is found only here, but the verbal root is found in cognate languages. *AV* 'tabret' follows Rashi, and connects the word with *tōp* (='timbrel'). This is manifestly less appropriate. Spitting in the face is a grievous insult (cf. Dt. 25.9; Isa. 50.6; Mt. 26.67). Targ. identified the word with Topheth (Jer. 7.31f.). Perles proposed to read *mōpēt* = 'a portent' and many editors follow this reading, and also read, with LXX, Syr. and Vulg. 'before them' instead of 'to the face'. But this is unnecessary. For the thought, cf. 30.9f.

7. has grown dim: the same verb is used of eyesight failing through age in Gen. 27.1; Dt. 34.7, and the adjective in 1 Sam. 3.2. Here it is grief which is the cause.

all my members: the Hebrew has 'my members . . . all of them'. Beer proposed to read 'all of them' as a verbal form, 'my members as a shadow fail' (cf. 33.21), and some editors, including Dhorme and Fohrer, follow this. The word for 'members' is found only here in *OT*. It means 'formed things'. With

⁸ Upright men are appalled at this,
   and the innocent stirs himself up against the godless.
⁹ Yet the righteous holds to his way,
   and he that has clean hands grows stronger and stronger.
¹⁰ But you, come on again, all of you,
   and I shall not find a wise man among you.

---

the same consonants Budde read 'my imaginations', on the basis of Syr. This is less good. It is the body of Job which has shrunk to a skeleton.

8. Many editors (Duhm, Gray, Ball, Hölscher, Stevenson, Fohrer) hold verses 8–10 to be out of place, while others (Peake, Kissane, Pope) hold at least verses 8f. to be out of place. It is noted that verse 11 gives a good connection with verse 7. Ball holds that they are certainly authentic, since there is an echo of them in Bildad's speech (18.20), and he transfers them to the end of the chapter. Others make different transfers (Duhm assigns them to Bildad, and places them after 18.3). Dhorme, however, defends their retention where they are. Similarly Davidson retains them where they are and finds here perhaps the most surprising and lofty passage in the book, warning against the temptation to let faith waver at the sufferings of the righteous through indignation against the wicked who thrive, and affirming that the truly righteous man will go on from strength to strength in unfaltering righteousness.

are appalled: the same verb as that found in Isa. 52.14, where *RSV* has 'astonished' (cf. *AV*, *RV* here). With the addition of a letter, Ehrlich reads 'rejoice'; but this is to be rejected.

innocent ... godless: Merx and Bickell would transpose these words, following one MS. of LXX; but this is rejected by Budde and Dhorme.

stirs himself up against: The verb means 'to rouse oneself to excitement'. In 31.29 it is to pleasurable excitement, and so some understand it here (whence the emendation to 'rejoice', see above). But here it is more likely that it means in displeasure, as *RSV*.

9. 'The human spirit rises to the height of moral grandeur, when it proclaims its resolution to hold on the way of righteousness independently both of men and God' (Davidson). 'These words of Job are like a rocket which shoots above the tragic darkness of the book, lighting it up suddenly, although only for a short time' (Delitzsch).

JOB'S ANTICIPATION OF DEATH AS THE END OF HIS TROUBLES 17.10–16

Job rejects the hopes of restoration which his friends had held out to him. Never again would he be able to achieve his purposes. Only Sheol was before him.

10. come on again: i.e. repeat your arguments. Job is undismayed by their assaults, and confident that they will only expose their folly.

¹¹ My days are past, my plans are broken off,
   the desires of my heart.
¹² They make night into day;
   "The light," they say, "is near to the darkness".
¹³ If I look for Sheol as my house,
   if I spread my couch in darkness,
¹⁴ if I say to the pit, "You are my father,"
   and to the worm, "My mother", or "My sister,"
¹⁵ where then is my hope?
   Who will see my hope?
¹⁶ Will it go down to the bars of Sheol?
   Shall we descend together into the dust?'

---

11. This verse again consists of three short lines (cf. verse 1), reflecting the strong emotion of Job. LXX has the normal rhythm and reads 'My days passed in roaring, and the joints of my heart were broken'. This has not satisfied editors, and very many emendations have been proposed, few of which have been acceptable to more than their proposers. It seems best, therefore, to leave the text as it is. The general sense is clear. Job feels that death is near, being perhaps once more convulsed with pain.

my plans. This word elsewhere has only a bad sense. But though the root from which it comes most often has a bad sense, it is also used of God's purposes, and in Zech. 8.15 of his purpose to bless. Another noun from the same root, which again is frequently used of evil purpose, is used in 42.2 of God's purposes, and in Prov. 1.4 it means 'discretion' (cf. Prov. 2.11; 3.21; 5.2; 8.12). There is no necessary evil nuance in the word.

desires. This word elsewhere means 'possessions', from the root *yāraš*. But it could equally well come from the root *'āraš*='desire', from which another noun, found in Ps. 21.2 (M.T. 3, *RSV* 'request') is derived. There is therefore no insuperable barrier to the retention of the text.

12. This verse did not stand originally in LXX. It is thought to represent the false comfort of Job's friends, who pretend that night is day and hold out false hopes that light is at hand (cf. 5.17ff.; 8.20ff.; 11.13ff.). Dhorme thinks the first line is a continuation of verse 11: 'The desires of my heart change the night into day'; but this is rhythmically impossible.

they make night into day: cf. Isa. 5.20.

they say. The words are supplied in the translation. The rendering **is near to the darkness** is questionable, and Dhorme omits one letter and renders 'is closer than darkness' (cf. Weiser and Fohrer).

13. Job here returns to his morbid longing for death. Duhm rejects the rendering of verses 13–15 represented by *RSV*, and so Dhorme, who says it yields 'a series

18

Then Bildad the Shuhite answered:
² 'How long will you hunt for words?

---

of truisms worthy of La Palisse' (cf. also Peake). They prefer the rendering represented by *RV* marg.: 'If I hope, Sheol is mine house' (Dhorme: 'Can I hope again? Sheol is my home'). On this view, Sheol is the best that Job can hope for. But Ball objects that the verb 'hope' requires an object. He therefore reads 'Yea' for 'If'.

spread: Ehrlich changed one letter to yield 'deck' (cf. Prov. 7.16). But this is unnecessary.

couch: This word is found in Gen. 49.4; Ps. 63.6 (M.T. 7); 132.3; 1 Chr. 5.1; the cognate verb stands in Ps. 139.8.

14. to the pit: this is better than *AV* and *RV* 'corruption', which derives the word from the root meaning 'act corruptly', instead of from that meaning 'sink down'. The word is found also in Ps. 16.10, where Sutcliffe (*The Old Testament and the Future Life*, 1946, pp. 76ff.) defends the translation 'corruption'. But the view of *RSV* is the more probable, and is accepted by almost all scholars. In Ezek. 19.4, 8 the meaning 'pit' is certain, and in Job 33.18, 22, 28, where it is used of the grave, *AV* and *RV* give it the meaning of 'pit'. Here it stands parallel to 'the worm', but in Ps. 16.10 it stands parallel to Sheol, and here there is nothing in the context to require the meaning 'decomposition'.

15. Poor is the prospect Job sees before him, quite other than the rosy hope of restoration which the friends predicted if only he would confess his sin and repent.

my hope (2°). LXX seems to have read two different words in this verse, and as the repetition is not good most editors change the second to 'my happiness'. Without change of text Guillaume (*Promise and Fulfilment*, edited by F. F. Bruce, 1963, p. 113) gives an Arabic sense to the word and renders 'my steadfast piety'.

16. the bars of Sheol. The meaning 'bars' is very doubtful, and if it is correct, the bars stand for the gates of Sheol. But LXX has 'with me to Sheol', and many editors follow this reading. Dahood (*The Bible in Current Catholic Thought*, p. 62) retains M.T., but regards the word *baddê* as a contraction for *bîdê*='into the hands (or power) of'.

Shall we descend? This rendering follows LXX and Syr., with the change of a vowel from M.T., and most editors follow this. M.T. has a noun, 'rest'; cf. *AV* 'when our rest together is in the dust', *RV* 'when once there is rest in the dust'. Neither of these is a true rendering of the Hebrew, and it is best to read as *RSV*. Job will carry such hope and happiness as are left to him, unworthy of such description as they are, to the grave.

THE SECOND SPEECH OF BILDAD 18

Bildad now returns to the attack with less subtlety than Eliphaz, though in no less doctrinaire a way. Whereas Eliphaz had described the fears bred of the evil

Consider, and then we will speak.
3 Why are we counted as cattle?
Why are we stupid in your sight?
4 You who tear yourself in your anger,
shall the earth be forsaken for you,
or the rock be removed out of its place?
5 'Yea, the light of the wicked is put out,
and the flame of his fire does not shine.

---

conscience of the wicked, Bildad describes the miserable experiences he en-
counters. He leaves it to be inferred that misfortune is the proof of wickedness,
which is the assumption of all the friends. Strahan says 'While Job, as a spiritual
pioneer, strikes out for himself a new path in every successive speech, and is
rewarded with wonderful vistas of hitherto unexplored and unimagined truth,
his friends keep to the beaten, monotonous tracks, which lead them through no
land of far distances. . . . On the present occasion Bildad the traditionalist is as
brilliant as he is truculent.' The speech falls into two parts: Why is Job so contemptuous of the friends? (verses 2-4); the fate of the wicked (verses 5-21).

WHY IS JOB SO CONTEMPTUOUS? 18.2-4
Briefly Bildad complains that Job has no respect for his friends, and is so egotistical
that he expects the order of nature to be changed in his favour.
  2. hunt for words: lit., as *RV*, 'lay snares for words'. The word for 'snares'
(*ḳinṣê*) is found only here, and is explained from an Arabic cognate, meaning
'ensnare (an animal)'. *AV* 'How long will it be ere you make an end of words?'
treated the word as equivalent to *ḳēṣ*, and by adding 'will it be ere' did violence
to the Hebrew. Job is curiously addressed in the plural here, and Ewald supposed
that this was because Bildad would only treat Job as belonging to the company
of the wicked. LXX read a singular verb, and editors in various ways restore a
singular. LXX has 'How long wilt thou not cease (talking)?' and from this Gray
reconstructs 'How long will you not be silent?' Ball keeps closer to the Hebrew,
but supplies a negative from the Greek and secures the sense of *AV* 'How long
wilt thou not make an end?', or alternatively proposes a conjectural reading 'How
long wilt thou not restrain words?' By different processes others reach a similar
result, while some think Bildad complains that Job is restraining words, but those
of the friends. They base this on an alleged Akkadian word *ḳinṣu*, to which the
meaning 'bridle' is assigned, but Driver (*SVT*, III, 1955, p. 79n.) says this is a
misreading, and *ḳinṣu* did not exist in this sense (cf., however, Dhorme). He
himself secures the same sense, however, by reversing the consonants and reading
ṣinōḳ (cf. Jer. 29.26, 'collar'), which he explains from Syriac. Tur-Sinai, adducing
Akkadian evidence (cf. also Dhorme), finds the opposite meaning, and gives to

the word *ḳinṣê* the meaning of 'whip': 'How long will you put the whip to words?' The general sense seems rather to be that Job set no restraint to his own speech than that he is restraining his friends, and it is hard to see what relevance to laying traps for words can be found in anything Job has said.

Consider: this again is plural, and editors substitute singular. With the change of a letter Dhorme reads 'Listen'. LXX has 'Leave off (sing.), that *we* may speak', and many editors follow this. This involves the reading of the pronoun 'we', used here for emphasis, instead of the word 'afterwards' (*RSV* 'then'). The debate between Job and his friends often lacks courtesy, and on both sides charges are bandied about. Dhorme says 'it is an ill-judged rhetorical device to say to one's listeners: be intelligent!' But harder things than this are said in the course of the debate. A. Guillaume (*ALUOS*, Supplement ii, 1968, p. 99) connects the verb with an Arabic root and renders 'express yourselves plainly'.

3. why are we stupid?: *AV* has 'reputed vile' and *RV* 'become unclean'. But this is not very appropriate. Hence many editors point the word differently, with some MSS., and derive it from a different root, yielding the sense of *RSV*. LXX has 'why have we been silent?'; but the friends have not been silent, and this is not appropriate. Reading the same consonants as LXX, but deriving from a different root, Dhorme secures 'why have we been likened?', and then completes the sense by adding 'to cattle', giving a good parallel to the previous line, and completing the rhythm (cf. Ball, Kissane). For the thought of the verse cf. Ps. 73.22.

4. Duhm transfers 17.8–10*a* to precede this verse (cf. note on 17.8). As this verse consists of three lines, some have thought a line has fallen out, while Fohrer deletes the first line as a gloss.

You who tear yourself: lit. 'O tearer of himself'. Job is here accused of letting his passion carry himself away, to his own injury. Kissane connects this line with the previous verse, and supposes that it is the brute beast that rends itself in wrath. This is less likely. In 16.9 Job said God tore him in his wrath, and to this Bildad retorts that Job tears himself.

shall the earth be forsaken?: Bildad means that Job's violent protests against his sufferings, which on the friends' view were but the working out of the moral principles on which the world is founded, were as unreasonable as it would be to expect the order of nature to be overturned for his convenience. Dahood (*JBL*, LXXVIII, 1959, p. 306) renders 'shall the earth be rearranged for your sake?' connecting the verb with a different root='repair', for which Arabic and Ugaritic evidence is offered.

the rock be removed: cf. 14.18*b*, where Job had said that in the course of nature the rock is removed. The point Bildad is making here is that this does not take place for Job's convenience.

THE FATE OF THE WICKED 18.5–21

Bildad describes in a speech 'studded with sententious and proverbial sayings' (Davidson) the misfortunes which befall the wicked and the blotting out of his family and the horror which his very memory arouses.

⁶ The light is dark in his tent,
  and his lamp above him is put out.
⁷ His strong steps are shortened
  and his own schemes throw him down.
⁸ For he is cast into a net by his own feet,
  and he walks on a pitfall.
⁹ A trap seizes him by the heel,
  a snare lays hold of him.

---

5. Cf. Prov. 13.9; 24.20. Job later takes up this word of Bildad's (21.17), and asks how often experience confirms it. The light burning in the house or the fire on the hearth are symbols of prosperity and happiness. Their extinction is the mark of disaster.

is put out: cf. on 17.1.

6. in his tent: the story is set in the patriarchal age, when the tent was the home; cf. 5.24; 8.22; 12.6; 15.34.

above him: hanging from the roof of the tent.

7. His strong steps: lit. 'the steps of his strength', i.e. the confident stride of the prosperous man (cf. Ps. 18.36 (M.T. 37)).

shortened: cf. Prov. 4.12.

his own schemes throw him down: his selfish and impious purpose recoils upon himself, to his own undoing. The word rendered 'schemes' is not the word Job had used in 17.11, but a word meaning 'counsel', commonly used in a good sense. The wisdom of the wicked is but folly. 'Throw him down' is represented in LXX by 'make him stumble', which many editors prefer. This involves the transposition of three letters.

8. This and the following verses develop the thought of the perils into which the wicked walks, and the hidden dangers that surround him. Note the variety of terms for traps and snares which Bildad uses to indicate how full of peril life is for the wicked.

a net: for catching birds (Prov. 1.17) or men (Lam. 1.13; Ps. 140.5 (M.T. 6)).

by his own feet: G. Gerleman (*JSS*, IV, 1959, p. 59) argues that this is an idiomatic expression, meaning 'on the spot'.

pitfall: *AV* 'a snare', *RV* 'the toils'. The word has this meaning only here. In 2 Kg. 1.2 it means a lattice window, and elsewhere it means an ornament of network. The root from which it comes means 'interweave'. Here it appears to mean a light network covering a pit.

9. a trap: a fowler's snare; cf. Hos. 9.8.

a snare: here only with this meaning. The word is found also in 5.9 (cf. note there), where it should be read differently. From the same root a word meaning 'veil' is derived (Isa. 47.2). It apparently denotes a trap with some kind of mesh.

¹⁰ A rope is hid for him in the ground,
  a trap for him in the path.
¹¹ Terrors frighten him on every side,
  and chase him at his heels.
¹² His strength is hunger-bitten,

---

10. a rope: the same word stands in Prov. 5.22 (*RSV* 'toils'); cf. also Ps. 18.5 (M.T. 6), where the same word is parallel to another word for 'snares'.
a trap: this word is found only here, but the root is common, meaning 'to capture', or 'catch'. It is probably a general term for any catching device.

11. Cf. Jer. 20.3f. Bildad is not here referring to imaginary fears conjured up by the conscience of the wicked, but to actual experiences he will have. Terrors are personified and represented as chasing him on every side and filling him with dread. Pope thinks the terrors here are demons.
chase him: the verb is usually employed to denote the scattering of a company. Here it is used of an individual, perhaps to indicate his bewilderment as to which direction to flee in, turning now hither and now thither. Voigt emended the text to read 'and surround (his feet)', but this adds nothing to the first line and is less graphic than M.T. Ehrlich and Driver (*ZAW*, N.F., xxiv, 1953, pp. 259f.) render the Hebrew 'and compel him to make water over his feet', but Dhorme dismisses this as needlessly coarse. LXX has a longer text, and Kissane picks up one of the additional words, 'many', but reads the Hebrew equivalent in the sense 'arrows' (cf. 16.13, where the same word stands), and renders 'from behind arrows shall discomfit him', but this is very doubtful. The Hebrew is much more vigorous as it stands. Terrors are on every side, and whichever way he turns to flee they are hard on his heels, so that they are completely unescapable.

12. His strength is hunger-bitten: the first word could be rendered 'his iniquity' (22.15, *RSV* 'wicked men', lit. 'men of iniquity') or his 'trouble' (5.6, *RSV* 'affliction'), or 'his strength' (verse 7), or 'his wealth' (20.10). Dhorme cites Le Hir for the first of these meanings 'his iniquity yawns before him'. Many editors have followed the second, e.g. Zöckler 'his calamity shows itself hungry', or, with a slight change of one word, Duhm, 'trouble is hungry for him' or, with a different slight change following Syr., Ball, 'Hunger shall be his sorrow'. Most have followed the third, as *RSV*. The meaning is then thought to be 'his strength becomes feeble', as happens through hunger. But this seems forced. By giving an Arabic sense to the verb Guillaume (*Promise and Fulfilment*, edited by F. F. Bruce, 1963, p. 114) secures the same sense. Reiske suggested the addition of a letter which could easily have fallen out by haplography, yielding 'he is hungry amid his strength' (so Szczygiel), and Dhorme adopted this, but with the fourth meaning 'he is hungry amid his wealth', and this is followed by Kissane and Pope. Driver (*ZAW*, N.F., xxiv, 1953, p. 260) derives the word rendered 'is hungry'

and calamity is ready for his stumbling.
¹³ By disease his skin is consumed,
   the first-born of death consumes his limbs.
¹⁴ He is torn from the tent in which he trusted,

---

from another root, for which he offers Arabic authority, meaning 'was terrified', yielding 'his strength was terrified'. Of these the view of Duhm seems the most likely, and the change it involves is very slight. The line is then excellently parallel to the following line.

calamity is ready for his stumbling: the last word could mean, as *RV* marg., 'at his side' (so Dhorme, Stevenson, and Pope). The view of *RSV* connects it with the verb meaning 'limp' (Gen. 32.31 (M.T. 32)). Some editors find this inappropriate, but it is supported by Ps. 35.15; Jer. 20.10 (*RSV* 'fall'), though Ball points out that the ancient versions nowhere recognize the meaning 'stumbling' or 'falling' for the word. Ball himself changes one consonant to get 'ready to swallow him up'. He notes that this is then a favourite word of the author's, but this would make the change more difficult to understand. Tur-Sinai renders 'ready for his rib', by which he understands 'his wife' (cf. the story of the creation of Eve)! Driver (loc. cit.) finds the same word, 'rib', but in the sense of 'force' or 'vigour', and renders 'with disaster waiting his vigour'. The general sense is clear. Calamity is ever ready to overwhelm him.

13. By disease his skin is consumed: the Hebrew is lit. 'It shall consume the limbs of his skin, The firstborn of death shall consume his limbs.' Here the repetition in the verse is not good, and the expression 'the limbs of his skin' is meaningless. In 41.12 (M.T. 4) the word 'limbs' is used of the limbs of Leviathan, and in Ezek. 17.6 the same word is used of the branches of the vine. LXX has here 'let the branches of his feet be eaten'; Syr. 'his cities will be swallowed up by force'; Vulg. 'let it devour the beauty of his skin'; Targ. 'it will devour the linen garments (understanding the word as its homonym='white linen') which cover his skin'. These renderings show that the translators were puzzled to understand the text. The rendering of *RSV* follows the reading proposed by Wright and accepted by very many scholars. This reads 'is consumed' (with LXX and Syriac) and *bideway* for *baddê*.

the first-born of death: this probably means death in its most terrible form. Dhorme thinks it means the demon of the plague. Marshall suggested the worm of corruption. After describing the menaces that beset the wicked man and the errors that affright him, Bildad pictures the disease that attacks his body. This is a savage thrust at Job, so sorely afflicted with disease, here so pointedly used as the evidence of his sin. Tur-Sinai's strange rendering of the verse is scarcely to be recommended: 'he shall eat the strips of his hide; the starving first-born shall eat his own flesh-strips'.

14. He is torn from the tent in which he trusted: lit. 'from his tent, his

and is brought to the king of terrors.
¹⁵ In his tent dwells that which is none of his;
   brimstone is scattered upon his habitation.

---

object of confidence'. The apposition is somewhat strange (but cf. Isa. 32.18, 'in
secure dwellings', lit. 'in dwellings, their objects of confidence'), and *AV* took 'his
confidence' as the subject: 'his confidence shall be rooted out of his tabernacle'.
The verb is used of pulling up tent pegs or cords. Hence Ball substituted 'his
tent-cords' for 'his confidence' and renders 'his cords are broken away from his
tent'. Dhorme, however, notes that verse 15 shows that he no longer inhabits his
tent, so that here it must be the wicked man who is plucked up, or torn away from,
his tent, and *RSV* most probably preserves the meaning.

is brought: the verb may be read as second person 'thou shalt bring him'
(so Dhorme), or third person 'it (or she) shall bring him'. Rashi unkindly suggested that this meant the wife of the wicked. With a very slight change it
reads 'one shall bring him' or 'they shall bring him', equivalent to the passive of
RSV.

the king of terrors: i.e. Death, the king of the underworld (cf. Virgil's *rex
tremendus*, *Georgics*, IV, 469). Pope identifies with the Ugaritic god, Mot.

15. that which is none of his: the Hebrew is strange, lit. 'things of what are
not his'. Kissane took the meaning to be personal, 'strangers'; Gray thought rather
of weeds and wild animals. Dhorme again read the verb as second person, 'thou
shalt dwell', and rendered 'because it is no longer his', meaning the tent. But the
second person is not easy. Duhm proposed *beliyya'al* for *mibbelî lô*, and then
assigned to this word the very doubtful meaning 'incurability'. Theod. renders
'in his night', which represents *belêlô*, which led Voigt, Beer and others to
read *lîlîth*=the Night-hag (Isa. 34.14), and so Ball, who renders 'the Vampire'.
Driver (*SVT*, III, 1955, p. 79) suggests *maḫlêl* or *maḫlûl*='mixed herbs', but this
does not seem likely. More promising is Dahood's suggestion (*Biblica*, XXXVIII,
1957, pp. 312ff.) to read *mabbēl* (vocalization uncertain) and to connect the word
with Akkadian *nablu*='fire' (cf. Ugaritic *nbl*). Fire and brimstone are frequently
associated (Gen. 19.24; Ps. 11.6; Ezek. 38.22). The interchange of *n* and *m* is
common and would provide no difficulty. The parallel with the next line would
then be excellent if Dahood's rendering '(fire) is set (in his tent)' can be accepted for
M.T. 'dwells'. But we should expect a better parallel to 'is scattered'. On the whole
it is best to accept the reading 'Night-hag', which can claim some support from
Theod.

brimstone: or sulphur. It is generally thought that the reference here is to the
destruction of Sodom and Gomorrah, while some find a reference to the calamity
Job had himself experienced (1.16). Ehrlich thought the use of sulphur was for
disinfectant purposes, and Dhorme follows, adducing testimony to show that the
disinfectant properties of sulphur were known to the ancients. Thus Homer

¹⁶ His roots dry up beneath,
and his branches wither above.
¹⁷ His memory perishes from the earth,
and he has no name in the street.
¹⁸ He is thrust from light into darkness,
and driven out of the world.
¹⁹ He has no offspring or descendant among his people,
and no survivor where he used to live.
²⁰ They of the west are appalled at his day,
and horror seizes them of the east.
²¹ Surely such are the dwellings of the ungodly,
such is the place of him who knows not God.'

(*Odyssey*, xxii, 481ff.) refers to the disinfection of a room in which a corpse had been as effected by sulphur.

16. Bildad returns to the comparison of the wicked with vegetable life (cf. 8.11ff.); cf. also 14.7ff. (Job), 15.30 (Eliphaz) for other uses of figures drawn from trees.

branches: a collective term, as in 14.9.

wither: this is a better parallel than *AV* and *RV* 'shall be cut off.' The word could be derived from either root.

17. street: the word may mean 'street' or 'countryside'; cf. on 5.10. Many editors prefer the latter meaning here, as there. They then take 'earth' here to mean inhabited places. For the thought, cf. Ps. 109.15*b*; also Ps. 9.6 (M.T. 7); 34.16 (M.T. 17).

18. The Hebrew has the verbs in the indefinite third person plural, equivalent to the passive, as *AV* and *RSV*. Duhm and Ball replace them by singulars 'He shall thrust him' and 'He shall drive him', understanding the subject to be God, while Beer adds the word 'God' in the second line for metrical reasons. But Dhorme notes that God has little place in this speech of Bildad. Light and darkness here represent life and death (cf. 3.20 and 17.13).

19. offspring or descendant: these words are only found together (Gen. 21.23; Isa. 14·22). They form an alliterative phrase, which Moffatt tries to catch with 'neither son nor scion', and Ball by 'neither chit nor child', and Tur-Sinai less successfully by 'neither breed nor brood'. The lack of descendants was a much-dreaded fate.

where he used to live: lit. 'in his sojournings'. Some take this to mean 'in his home'. As this has already been mentioned as destroyed, it is more probable that it has a wider reference. Peake understands it to mean that no survivor of his family would escape to take refuge with friends, and Dhorme that even where he has made temporary stay no one would be able to perpetuate his memory.

19 Then Job answered:
² 'How long will you torment me,
   and break me in pieces with words?

---

20. of the west ... of the east. *AV* and *RV* have 'they that come after ...
they that went before'. It is difficult to see how those that should come after could
be appalled if all memory of him was lost, and even more difficult to see how
those who preceded him could know of his end, unless with Budde we understand it to mean in Sheol. Ball would avoid the difficulty by understanding the
meaning to be 'his juniors' and 'his seniors'. But this is not the natural meaning.
It is far better to understand the terms as in *RSV*, and so most modern scholars.
Elsewhere we find 'the hinder sea' for the Mediterranean, and 'the front sea' for
the Dead Sea (cf. Zech. 14.8), and this probably supplies the key to the terms here.
Stevenson objects that as applied to persons the terms elsewhere express a time
relationship and not a local sense, and LXX, Syr., Vulg. and Targ. all understood
them as temporal here. He thinks the intention was to speak comprehensively and
to include all men, but this is so on any interpretation.
his day: here equivalent to 'his fate', or the day of his ruin.
horror seizes them: lit. 'they laid hold on horror'. The same idiom is found in
21.6 'laid hold on shuddering'.
21. This verse summarily assures Job that the facts are as Bildad has stated them,
and that wickedness and the fate he has described are directly linked as cause and
effect.

JOB ANSWERS BILDAD 19

Stung by Bildad's speech, Job feels his utter loneliness. Deserted by God and men,
he is utterly friendless. Yet from his very despair, new hope is born, and after a
vain cry to his friends to relent and have pity on him, he rises to a new height of
faith. Though he feels that he will die in his innocence, his faith in God returns
to the thought of the Witness in heaven, and he is confident that God will vindicate
him after his death, and that he will be conscious of his vindication. The speech
falls into four parts: Job's impatience with his friends (verses 2–6); God's abandonment and assault (verses 7–12); he laments his forsaken state and appeals to his
friends (verses 13–22); his assurance of vindication (verses 23–9).

JOB'S IMPATIENCE WITH HIS FRIENDS 19.2–6
Briefly he rebukes them for their cruel words, and reiterates his assurance that God
has unjustly persecuted him.
2. How long? Bildad had begun both his speeches with this expression, and
Job retorts by turning it against him and the other friends.
torment ... break me in pieces: these verbs indicate how crushed Job feels at
the bitter and unfeeling words of his friends. *AV* and *RV* have 'vex' for the
former, but it is much stronger than this. The latter is found with a different

³ These ten times you have cast reproach upon me;
   are you not ashamed to wrong me?
⁴ And even if it be true that I have erred,
   my error remains with myself.
⁵ If indeed you magnify yourselves against me,
   and make my humiliation an argument against me,
⁶ know then that God has put me in the wrong,
   and closed his net about me.
⁷ Behold, I cry out, "Violence!" but I am not answered;
   I call aloud, but there is no justice.
⁸ He has walled up my way, so that I cannot pass,
   and he has set darkness upon my paths.
⁹ He has stripped from me my glory,
   and taken the crown from my head.
¹⁰ He breaks me down on every side, and I am gone,

---

nuance in Isa. 57.15, where the 'crushed', like the man of broken spirit in Ps. 51.17 (M.T. 19), is the contrite. Here the words of the friends do not lead him to contrition, but grievously add to his pain.

3. ten times: a round number, meaning 'often', and not to be taken literally (cf. Gen. 31.7; Num. 14.22).

wrong me: this verb is found only here in OT. The Jewish commentator Ķimḥi rendered 'wonder at me', which connects with the Arabic root hakara, while Delitzsch took it in the causative sense 'astonish me'. Three MSS. have ḥ for h in the word, and this has led Budde, Duhm and others to connect it with the Arabic ḥakara='wrong', 'deal hardly with' (usually by following the three MSS., but Dhorme retains the reading h and justifies the weakening of the consonant), and this is represented in RV and RSV, and is probably right. LXX has 'press upon me' and this Beer follows, emending to secure it. Targ. has 'to acknowledge me as an acquaintance', and Syr. 'sadden me', both involving different readings from M.T. Innumerable emendations have been proposed, to yield 'insult' (Olshausen), 'league yourselves against' (Merx and Siegfried), 'dissemble (lit., makes yourselves strange)' (Graetz; cf. AV), 'trouble' (Bickell and Ball), 'slight' (Tur-Sinai). AV marg. 'harden your faces against' goes back to Ķimḥi's father, as cited by Ķimḥi. Where so appropriate a sense can be secured from M.T., preferably by following the three MSS., it is gratuitous to proliferate emendations.

4. The meaning of this verse is far from clear. It can hardly be an admission of sin on Job's part, and certainly not an admission of secret sin, which is what the friends accuse him of. It is probably a hypothetical sentence, as RSV, though there is no hypothetical particle. Dhorme takes it to mean 'Even if I have erred, that is my concern'. This does not seem very satisfactory, since Job does not complain of the friends for their interference, but for their hostility. Hence it is better to understand it to mean 'Even if I have erred, I have not injured you' (cf. 7.20).

5. According to *RSV*, this verse carries on into verse 6. Dhorme and Fohrer follow some earlier scholars who took this verse as a question 'Will you really magnify yourselves . . . and reproach me . . . ?'

magnify yourselves against: Dhorme renders 'treat me insolently'. The verb has a bad sense, as in Ps. 35.26; 38.16 (M.T. 17, *RSV* 'boast against'); 55.12 (M.T. 13, *RSV* 'deal insolently with').

make . . . an argument against me: this is the verb used in 16.21; see note there. Here it has the sense 'plead (my disgrace) against me'. Job's present humiliation is used by the friends as an argument proving his guilt.

6. This verse confirms that verse 4 is no confession of sin on Job's part. He protests that his misfortunes arise from the caprice of God. In 8.3 Bildad had asked if God perverts justice, and here, using the same verb, Job solemnly declares that in his case God has so perverted it. So far from Job's wayward steps having led him into the toils (cf. 18.8), it is God who has thrown the net around him. The word for 'net' used here is different from any used by Bildad. This is the hunter's net, into which he drives animals.

GOD'S ABANDONMENT AND ASSAULT 19.7–12

In verse 6 Job's thought had passed from the friends to God. This brings him to the thought of his vain cry to God for help, and of the violence of God's attack upon him. Job is as sure as his friends that God is the source of his troubles. But whereas they build everything on the doctrine of divine justice, he builds all on his consciousness of innocence.

7. Violence: i.e. 'Help!' Cf. Jer. 20.8; Hab. 1.2.

cry aloud: better, as *RV*, 'cry for help'; cf. 24.12; 29.12; 30.28; 35.9; 36.13, where the same verb appears.

8. walled up my way: cf. Lam. 3.7, 9; Hos. 2.6 (M.T. 8). See also Job 3.23; 13.27; 14.5, where Job had complained of restrictions which hemmed him in. In 1.10 the Satan had spoken of protective barriers raised by God around Job.

darkness: cf. Lam. 3.2. Guillaume (*Promise and Fulfilment*, edited by F. F. Bruce, 1963, p. 114) with different vowels gives to the word an Arabic sense 'thorn hedge'.

9. God has stripped Job of the honourable reputation he once enjoyed, and has removed from his head the crown which serves as the metaphor for the esteem in which he was once held. Honour is a garment to be worn or stripped off; cf. 29.14; Isa. 61.3 (for shame as a garment cf. Job 8.22). For glory as a crown, cf. Ps. 8.5 (M.T. 6).

10. The metaphor is constantly changed. Here Job uses the figure of a building which is demolished and of a tree which is torn up by the roots; cf. Ps. 52.5 (M.T. 7).

I am gone: i.e. I perish, as in 14.20. The very common verb *hālak* = 'walk', 'go', in several passages has the special nuance 'pass away', 'die', found also in Arabic.

and my hope has he pulled up like a tree.
¹¹ He has kindled his wrath against me,
   and counts me as his adversary.
¹² His troops come on together;
   they have cast up siegeworks against me,
   and encamp round about my tent.
¹³ 'He has put my brethren far from me,
   and my acquaintances are wholly estranged from me.
¹⁴ My kinsfolk and my close friends have failed me;

---

11. his adversary: the Hebrew has 'his adversaries'. *AV* and *RV* interpret 'one of his adversaries'. It is better to omit one letter, with Vulg. and Targ., and to render as *RSV* (LXX and Syr. have 'an adversary'). Note that here and in verse 12 the metaphor changes again, this time to a military one (cf. 10.17; 16.12ff.).

12. siegeworks: lit. their way; the meaning is that they raise a rampart, by which they can come to the attack. The verse is a tristich, and Fohrer deletes the second line as a gloss based on 30.12, in order to restore to a distich. Ball reconstructs a distich, following LXX, to read 'Together his troops fell upon me, they beset my ways with an ambush'.

tent: this word reads oddly. A rampart would hardly be required to attack a tent. It is due to the incompatibility of the military metaphor of siege with the representation elsewhere, as well as here, of Job's residence as a tent.

JOB LAMENTS HIS FORSAKEN STATE AND APPEALS TO HIS FRIENDS **19.13–22**

Deserted by his brethren and kinsmen, his closest friends, his servants and his wife, and despised by children, he cries to his friends to have pity on him and to give him their sympathy and comfort. But they are as unmoved by his appeal as they had been by his reproaches and he finds their inhumanity adds to his affliction. Davidson observes: 'There is something more breaking to the heart in the turning away of men from us than in the severest sufferings. It crushes us quite. We steel ourselves against it for a time and rise to it in bitterness and resentment, but gradually it breaks us and we are crushed at last'.

13. He has put my brethren far: LXX has 'my brethren have gone far', and some editors follow this.

are wholly estranged: LXX appears to have read as one word ('*akzārû* for '*ak zārû*) and to have understood it as a denominative from '*akzār*='cruel', 'have become cruel'. But 'from me' is against this, and the verb is not elsewhere known.

14. M.T. reads, as *AV* and *RV*, 'My kinsfolk have failed, and my familiar friends have forgotten me'. The first line is thus short and verse 15 is overloaded.

¹⁵   the guests in my house have forgotten me;
      my maidservants count me as a stranger;
      I have become an alien in their eyes.
¹⁶ I call to my servant, but he gives me no answer;
      I must beseech him with my mouth.
¹⁷ I am repulsive to my wife,
      loathsome to the sons of my own mother.
¹⁸ Even young children despise me;
      when I rise they talk against me.

Most modern editors redivide to yield four normal lines in the two verses, as *RSV*. For the first line, then, Duhm proposed to read 'My kinsfolk have ceased to know me', which Peake and Strahan approve, but Gray and Dhorme reject. As re-divided, the verses are excellently balanced.

15. The guests I entertained: lit. 'the sojourners of my house'. Davidson took this to mean menials, but *RSV* is to be preferred.

maidservants: to lose the respect and obedience of slaves is the very depth of humiliation.

16. Instead of Job's slaves obeying the slightest sign of his hand (cf. Ps. 123.2), they ignore his wishes when he humbles himself to implore them to attend him.

17. I am repulsive: *AV* and *RV* 'my breath is strange'. The verb is probably to be connected with a different root, meaning 'be loathsome'. For 'my breath' Beer needlessly proposed to read, with a slight change, 'my smell'.

I am offensive: *AV* 'though I intreated'; *RV* 'my supplication'. *AV* and *RV* connected the word with the root *ḥānan* = 'be gracious'. But it is probably to be connected with a different root, meaning 'be offensive', giving the sense of *RSV*. Duhm emended to read 'my stink' and has been followed by some scholars. Others secure the same sense without emendation, by looking to the root 'be offensive'.

the sons of my mother: lit. 'the sons of my womb'. This cannot refer to Job's children, as they were all dead—unless we ascribe to the poet forgetfulness of this. It is unlikely that the reference can be to children of Job's concubines, since there is no suggestion that Job had concubines. The suggestion that the reference is to members of Job's clan is inappropriate, especially since his kinsmen had already been mentioned. The meaning is best understood to be to the womb from which Job himself emerged, i.e. his mother's womb (cf. 3.10).

18. young children: this word is found only here and in 21.11 (in 16.11 it should probably be read differently; see note there). When Job painfully rises and tries to walk, the children jeer at him and laugh at his agony. I. Eitan (*JQR*, N.S., XIV, 1923-24, pp. 38f.) gives a different meaning to the verb, and renders 'run

¹⁹ All my intimate friends abhor me,
   and those whom I have loved have turned against me.
²⁰ My bones cleave to my skin and to my flesh,
   and I have escaped by the skin of my teeth.

---

away from me', or 'turn the back on me', instead of 'talk against me'. This meaning can be justified from Arabic.

19. my intimate friends: lit. 'men of my confidence', i.e. my bosom friends. Cf. Ps. 55.12ff. (M.T. 13ff.).

have turned against me: T. Penar (*Biblica*, XLVIII, 1967, pp. 293ff.) translates 'turn away from me', which would well fit the context.

20. The first line is too long, and the second half is obscure, though it has provided our speech with a proverbial phrase. Also the repetition of 'skin' is not good. Many editors delete 'and to my flesh' in the first line, and read 'with my flesh in my teeth' for 'by the skin of my teeth' in the second. The first line gives the picture of an emaciated form, with bones projecting under the skin (cf. Ps. 22.17). The general sense of the second line must be that he has barely escaped. The suggestion that 'the skin of the teeth' means the gums (so *BDB*) is not convincing. More commonly the line is understood to be a picture of an animal escaping with its young in its mouth, and hence impeded in its flight. But 'my flesh' would be a strange way of referring to its cubs, and the relevance on Job's lips would not be obvious. Some adduce 1 Sam. 28.21 ('I have taken my life in my hand'), and think the flesh in the teeth means the same as the life in the hand. But Job is not saying that he has risked his life, but that he has barely escaped. In 13.14 (see note there) Job was using 'my flesh in my teeth' in the sense of risking his life, but that will not do here. Dhorme follows LXX in the first line, 'In my skin my flesh has rotted away' (reading *beśārî rāḳāḇ* for *ûḇiḇeśārî daḇeḳāh*), and in the second line takes the verb from a different root and renders 'I have gnawed my bone with my teeth' (transferring 'my bone' from the first line and omitting 'skin'). Driver (*SVT*, III, 1955, p. 80) finds the same meaning for the verb, but omits 'my skin' from the first line and renders the second 'I gnawed myself on the skin with my teeth'. Of the innumerable other emendations may be mentioned: 'I escape, my bones in my teeth' (Merx); 'my teeth fall out' (Duhm; cf. Pope, 'my teeth fall from my gums'); 'I am stuck to the skin of my teeth' (Tur-Sinai); 'my bones protrude in sharp points' (Kissane). None of these is convincing, and the precise figure is irrecoverable. What Job is apparently saying in the verse is that he has been reduced by disease to a shadow of his former self and that he has barely survived at all. D. R. Blumenthal (*VT*, XVI, 1966, pp. 497ff.) derives the word rendered 'skin' from two different roots and so finds a pun here. In the first line he follows *RSV*, and in the second renders 'I am left with only the bone in which my teeth are set'.

²¹ Have pity on me, have pity on me, O you my friends,
    for the hand of God has touched me!
²² Why do you, like God, pursue me?
    Why are you not satisfied with my flesh?
²³ 'Oh that my words were written!
    Oh that they were inscribed in a book!

---

21. The repetition of 'Have pity on me' is rhetorically effective, and there is no need to omit the second, with Ball. Peake finely notes that the supreme art of the poet in placing this passage here 'lies in this, that it greatly heightens the effect of the wonderful passage that is to follow. From God he (i.e., Job) turns to man in his desperation, but man fails him, and in a burst of sublime confidence he returns from man to God.'

touched: better 'struck'. This is the verb that stands in Isa. 53.4 (*RSV* 'stricken').

22. like God: Strahan says 'The whole tragedy of the book is packed into these extraordinary words. Job's complaint of his friends is that they are too God-like. What higher ideal can men have than the imitation of God? And yet their conduct may be most inhuman just when it seems to them most divine' (cf. Jn 16.2). It is needless to weaken the meaning here. Reiske and Beer would read 'like a hart', and Neubauer (*Athenaeum*, June 1885, p. 823n.) 'like an avenger'; Fohrer 'like a demon'.

not satisfied with my flesh. In Akkadian, Aramaic (Dan. 3.8, *RSV* 'maliciously accuse'); 6.24 (M.T. 25)), and Arabic 'to eat the pieces' of anyone means 'to slander'. Something of this nuance is to be found here. The friends ceaselessly calumniate Job.

JOB'S ASSURANCE OF VINDICATION 19.23–29

Job desires his avowal of his innocence to be inscribed for future generations. For he is sure that God will vindicate him, and that he will be conscious of his vindication. The passage is very difficult, but this much seems certain. Some editors emend a clearer conception of resurrection into the passage, while others emend out of it any element of such conception. It seems wiser to find Job's leap of faith that reaches, but does not securely grasp, this thought. In whatever condition Job may be, there is no thought of more than the moment of his consciousness of his vindication, and certainly not the thought that the bliss of the Afterlife will make amends for the sufferings of this life. It is not bliss for which Job longs, but vindication. Finally, he warns the friends that for their persecution they will one day stand under judgment.

23. my words: Job is thinking of his protestation of his innocence, which he longs to be preserved after his death.

in a book: usually understood to mean 'a scroll'. But Gehman (*JBL*, LXIII, 1944,

24 Oh that with an iron pen and lead
    they were graven in the rock for ever!
25 For I know that my Redeemer lives,
    and at last he will stand upon the earth;
26 and after my skin has been thus destroyed,

---

pp. 303ff.) notes that in Phoenician the word means 'inscription' and this better accords with the verb used for 'inscribe' (cf. Isa. 30.8) and with the following verse (cf. earlier J. A. Montgomery, *Arabia and the Bible*, 1934, p. 165n.). Pope cites Akkadian *siparru*='bronze' or 'copper' and thinks of something like the Copper Scroll from Qumran. Strahan observes 'how splendidly his idea has been realised! His singular fancy of a testimony in the rocks could not be gratified, but he has his *apologia* in a book which is the masterpiece of Hebrew poetic genius.' Cf. Horace, *Odes* III, xxx, 1: *Exegi monumentum aere perennius.*

24. with an iron pen and lead. Rashi supposed that the meaning was that lead was run into the cut-out letters, and this is followed by Dillmann, Duhm, and Peake. It is often said that there was no evidence that this practice is ancient, but such evidence has been found (cf. K. Galling, *WO*, II, 1954–59, p. 6). Others have thought the writing was on leaden tablets (so Gray, Buttenwieser, Pope), but Dhorme objects that the text should then read 'on lead' rather than 'and lead'. He himself thinks we should translate 'with a tool of iron and lead', and that an alloy of iron and lead was used to mark out the letters before cutting the rock. Tur-Sinai renders 'on a plaque of iron and lead'. Writing on leaden tablets is referred to by Classical writers, and if we follow this we must find two forms of inscription indicated, on leaden tablets and on rock. On the whole, however, it seems best to follow the first view above. C. R. Conder (*PEFQS*, 1905, p. 156) holds that the meaning here is 'red lead', and that the reference is to painting the letters in red after being incised. Cases of this from the third and second centuries B.C. are known.

25. This and the following verses are unusually difficult, and an incredible number of different translations have been offered (for a selection of these, cf. H. H. Rowley, *From Moses to Qumran*, 1963, pp. 180f. n., and for a history of interpretation of the passage to the beginning of this century, cf. J. Speer, *ZAW*, xxv, 1905, pp. 47ff.).

Redeemer. The Hebrew word is used for the next-of-kin, upon whom the duties of avenger of blood, or of levirate marriage, or of redeeming property in danger of sequestration, fell. The word 'Redeemer' evokes wrong ideas, since what Job wanted was not deliverance from Sheol, but the vindication of his name before men. Hence Vindicator is the most appropriate term here. Irwin (and so Pope) finds in the redeemer or vindicator a further allusion to the mediator he found in 16.19 (see note there), but most hold that Job thinks of God himself as the

Vindicator, and that seems most probable (cf. Ps. 19.14 (M.T. 15), where the same term is used of God). Commentators differ as to whether the vindication is to be on this side of the grave or after death, and this affects their approach to the textual problems. Budde finds the anticipated vindication to be in this life, and so Ball who finds merely an anticipation of the actual denouement of the book, when God speaks from the whirlwind. But in the preceding verses Job had recognised that he would see no vindication in this life, and so had sighed for a record of his defence to be preserved for after generations. It therefore seems most likely that his hope was for vindication after death.

at last: this is an adjectival term and not adverbial, and it is an epithet of the Vindicator. Dhorme therefore renders 'as the Last' recalling such passages as Isa. 44.6; 48.12, where God is declared to be the First and the Last. Ball would change the term to make it adverbial, as *RSV*. Siegfried (and so Strahan) would make it clearer that the vindication is to be after Job's death by rendering 'my successor' (cf. Pope 'my guarantor'). Gray and Dhorme dismiss this as without evidence. T. H. Gaster (*VT*, IV, 1954, p. 78n.) renders 'even if he were the last person to exist'.

he will stand: Vulg. has 'I shall arise', thus importing the idea of Job's resurrection. Gray doubts if it points to a different Hebrew reading.

upon the earth: lit. 'upon dust', probably to be understood as in 41.33 (M.T. 25). Some render 'upon my grave', and thus make it explicit that the vindication will be after death (Bickell, Siegfried and Klostermann read 'upon my dust'). This view is rejected by Budde, and Dhorme observes that wherever the word is used of Sheol or the tomb, the context leaves no room for ambiguity.

26. It is in this verse that the problems of translation and interpretation are the greatest, and the versions offered by different scholars diverge most widely.

after my skin has been thus destroyed: it is difficult to see what this can be supposed to mean. Meek (*VT*, VI, 1956, pp. 100ff.) takes it to mean 'after my skin has been struck off', and thinks this meant in this life. Cf. Kissane 'after my skin is stripped off'; Sutcliffe (*Biblica*, XXXI, 1950, p. 377) 'shall my skin be stripped from my flesh?'; Pope 'after my skin is flayed'. But Job was scarcely expecting to be flayed alive, and his disease could not 'strike' his skin off. For 'after' Ball would read 'I shall see' (with a difference of vowels only), and then for 'my skin' he suggests 'while I live' (reading *beʿôḏî* for *ʿōrî*). This makes it more explicit that the thought is of this life. Dhorme, on the other hand would make it more explicit that the thought is of something after death. He therefore emends the verb, to yield 'behind my skin I shall be raised up'. The relevance of 'behind my skin' is not clear. In M.T. the text means 'they strike off this', with indefinite subject, equivalent to 'this is struck off'. *AV* supplies 'worms' as the subject of the verb 'though after my skin worms destroy this body', but there is no justification for this, which again makes much more specific than the Hebrew the view that something which should follow death is in mind. Indeed it would postpone the vindication to the distant future, after the decomposition of the body. Vulg., so far from seeing the destruction of the skin, has 'I shall be surrounded by my skin'. Ball,

> then from my flesh I shall see God,
> 27 whom I shall see on my side,
>   and my eyes shall behold, and not another.

---

with his usual boldness, changes the text to produce 'I shall see, while I yet live, El's revenges', but this has little to commend it. Still less has Tur-Sinai's 'After my body let them break it up!' Duhm brings into this verse the last word of verse 25 and emends to secure 'and another (*'aḥēr* for *weʾaḥar*) shall arise as my witness (*'ēḏî* for *'ôrî*)'. D. R. Blumenthal (loc. cit.) finds here a third meaning for the word rendered 'skin' (see on verse 20), invoking a third root, and translates 'when the period of my abuse is at an end'. It is unnecessary to traverse the innumerable other proposed emendations.

from my flesh: this could mean 'without my flesh' (so *RSV* marg.), or 'in my flesh' (so *AV*). This lends itself to either type of interpretation. The rendering 'without my flesh' is rejected by some of those who favour the interpretation in terms of the doctrine of resurrection as strongly as by those who think of a vindication in this life, since the idea of a non-corporeal posthumous experience in a momentary rising from the dullness of Sheol is unlikely to be in mind. G. R. Driver (*Alttestamentliche Studien*, Nötscher Festschrift, 1950, pp. 46f.), who follows Beer in reading the preceding line as 'I shall see my witness standing beside me', with a change of vowels here secures for this line the meaning 'and shall behold one refuting (the opponent) for me, even God.'

I shall see God. The text of this verse is so difficult, and any convincing reconstruction is so unlikely, that it seems best not to attempt it. That it is in its original form is very improbable. To remove any trace of the thought of resurrection is as improper as it is to strengthen it. Two things seem to be clear. Job is assured that his Vindicator will arise to vindicate his innocence, and that he himself will see God. If, as seems probable, the Vindicator is God, this means that he will be aware of his vindication. That this vindication is not expected until after Job's death is likely, since he has cried for his blood to demand satisfaction. But in what form Job will be conscious of vindication must remain obscure. Peake says: 'The hope of immortality is not expressed here, but only of a momentary vision of God, assuring him of his vindication'. In 14.21f. Job had spoken of the ignorance of the dead of all that transpires on earth. Here he is borne by the inner logic of his faith in God, despite the suffering he believes to come from the hand of God, to look for a break in that ignorance, and the immense relief of knowing that his innocence has been vindicated. Though there is no full grasping of a belief in a worthwhile Afterlife with God, this passage is a notable landmark in the progress toward such a belief.

27. on my side: so Budde, Duhm, Gray and others; *AV* and *RV* 'for myself' (so Dhorme) is equally possible.

and not another: this appears to mean that Job's own eyes, and no one else's

My heart faints within me!
28 If you say, "How we will pursue him!"
  and, "The root of the matter is found in him";
29 be afraid of the sword,
  for wrath brings the punishment of the sword.
  that you may know there is a judgment.'

20 Then Zophar the Na'amathite answered:
    2 'Therefore my thoughts answer me,

---

will see God. Hitzig (so also Gray) thinks the meaning is that Job's eyes shall see God, and not as one estranged from him, an enemy.

My heart faints within me: lit. 'my reins fail in my bosom'. Job is overcome at the thought he has just expressed, which seems to him too wonderful to be possible, though he has been irresistibly carried forward to it.

28. The meaning of this verse and verse 29 appears to be a warning to the friends against persisting in persecuting Job under the mistaken idea that the *fons et origo* of all his sufferings is in himself. Ehrlich declared them hopelessly corrupt.

in him: M.T. changes to indirect speech and has 'in me'. But about 100 MSS. have 'in him', and this is represented in Theod., Targ. and Vulg., and is followed by most editors.

29. wrath. Many editors read 'these things' (*hēmmāh* for *ḥēmāh*); so Budde, Beer, Gray, Weiser, Fohrer.

brings the punishment of the sword: i.e. '(these things) are offences punishable by death'. Dhorme changes M.T. to yield '(wrath) is kindled against iniquities' (cf. Kissane). With greater change Dillmann proposed 'for the sword avengeth iniquities', and Duhm 'for wrath will destroy the ungodly'.

there is a judgment. The Hebrew is here unusual and doubtful. Reading *šadday* for *šaddîn*, Ewald, Wright and Ball secured 'that ye may know Shaddai', and then deleted as a gloss (cf. Weiser). Klostermann, Budde, Gray, and Fohrer read *yēš dayyān*, 'that ye may know there is a judge'. Dhorme defends the rendering of RSV. L. R. Fisher (*VT*, XI, 1961, pp. 342f.) argued that M.T. *šaddîn* is really an alternative form of the name Shaddai, appealing to Ugaritic for evidence. But elsewhere in Job the name is spelt in the normal way, and this view is very improbable (this revival of a view propounded by Eichhorn, who rendered 'he is mighty', and Hahn was already rejected by Zöckler).

THE SECOND SPEECH OF ZOPHAR 20

Hot to take up the argument, Zophar bursts out in passionate and intemperate speech to dwell on the brevity of the prosperity of the wicked and the retribution he brings on himself. 'Every syllable of his remorseless invective', says Strahan,

because of my haste within me.
³ I hear censure which insults me,
    and out of my understanding a spirit answers me.

'whether true or false in the abstract, is tragically irrelevant and cruelly unjust in its application.' He is sure that God is as hot and impatient as himself. For 'when the zealot makes his own opinions and sentiments the standard of divinity, there is a magnified Zophar on the throne of the universe' (Strahan). The speech falls into four parts: a brief preface (verses 2f.); the brevity of the triumph of the wicked (verses 4–11); the self-entailed retribution of sin (verses 12–22); the swift stroke of God upon the wicked (verses 23–29).

PREFACE 20.2f.

Roused by Job's words, Zophar impetuously bursts out upon him.

2. my thoughts: see on 4.13.

answer me: Peake observes that the idea of a colloquy between Zophar and his thoughts is artificial. Duhm proposed to read 'disturb me', and so Strahan and Gray; Kissane changes to read 'appal me', which is a slighter change. But Dhorme retains M.T. and understands it to mean 'bring me back', i.e. cause me to intervene again in the discussion.

because of mine haste within me: *AV* and *RV* 'because of this'; so a number of editors, with the addition of a word. Delitzsch derived the word rendered 'haste' from a different root, giving the meaning 'emotion' (similarly Dhorme). 'Zophar is boiling over and can no longer contain himself. Voigt proposed *tûšiyyāh* ('wisdom'; cf. on 5.12) for *ḥûšî* ('my haste').

3. censure: *AV* 'check', obsolete for the same meaning. The word commonly means 'correction or 'chastisement' (cf. Isa. 53.5). When the correction is by word, it becomes 'reproof'.

insults: better than *RV* 'putteth me to shame', which suggests that Zophar feels shame. Rather is he complaining that he is humiliated by Job's words, perhaps especially by his concluding words, in 19.28f.

out of my understanding a spirit answers me: this is not very lucid. The word rendered 'spirit' means also wind, and the friends had previously called Job's speech windy (cf. 8.2; 15.2). With a slight change Duhm read 'with wind void of understanding thou answerest me', while Budde reads 'wind answers my understanding'. With a slighter change, Dahood (*The Bible in Current Catholic Thought*, 1962, pp. 63f.) renders 'the spirit in my frame answers me', adducing a passage from the Qumran Hymns Scroll (so Pope). Without change of the text, Dhorme renders 'a wind (or impulse) arising from my understanding prompts me to reply', taking the verb in a causative sense. This is fully relevant to the context. Zophar is irresistibly driven to reply to Job.

⁴ Do you not know this from of old,
   since man was placed upon earth,
⁵ that the exulting of the wicked is short,
   and the joy of the godless but for a moment?
⁶ Though his height mount up to the heavens,
   and his head reach to the clouds,
⁷ he will perish for ever like his own dung;
   those who have seen him will say, "Where is he?"
⁸ He will fly away like a dream, and not be found;

THE BREVITY OF THE TRIUMPH OF THE WICKED 20.4-11

Still refusing to consider the particular case of Job before him, Zophar continues
to dwell on the theoretical generalities of his theology, and to maintain the
invariable nexus between wickedness and disaster. He declares that the wicked
dies before his time, being cut off with dramatic swiftness and leaving his children
to inherit poverty.

4. Do you not know?: M.T. has 'Do you know?' Budde takes this to imply
that what Job has been saying is but new-fangled ideas, and not based on the
wisdom of the ages. This seems very forced. Syr. and Vulg. have 'I know' for
'you know', and Merx follows this. But Dhorme observes that Zophar does not
ask himself what he knows. Kissane also follows Vulg. and takes this verse to be
the utterance of the inner voice which speaks to Zophar. It seems better to render
as *RSV* (so also *AV*, *RV*). Rosenmüller and Duhm alter the Hebrew text to secure
this, but R. Gordis (*HTR*, xxxiii, 1940, p. 244) justifies this without change of
text.
since man was placed upon earth: cf. Dt. 4.32.

5. Cf. 8.13ff. (Bildad); 15.29ff. (Eliphaz); also Ps. 37. In Ps. 73 the Psalmist
toyed with the same thought (verses 18ff.), until he went on to penetrate more
deeply into the true consolations of the righteous (verses 21ff.).

6. Cf. Am. 9.2; Isa. 14.13ff.; Ob. 4; Mt. 11.23; Lk. 10.15. 'It is not Zophar's
sermon against pride that makes him a false prophet, but his application of it to
Job' (Strahan).
his height: Guillaume (*Promise and Fulfilment*, ed. F. F. Bruce, 1963, pp. 114f.)
gives the word an Arabic sense, 'his skull', or 'his crown'.

7. like his own dung: Syr. has 'like a whirlwind'. Ewald renders 'according
to his greatness'; Dhorme 'like a ghost' (adducing Akk. *gallû*='an evil spirit').
But Peake holds it unnecessary to eliminate the vigorous coarseness, so characteristic of Zophar.
Where is he?: cf. 14.10.

8. Cf. Ps. 73.20; Isa. 29.7.

    he will be chased away like a vision of the night.
⁹ The eye which saw him will see him no more,
    nor will his place any more behold him.
¹⁰ His children will seek the favour of the poor,
    and his hands will give back his wealth.
¹¹ His bones are full of youthful vigour,
    but it will lie down with him in the dust.
¹² 'Though wickedness is sweet in his mouth,
    though he hides it under his tongue,
¹³ though he is loath to let it go,
    and holds it in his mouth,

---

9. Cf. 7.8ff.; Ps. 103.16, where the brevity of life in general, and not specifically of the wicked, is in mind.

saw: this verb (*šāzap*) recurs in 28.7 and Ca. 1.6 (*RV* and *RSV* 'scorched' treat it here as a synonym of *šādap*, found in Gen. 41.6, *RSV* 'blighted').

10. His children will seek the favour of the poor: i.e. they will be so reduced that they will look up to the poor for relief. *AV* marg. and *RV* marg. 'the poor shall oppress his children' follow LXX in deriving the verb from the root found in verse 19 (*RSV* 'crushed'), and so some editors. Dhorme transfers the verse to follow verse 19, and renders 'his sons will compensate the poor' (cf. Tur-Sinai 'will indemnify'; Pope 'must redress'). On this view Zophar says that the sons of the wicked man will be compelled to return to those whom he has impoverished the ill-gotten gains he has acquired at their expense. This makes the line excellently parallel to the following line, but is a less effective picture of the straits to which they will be reduced.

his hands: this reads surprisingly. We should not expect to return to his own lifetime after the previous line. Budde suggested adding one letter to read 'his children', which would improve the parallel with 'his sons' (so lit.) of the previous line. Gordis (*JBL*, LXII, 1943, p. 343) renders the text without change, 'his offspring', arguing that in several passages 'hand' stands for offspring.

11. full of youthful vigour: i.e. he will die prematurely. *AV* 'full of the sin of his youth' follows Vulg. (cf. Sym.), but is without basis in M.T.

THE SELF-ENTAILED RETRIBUTION OF SIN 20.12-22

The sweetness of sin turns into the gall of retribution, and riches wrongfully acquired must be vomited up again.

12. hides it: to retain it in his mouth as long as possible, so as to extract the maximum pleasure from its taste

14 yet his food is turned in his stomach;
     it is the gall of asps within him.
15 He swallows down riches and vomits them up again;
     God casts them out of his belly.
16 He will suck the poison of asps;
     the tongue of a viper will kill him.
17 He will not look upon the rivers,
     the streams flowing with honey and curds.
18 He will give back the fruit of his toil,
     and will not swallow it down;

---

14. The food that tasted so sweet proves to be poison. So the enjoyment of the sinner in his sin turns to destroy him.

the gall of asps: the ancients believed that serpents secreted poison in the gall bladder.

15. 'The figure of God administering the emetic is coarse and powerful, as befits Zophar' (Peake).

16. Budde held this verse to be a gloss on verse 14. But it is improbable that the rarer word viper (found elsewhere only in Isa. 30.6; 59.5) would be used in a gloss. The thought is similar to that of verse 14. The wealth which the wicked greedily sucked in by his oppression proved to be his undoing, as poison destroys him who takes it. Strahan prefers to understand the verse to mean that asps shall sting him and his body shall suck the poison. But it is doubtful if the verb 'suck' would have been used in that case.

tongue: this is not strictly correct, but the darting tongue of the viper may have been popularly regarded as the source of the poison.

17. The time of enjoyment to which the wicked looked forward, he will not live to see.

the streams flowing: lit. 'rivers of, torrents of'. Some editors have thought these to be alternative readings, naharê or nahalê. Klostermann suggested that the first of these words was a corruption of yiṣhār='oil', and that it belonged to the first line 'rivers of oil'. This yields a good parallel to 'streams of honey and curds', and Peake, Gray, Dhorme and others follow. For the reference to oil and honey together, de Vaux (RB, XLVI, 1937, p. 533) cites a passage in the Baal text from Ras Shamra.

honey and curds: the same words in reverse order stand in Isa. 7.14. 'Curds' means 'curdled milk', much esteemed for refreshment (cf. Jg. 5.25).

18. Strahan speaks of the lumbering lines of this verse, so unlike the poet's artistic work. But the fruit of his toil is a single short word in the Hebrew. It is found only here and it means 'the profit of labour'. If we render 'He must restore

from the profit of his trading
    he will get no enjoyment.
¹⁹ For he has crushed and abandoned the poor,
    he has seized a house which he did not build.
²⁰ 'Because his greed knew no rest,

---

his gains unenjoyed', the line does not appear lumbering. The wicked is depicted
as seeking to engulf in his maw (the verb 'swallow' as in verse 15) the wealth he
wrongly acquires, but failing to do so.

from the profit of his trading: lit. 'according to the wealth of his exchange'.
Dhorme reads *b* for *k*, with some MSS., to secure the sense of *RSV*.

   19. and abandoned: if the reading is correct, it means that the wicked has
callously left the poor to their fate after he has oppressively treated them. Ehrlich
with a change of vowels read a noun, which he rendered 'the mud hut (of the
poor)'. Kissane read the same word, which he connected with a root found in
Neh. 3.8 (*RSV* 'repaired') and rendered '(he hath broken down) the hovel (of the
poor)'. M. Dahood (*JBL*, LXXVIII, 1959, pp. 306f.) similarly renders 'hovel'. But
the meaning is hazardous. J. Reider (*HUCA*, XXIV, 1952–53, pp. 103f.) also read
the same noun, but connected it with the root 'forsake' and rendered '(he hath
squeezed) the leavings (of the poor)'. Dhorme cleverly suggests reading *beʿōz* for
ʿāzaḇ, and renders '(he has crushed) with violence (the poor)'. Tur-Sinai connected the verb of M.T. with a cognate Arabic root meaning, in the third form,
'torture', and renders '(he hath oppressed) and maltreated (the poor)'; and this
is the simplest suggestion and yields an appropriate sense.

which he did not build: Duhm secures this sense by a slight modification of the
text to agree with Vulg. As M.T. stands it means 'he seized a house, but doth not
go on to build it', and this is followed by a number of editors. The sense then is
that he does not enjoy the fruit of his violence. But the sense of *RSV* is to be
preferred, though it is doubtful if it can be sustained without emendation.

   20. his greed knew no rest: lit. 'he knew no quietness in his belly', i.e. his
greed was insatiable. D. Winton Thomas (*JTS*, XXXVI, 1935, pp. 409ff.) deleted
the noun 'quietness', and argued that the verb here means 'be quiet', rendering
'he is not quiet' (within himself).

he will not save anything in which he delights: lit. 'he will not cause his
valued possessions to escape'. Cf. N. M. Sarna (*JBL*, LXXVIII, 1959, pp. 315f.):
'Of his most cherished possessions he shall save nothing.' Many editors read 'he
will not escape with his valued possessions' (so Gray). Dhorme renders: 'it was
impossible to escape his appetite'; but this is of doubtful justification. Kissane's
'By his precious things he shall not escape' is not convincing. Pope's 'In his greed
he let nothing escape' yields an excellent sense, if 'because' is omitted at the
beginning of the verse. If that is retained, *RSV* gives the most probable sense.
His very greed overreaches itself, and leaves him in the end with nothing.

he will not save anything in which he delights.
21 There was nothing left after he had eaten;
   therefore his prosperity will not endure.
22 In the fulness of his sufficiency he will be in straits;
   all the force of misery will come upon him.
23 To fill his belly to the full
   God will send his fierce anger into him,
   and rain it upon him as his food.

---

21. This verse repeats the same thought. His insatiable appetite defeats itself. For **nothing**, Dhorme has 'no one' (and so Kissane), which the Hebrew equally allows. It is not his gluttony for food, but his eagerness to swallow up the weak, which is in mind.

22. Again the thought is of the boomerang effect of his avarice. Like apples of Sodom, his satisfaction fails him in the moment when he grasps it.

the force of misery: this follows LXX and Vulg. So many editors. Dhorme excellently renders 'all the blows of misfortune pour upon him'. M.T. has 'every hand of one in misery'.

THE SWIFT STROKE OF GOD UPON THE WICKED 20.23-29

All this self-destruction which the wicked brings upon himself is really the judgment of God upon him.

23. This verse is a tristich, and Duhm and others omit the first line as a gloss. *RV* marg. renders literally 'Let it be for the filling of his belly'. Wright proposed for the first word (*y*ᵉ*hî*) to read Yahweh (*yhwh*), and so Budde; but as this divine name is avoided in the dialogue (see p. 24), this is to be rejected. Dhorme thinks the meaning is that, in the moment when he is occupied in filling his belly, the stroke of God will fall upon him. This is in full harmony with the thought of the preceding verses.

God: M.T. 'he'; that God is understood is doubtless correct.

as his food: *AV* and *RV* 'while he is eating'. The word stands elsewhere only in Zeph. 1.17 (*RSV* 'flesh'), and Hitzig and Delitzsch render 'upon his flesh'. Others read the ordinary word for 'bread' (*laḥmô* for *lᵉḥûmô*), and secure the sense of *RV* marg. and *RSV*. Peake comments 'Just as God rained manna on his people, so He will rain his fierce wrath to glut the hunger of the greedy.' Many emendations have been proposed, of which the following may be mentioned: '(rain upon him) the fire of his wrath' (Dahood (*Biblica*, XXXVIII, 1957, pp. 314f.), reading '*ālaw mabbēl ḥammô*, the last two words not found elsewhere in OT, for '*ālêmô bilᵉḥûmô*; so also Pope); 'rain his arrows upon his flesh' (Dhorme, reading '*olmāw* for '*ālêmô*, and interpreting from Akkadian). *RSV* yields a satisfactory sense and involves but slight change.

²⁴ He will flee from an iron weapon;
    a bronze arrow will strike him through.
²⁵ It is drawn forth and comes out of his body,
    the glittering point comes out of his gall;
    terrors come upon him.
²⁶ Utter darkness is laid up for his treasures;
    a fire not blown upon will devour him;
    what is left in his tent will be consumed.
²⁷ The heavens will reveal his iniquity,
    and the earth will rise up against him.
²⁸ The possessions of his house will be carried away,

---

24. Cf. Am. 5.19; Isa. 24.18.
He will flee: G. R. Driver (*SVT*, III, 1955, p. 81) revocalizes and renders 'he shall be wounded', a meaning supported by Arabic.

25. It is drawn forth and comes out of his body: we should render 'out of his back'. For the first verb Duhm renders 'a shaft (comes)', reading *šelaḥ* with LXX for *šālap* (so Dhorme, Kissane, Fohrer, Pope), and this is to be preferred. It would seem probable that the meaning is that the shaft penetrates right through his body.

the glittering point: lit. 'lightning', here the flashing point of the arrow, which penetrates his vitals.

gall: the same word as in verse 14.

26. Utter darkness is laid up for his treasures: lit. 'all darkness is hidden for his laid up things'. LXX omits the word 'hidden', and for 'for laid up things' (*liṣᵉpûnāw*) reads 'laid up for him' (*lô ṣāpûn*), and so many editors. This yields a clearer sense than M.T.

not blown upon: not kindled by man, i.e. a fire of divine origin (cf. Num. 16.35; 26.10). G. R. Driver (*JBL*, LIII, 1934, p. 289) reads 'unquenched'.

what is left: Dhorme takes the meaning to be 'whoever survives', and so Kissane and Pope. The Hebrew is patient of either rendering.

27. Heaven and earth will combine against him. Some editors think there may be a reference to Job's claim that his Witness is in heaven and appeal to earth not to cover his blood, but Gray thinks this is doubtful. Budde transposed this verse to follow verse 28, and so Dhorme.

28. The possessions of his house will be carried away. The word rendered 'possessions' elsewhere denotes the produce of the soil, and the verb (*yiḡel*) means 'will go into exile'. Duhm emended to read with LXX 'destruction will sweep away his house', and Dhorme to read 'a flood will sweep away his house', adducing Akkadian evidence for the meaning 'flood' (so also Kissane and Pope). The flood,

dragged off in the day of God's wrath.
²⁹ This is the wicked man's portion from God,
   the heritage decreed for him by God.'

21 Then Job answered:
       ² 'Listen carefully to my words,
         and let this be your consolation.

---

like the unblown fire of verse 26, is produced by divine action, unleashing the waters.

dragged off: some editors derive this word from the root 'drag away', and others from the root 'pour out'. Hence Kissane 'a downpour', Dhorme 'waters which flow', and Pope 'torrents' (cf. 2 Sam. 14.14, *RSV* 'spilt'). The general sense of the verse is either, with *RSV*, that all his property will be seized and carried off by others, or that everything will be swept away by the overwhelming ruin which will be poured out on him by God. In either case total destruction will be his lot, and it will be the expression of the divine judgment upon him.

29. For the summary conclusion of the speech, cf. 5.27; 18.21.

JOB ANSWERS ZOPHAR 21

Job now answers the doctrinaire utterances of the three friends. To their *a priori* theories he opposes the realism of experience, and, whereas they had sharply distinguished between the happiness of the righteous and the misery of the sinner, Job points to the fact that the wicked are often the prosperous. 'It is only the corrosive language of Zophar that awakens him on each occasion to the particular meaning of his friends' addresses' (Davidson). It is to be noted that in his previous speech, when he looked at his own suffering in the light of his consciousness of his innocence, he rose to a new height of faith in God. In this present speech, when he looks out on the divine government of the world, he is bewildered and attacked by doubt. The speech falls into five parts: Job appeals for a hearing (verses 2–6); the wicked who renounce God prosper (verses 7–16); how often do the godless suffer? (verses 17–22); death levels all (verses 23–26); the arguments of the friends are contradicted by universal experience (verses 27–34).

JOB APPEALS FOR A HEARING 21.2–6

When he has spoken, the friends may continue to mock; but meanwhile they will share the dismay which Job feels when he unfolds the realities of experience.

2. your consolation: i.e. the consolation you give. Eliphaz had professed to offer Job the consolations of God (15.11). If they will listen to what Job has to say, they will console him more.

³ Bear with me, and I will speak,
    and after I have spoken, mock on.
⁴ As for me, is my complaint against man?
    Why should I not be impatient?
⁵ Look at me, and be appalled,
    and lay your hand upon your mouth.
⁶ When I think of it I am dismayed,
    and shuddering seizes my flesh.
⁷ Why do the wicked live,
    reach old age, and grow mighty in power?
⁸ Their children are established in their presence,
    and their offspring before their eyes.
⁹ Their houses are safe from fear,
    and no rod of God is upon them.
¹⁰ Their bull breeds without fail;
    their cow calves, and does not cast her calf.
¹¹ They send forth their little ones like a flock,
    and their children dance.
¹² They sing to the tambourine and the lyre,
    and rejoice to the sound of the pipe.
¹³ They spend their days in prosperity,

---

3. mock on: the verb changes from the plural to the singular, and it would seem that here Job is addressing Zophar in particular. But the versions, except Targ., have plural, and many editors follow this.

4. is my complaint against man? Job's complaint is against God and not against men. If it were against men, he might expect sympathy from other men; but none dare offer him sympathy when his complaint is against God. From neither God nor man, then, can he find consolation. He will therefore give free expression to his unsoothed spirit.

be impatient: lit. 'my spirit be short'. This is not the expression used in 4.5 (see note there).

5. be appalled: what Job has to say will astound his friends, as it has astounded him. God's government of the world is quite other than their vain theorizings have suggested.

lay your hand upon your mouth: a gesture of awed silence; cf. 29.9; 40.4; Mic. 7.16. Harpocrates (Horus the child) is represented with his finger held to his mouth, and by a misunderstanding of this symbol of childhood he became for the Greeks the god of silence. But Dahood (*The Bible in Current Catholic Thought*,

1962, p. 64) holds that we have here a gesture of amazement rather than of silence.

6. I am dismayed: Job's old faith in God is shattered when he faces the facts of experience, and he shudders at the thought that there is no moral basis of the universe.

THE WICKED WHO RENOUNCE GOD PROSPER 21.7–16

Job begins his attack on the theodicy of the friends by asking why the wicked prosper and live long. Their children thrive and their homes are happy. Their end is peaceful, though they openly renounce God. This is a flat contradiction of all the pictures of the godless drawn by the friends, but, like the friends, Job speaks in general terms, as if all experience is of a single pattern. Neither he nor the friends have yet resolved the tension between Job's faith and his experience.

7. In contrast to what Zophar had said (20.11), that the wicked die prematurely, Job declares that they live to old age. Their prosperity continues unbroken, and is not the fleeting thing the friends had supposed (15.20; 18.5; 20.5). This problem of the prosperity of the wicked is one that troubled others; cf. Jer. 12.1f.; Mal. 3.15; Ps. 73.3ff.; Hab. 1.13.

8. in their presence: lit. 'before them, with them' (cf. *AV, RV*). Many editors think these are alternative readings, and omit one or the other of them, as *RSV*. Kissane transferred 'with them' to the second line and with a change of vowel secured 'their kinsfolk (and their offspring)'. Ball similarly transferred, but added a consonant to secure '(their offspring) abide', comparing Isa. 66.22, and so Dhorme. Job here still contests the statements of the friends (15.33f.; 18.19; 20.21).

9. In 5.24 Eliphaz had promised Job safety in his tent if he accepted his misfortunes as divine chastisement, and repented. Job here sets the security of the wicked against this.

no rod of God: in 9.34 Job complained that there was no umpire to remove the rod of God from him; here he declares that the wicked do not feel this rod.

10. Fertility in herds and flocks was regarded as a mark of divine blessing; cf. Dt. 28.14; Ps. 144.13f. But Job finds this to be given to the wicked.

11f. Cf. Zech. 8.5. The picture of the children frolicking like lambs and singing and playing suggests most vividly peace and happiness. The instruments mentioned are a percussion instrument, a stringed instrument, and a wind instrument. The first two are mentioned in connection with rejoicing in Gen. 31.27; Isa. 24.8. Dahood (*The Bible in Current Catholic Thought*, p. 65) needlessly emends to introduce a sword dance. For **sing** A. Guillaume (*JTS*, N.S., XVII, 1966, pp. 53f.) renders 'rejoice', adducing an Arabic root to justify the meaning.

13. Not only do the wicked know unbroken prosperity, but they come to a peaceful end in their ripe old age.

spend: Kt. has 'wear out'; Ķr. and the versions have 'bring to an end' (the same verb as in Ps. 90.9).

and in peace they go down to Sheol.
14 They say to God, "Depart from us!
We do not desire the knowledge of thy ways.
15 What is the Almighty, that we should serve him?
And what profit do we get if we pray to him?"
16 Behold, is not their prosperity in their hand?
The counsel of the wicked is far from me.
17 'How often is it that the lamp of the wicked is put out?
That their calamity comes upon them?
That God distributes pains in his anger?
18 That they are like straw before the wind,
and like chaff that the storm carries away?
19 You say, "God stores up their iniquity for their sons".
Let them recompense it to themselves, that they may know it.

---

in peace: *AV* and *RV* 'in a moment'. The word commonly means 'in a moment', and the thought is then of the swift death, with no lingering illness or period of suffering. But some connect the word here with a root meaning 'be at rest', and secure the sense of *RSV* (so also LXX). The sense is not greatly different, but 'in a moment' suggests to the English reader an untimely death, which is not in mind here.

go down: M.T. has 'they are frightened', but by a slight change of vowels the meaning 'go down' is obtained. This is represented in the versions and followed generally by editors, as being more appropriate to the context. With a different vocalization O. Rössler (*ZAW*, N.F., xxxiii, 1962, p. 127) derives the word from a different root and renders 'they are snatched away'. But this yields an inappropriate sense, suggesting that death comes as an enemy, whereas Job is saying that it comes when they have lived a complete life.

14. Depart from us: these are not the people who drift away from God, but men who deliberately reject him, and turn away from him. In spite of this, Job says, their lot is happy. Eliphaz repeats this line in 22.17.

thy ways: contrast the attitude of the Psalmist in Ps. 25.4. To walk in God's ways is to obey his will.

15. This verse was omitted in LXX (later supplied from Theod.), probably because it seemed blasphemous. Davidson cites Coverdale's rendering 'What maner of felowe is the Almightie that we shulde serve him?'

pray to: the verb commonly means 'meet', 'encounter' (cf. Gen. 32.1 (M.T. 2)). But occasionally it means, as here, 'meet with a request', i.e. 'entreat', or 'pray to' (cf. Jer. 7.16; Ru. 1.16).

16. Is not? M.T. has '(their prosperity) is not' (cf. *AV*, *RV*), and some editors follow this (so Pope), finding the meaning to be that Job implies that their prosperity comes from God. Others (so Kissane) think Job is anticipating an objection of the friends, who believe that the wicked has no secure control of his own prosperity, and Job then replies to this in verse 17. Yet others take the sentence as a question, as *RSV* (so Duhm, Gray, Dhorme), the meaning then being that God does not concern himself with them, but leaves them their prosperity as their own achievement. LXX omits the negative and gets the same result.

from me: this yields the fine sense that despite the prosperity of the wicked, Job does not desire it on their terms. He still holds fast to his integrity and his piety, and so far from crying to God to depart from him, he continually desires the fellowship he feels is denied him. Many editors follow LXX in reading 'him', i.e. God, instead of 'me', but this reduces the line to a platitude.

counsel of the wicked: see on 10.3.

HOW OFTEN DO THE GODLESS SUFFER? **21.17–22**

How rarely do visitations from God befall the wicked, such as the friends had described, or their children suffer for their misdeeds! Even if they did, this would be no fitting judgment on the wicked themselves. If there is any moral government of the world, they should suffer in their own persons.

17. In 18.5 Bildad had said that the light of the wicked is put out (see note there). Job asks how often this happens. He does not deny that this ever happens, but implies that it is too rare to be significant.

God: the subject is unexpressed, but is implied.

pains: the Hebrew word can mean 'cords' (in 18.10 to ensnare), but the verb ('apportion') is against this here; or 'measured plots of land' (cf. Ps 16.6), but this is not very probable here; or 'pangs' (elsewhere only of birth-pangs). It is most probable that it has the last of these meanings, but in a wider sense, here: how often does God send physical agony on the wicked (cf. Ps. 73.4, where, however, different words are used)? In Mic. 2.10 the singular is used in the sense of 'destruction', and Weiser finds that sense here. This is a possible meaning, and it would yield a good parallel to 'calamity'. Duhm emended the verb to read 'cords seize them', and so Gray; but this seems less effective. Dhorme without change of text renders 'does he destroy evil-doers', giving to both the verb and the noun meanings not elsewhere found in Hebrew, but for which he adduces Akkadian evidence (the verbal root with which he connects the noun is found in *OT* meaning 'act corruptly'). But this seems hazardous. Bickell and Fohrer delete the line.

18. For the figures in this verse cf. Ps. 1.4; Isa. 17.13; Job 27.20. But note that Job questions what the Psalmist affirms.

19. You say: these words are not in the Hebrew, but it is probable that the verse is rightly understood as a reply to an objection which Job supposes the friends might offer, namely, that even if the wicked man should escape punishment himself, his children will have to suffer it (cf. Exod. 20.5; Dt. 5.9). In 5.4;

²⁰ Let their own eyes see their destruction,
   and let them drink of the wrath of the Almighty.
²¹ For what do they care for their houses after them,
   when the number of their months is cut off?
²² Will any teach God knowledge,
   seeing that he judges those that are on high?
²³ One dies in full prosperity,
   being wholly at ease and secure,
²⁴ his body full of fat

20.10 the friends had spoken of the inheritance of suffering the wicked leaves to his children, though there it was in addition to the disaster he brings on himself. Jeremiah (31.29f.) and Ezekiel (18.2ff.) both rejected the view that a man's sin was visited on his children (cf. also Jn 9.1ff.), though it is beyond doubt that experience shows a man's family often suffers for his sin (cf. H. H. Rowley, *The Faith of Israel*, 1956, pp. 112ff.). Job here protests that it would be no justice for one to sin and his children to suffer. The sinner himself should be corrected and disciplined. Neither doctrine alone expresses the whole truth. For Scripture and experience show that the children of the righteous are blessed no less than the children of the unrighteous suffer; yet at the same time every man is responsible to God for his own character and conduct. The issue is more complex than the friends or Job realised, and while they are wrong in tracing punishment in father or son to sin, Job is wrong in assuming that righteousness should ensure the absence of suffering. Duhm transformed the meaning by reading *'al*='do not' for *'elôah*='God'. He then renders 'Let him not lay up iniquity for his children'. This would imply the view that any unpunished sins of the father were visited upon his children. Though several editors follow this view, it does not seem so relevant to Job's position as the view of *RSV*. In Job's view (14.21) the dead are completely ignorant of what happens to their children, so that no sufferings of their families could be regarded as affecting them in any way.

   20. destruction: this word is found only here, and is often held to mean 'craft' and so changed by many editors to 'ruin' (cf. on 12.5), or 'misfortune', or 'cup' (so Ehrlich; with a different word for 'cup', Dahood (*Biblica*, XXXVIII, 1957, p. 316) and Pope), or 'weapons' (so Wright). But A. F. L. Beeston (*Le Muséon*, LXVII, 1954, pp. 315f.) has argued for the meaning 'condemnation' for M.T., so that no change of text is necessary. For the figure of the second line cf. Isa. 51.17; Jer. 25.15; Rev. 16.19. Job is here continuing to express his view that the wicked ought to experience retribution themselves (but commonly do not), rather than entail it for their children.

21. do they care: better than *AV* and *RV* 'pleasure hath he'. Job asks what interest a man takes in the affairs of his family, once he is dead (cf. 14.21). The Hebrew can mean 'pleasure', but here it is probably used in a wider sense.

the number of their months: their life span; Pope 'his quota of months'.

is cut off: a rare verb explained from an Akkadian root='cut in two', and an Ethiopic root='curtail', 'diminish', or an Arabic root='be apportioned'. Hence the line is variously interpreted to mean 'when his life span has been allotted him', or 'when his life span is cut short'. The latter seems the more appropriate meaning here.

22. Gray regards this verse as a gloss, while Hitzig and Tur-Sinai think it is an objection of the friends which Job is expressing. But Dhorme defends it, holding that Job is here reproaching the friends for imposing on God himself their own rigid doctrine. They maintain that there is an invariable nexus between desert and experience, while Job maintains that the facts of experience show that moral considerations do not explain diversities of fortune. God, who is the judge of angels and men, is too exalted to be taught by the friends how he should act.

those that are on high: i.e. the angels. Dahood (*Biblica*, xxxviii, 1957, pp. 316f.) renders 'the Most High', i.e. God, holding that the word is singular, with an enclitic *-m*. It is unnecessary to multiply examples of enclitic *-m* where it may more naturally be the normal plural ending. Moreover the 'he' is here emphatic and not naturally to be equated with the unexpressed subject of the first line (Dahood renders 'will he judge the Most High?'). The usual interpretation is much more probable.

DEATH LEVELS ALL **21.23–26**

One man dies in prosperity and another in bitterness and suffering. But in the grave the bodies of both moulder alike. In life no moral differences explain their diversity of fortune; in death as little do they explain their common fate.

23. One dies: it is needless to suppose that here Job is thinking only of the wicked and in verse 25 only of the good. Job is not arguing that the wicked always prosper and the good are always unfortunate, but that merit and experience are not directly matched. One man dies in prosperity and another in misery, and both may be wicked or both good. Their character cannot be inferred from their lot.

in full prosperity: lit. 'in the bone (i.e. the essence) of his perfection'. In 2.3 the word is used of the moral integrity of Job's character; here of the physical state of men.

24. his body: *AV* and *RV* follow Targ. in reading 'his breasts'. Most modern editors hold the meaning to be 'his pails'. But both are very doubtful. The word is found only here, and its meaning can only be conjectured. Syr. has 'his sides', and some editors (Beer, Klostermann, Dhorme, Kissane, Fohrer, Pope) follow this meaning, and with slight alteration connect the word with an Aramaic word meaning 'flank'. *RSV* reflects this view. Gray pronounces it precarious and

and the marrow of his bones moist.
25 Another dies in bitterness of soul,
    never having tasted of good.
26 They lie down alike in the dust,
    and the worms cover them.
27 'Behold, I know your thoughts,
    and your schemes to wrong me.
28 For you say, "Where is the house of the prince?
    Where is the tent in which the wicked dwelt?"
29 Have you not asked those who travel the roads,
    and do you not accept their testimony
30 that the wicked man is spared in the day of calamity,
    that he is rescued in the day of wrath?
31 Who declares his way to his face,
    and who requites him for what he has done?
32 When he is borne to the grave,
    watch is kept over his tomb.

---

unnecessary, but it is no more so than 'pails', for which the post-biblical support claimed is associated only with olives and not with milk.
fat: M.T. has 'milk' (the change being merely of vowels), and editors follow the one or the other reading according to their view of the rendering of the word discussed in the preceding note. For the thought of the prosperity of a man being reflected in his bloated body, cf. Ps. 73.4, 6. For the second line cf. Prov. 3.8.
   25. bitterness of soul: cf. 3.20; 7.11; 10.1.
   26. Cf. Ec. 2.15ff.; also Isa. 14.11.

THE ARGUMENTS OF THE FRIENDS ARE CONTRADICTED BY UNIVERSAL EXPERIENCE
21.27–34
Job's observation and experience are confirmed by the testimony of those who had travelled. They can tell of wicked men who came to the grave with honour, and whose tomb is maintained with care.
   27. Job's meaning is that he knows that when his friends talked of the fate of the wicked they really meant himself, and that they concluded from his sufferings that he must be paying the price of his sins.
to wrong me: or perhaps, 'which you think up against me'.
   28. the prince: probably used in a bad sense here, meaning 'the oppressor'; cf. its parallel 'the wicked'. Job anticipates that his friends will bring forward against him once more their declarations that the wicked leave no memory among

men (cf. 8.14f.; 15.34; 18.15ff.; 20.26ff.). It is for this reason that he appeals in the following verses to independent testimony by those qualified to speak, which he maintains will support his case.

29. those who travel the roads: this is generally taken to mean those who have travelled far and had wide experience. But Kissane takes it to mean the man in the street. This seems less likely, though in itself the phrase could possibly mean either.

accept: lit. 'recognise'. Pope connects the word with a homonymous root and renders 'find strange'. It is more likely that the word here has the same sense as in 34.19, where it means 'regard'.

their testimony: lit. 'their signs'. Dhorme thinks it means the marks or scribblings of tramps or wandering labourers at the cross-roads. It is doubtful if Job would regard these as the repositories of wisdom, and equally doubtful if such persons would record instances relevant to what Job is discussing. It is more likely that widely travelled merchants would talk of the things they had seen and heard, so that *RSV* conveys the sense (cf. Pope 'their tales'—which, however, suggests to us 'tall stories').

30. spared: lit. 'is withheld'. *AV* and *RV* make Job say the opposite of what he is contending: 'reserved to (the day)'. In 38.23 it has this meaning, but in 33.18 it has the meaning which is more relevant here.

he is rescued: lit. 'led forth'. Again *AV* and *RV* give the wrong picture in rendering 'brought (led) forth to (the day)'. Kissane follows *AV* and *RV* but thinks verses 30f. are out of place where they stand, and so transfers them to precede verse 13. The Hebrew is fully patient of the meaning of *RSV*, which is appropriate to the context. To be led forth in the day of wrath is to be delivered from it. Some editors have tried by emendation to make the sense clearer: 'he is saved' (Dillmann, Gray, Fohrer); 'he escapes' (Ball). Dhorme by emendation secures a wider difference of sense 'he is merry'. But the parallelism favours *RSV*.

31. Some rabbinical commentators thought the reference was to denouncing God to his face, but most modern commentators think we revert here to Job's own words about the prosperous wicked oppressor. None dare oppose him to his face for fear of the consequences. The following verse cannot refer to God and makes the view that the wicked man is in mind here most probable.

32. Not only in life, but also in death the sinner is honoured. He is ceremoniously buried, and his tomb is carefully guarded.

watch is kept: *AV* 'shall remain' is inadequate. The verb means 'wake' or 'watch' (cf. Jer. 1.12). Some editors understand the subject to be the dead man: 'he shall watch', but more probably it is impersonal: 'one shall watch'. Yet others take it to be the dead man's effigy (see next note).

over his tomb: this word is found only here, and is explained by an Arabic cognate word. A Hebrew homonym means 'sheaf', which is inappropriate here. Many editors refer to the custom of setting up an effigy of a nobleman on his tomb, for which there is evidence from various ancient Near Eastern countries, and suppose that the dead man through his effigy is thought of as keeping watch

³³ The clods of the valley are sweet to him;
   all men follow after him,
   and those who go before him are innumerable.
³⁴ How then will you comfort me with empty nothings?
   There is nothing left of your answers but falsehood.'

---

on his own tomb. This seems very unlikely, and Job can scarcely be supposed to have thought of the dead as effective guardians of any thing, since he believed they were ignorant of all that transpired on earth (14.21). Zöckler rejected this view (so Strahan), but with equal improbability thought the dead man was conceived of as watching over his own grave from within the mound which was erected over his body.

33. The clods of the valley: for burial in a valley, cf. Dt. 34.6. The clods are those used to make the mound over the body. (Alfrink (*Biblica*, XIII, 1932, pp. 77ff.) favours the meaning 'stones', but has found no following. Cf. note in Rosenmüller.) The dead man is poetically depicted as consciously sharing in his own funeral, rejoicing in the splendid mound that covers him, proud of the hosts that precede and follow him to the grave. For 'are sweet to him' Ball reads 'he is quiet among (the clods)'. Stevenson dismisses this as weak, but himself suggests the no more convincing '(clods) are laid in order'. Many commentators quote the Latin *sit tibi terra levis*, 'Light fall the earth on thee'.

34. In view of all this and the lack of moral principles to explain the inequalities among men, Job dismisses the arguments of the friends as hollow and meaningless.

THE THIRD SPEECH OF ELIPHAZ 22

The third cycle of speeches now begins. In the first cycle the friends had argued from their conception of God that Job must have fallen into some sin, and assured him that repentance would lead to the restoration of his fortunes. In the second cycle they develop their ideas on the fate of the wicked, and maintain that there is a moral government of the world. In the third cycle they turn more sharply on Job and charge him openly with heinous sins. It is clear that these sins are no more than their deductions, based on their theological conceptions. They rest on no evidence, but only on their presuppositions, which are more important to them than any evidence. Eliphaz once more opens the cycle, repudiating Job's argument in the preceding speech that there is no moral government of the world by maintaining that since God was untouched by man's behaviour, the source of man's ills must lie in himself. He then proceeds to deduce from Job's suffering the sins he must have committed and the impious assumption that God was indifferent to what happened on earth that must have encouraged him. Finally, Eliphaz returns to the thought that repentance might lead to the restoration of his fortunes. The speech falls into four parts: since God is disinterested, Job's suffering

22 Then Eli'phaz the Te'manite answered:
   2 'Can a man be profitable to God?
      Surely he who is wise is profitable to himself.
   3 Is it any pleasure to the Almighty if you are righteous,
      or is it gain to him if you make your ways blameless?
   4 Is it for your fear of him that he reproves you,
      and enters into judgment with you?
   5 Is not your wickedness great?
      There is no end to your iniquities.
   6 For you have exacted pledges of your brothers for nothing,
      and stripped the naked of their clothing.

---

is proof of his sin (verses 2–5); Job's sin, as deduced by Eliphaz (verses 6–11); Job's assumption of divine indifference, as envisaged by Eliphaz (verses 12–20); Eliphaz's appeal and promise to Job (verses 21–30).

SINCE GOD IS DISINTERESTED, JOB'S SUFFERING IS PROOF OF HIS SIN 22.2–5

God is too far above man to be affected by anything he does, and therefore his treatment of man is objective and impartial, and hence when he sends suffering, it is evidence of sin.

2. God can derive no possible advantage from man, Eliphaz says, but virtuous conduct can benefit a man himself. There can be no temptation to God to deviate from strict justice, since he could not gain anything from it. Cf. 7.20, where Job had drawn the opposite conclusion, arguing that if he had sinned his sin could not injure God, and so there was no reason why God should bother himself about it.

profitable: cf. on 15.3.

3. pleasure: better 'advantage', 'concern'; cf. on 21.21, and note the parallel term here, 'gain'.

4. your fear of him: i.e. 'your piety'; cf. on 4.6. Since God is disinterested, his treatment of men must be for their advantage and not his. It is therefore inconceivable that he should correct the righteous. *AV* 'for fear of thee' is quite inappropriate here.

5. If correction is not for piety, then it must be for wickedness, and hence Job's sufferings must prove his sin. Such is the simple argument of Eliphaz. As Strahan says, he attempts to be logical but only succeeds in being fallacious. Note how carried away Eliphaz is by his own argument, and concludes from Job's great sufferings that his sins must be without limit.

JOB'S SIN, AS DEDUCED BY ELIPHAZ 22.6–11

Eliphaz proceeds to specify the particular sins of which he supposes Job must

⁷ You have given no water to the weary to drink,
    and you have withheld bread from the hungry.
⁸ The man with power possessed the land,
    and the favoured man dwelt in it.
⁹ You have sent widows away empty,
    and the arms of the fatherless were crushed.
¹⁰ Therefore snares are round about you,
    and sudden terror overwhelms you;
¹¹ your light is darkened, so that you cannot see,
    and a flood of water covers you.
¹² 'Is not God high in the heavens?
    See the highest stars, how lofty they are!
¹³ Therefore you say, "What does God know?
    Can he judge through the deep darkness?
¹⁴ Thick clouds enwrap him, so that he does not see,
    and he walks on the vault of heaven".
¹⁵ Will you keep to the old way
    which wicked men have trod?

---

have been guilty. They are such as corrupting power might lead a man into. For Job's repudiation of the sins with which he is charged, cf. chapter 31.

6. The pledges were commonly outer garments, which were especially needed for a covering at night, and which therefore should be returned nightly (cf. Exod. 22.26f.; Dt. 24.10ff.). In wrongfully retaining these, Job is thought to have violated this law, and so to have stripped men of their covering. Moreover, he is held to have done this oppressively and without justification or cause. Job replies in 31.19.

for nothing: cf. on 1.9; 2.3.

7. For the inculcation of what Job is here said to have neglected, cf. Isa. 58.7; Ezek. 18.7. Cf. also Mt. 25.42f. and 10.42. For Job's reply, cf. 31.17.

weary: an adjective used of the thirsty in Isa. 29.8; Jer. 31.25; Prov. 25.15.

8. Job is no longer addressed here in the second person, and some editors (Siegfried, Budde, Beer, Peake) delete the verse as a gloss. Others (Dillmann, Strahan, Gray) find an oblique reference to Job, who is thought to have oppressively used his power to seize the lands of the defenceless (cf. Isa. 5.8). Dhorme thinks Job is here only accused of being the accomplice of the rapacious. Against this Kissane objects that it reads too much into the text, since nothing is said about connivance. It seems best to see here the suggestion that Job's great wealth had been acquired by the seizure of lands as well as by oppressive acts of personal inhumanity. Ball proposed 'you favour' for 'possessed the land', and so secured the second person here. But this has found no following.

man with power: lit. 'man of arm', the arm being the symbol of might; cf. Ps. 10.15.

the favoured man: lit. 'lifted of face'; cf. Isa. 3.3 (*RSV* 'the man of rank').

9. Oppression of the widow and orphan is frequently condemned in the OT (Exod. 22.22; Dt. 27.19; Jer. 7.6; 22.3; Zech.7.10) and compassion on them commended (Dt. 10.18; 14.29; 16.11, 14; 24.19; 26.12; Isa. 1.17). The orphan is strictly the fatherless, who is normally with his widowed mother. Their defence-lessness exposed them to the exploitation of the ruthless. Job repudiates this charge in 31.16.

were crushed: LXX, Vulg., Syr. and Targ. all have 'you crushed', and so some editors. But the change is needless, and it is easier to see why the versions should have assimilated this to the previous line than why anyone should have changed from that form.

10. Cf. 18.8ff. Eliphaz now directly applies the thought of Bildad to Job.

11. Your light is darkened: M.T. 'or darkness' (so *AV*, *RV*). *RSV* follows LXX (reading 'ôr (or 'ôreḵā) ḥāšaḵ for 'ô ḥōšeḵ), and so many editors. The second line is repeated in 38.34.

JOB'S ASSUMPTION OF DIVINE INDIFFERENCE, AS ENVISAGED BY ELIPHAZ 22.12–20

Eliphaz now proceeds from Job's presumed sins to the attitude to God which he supposes must have inspired them, and tells him how the wicked had been punished for their sin, to the satisfaction of the righteous.

12. Duhm would suppress this verse as a gloss (so Hölscher and Fohrer). But without it verse 13 is left without connection with what precedes. That God is enthroned on high led psalmists to conclude that he perceived all that is done on earth (Ps. 14.2; 33.13f.), but Eliphaz supposes that Job infers that he is too far off to concern himself with what men do (cf. Ps. 10.4; 73.11; Isa. 29.15).

the highest stars: lit. 'the head of the stars'. Budde, Strahan and Gray omit 'the head of'.

13. Job has not said this, but has recognized that God sees him, and besought him to look away from him (7.19; cf. 10.14).

14. the vault: *AV* and *RV* 'the circuit', lit. 'circle' (cf. Prov. 8.27; Isa. 40.22). Here it must mean the dome which was thought to cover the earth, beyond which God sat afar off. Elsewhere God is depicted as riding upon the clouds (Isa. 19.1), or making the clouds his chariot (Ps. 104.3).

15. Eliphaz finds nothing new in the attitude he attributes to Job, but reminds him that it has been adopted by wicked men of old, to their undoing. Many editors find here a reference to the wickedness that brought the Flood as its punishment. But elsewhere a flood is the means of destruction, where there is no allusion to the Flood (cf. 20.28; 27.20).

the old way: Chajes (*GSAI*, xix, 1906, pp. 182f.) proposed to read (with a change

16 They were snatched away before their time;
   their foundation was washed away.
17 They said to God, "Depart from us,"
   and "What can the Almighty do to us?"
18 Yet he filled their houses with good things—
   but the counsel of the wicked is far from me.
19 The righteous see it and are glad;
   the innocent laugh them to scorn,
20 saying, "Surely our adversaries are cut off,
   and what they left the fire has consumed".

---

of vowels only) 'the way of evil-doers' (so Ball, Tur-Sinai). But this loses something and has no support in the Versions, and it is not generally followed. Dahood (*The Bible in Current Catholic Thought*, 1962, p. 65) renders 'the way of ignorance'.

16. snatched away: cf. on 16.8.

their foundation was washed away: the Hebrew is obscure. It may be rendered, as *RV*, 'whose foundation was poured out as a stream' (so Gray; cf. Dillmann, Budde), or 'upon whose foundation a stream was poured out' (so Rosenmüller, Dhorme, Kissane; cf. *AV*). The second of these yields a clearer picture, and it lies behind RSV. Ewald finds here a reference to Sodom and Gomorrah, while others think of the Flood.

17. Many editors delete verses 17f. on the ground of their reminiscences of 21.14ff. But Eliphaz recalls what Job had said, in order to say that the prosperity to which Job had alluded was but the prelude to a disaster he had denied.

to us: so LXX and Syr. M.T. has 'to them'.

18. Eliphaz here varies the words of Job (cf. 21.16) to affirm that their prosperity came from the God they scorned. They therefore merited the disaster he sent upon them.

counsel of the wicked: see on 10.3.

far from me: LXX has 'from him' (so Dhorme). But M.T. is far more effective. Eliphaz repeats the words of Job, but with a different intention. Job rejected the way of the wicked despite their prosperity, Eliphaz to avoid disaster. He could not rise to Job's clinging to piety for its own sake.

19. For the rejoicing of the righteous over the misfortunes of the wicked, cf. Ps. 52.6f. (M.T. 8f.); 69.32 (M.T. 33). Cf. also Ps. 107.42 for their rejoicing over the exaltation of the righteous.

laugh them to scorn: the same expression stands in Ps. 2.4.

20. our adversaries: a word found only here, and if correct a curious collective term. Merx emends to read 'their possessions (cf. LXX)', and so Wright, Gray, Dhorme, Weiser, Fohrer. This is preferable to Kissane's 'their greatness', but a very slight change would yield a more ordinary word for 'our adversaries'. Since

²¹ 'Agree with God, and be at peace;
     thereby good will come to you.
²² Receive instruction from his mouth,
     and lay up his words in your heart.
²³ If you return to the Almighty and humble yourself,
     if you remove unrighteousness far from your tents,
²⁴ if you lay gold in the dust,

---

both the wicked and their possessions were destroyed (verse 16), we should expect
the rejoicing to be at both.

ELIPHAZ'S APPEAL AND PROMISE TO JOB 22.21–30

If only Job will be instructed and humble himself before God, repenting and
abandoning his sin, then he will be restored to favour and fortune. All the friends'
speeches in the first cycle had ended with advice and promise, but none of those
in the second cycle. Peake suggests that the poet may have wished to represent
Eliphaz as conscious of the harshness of his speech, feeling he had perhaps gone
too far.

21. Agree with God: the verb means 'be accustomed to' in Num. 22.30 and
'be acquainted with' in Ps. 139.3 (cf. AV and RV here). Delitzsch renders 'make
friends with', but Strahan caustically observes that the God of Eliphaz has no
friends. W. B. Bishai (*JNES*, xx, 1961, pp. 258f.) cites Arabic and Ugaritic
evidence for the meaning 'acquiesce', and so Pope: 'yield to'.

will come to you: the Hebrew is anomalous. Some editors restore the normal
form for the sense of *RSV*, while others vocalize to yield 'your increase (will be
good)'. For Eliphaz the good dividends of righteousness constitute its attraction.

22. his mouth: Eliphaz clearly thinks of himself as the mouthpiece of God.
Elsewhere he refers to revelation he has received (4.12ff.), and he declares his
own words to be the consolations of God (15.11).

lay up his words: M. Dahood (*Biblica*, XLVII, 1966, pp. 108f.) renders 'write
his words'.

23. and humble yourself: M.T. 'you will be built up' (cf. AV, RV). RSV
follows LXX (reading *tēʿāneh* for *tibbāneh*), and so many editors. Dahood (*The
Bible in Current Catholic Thought*, 1962, p. 66), citing Ugaritic evidence, renders
'you will be healed', and so Pope; but this is not convincing.

24. if you lay gold in: this is thought to mean that Job must renounce his
wealth and find his treasure in God alone. It is highly improbable that such a
thought would occur to Eliphaz, and if it did he might reflect that Job was already
stripped of all he had. The reading of Theod. and Syr. is closer to Eliphaz's
thought 'you will esteem gold as (dust)'. Eliphaz is promising Job the restoration
of his fortune; gold will be as common as dirt.

and gold of Ophir among the stones of the torrent bed,
25 and if the Almighty is your gold,
    and your precious silver;
26 then you will delight yourself in the Almighty,
    and lift up your face to God.
27 You will make your prayer to him, and he will hear you;
    and you will pay your vows.
28 You will decide on a matter, and it will be established for you,
    and light will shine on your ways.

---

gold of Ophir: M.T. simply 'Ophir'. The gold of Ophir was highly valued, but where Ophir lay is not known. It has been variously located in India, Elam, S. Arabia, and Africa. Gen. 10.29 places it between Sheba and Havilah, i.e. in S. Arabia, and Havilah is also a source of gold (Gen. 2.11f.).

among the stones: Theod. and Syr. have 'as the stones'.

25. if: this is not expressed in M.T., and we should probably render as *AV* and *RV* 'the Almighty shall be'. Dhorme says 'If the converted believer can despise money, it is because the Almighty takes the place of all the treasures in the world.' This edifying thought can scarcely be credited to Eliphaz, who had already in 5.17ff. promised Job a restoration of prosperity if he repented. What he here means most probably is that God's favour brings wealth.

your gold: this is the plural of the word in verse 24*a*, and hence Dhorme renders 'ingots of gold'. It occurs only in these two verses, and its exact meaning is unknown. That it is a term for gold is almost certain, and Dhorme thinks it means gold as it leaves the crucible. *AV* derives the word here from a different root and renders 'defence'. This is not to be preferred.

precious: the meaning of the word is uncertain. *BDB* renders 'heaps of', and so Dhorme. Cf. Pope: 'silver piled high'. With the change of one letter Voigt secured the sense 'and silver will be an abomination to you'.

26. Strahan says 'Nothing could well be finer than Eliphaz's picture of a religious life in days of prosperity.' But the days of prosperity are essential to it. Job had already lived this life in prosperity, and now in adversity he nowhere regrets his integrity or abandons it, despite the harsh judgment of his friends.

delight yourself: the same verb as in Ps. 37.4. Driver (*SVT*, III, 1955, p. 84) would derive from another root and renders 'depend on' (cf. P. Joüon (*MFO*, III, 1, 1908, pp. 323–5), who renders 'abandon oneself to', 'trust in').

27. he will hear you: Job's present complaint is that God hides his face from him and will not hear him.

pay your vows: because your requests will be granted.

28. All his undertakings will prosper, and instead of the darkness in which he now walks (19.8; 22.11) his paths will be light.

²⁹ For God abases the proud,
    but he saves the lowly.
³⁰ He delivers the innocent man;
    you will be delivered through the cleanness of your hands.'

---

29. God abases the proud: M.T. has 'when they humble, you shall say: Pride' (cf. *AV*). This is supposed somehow to mean that when men abase Job, either God will defend him, or his confidence in God will fill him with courage. It is probable that the line should provide a parallel to the following line and that 'he humbles' should be read, parallel to 'he saves'. For 'you will say' (*wattômer*) Dhorme reads '*eṭ* and deletes '*ōmer* as a repetition from the previous verse ('matter' or 'word'). But this leaves the line short: 'He abases pride'. Other proposals are '(He abases) the lofty and the proud' ('*eṭ-rām wᵉgē'eh*, Beer); '(He abases) the word of pride' ('*ōmer ga'ᵃwāh*, Duhm); '(He abases) the haughtiness of pride' (*rômaṭ gēwāh*, Steuernagel, Hölscher, Steinmann, Fohrer); '(He abases) the one who speaks proudly' ('*ōmēr gēwāh*, Richter; cf. Weiser); '(He abases) the one who boasts in pride' (*miṭ'ammēr gēwāh*, Kissane, Larcher); 'God (abases) pride' ('*elôah ga'ᵃwāh*, Budde, Gray). With this *RSV* agrees, save that it reads *gē'eh*='the proud' for *gēwāh*='pride' (so Stevenson). The proposal of Kissane involves very slight change, and is perhaps the best.

the lowly: lit. 'lowly of eyes'; contrast 'haughty of eyes' in Ps. 101.5.

30. the innocent man: the Hebrew has '*î nāqî*, which could be rendered 'island of the innocent' (so Ibn-Ezra and *AV*) or 'him that is not innocent (so Rashi and *RV*). On the latter view the verse is held to mean that by the cleanness of Job's hands the guilty will be saved. Reiske proposed to read '*iš* for '*î*, and this is followed by many editors (so *RSV*). This seems to accord more closely with Eliphaz's thought. Guillaume (*Promise and Fulfilment*, ed. by F. F. Bruce, 1963, p. 115) secures this sense without emendation by equating '*î* with Arabic '*ayya*, 'whoso-ever'. M. Dahood (*Biblica*, XLIX, 1968, p. 363) secures the same sense by resorting to Ugaritic and reading '*ê*. When Job through confession and the amendment of his life is restored to innocence, he may expect deliverance from his misfortunes.

you will be delivered: M.T. 'he will be delivered'. Theod. has second person, and so many editors. Duhm and Ball retain M.T. here, and change 'your hands' to 'his hands'. In either case the vicarious element of *RV*, which is out of place here, is removed. The man whose hands are clean delivers but himself. In the sequel Job intercedes for his friends and they are forgiven (42.8), and the principle of vicarious intercessory prayer is fully Scriptural (Gen. 18.22ff.; I Sam. 12.23). But it is improbable that Eliphaz, whose own consciousness of superior rectitude had not led him to intercede for Job or to think he had any merit to spare for Job, was thinking of this. C. Thexton (*ET*, LXXVIII, 1966–67, pp. 342f.) retains the negative in the first half and takes the second half as a rhetorical question: 'He (God) delivers the man who is not innocent; And wilt thou be delivered by the cleanness of thy hands?' This seems less appropriate than *RSV*.

23 Then Job answered:
  2 'Today also my complaint is bitter,
    his hand is heavy in spite of my groaning.
  3 Oh, that I knew where I might find him,
    that I might come even to his seat!
  4 I would lay my case before him
    and fill my mouth with arguments.
  5 I would learn what he would answer me,
    and understand what he would say to me.
  6 Would he contend with me in the greatness of his power?
    No; he would give heed to me.
  7 There an upright man could reason with him,
    and I should be acquitted for ever by my judge.
  8 'Behold, I go forward, but he is not there;
    and backward, but I cannot perceive him;

JOB ANSWERS ELIPHAZ 23; 24.1–17, 25

In the first part of his reply Job leaves aside what Eliphaz has said and gives new expression to his consciousness of undeserved suffering, and yearns afresh for the opportunity to argue his case with God, though at the same time he is afraid of God. He then turns again to the injustices of the world, where the strong oppress the weak while God does nothing. Nowhere in this speech does Job directly address the friends. Some verses, 24.18–24, do not seem appropriate to the lips of Job, and some editors think they are out of place here (see p. 210). The speech falls into four parts: Job's longing to meet God (23.2–7); the inaccessibility and power of God (verses 8–17); the inactivity of God in the face of human oppression and injustice (24.1–17, 25). On verses 18–24 see below.

JOB'S LONGING TO MEET GOD 23.2–7

Protesting anew against his sore affliction, Job desires that he might meet God, and is sure that if he did so he could convince him of his innocence. 'The undimmed light of his moral consciousness illuminates for him the way that leads unto God' (Strahan).

2. bitter: M.T. 'rebellion', used adjectivally, i.e. 'rebellious' (so *RV*, Dhorme and others). 'Bitter' (so *AV* and many editors) follows Vulg., Targ. and Syr., reading *mar* (as in 7.11) for *merî*. Ball would read 'of Shaddai'. But M.T. yields a good sense. The friends regard Job's questioning of the divine government of the world and protestation of his innocence as impious rebellion against God, and Job here declares that he will continue to be a rebel in their eyes.
his hand: M.T. 'my hand', whence *AV* and *RV* 'my stroke', following the

improbable interpretation of the Targ. of 'hand' by 'stroke'. LXX and Syr. have 'his hand', and this is followed by many editors. Budde, Dhorme and Kissane retain M.T., and find the meaning to be that Job tries to suppress his groans, but the hand with which he controls them presses too heavily on him.

heavy: *AV* and *RV* 'heavier' is without justification.

in spite of: the preposition may have this meaning, or simply 'upon', which is more natural if 'my hand' is read.

3. 'It is the chief distinction between Job and his friends that he desires to meet God and they do not' (Strahan). Cf. 9.34f.; 13.15ff.

seat: i.e. his judgment seat, or tribunal. The word means a fixed or prepared place, and some render 'dwelling'.

4. lay: lit. 'set in order', prepare my case.

5. Job is ready not alone to face God with his charges, but to hear any counter-charges God might bring against him; cf. 13.22. If only God would give him a chance to understand why he was suffering he would be satisfied.

6. He is confident that God would give him a fair hearing, and would not simply overwhelm him by his power. Earlier he had feared that God would do just that (9.34f.; 13.21). 'The magnanimity he here ascribes to God contrasts remarkably with the pettiness of which he had before accused Him' (Peake).

give heed: M.T. 'pay (attention)', an elliptic expression. Some would add a letter to give 'hear', but this implies an idiom not elsewhere found and is unnecessary.

7. An unshakable confidence in the strength of his case and the certainty of his acquittal possesses Job.

an upright man could reason with him: G. R. Driver (*AJSL*, LII, 1935-36, p. 160) with slight changes reads 'there would he affirm his case and argue with me'.

by my judge: with a change of vowels some editors read 'my suit', and take the meaning to be 'I should recover my right', or 'I should win my acquittal'. Strahan says Job does not want to be delivered from his Judge, but wants his innocence vindicated. But the one inevitably follows from the other, and since Job conceives of God as his adversary at law and also his Judge, it is meaningful that his acquittal from the charges the friends are making against him should be pronounced by God.

THE INACCESSIBILITY AND POWER OF GOD 23.8-17

Though Job cannot find God wherever he seeks him, he is assured that God knows his ways and that in the end he will be vindicated and come forth as gold from the refiner. His mind then reverts to the arbitrariness of God and his power, before which Job trembles in fear.

8f. The Psalmist can conceive of no place where he may escape God (Ps. 139.7ff.); Job finds him ever elusive (cf. 9.11). Many editors (Budde, Duhm, Gray, Ball, Fohrer) find verses 8f. to be intrusive, but Dhorme defends their retention. The thought picks up that of verse 3, which was followed by the purpose for which Job desired to find God. **Forward** is to the east, and **backward**

⁹ on the left hand I seek him, but I cannot behold him;
    I turn to the right hand, but I cannot see him.
¹⁰ But he knows the way that I take;
    when he has tried me, I shall come forth as gold.
¹¹ My foot has held fast to his steps;
    I have kept his way and have not turned aside.
¹² I have not departed from the commandment of his lips;
    I have treasured in my bosom the words of his mouth.
¹³ But he is unchangeable and who can turn him?

---

to the west; **on the left** is to the north, and **on the right** to the south. Duhm prosaically asks if any man would seek God in this fashion.

9. I seek him: M.T. 'when he works' (cf. *AV*, *RV*). Syr. has 'I seek him', and so many editors. LXX renders by '(when) he turns', and G. R. Driver (*Studies in O.T. Prophecy*, ed. H. H. Rowley, 1950, p. 54) defends this meaning for M.T. from Arabic (cf. Guillaume, *Promise and Fulfilment*, ed. F. F. Bruce, 1963, pp. 115f.). **I turn:** M.T. 'he turns'. Syr. and Vulg. have 'I turn', and so many editors. *AV* and *RV* have 'he hideth himself', giving to the verb the sense it has in Ps. 65.13 (M.T. 14); 73.6, where it means 'cover (with a mantle)'. But the verb here is a homonym meaning 'turn'.

10. the way that I take: M.T. 'the way with me' is peculiar. Syr. has 'my way and my standing', and so Houbigant, Graetz, Beer, Dhorme. S. T. Byington (*ET*, LVII, 1945–46, p. 110*a*) prefers 'the way of my standing', i.e. in which quarter to look for me. J. Reider (*HUCA*, III, 1926, p. 115) renders 'the way of my life'. The meaning is in any case clear. In contrast to Job's inability to find God, he is sure that God knows where he can find Job.
tried me: cf. on 7.18.
come forth: Dahood (*The Bible in Current Catholic Thought*, 1962, p. 67), adducing Arabic and Ugaritic evidence, holds that here this verb does not have its ordinary sense, but means 'shine'. The reference would then be to the shining surface of the gold in the crucible when the dross is removed.

11. Cf. Ps. 17.5. The divine testimony to the unswerving integrity of Job (2.3) is matched by his unwavering loyalty to the law of God.

12. in my bosom: this follows LXX and Vulg. (so most editors) in reading *beḥēḳî* instead of M.T. *mēḥuḳḳî*='more than my law'. *AV* and *RV* expand M.T. to yield 'more than my necessary food'. For the thought cf. Ps. 119.11.

13. is unchangeable: lit. 'in one' or 'as one'. *AV* and *RV* 'in one mind' supplies the word 'mind'. Most editors follow Budde and Beer in reading *bāḥar*='has chosen' instead of *be'eḥād*, and so most editors. The meaning then is that God freely chooses his course, and his power is irresistible.

What he desires, that he does.
14 For he will complete what he appoints for me;
   and many such things are in his mind.
15 Therefore I am terrified at his presence;
   when I consider, I am in dread of him.
16 God has made my heart faint;
   the Almighty has terrified me;
17 for I am hemmed in by darkness,
   and thick darkness covers my face.

---

14. what he appoints for me: lit. 'my decree'. Vulg. and Syr. have 'his decree', and so Dhorme. But this is unnecessary. The one is objective genitive and the other subjective. What Job is here saying is that whatever lot God has decreed for Job will be experienced by him. God's decree is irresistible.

many such things: Job recognizes that he is not alone in being the victim of the inscrutable will of God.

15. When Job thinks of this inexplicable way of God with men, his terror returns; cf. 21.6.

16. made . . . faint: the verb means 'be tender', and then 'be fearful'. It is used parallel to 'fear' in Dt. 20.3; Isa. 7.4; Jer. 51.46; here it is parallel to a stronger word (cf. 22.10, 'overwhelms').

17. This is a difficult verse. M.T. has 'Because I was not annihilated by reason of darkness, and by reason of my face which thick darkness covered' (cf. *AV*, *RV*). Most modern editors omit the negative, as *RSV*, though 'hemmed in' is somewhat free. In the second line the omission of one letter gives the sense of *RSV*. The meaning is then held to be that Job is enveloped in darkness by God and reduced to terror. But the verb 'be annihilated' means in Arabic and Aramaic 'be silent' and it is so rendered by Syr. here. Hence Dhorme retains the negative and renders 'I have not been silent because of darkness' (so Fohrer), and in the second line finds hypallage and renders 'and because of the gloom which has veiled my face'. He then finds the meaning to be that, despite his sufferings and the darkness which surrounds him, Job has not been reduced to silence but has freely uttered his complaints. Kissane reads 'to him' (*lô*) for 'not' (*lō'*) and renders 'to him I am blotted out by the darkness, and from me the gloom hath veiled him'. This does not seem probable, since Job has just said that he is not hidden from God. The Confraternity Version reads *lū'* for *lō'* and renders. 'Would that I had vanished in darkness, and that thick gloom were before me to conceal me'. On the whole the sense of *RSV* is to be preferred. In fear and darkness, through which he cannot see the God for whom he so yearns, Job is reduced to despair.

24 'Why are not times of judgment kept by the Almighty,
and why do those who know him never see his days?
² Men remove landmarks;
    they seize flocks and pasture them.
³ They drive away the ass of the fatherless;
    they take the widow's ox for a pledge.
⁴ They thrust the poor off the road;
    the poor of the earth all hide themselves.
⁵ Behold, like wild asses in the desert
    they go forth to their toil,
seeking prey in the wilderness
    as food for their children.

THE INACTIVITY OF GOD IN THE FACE OF HUMAN OPPRESSION AND INJUSTICE
24.1–17, 25

Job now looks beyond his own case to the world around him, and asks why God does not fix times of judgment on all the ruthless oppressors who dispossess others and whose victims are reduced by poverty to misery and robbery. Murder and adultery abound, yet God does nothing about it. Finally Job asks who can gainsay what he has stated. Apart from verses 18–24, on which see below, many editors dispute the unity of this chapter. Merx (cf. also Strahan) thought that verses 9–24 were substituted for part of Job's speech because it was too heretical to be preserved, and found its sketches of human behaviour to be without moral judgment. But the question why God does not fix times of judgment implies that it was on these things that he thought it was called for. Hoffmann transferred verses 13–25 to Bildad, following 25.6, while Siegfried held verses 13–24 to be a correcting interpolation to conform the speech to the orthodox doctrine, and Steinmann verses 1–24 to be an interpolated social satire. Westermann (*Der Aufbau des Buches Hiob*, 1956, p. 103) rejected verses 5–8, 10f., 13–17 as later interpolations. Duhm found in the chapter a collection of isolated poems rather than a single speech, and similarly Fohrer, who distinguishes the following four poems: verses 1–4, 10–12, 22f.; 5–8; 13–14, 16*a*, 15, 16*b*, 17; 18*aα*, 20*b*, 18*aβ*, *b*, 19, 20*a*, 21. G. A. Barton (*JBL*, xxx, 1911, pp. 70ff.) assigned verses 5–8, 17–22, 24 (but not in that order) to Bildad. Budde, on the contrary, finds no reason to reject the chapter as a whole, and so Gray (save for 13–17 and parts of 18–24) and Dhorme (save 18–24; so Pfeiffer, *Introduction to the Old Testament*, 1941, p. 664), while Peake says 'the coincidence of unusual form and unexpected content suffices to justify a measure of uncertainty, but hardly more than a suspended judgment'. Kissane transfers some verses within the chapter, but finds no reason to reject them.

    1. LXX reads 'Why are times hidden from the Almighty?' and this is followed by Dhorme, who thinks the meaning is that God is not interested in the events

on earth. But if these were hidden from God the sense would be that he *could* not see them, and not that he did not wish to. The verb could mean 'be hidden' (Jer. 16.17), but it can also mean 'be laid up' (15.20), and so most editors here. The meaning then is: 'Why does not God reserve fixed times (for judgment)?' What troubles Job is that God not only does not interfere with all the things he is going to describe, but that he has no days of assize or reckoning with men, so that those who are loyal to him never see him in judgment on the lawless. Note that in Ps. 36.10 (M.T. 11) 'those who know' God are parallel to 'the upright of heart'. For **his days** Kt. has 'his day', and Duhm follows this and gives an eschatological turn to the verse. But this is unnecessary.

2. The first line is short, and many editors follow LXX in reading 'The wicked remove landmarks'. This means the removing of boundary stones and hence the encroachment on the lands of others. For the condemnation of this cf. Dt. 19.14; 27.17 (cf. also Prov. 22.28; 23.10; Hos. 5.10).

and pasture them: LXX reads 'and their shepherd', and so many editors. If M.T. is retained (so Duhm, Strahan, Kissane, Fohrer), the meaning is that the powerful seize the flocks as well as the lands of their weaker neighbours, and openly pasture them, perhaps on the lands they have stolen. Whichever reading is adopted, the powerful are presented as brazenly dispossessing the weak of their property.

3. The most defenceless of persons were the widow and orphan, who are frequently commended in the *OT* to the conscience of men. To drive away the ass of the fatherless was as cruel as the seizure of the poor man's ewe lamb in Nathan's parable (2 Sam. 12.4), and to seize the widow's ox in pledge was far harsher than to take her garments, which is forbidden in Dt. 24.17. For garments taken in pledge were returned at night when they were most needed (Exod. 22.26; Dt. 24.10ff.). But the ox, like the millstone (cf. Dt. 24.6), was needed for livelihood. Job is here describing the behaviour of the most callous of men.

4. thrust: Dhorme takes the verb to be intransitive, '(The poor) turn aside', but most take as *RSV*. The line is variously taken to mean that the rights of the poor on the public highway are denied them, or that this is a figure for the deprivation of the poor of their rights in general. Hitzig, with an excess of imagination, thought it referred to the dispossessed poor begging for the restoration of their property.

hide themselves: M.T. 'are hidden together'. Dhorme thinks the form of the verb (found only here) indicates that they were compelled to hide themselves. But Gray rejects this and, with many others, reads the normal reflexive form for the two words of the Hebrew, as *RSV*. The general thought is that the poor, deprived of their rights, betake themselves where they may and no one cares.

5. The thought now turns to the victims of oppression, and the life of misery and crime to which they are driven. The text is very difficult, as may be seen by comparing *AV*, *RV*, and *RSV*. Innumerable emendations have been proposed, but none has been generally accepted.

to their work: M.T. has 'in their work' or 'when they work', but the change of

⁶ They gather their fodder in the field
   and they glean the vineyard of the wicked man.
⁷ They lie all night naked, without clothing,
   and have no covering in the cold.
⁸ They are wet with the rain of the mountains,
   and cling to the rock for want of shelter.
⁹ (There are those who snatch the fatherless child from the breast,
   and take in pledge the infant of the poor.)
¹⁰ They go about naked, without clothing;
   hungry, they carry the sheaves;

---

preposition is slight and is found in some MSS. Some editors (so Peake, Strahan, Stevenson) omit these words, while Dhorme retains M.T., but transfers to follow 'seeking prey', and for 'in the wilderness' reads 'until evening': 'although they work until the evening'. Then, with many editors, he reads *lō'* for *lô*, securing 'no bread for the children'. The picture then is of desperate people seeking a meagre existence in the desert, but in vain. *RSV*, with less change of the text, presents a less desperate picture, since here some prey for the maintenance of the family is found. *AV* and *RV* more vaguely allow the wilderness to provide some food. The general sense of the verse seems to be that as the wild asses roam the desert in search of food, so these wretched people, who have no land to cultivate, eagerly seek such wild food as the wilderness provides to maintain themselves and their families. A precarious livelihood indeed! Kissane emends to secure a poorer verse: 'Like wild asses in the desert they go forth, By their labour they seek food, They work to get bread for their children'. More violent is Ball's treatment: 'Like wild asses into the waste they go forth, Like ass-colts in quest of forage', with the suppression of the rest of the verse. Guillaume (*Promise and Fulfilment*, ed. F. F. Bruce, 1963, p. 116) reads *lû* for *lô* and renders 'they go early to the steppe for meat, (To see) if there be food for the(ir) children.'

6. They gather their fodder: M.T. 'they reap his mixed fodder'. This is thought to mean that they can only get cattle food to eat. But some ellipsis is involved in *reaping* mixed fodder. LXX, Vulg., Targ., Syr. have 'They reap (in a field which) is not his' (*bᵉlî lô* for *bᵉlîlô*), and this is followed by Hitzig (so Kissane). But the change from plural to singular in M.T. is to be noted. Houbigant suggested reading '(They reap) in the night' (*ballaylāh* for *bᵉlîlô*), and so Budde, Dhorme, Fohrer (Merx, Duhm, and Hölscher *ballayil* with the same meaning). The meaning is then thought to be either that they work as labourers for someone else (or perhaps by night), or that they steal from someone else's field (perhaps by night). It is more probable that the meaning is that they eke out the poor provision they get from the wilderness by night prowling wherever they can see a chance to secure some food. That night prowling had to be guarded against at harvest time is clear from Isa. 1.8. Ball thought a closer parallel to 'the wicked man' was needed here, and suggested *b^eliyya'al*='worthless man' (so also Larcher, Steinmann, Pope). But this was the good-for-nothing, and the thief is less concerned with the character than with the possessions of his victim.

glean: the word is found only here, and its meaning is not certain. Gleaning was a legitimate occupation of the poor. If the reaping of the previous line was as a hired labourer, we should expect here the gathering of the grapes as a paid labourer (so Dhorme). On the other hand, if the reaping was unauthorized, we should expect more than gleaning here, and *BDB* gives 'despoil'.

the wicked man: many editors change this to 'the rich man', but this is unnecessary. To the poor the rich are often the wicked, and there may here be some suggestion that the people who are being despoiled deserved it by the way they acquired their wealth. Without change of text Guillaume (loc. cit.) secures this meaning by importing an Arabic sense.

7f. To the misery of hunger is added that of lack of clothing, and lack of shelter against the storms. Unhoused and barely clad they live their wretched lives in stark contrast with the ruthless who have been described in verses 2–4.

cling: lit. 'embrace', the word used in Gen. 29.13. Nothing could better express the exposure and wretchedness of these people than the picture of them embracing the rock as though it were their dearest friend.

9. This verse is commonly held to interrupt the account of the plight of the outcasts, and may be out of place. Gray, Dhorme and others transfer it to follow verse 3, while Kissane transfers it to follow verse 12. Fohrer, following Siegfried, Budde, Duhm, regards it as a misplaced gloss on verse 3. But cf. on verse 10.

from the breast: the Hebrew word normally means 'violence', 'ruin', and Syr. and Vulg. so understand here. But this is inappropriate. The word is occasionally found elsewhere for 'breast' (Isa. 60.16; 66.11), however, and that is doubtless the meaning here (so LXX, Targ.). The heartlessness of the creditor is seen in the cruel snatching of the babe from its widowed mother, to be brought up as a slave. Larcher adds a letter to yield 'from his field', but this is much inferior.

the infant: M.T. has the strange construction 'take as a pledge upon the poor'. Kamphausen proposed to read *'ūl*='suckling' instead of *'al*, giving the sense of RSV. This has been generally followed, and is supported by the parallelism J. D. Michaelis (*Orientalische und exegetische Bibliothek*, VIII, 1775, p. 196) anticipated Kamphausen, but erroneously proposed *'ōl* for *'ūl*). Less probably Larcher reads *m^e'īl* for *w^e'al* and renders 'the mantle (of the poor)'. But the *m^e'īl* was a garment worn by men of rank and it is quite inappropriate here.

10. Here, it is sometimes thought, we have the picture of labourers in the fields of others, reinforcing the view that in verse 6 it is a question of hired labourers. But it is more probable that here the condition of slaves is described. In verses 6–8 the state of outcasts is depicted, and there is no reason to link verses 10f. directly with verses 6–8. The author passes from one group of exploited people to another, and draws a series of sketches of wretched and downtrodden people,

¹¹ among the olive rows of the wicked they make oil;
    they tread the wine presses, but suffer thirst.
¹² From out of the city the dying groan,
    and the soul of the wounded cries for help;
    yet God pays no attention to their prayer.
¹³ 'There are those who rebel against the light,

---

to expose the many injustices of the world. Here the scarcely clad who work in
the fields are more likely to be slaves than day-labourers. 'It is a torture of
Tantalus', says Dhorme, 'to have to carry sheaves when one suffers from hunger'.
E. F. Sutcliffe (*JTS*, L, 1949, p. 174) rejects verse 10*a* as tautologous, while Gray
rejects verses 10*a* and 11*a* as out of place or corrupt. But nakedness and hunger
do not make a surprising combination. Tur-Sinai, with the greatest improbability,
finds the sense 'Naked, they spin without clothing'. This depends upon the
assumption that the Hebrew word is the translation of an Aramaic word wrongly
substituted for another Aramaic word which had the requisite meaning!

11. among the olive-rows of the wicked they make oil: *AV* and *RV*
understood the meaning to be 'between their walls', which is a possible translation.
The reference then is supposed to be within the walled enclosure of their masters.
But M.T. can equally be rendered 'between their rows', and this is understood by
RSV and many editors. But this would be a curious place to press the oil. Dhorme
with a very slight change proposed to read 'between two millstones', and so
Steinmann and Pope (Larcher 'without the two millstones'). But this meaning is
hazardously conjectured, and the word is nowhere else found for 'millstones'.
Bickell cleverly suggested, with the change of two letters, 'between their songs'
(cf. E. F. Sutcliffe, loc. cit., p. 176, 'without their songs'). It is well known that
songs characterized the vintage and olive harvest, and the absence of such songs
would well express the misery of the labourers. The verb 'they make oil' is
found only here, but it is probably a denominative from the well-known word
for 'oil' *yiṣhār* (so *AV*, *RV* and almost all editors). Alternatively it has been derived
from the word for 'noonday' (cf. Vulg. and Syr.), and Kissane follows this,
finding the meaning to be that they are forced to work through the heat of the day.

12. the dying: M.T. has 'the city of men', but the change of a vowel ($\bar{e}$ for ^{e}),
following Syr., improves the sense and is generally followed (so *RSV*).
pays no attention: the same idiom as in 23.6 (see note there). There is no need
to alter the text to 'does not hear'.
prayer: M.T. has 'folly', 'tastelessness' (cf. on 1.22), in which case the verb may
be rendered 'impute' (cf. *AV*, *RV*). But Syr. has 'prayer' (so two Hebrew MSS.)
and so many editors. The verse describes the apparent indifference of God to the
groans and cries of suffering mortals.

13. Job now turns to fresh groups of evil-doers who escape judgment:

who are not acquainted with its ways,
and do not stay in its paths.
¹⁴ The murderer rises in the dark,
that he may kill the poor and needy;
and in the night he is as a thief.
¹⁵ The eye of the adulterer also waits for the twilight,
saying, "No eye will see me";
and he disguises his face.
¹⁶ In the dark they dig through houses;
by day they shut themselves up;

---

murderers, adulterers, housebreakers. Above he has referred to those who are driven by poverty to steal in order to survive; but here he thinks of those who are driven by the wickedness of their heart to rebel against the law of God.

stay: Dhorme and some others read 'return' with Vulg. But this is not to be preferred. The classes to be mentioned are singled out because they leave the path of rectitude, not because they do not return to it. The sin of an adulterer is not that he does not return to chastity, but that he did not abide in it.

14. in the dark: M.T. has 'at the light' (cf. *AV*, *RV* 'with the light'). But since verse 13 indicates that here we have classes of men who avoid the light, very many editors add one letter (believed lost by haplography) to read '(when there was) no light'. The murderer seeks the cloak of darkness for his crime.

the poor and needy: Duhm changes this to 'his adversary and his enemy', and is followed by Strahan. But the murderer is not here thought of as killing in order to avenge himself, or in order to rob, but because he loves murder, and chooses the defenceless as his victims (cf. Ps. 10.8f.; 37.14).

he is as a thief: this could only mean that the murderer is like the thief in working in the night. But his crime is so much greater than that of the thief that almost all modern editors accept the emendation of Merx, which, with the change of one letter and the redivision of the words, yields 'the thief prowls'. This line is then transferred to precede verse 16, where the activity of the burglar is described.

15. Cf. Prov. 7.9, where the prostitute is represented as beginning operations at dusk. Here the adulterer seeks the double protection of darkness and disguise.

16. they dig: M.T. has 'he digs', which is not the way an adulterer secures entrance to a house, but which is the way a thief found entrance (cf. Mt. 6.19). This therefore favours the view that verse 14c belongs with verse 16.

they shut themselves up: the verb here changes to the plural, the reference from here on being to the three groups first mentioned, all of whom work the works of darkness and shut themselves up by day. The verb here means 'seal', i.e. set a seal upon, or 'seal up'. *AV* and *RV* marg. take it in the former sense,

they do not know the light.
¹⁷ For deep darkness is morning to all of them;
   for they are friends with the terrors of deep darkness.
¹⁸ 'You say, "They are swiftly carried away upon the

---

and suppose the thief had marked in the daylight the house he would enter at night, and so Dhorme. But the seal identifies the person whose seal it is, and is not appropriate to such marks as thieves might make. When something is sealed up, the purpose of the seal is to prevent unauthorized opening by the identifiable unbroken seal. It is therefore to ensure security. Here it is appropriate, for it implies that these classes of criminals lie during the day as secure as if their houses were sealed.

they do not know the light: this line is short, but the next line is long, and it is probable that its opening, 'for together', i.e. all of them, should be transferred to precede this line.

   17. deep darkness: see on 3.5.

to all of them: M.T. 'for together to them'. The first two of these words should be transferred to verse 16, leaving 'to them'.

are friends: M.T. has singular. The verb is the same as in verse 13 ('are acquainted'), and in both it has the nuance of friendly acquaintance. The meaning is that the darkness which holds only terrors for others is to them a friend. Dhorme emends to read 'When its (i.e. morning's) light shines, terrors seize them', meaning that daylight, which dispels the terrors of others, brings them upon them. But this is a needless effort to secure essentially the same meaning.

MISPLACED PART OF THE THIRD SPEECH OF ZOPHAR 24.18–24

THE DIVINE PUNISHMENT OF THE WICKED 24.18–24

These verses are very perplexing on the lips of Job. They express rather the sentiments of the friends, that the wicked are swiftly cut off, and though they may flourish for a time this is but the prelude to their inevitable doom. RSV represents verses 18–21 as Job's citation of the views of the friends, though there is no indication of this in the text, and verses 22–24 as Job's reply. But they are not really a reply, for they end with the assurance of retribution on the wicked, whereas Job is arguing that experience does not justify this assurance. Peake regards verses 18–21, 24 as glosses added to correct the views of Job. As the third cycle of speeches is certainly in some disorder (see pp. 213f.), it seems better with Dhorme to transfer them to Zophar's third speech, following 27.13 (so Terrien; also H. Rongy, *Revue Ecclésiastique de Liége*, xxv, 1933, pp. 97f.). Larcher assigns them to Zophar, but after 27.23 (cf. Pope). Stevenson declares these verses corrupt beyond any plausible reconstruction.

   18. You say: this is not in the Hebrew or in the versions.

they are swiftly: M.T. 'he is swift'. Many editors read as RSV (*kallû* for *kal hû*').

    face of the waters;
  their portion is cursed in the land;
  no treader turns toward their vineyards.
¹⁹ Drought and heat snatch away the snow waters;
  so does Sheol those who have sinned.
²⁰ The squares of the town forget them;

Dhorme, transferring this verse to follow 27.13, retains M.T. and takes the
singular to refer to the 'wicked man' and the plural in 'their portion' to refer to
the 'oppressors'. The wicked man is likened to a light thing on the surface of the
water, borne swiftly away by the current and vanishing before one's eyes (cf.
Hos. 10.7).

their portion: i.e. their estates. These lie under a curse, and are therefore not
fruitful (cf. 5.3).

no treader turns: M.T. has 'he turneth not by the way of', which is then
held to mean that he knows his vineyards are unfruitful and so does not visit
them. Bickell suggested reading *dōrēk karmām* for *derek kᵉrāmîm*, yielding the
sense of *RSV*, and so very many editors. The meaning then is that there are
no grapes to tread. The whole thought of the verse is alien to the contention of
Job.

  19. The meaning of the verse is clear. As drought and heat melt the snow, so
Sheol carries off the sinner. But the two halves of the verse are not balanced, and
innumerable emendations have been proposed. Dhorme transfers the verb to the
second line, where it is more appropriate to Sheol's snatching of the sinners,
though by zeugma it is understood with both halves: 'Drought and heat the
snow waters, and Sheol the sinner snatches'. Pope omits 'drought' and 'waters'
but that leaves the second line short. Duhm omitted 'waters', and so several
editors, who think that originally 'snow' and 'waters' were alternative readings.
Gray thinks 'snow waters' were specified as not fed from a source and so easily
dried up. Guillaume (*Promise and Fulfilment*, ed. Bruce, 1963, pp. 116f.) secures
the unconvincing sense: 'When drought and heat are great The snow waters fail
to flow.'

  20. The squares of the town: M.T. has 'the womb (*reḥem*) (forgets him, the
worm) sucks him (*mᵉtāḳô*)' (cf. *AV, RV*). But the arrangement of the verse is
unusual, and 'is not remembered' is parallel to 'forgets him'. Beer proposed
rᵉḥōb mᵉḳōmô='the square of his place', giving the sense of *RSV*, and this has
been widely followed. Dhorme thinks 'womb' more appropriate (cf. Isa. 49.15),
and for *mᵉtāḳô* suggests *pᵉtāḳô*='which has formed him (forgets him)', using a
known Akkadian root to provide a lost Hebrew verb. But Beer's suggestion is
more probable. The wicked man is unremembered in the place where he was
once so powerful. M.T. 'sucks him' is from the root 'be sweet' (21.33) or 'suck

their name is no longer remembered;
     so wickedness is broken like a tree".

21 'They feed on the barren childless woman,
     and do no good to the widow.

22 Yet God prolongs the life of the mighty by his power;
     they rise up when they despair of life.

23 He gives them security, and they are supported;
     and his eyes are upon their ways.

(*AV* and *RV* 'feed sweetly on')', though the latter sense is doubtful and is found only here in *OT*.

their name: M.T. has 'the worm (feeds sweetly on)'. Gray proposed the reading followed by *RSV*, and is followed by Ball, Dhorme, Fohrer and others. This is more appropriate to the verb (cf. Ps. 83.4 (M.T. 5)), if the first line is read as above. For the third line cf. 19.10.

21. feed on: this is a strange figure and many editors follow LXX in reading 'ill-treat' (*hēra'* for *rō'eh*). This gives a better parallel. The reference is once more to the wicked man who exploits and oppresses the weak and the unfortunate. But here he meets with swift retribution (verse 24).

22. This verse has been most variously interpreted. *RSV* presents the picture of God recovering the wicked to health when they are at death's door. On the other hand, *AV* and *RV* present the picture of God using his power over the mighty to destroy their confidence. It is a question whether it is God who rises in judgment or the wicked who rises in health.

God prolongs: M.T. 'he draws'. Most editors agree that the understood subject is God, but Kissane thinks it is the tyrant. The verb may mean 'drag off' or 'prolong'; if the latter is understood, 'his life' must be supplied. Dhorme takes it in the former sense, and reads the participle, 'he who seizes (the mighty by his power) rises)'. On the one view God here is gracious to the wicked, only to destroy them in the next verse; on the other he here swiftly intervenes to punish them for their harshness to the weak. The latter seems most relevant here, if these verses are rightly to be transferred to Zophar.

they rise: M.T. 'he rises', probably with God as subject.

when they despair of life: M.T. 'and he does not believe (or trust) in life'. The same idiom is found in Dt. 28.66 'and have no assurance of life'. This is more naturally taken to be the consequence of the rising (of God), than the time of the rising (of the wicked man). When God rises against a man, he is uncertain of his very life.

23. The difference in interpretation here rests on whether the second line should read 'and his eyes' (*RSV*) or 'but his eyes' (*AV*). On the former view God grants the wicked support and a sense of security and watches over them with care; on

²⁴ They are exalted a little while, and then are gone;
  they wither and fade like the mallow;
  they are cut off like the heads of grain.
²⁵ If it is not so, who will prove me a liar,
  and show that there is nothing in what I say?'

25 Then Bildad the Shuhite answered:
  ² 'Dominion and fear are with God;

---

the latter though God allows them to feel secure, he is in fact watching them closely. The latter view (Dhorme, Larcher, Pope) leads on better to verse 24.

24. Here the Hebrew is strange in reading 'they are exalted . . . and he is not'. But throughout this passage there is some confusion between singular and plural. The sense here is quite clear. The wicked in the midst of their exaltation are cut off like a flower, or like the heads of grain before the reaping knife (cf. Ps.103. 15f., where the thought is not of the wicked, but of all men). There are, however, some difficulties in the Hebrew forms of the verse, which have given rise to various emendations, which need not be considered here.

they wither and fade: the Hebrew has 'they are brought low' (cf. Ps. 106.43) 'and are drawn together' (cf. 5.16 of shutting the mouth). For the second verb many editors substitute the verb used of the mallow in 30.4, 'they are plucked'.

like the mallow: M.T. has 'as all'; cf. *AV* and *RV* 'as all other'. Here LXX has 'as the mallow' (cf. 30.4), and this is widely followed by editors. J. Reider (*ZAW*, N.F., xII, 1935, pp. 273ff.) without change of text argues for the meaning 'umbel of the mallow').

heads of grain: the grain was cut off near the ear by a knife, and not by a scythe (cf. Wetzstein in Delitzsch).

25. This verse probably returns to the speech of Job and concludes it.

THE THIRD SPEECH OF BILDAD 25;26.5–14

As the book stands, this speech of Bildad's consists of five verses only, and it is followed by two speeches of Job's, while Zophar disappears from the discussion. Some scholars have thought the author intended to suggest that the friends had run out of arguments (cf. A. Schultens, *Liber Jobi*, II, 1737, p. 729), but this is improbable (cf. K. Fullerton, *ZAW*, N.F., I, 1924, p. 121). In chapter 26 and again in chapter 27, as in chapter 24, there is material which is not appropriate to the lips of Job, and so many scholars have rearranged these chapters to yield a complete third cycle of speeches, though with the recognition that part of the speeches may be lost. But there are wide diversities in the reconstructions. The most probable view is that Bildad's speech consisted originally of 25.2–6; 26.5–14 (so Reuss, Siegfried, Ball, Dhorme, Stevenson, Terrien, Larcher, Pope; Lefèvre

he makes peace in his high heaven.
3 Is there any number to his armies?
  Upon whom does his light not arise?
4 How then can man be righteous before God?
  How can he who is born of woman be clean?
5 Behold, even the moon is not bright
  and the stars are not clean in his sight;
6 how much less man, who is a maggot,
  and the son of man, who is a worm!'

(SDB, IV, 1949, cols. 1078f.) reverses the order, 26.5–14, 25.2–6, while Tournay (RB, LXIV, 1957, pp. 321ff.) does the same but assigns 26.2–4 also to Bildad, and so Strahan, the former placing these verses at the end and the latter at the beginning of the speech, while Löhr (BZAW, no. XXXIV, 1922, pp. 107ff.) and Steinmann have the order 26.2–4; 25.2–6; 26.5–14). Duhm and Hölscher give Bildad 26.2–4, 25.2–6, 26.5f., 11–14, while Gray gives him 25.2–6 and perhaps chapter 26. Peake rejects all of these views, and assigns to Bildad 26.2f.; 26.5–14, while Fohrer limits Bildad's speech to 25.2–6 and regards 26.5–14 as an interpolated hymn (cf. Irwin). Marshall and Kissane suppose that 25.2–6; 26.5–14 belong to Zophar, while Pfeiffer with great improbability assigns these verses to Job. Laue (Die Composition des Buches Hiob, 1895, pp. 75–90) rejects chapter 25 altogether, and gives to Bildad 27.13–23. While all reconstructions must be hazardous, it will be seen that there is much support for that here adopted.

It is to be noted that Bildad's speech has no proper beginning, and it resumes some of the things that have been already said by Eliphaz. Its theme throughout is the power of God and the universality of his dominion in the netherworld, on earth and in heaven. It falls into two parts: God's might and purity (25.2–6); God's all-embracing rule (26.5–14). These two parts are separated by the beginning of Job's response.

GOD'S MIGHT AND PURITY 25.2–6

Shocked at Job's catalogue of the miseries and inequalities on earth, Bildad directs Job's thought to the exalted character of God, whose power is matched by a purity which is awe-inspiring and before which even the stars are impure.

2. **Dominion and fear:** cf. 13.11. God is the supreme Lord of the universe, and his power inspires terror.

with God: M.T. 'with him'. It is probable that the real beginning of the speech is lost, since here we have none of the reproach or impatience which usually marks the opening words of the speeches. Some antecedent to the pronoun may have stood in the lost opening.

peace in his high heaven: lit. 'peace in his heights'. This may refer to mytho-

26 Then Job answered:
2 'How you have helped him who has no power!

---

logical stories of wars between the angels or of rebellion against God. For conflicts between angels cf. Dan. 10.13, 20f.; 11.1; for rebellion against God cf. 26.12f.; also 8.13; Isa. 51.9; 24.21.

3. armies: the hosts of God are not merely the angels, but the stars with whom they were associated; cf. Isa. 40.26.

light: LXX has 'his ambush' (a change of one letter), and so Duhm, Dhorme, Fohrer. This is not to be preferred. If the armies are linked with stars, light is relevant here. God is in control of all heavenly bodies, spiritual and material, and his will is everywhere supreme.

4. It is hard to escape the feeling that for Bildad the power of God was equated with his purity. Cf. 4.17; 15.14.

5. Cf. 15.15. Here physical brightness is linked with ethical purity. The heavenly bodies are again linked in thought with the angels associated with them, and the clearness of their light accepted as the proof of their moral perfection. For the first line, which shows some peculiarities, Driver (*AJSL*, LII, 1935–36, p. 161) offers the rendering 'Lo, the moon goes round her course and shows herself unworthy'. This involves the change of one vowel and the derivation of the second verb from a different root, for which Arabic evidence is adduced.

6. Cf. 4.19; 15.16. The littleness of man, and his humble origin, are evidence to Bildad of his moral worthlessness. It is hard to see how Bildad could suppose that any of this was an answer to Job. When God speaks to Job from the whirlwind, it is not to say that because he is weak he should not question or challenge the might of God, but to say that because he is ignorant he should not judge God.

JOB ANSWERS BILDAD 26.1–4; 27.2–6

At this point difficulties and disagreements increase. Part of chapter 26 is probably to be assigned to Bildad (see pp. 213f.), and part of chapter 27 is to be assigned to Zophar (see p. 221). But there is considerable divergence of view as to how much is to be attributed to Job. Dhorme, Lefèvre (loc. cit.), Terrien and Larcher think 26.2–4; 27.2–12 constitute all that has survived of his speech, while Gray, Ball and Fohrer allow him only 26.2–4; 27.2–6, 11f., to which Stevenson adds also 27.22, while Reuss allows 26.2–4; 27.2–23. Siegfried and Peake reduce his speech to 26.2–4; 27.2–6 (Pope adds 27.7), and this view is accepted here as the most satisfactory. Hertzberg (*Festschrift Alfred Bertholet*, 1950, pp. 238ff.) extends the speech to 26.2–4; 27.11f.; 26.5–12; 27.2–6. Others allow Job no part of chapter 26. Thus Strahan assigns him 27.2–6; Duhm 27.2–6, 12; Gray 27.2–6, 11f.; Hölscher and Stevenson 27.2–12. Laue (loc. cit.) improbably transfers 9.2–24 to follow 26.2f. to form the whole of Job's speech here, and with greater improbability Kissane assigns 26.2–4; 27.7–23 to Bildad. Pfeiffer attributes 26.2–4; 27.11f.;

How you have saved the arm that has no strength!

³ How you have counselled him who has no wisdom,
    and plentifully declared sound knowledge!
⁴ With whose help have you uttered words,
    and whose spirit has come forth from you?
⁵ The shades below tremble,
    the waters and their inhabitants.
⁶ Sheol is naked before God,
    and Abad'don has no covering.
⁷ He stretches out the north over the void,

25.2–6; 26.5–14 to Job here, and 27.2–6 to Job in answer to Zophar, but this includes what is probably to be assigned to Bildad.

Job opens his speech with biting sarcasm at the irrelevance of Bildad's speech, and then renews his declaration of his own innocence. The speech falls into two parts: Job's scorn for Bildad (26.2–4); Job's inflexible protestation of innocence (27.2–6).

JOB'S SCORN FOR BILDAD 26.2–4

Job asks what is the relevance of Bildad's speech. To whom has it been directed, and what is the source of its inspiration? Some think the meaning is that Job is taunting Bildad with having rallied to the defence of God as though he needed Bildad's help, while others think he is asking Bildad how he thinks his words could possibly bring help and relief to Job. As has been said above (p. 215), some think these verses belong to Bildad's speech and their sarcasm to be directed against Job. But Job's last speech could hardly be supposed to be a defence of God. It was rather a denial that there is any moral government of the world.

2. you: the Hebrew is here singular, and so in verses 3f. Job elsewhere addresses the friends together in the plural (save in 16.3; 12.7f.; 21.3).

him who has no power: it is hard to see how Job could be thought to be reproaching Bildad for thinking God needed his help when the burden of Bildad's speech was the all-ruling might of God. It is more likely that Job is asking what consolation Bildad imagines he has ministered to Job.

3. sound knowledge: cf. on 5.12.

plentifully: as the text stands, Bildad's speech is remarkably short, and even if we transfer to him 26.5–14 it is still not one of the long speeches. Job is thus ironically saying that, short as it is, its wisdom is superabundant. Reiske thought we should read a word directly parallel to the first line, and suggested 'to the tender' (and so Kissane). This is from the root found in 23.16 (see note there). But the timid are not the same as the unwise, and this is not to be preferred.

Graetz desiderated the meaning 'to the boorish' which he secured by reading *leḥaʿar* for *lārōḥ*. With the slighter change to *labbōr*, Driver (*HTR*, XXIX, 1936, p. 172) justifies the same meaning.

4. With whose help? *AV* and *RV* have 'To whom?' Either is a possible rendering. If the latter is read, the meaning is that Job is as well informed as the friends and does not need instructing in elementary truths (cf. 12.3; 13.2). If the former, the line is more closely parallel to the following line, and it challenges by implication the idea that Bildad's wisdom has any deeper source than his own heart.

Misplaced Part of Bildad's Third Speech 26.5–14

GOD'S ALL-EMBRACING RULE **26.5–14**

As noted above (pp. 213f.), these verses are probably a part of Bildad's speech, continuing his affirmation of the omnipotence of God. The nether world is subject to his authority and the earth and the heavens are governed by him. Yet all that we can know of his might is but a fragment of a vaster whole.

5. shades: these are the dead (*Repā'îm*), or perhaps the élite among the dead (cf. Isa. 14.9; 26.14; Ps. 88.10 (M.T. 11)), experiencing the attenuated half-life of Sheol. The term is also used of giants (Gen. 14.5; 15.20; Dt. 2.11, 20), and some think these are referred to here (so Strahan). It is suggested that they were rebels against God who were banished to Sheol. But the Biblical references to them do not suggest this, and the thought here seems to be of the power of God over those who are in Sheol rather than to the power that consigned them there. On the Rephaim and the theories about them cf. A. R. Johnson, *The Vitality of the Individual*, 2nd edn., 1964, pp. 88ff., where full references to the literature will be found.

below: in M.T. this word belongs to the following line; cf. *RV* 'beneath the waters'. It should perhaps be read with the first line. Dhorme then supplies a verb for the second line, *yēḥattû*='become terrified', which could easily have been lost after *mittāḥat*='below' (cf. Beer). This adds nothing to the sense, but improves the parallelism and the rhythm. The second line is commonly held to refer to the denizens of the sea, or perhaps to the great sea-monsters, though there is nothing to indicate the latter. But the mention of fishes between the Shades and Sheol is unnatural. It is therefore more probable that the reference here is also to Sheol, and if the Rephaim are the élite among the dead (cf. above) we have here mention of the ordinary dead in the nether world, entrance to which is often depicted in terms of being overwhelmed by waters (cf. 2 Sam. 22.5 =Ps. 18.4f. (M.T. 5f.)).

6. Cf. Prov. 15.11; Ps. 139.8; Am. 9.2.

Abaddon: another name for Sheol, found only in the Wisdom Literature (cf. 28.22; 31.12; Ps. 88.11 (M.T. 1); Prov. 15.11; 27.20). The word is derived from the root meaning 'destroy' (cf. *AV*). In Rev. 9.11 it is a personal name, translated as Apollyon.

7. the north: Hebrew *Ṣāpôn*. Some have thought the reference here was to

and hangs the earth upon nothing.
⁸ He binds up the waters in his thick clouds,
and the cloud is not rent under them.
⁹ He covers the face of the moon,
and spreads over it his cloud.

---

the northern heavens, with the great constellations (so Davidson). Others have
thought the reference was to the mysterious north of the earth, with its great
mountains (so Peake). In the Ras Shamra texts *Şāpôn* is the name of the mythological mountain (cf. Isa. 14.13), where Baal was enthroned (cf. Eissfeldt, *Baal
Zaphon, Zeus Kasios und der Durchzug der Israeliten durchs Meer*, 1932), and it is
possible that here there are overtones of this conception (so Pope). In Ps. 48.2
(M.T. 3) Zion, the seat of Yahweh, is equated with this mountain. It is to be
noted, however, that elsewhere we read of the heavens being 'stretched out'
(Ps. 104.2; Isa. 40.22; 44.24; 45.12; Jer. 10.12; 51.15), but not of the earth or the
mountains; and, since the parallel line speaks of the earth, it is more probable that
there is no mythological implication here and that the reference is to the heavens
in contrast to the earth.

upon nothing: elsewhere we read of the earth being supported by pillars
(1 Sam. 2.8; Ps. 75.3 (M.T. 4)). Buttenwieser thinks the author 'had outgrown
the naïve view of his age about the universe, and conceived of the earth as 'a
heavenly body floating in space', and notes that Pythagoras, as early as 540–510 B.C.,
on his travels in Egypt and the East, 'acquired the knowledge of the obliquity of
the ecliptic and of the earth's being a sphere freely poised in space'. The reference
to the pillars of heaven in verse 11, however, make this improbable. Dhorme
observes that even if the earth were thought of as standing upon pillars, unless
these were thought of as standing upon others, and those on yet others *ad infinitum*,
the whole must be thought of as poised upon nothing.

8. The clouds are here thought of as the water-skins of the sky; cf. 38.37 (also
cf. Prov. 30.4; Ps. 33.7).

9. He covers the face of the moon: for 'moon', *AV* and *RV* have 'throne'
(*kissēh*, normally written *kisse'*). The verb may mean 'enclose' (so *RV*) or 'fasten'.
But 'the face of his throne' is a curious expression. With a change of vowels
Duhm (so Strahan) secured the meaning 'he holds firm the pillars of his throne',
but the word for 'pillars' is doubtful. Houbigant and Reiske suggested reading
keseh='full moon' (Ps. 81.3 (M.T. 4); Prov. 7.20 (written *kese'*)), and this has
been followed by many editors. The meaning then, as is made clear by the
following line, is that God covers the face of the full moon by hiding it behind
the clouds. Even the bright light of the full moon is under his control. Less
probable is Kissane's reading *sukkōh*='his tent' for *kissēh*. For the meaning 'covers'
it is best to connect the verb not with the common root 'grasp', but with an
Akkadian root, meaning 'cover' (with gold or silver).

¹⁰ He has described a circle upon the face of the waters
    at the boundary between light and darkness.
¹¹ The pillars of heaven tremble,
    and are astounded at his rebuke.
¹² By his power he stilled the sea;
    by his understanding he smote Rahab.
¹³ By his wind the heavens were made fair;
    his hand pierced the fleeing serpent.

---

10. **He has described a circle:** this rendering rests on a change of vowels, and is to be preferred to M.T., which means 'he has drawn a limit as a circle' (cf. *AV*, *RV*).

upon the face of the waters: the earth was conceived of as surrounded by waters upon which the vault of heaven came down. Within the vault light and darkness alternated, as the sun entered from without and passed across the sky (cf. Ps. 19.4ff. (MT. 5ff.)).

11. **The pillars of heaven:** these are the great mountains which support the sky (cf. the Atlas mountain in classical mythology). The vault of heaven came down upon the waters (verse 10), but its weight was sustained by the mountains. Yet even their strength failed when God rebuked them.

tremble: the verb is found only here, but its meaning is not in doubt.

12. **stilled:** this verb can mean 'stir up' (so *RV*), as in Isa. 51.15; Jer. 31.35. A separate root, with the same spelling, means 'be stilled', and this is the sense most appropriate here (cf. *RV* marg.), with 'the sea' as subject. The reference to Rahab, who needed no incitement, but in whose quelling the power of God was shown, favours this view. What the author has in mind is the control of the primeval waters in creation. Dhorme defends the meaning 'divide' (cf. *AV*); cf. on 7.5. But this is not probable here.

Rahab: cf. on 9.13. Not by power alone, but by wisdom and understanding God's victory was won. For the parallel of strength and understanding, cf. Jer. 10.12.

13. **By his wind:** *AV* and *RV* 'by his spirit'. Either rendering is possible, but the reference is probably to the wind which blows away the clouds and brings the clear sky.

were made fair: *AV* and *RV* 'garnished'; lit. 'becomes fairness'.

pierced: *AV* 'formed' rests on Targ. and Vulg., and derives the word from the root 'writhe', 'be in birth pangs', which is unsuitable here. The verb should certainly be rendered as in Isa. 51.9, 'pierced' or 'wounded' (cf. *AV* there).

the fleeing serpent: cf. on 3.8. The reference here is to the defeat of the flying serpent, or Leviathan; cf. Isa. 27.1. Here and in verse 12 God's power over nature is associated with mythological motifs. Albright (*BASOR*, no. 53, Oct. 1941, p. 39) argues for the meaning in Ugaritic and here 'the primeval serpent'.

¹⁴ Lo, these are but the outskirts of his ways;
   and how small a whisper do we hear of him!
   But the thunder of his power who can understand?'

27 And Job again took up his discourse, and said:
   ² 'As God lives, who has taken away my right,
   and the Almighty, who has made my soul bitter;
   ³ as long as my breath is in me,

---

14. The fine poetic quality of this verse is to be noted. Skilfully the author evokes the sense of the infinite range of God's power, of which he has mentioned but an insignificant whisper. But the speech, like others, fails to come to grips with the problem of Job, contenting itself with generalities, which, however true and poetically expressed, are completely beside the point.

his ways: here equivalent to 'his works'.

whisper: cf. on 4.12.

JOB'S ANSWER TO BILDAD RESUMED 27.1–6

JOB'S INFLEXIBLE PROTESTATION OF INNOCENCE 27.1–6

Solemnly swearing by the life of God himself that he will utter the truth, Job reaffirms his innocence, and says he will maintain it so long as he lives.

1. The unusual formula here at once arouses suspicion, especially as it occurs in the middle of Job's speech, as the text now stands. It is probable (see pp. 213f.) that the preceding verses should be assigned to Bildad and that this verse resumes the speech of Job begun in 26.2–4, and this may account for this formula. It is likely that part of the speech has been lost altogether.

discourse: the Hebrew word *māšāl* is variously rendered 'proverb', 'parable', 'by-word', 'taunt'. It is used for a brief saying (cf. 1 Sam. 10.12) or for a longer composition (Isa. 14.4). For an examination of the meaning of the term cf. A. R. Johnson, *SVT*, III, 1955, pp. 162ff. (and the literature there cited). For the expression 'take up a *māšāl*', cf. Num. 23.7, 18; 24.3, etc.; Isa. 14.4; Hab. 2.6.

2. As God lives: this formula introduces an oath (cf. 1 Sam. 14.39, 45; 2 Sam. 2.27).

who has taken away: note that Job swears by the God who has wronged him. Once more the two conceptions of God, against whom and to whom he appeals, lie side by side in Job's thought.

made my soul bitter: cf. 7.11; 10.1; 21.25.

3. It is probable that Job is not swearing that he will speak the truth as long as he lives, but that this verse should be read as a parenthesis (so in *RV*), and that he is affirming that though he is racked with pain he is still in possession of his powers.

my breath: this derives from God (Gen. 2.7) and returns to God (34.14).

and the spirit of God is in my nostrils;
4 my lips will not speak falsehood,
    and my tongue will not utter deceit.
5 Far be it from me to say that you are right;
    till I die I will not put away my integrity from me.
6 I hold fast my righteousness, and will not let it go;
    my heart does not reproach me for any of my days.
7 'Let my enemy be as the wicked,
    and let him that rises up against me be as the unrighteous.

---

spirit: this word means 'wind', 'breath', or 'spirit'. The reference to 'nostrils' here shows that the meaning is 'breath', and that the line is synonymously parallel with the preceding line; 'spirit' is simply for stylistic variation.

4. This verse gives the content of Job's oath. He swears to speak the truth. Some editors prefer the present tense: Job swears that he habitually tells the truth. More probably he swears that what he is now about to say is the solemn truth. **utter:** the verb means 'meditate' (Ps. 1.2), 'devise' (Ps. 2.1), 'moan' (Isa. 38.14), or, as here, 'speak' (Ps. 71.24).

5. Far be it from me: this formula implies that there is something sacrilegious or profane in the idea that is repudiated (cf. 2 Sam. 20.20, where 'from Yahweh' is added). Here Job declares that to admit that the friends' charges were true would be a violation of his duty to God, and that so long as he lived he could not repudiate his integrity by the lie in his soul that such an admission would involve.

6. Job affirms that, as he looks back over his life, his conscience does not reproach him. In what has survived of this speech Job advances nothing new, but merely scorns Bildad's defence of God and reaffirms his own innocence. It is this which makes it probable that part of the speech has been lost.

THE THIRD SPEECH OF ZOPHAR 27.7–12; 24.18–24; 27.13–23

In the present text Zophar is given no third speech. It has been said above (p. 210) that 24.18–24 should probably be assigned to him. Now here we find that 27.7–23 is quite inappropriate on the lips of Job. For here again the speaker dwells on Gods' deafness to the cry of the wicked, whereas Job has complained that God will not hear his cry, though he is innocent, and describes the swift retribution on the wicked, which he has hitherto denied. Hence Peake, Strahan and Ball attribute 27.7–23 to Zophar (Stevenson assigns most of these verses to Zophar; Bickell 7–10, 14–20; Gray and Hertzberg 7–10, 13–23; Duhm and Barton 7–11, 13–23), while Kissane attributes them to Bildad (cf. Laue, loc. cit., where 27.13–23 are assigned to Bildad). As long ago as 1780, Kennicott held 27.13–23 to belong to Zophar (*V.T. Hebraicum cum variis lectionibus*, II, Diss. generalis, p. 115), and so Hölscher. To these verses Dhorme and Rongy add 24.18–24 following 27.13

⁸ For what is the hope of the godless when God cuts him off,
   when God takes away his life?
⁹ Will God hear his cry,

(cf. Pfeiffer, loc. cit.: 27.13; 24.21–24, 18–20; 27.14), while Lefèvre and Tournay
add them after 27.23, and Pope gives to Zophar 27.8–23; 24.18–25. Siegfried
dismissed 27.7–23 as unoriginal, and so Fohrer (save verses 11f.). It seems probable
that 27.7–23 should be assigned to Zophar, and 24.18–24 can best be added after
27.13. But in the present disordered state of the text something may have been
lost, and clues for the complete reconstruction of the text are no longer available.

The burden of Zophar's speech is that the godless man has no access to God
and his prayer is unheeded. Disaster comes upon him and he leaves no memory,
or if he flourishes for a time it is but the prelude to destruction. His family inherit
want and sorrow, and whatever he amasses is divided by the righteous. Swiftly
he is carried away unpitied and unmourned. The speech falls into two parts: the
desolate state of the godless (27.7–12); the fate of the godless (13–23, into which
24.18–24 should be inserted).

THE DESOLATE STATE OF THE GODLESS 27.7–12

The speech has no proper beginning, and this is doubtless lost. Zophar invokes
on his enemies the lot of the wicked, who is without God and without hope. It
is possible that verses 11f. (cf. above), in which the speaker promises to unfold
the ways of God, may be a fragment of Job's speech, since it is addressed to a
plurality of hearers, but both Job and the friends claim a monopoly of understanding of the ways of God.

7. So sure is the speaker of the misery that is the lot of the wicked that he can
think of nothing worse to call down on his enemies than this. This stands in stark
contrast with the picture drawn by Job in 24.1–17, and it cannot with any probability be supposed to come from him. Marshall, who retains verses 7–23 for
Job, thinks he is here retracting his earlier views, but of this there is no indication,
and it is most improbable.

8. cuts him off: the root is associated with dishonest gains (cf. Ezek. 22.27),
and so AV and RV here; or with cutting off (6.9), as RSV and many editors here.
But this would seem to imply that there is hope for the righteous when he dies,
and this is unlikely to be the meaning of Zophar. The following verse speaks of
God's deafness to the prayer of the wicked, and Mandelkern (V.T. Concordantiae,
p. 228b) suggested that we should here read 'when he prays' (yipga' for yibsa').
'God' is not expressed in M.T. Dhorme follows this reading, and so Larcher, and
it is probably to be read. Driver (AJSL, LII, 1935–36, p. 162) retains M.T. and
renders 'when he comes to an end'. But this keeps the idea of death, which is
inappropriate here, where the speaker is saying that in life the wicked is alone
and desolate.

when trouble comes upon him?
10 Will he take delight in the Almighty?
Will he call upon God at all times?
11 I will teach you concerning the hand of God;
what is with the Almighty I will not conceal.
12 Behold, all of you have seen it yourselves;
why then have you become altogether vain?
13 'This is the portion of a wicked man with God,

---

takes away: the verb is found only here, and it is thought to be a by-form of that used in Ru. 2.16 ('pull out'). But this is a curious expression. Many editors, with the addition of a letter, read 'asks (his soul)', and then compare Lk. 12.20. Both of these interpretations understand the reference to be to the death of the wicked. Perles (*Analekten zur Textkritik des ATs*, 1895, p. 48), with the addition of one letter and the redivision of words, rendered 'lifts (his soul) to (God)', which gives a good parallel to 'prays', and is relevant to the context (so Dhorme, Larcher). The godless man has none to whom he can pray. Cf. Confucius, *Analects*, III, xiii: 'He who offends against Heaven has none to whom he can pray'.

10. delight himself: the same verb as in 22.26.
at all times: it is useless to cry to God in the crises of life, if he is ignored at all other times.

11. you. This is plural, and those who retain verses 11f. for Job (see above) stress this. Peake thinks they introduced a description of the immorality of God's government of the world which was suppressed on account of its boldness. Some editors read singular for plural, and it is possible that the disordering of the text and attribution of the verses to Job may have led to the slight change involved. But in verse 12 the changes are greater and less easy to explain. The assumption of superior insight marked all the parties to the debate.

12. become altogether vain: the Hebrew has the noun 'vain thing', or 'breath' (cf. on 7.16) and a denominative verb formed from it, i.e. 'become vain with a vain thing'. This intensifies the idea of the futility attributed by the speaker to his hearers.

THE FATE OF THE GODLESS 27.13–23

Zophar here describes the fate of the wicked man's family, the transfer of his wealth to the righteous and the disappearance of his house, and the terrors which overwhelm him in the hour of his punishment. Into this speech 24.18–24 should probably be fitted, though in the disordered and incomplete state of the text it is impossible to fit it in with certainty. The best place seems to be after verse 13.

13. with God: we should perhaps read 'from God' (omitting one letter duplicated by dittography).

and the heritage which oppressors receive from the Almighty:
14 If his children are multiplied, it is for the sword;
   and his offspring have not enough to eat.
15 Those who survive him the pestilence buries,
   and their widows make no lamentation.
16 Though he heap up silver like dust,
   and pile up clothing like clay;
17 he may pile it up, but the just will wear it,
   and the innocent will divide the silver.
18 The house which he builds is like a spider's web,

---

oppressors: whereas 'wicked man' is singular, this is plural. Duhm and others change to singular. But cf. note on 24.18.

14. If 24.18–24 are transferred to follow verse 13, we now pass from the thought of the fate of the wicked man himself to the thought of his family. A numerous family was accounted a great blessing, but here they are destined only for destruction. For such sentiments on the lips of the friends cf. 5.4; 18.19. Job's views were quite other (21.8, 11). Job's own children had been suddenly cut off, and it is improbable that he uttered these words.

15. the pestilence buries: lit. 'will be buried by death', i.e. by pestilence, with the implication that they will have no other burial. Some editors add the negative 'will not be buried in death', but the omission of the negative would be surprising. Pope reads *babbāmôt*='in tombs' for *bammāwet*='in (or by) death' and also supplies the negative, 'will not be buried in tombs'.

their widows: M.T. has 'his widows', i.e. the widows of the wicked man, who are indifferent to his fate. LXX has 'their widows', and many editors follow this, making them the widows of the surviving members of his family.

16. Having disposed of the family of the wicked man, Zophar now turns to his possessions. All that he has amassed, whether in treasure or fine clothes, will be possessed by others.

heap up: the verb used in Gen. 41.49; Ps. 39.6 (M.T. 7), and in Zech. 14.14, where it is used of silver, as here.

like dust . . . like clay: for the parallelism cf. 4.19; 10.9; 30.19 (*RSV* 'mire').

clothing: fine clothing was greatly valued; cf. Gen. 24.53; Jos. 7.21; 2 Kg. 5.22f.; 7.8; Zech. 14.14.

17. Cf. Ps. 39.6 (M.T. 7); Prov. 13.22.

18. like a spider's web: M.T. 'like a moth's'. But this is inappropriate, as the moth does not build a house. Ehrlich proposed to find here a homonym with the meaning 'bird's nest', and so Dhorme. This would make a good parallel to the flimsy watchman's booth of the following line, but the word is not found else-

like a booth which a watchman makes.
¹⁹ He goes to bed rich, but will do so no more;
    he opens his eyes, and his wealth is gone.
²⁰ Terrors overtake him like a flood;
    in the night a whirlwind carries him off.
²¹ The east wind lifts him up and he is gone;
    it sweeps him out of his place.
²² It hurls at him without pity;
    he flees from its power in headlong flight.

---

where in Hebrew. LXX has a double rendering 'as moths, as a spider', and Syr. has only the latter. Hence many editors since Merx adopt this reading ('akkābîš for 'āš). In 8.14 the spider's web is mentioned as something insubstantial, and this is appropriate here.

booth: the temporary shelter erected towards harvest time for the watching of the fields; cf. Isa. 1.8. Wetzstein (in Delitzsch) thus describes its construction: 'Four poles are set up so as to form the corners of a square, the sides of which are about eight feet in length. Eight feet above the ground, four cross pieces of wood are tightly bound to these with cords, on which planks, if they are to be had, are laid. Here is the watcher's bed. . . . Six or seven feet above this, cross-beams are again bound to the four poles, on which boughs, or reeds, or a mat forms a roof. . . . Between the roof and the bed, three sides . . . are hung round with a mat. . . . A small ladder . . . frequently leads to the bed-chamber'.

19. will do so no more: this rendering rests on LXX and Syr., reading *yôsîp* for M.T. *yēʾāsēp* = 'he will not be gathered'. Very many editors follow this reading. Cf. then 14.12; Ps. 41.8 (M.T. 9). The swiftness of the doom which overtakes the wicked is here vividly expressed.

his wealth is gone: the Hebrew says 'it is not', or 'he is not' (so *AV, RV*). Dhorme takes the latter view, and finds here the last look of the dying man, who is thus conscious of the swiftness of his destruction.

20. like a flood: many editors desiderate a word parallel to 'in the night', and Merx proposed to read *bayyôm* for *kammayim* (= 'as waters'), while Wright proposed *yômām* (so Budde, Dhorme and others), both with the meaning 'by day'. The meaning then is that he is haunted by terrors night and day. Duhm and Gray retain M.T. Waters sometimes stand for an overwhelming torrent; cf. 2 Sam. 5.20; Isa. 28.17; Hos. 5.10; Am. 5.24.

21. The east wind: Wetzstein (in Delitzsch) says: 'The east wind is dry; it excites the blood, contracts the chest, causes restlessness and anxiety, and sleepless nights or evil dreams. Both man and beast feel weak and sickly while it prevails. Hence that which is unpleasant and revolting in life is compared to the east wind'.

²³ It claps its hands at him,
  and hisses at him from its place.

---

22. It claps: it is improbable that the east wind is represented as clapping its hands. Some editors (so Peake) take the view of *RSV* marg. 'he (i.e. God) claps'. More probably it is indefinite third person 'one claps', i.e. 'men clap' (so *AV*, *RV*). When disaster overtakes the wicked man all men rejoice, clapping their hands in scorn, and hissing at the thought of him; cf. Lam. 2.15.

POEM ON WISDOM 28

This chapter forms what Duesberg (*Les scribes inspirés*, II, 1939, p. 156) calls an 'erratic block', and it is generally believed to be an intrusion into the book of Job. As the book stands now it is the utterance of Job, and Budde defends it as such, holding that Job here gives up his problem, but in despair. But despair does not seem the mood of the chapter. Lefèvre (*SDB*, IV, col. 1079) also retains it and thinks it marks a pause, indicating that the dialogue is at an end, while Junker compares it with the Chorus in a Greek tragedy. The objection to all of these views is that if this chapter belonged to the original book, the Divine speeches were unnecessary. If Job had unaided reached the recognition that the wonders of the world surpassed man's understanding and that the way of wisdom lay in humble submission to God and obedience to him, the Divine irony in the speeches from the whirlwind would scarcely have been called for. If a Chorus had similarly anticipated the divine speeches and enlightened Job and his friends, the Divine speeches would not be the climax of the book. Szczygiel recognized this, and so transferred this chapter to follow 42.6. But there is no evidence that it ever stood there, and the stammered submission of Job is more appropriate than the calm air of this poem.

If 27.7–23 is attributed to Zophar, this chapter might be thought to belong to him (so Hoffmann). In 11.7f. Zophar had declared the divine wisdom to be unfathomable. But, as Peake says, the temper of chapter 28 is too calm and serene for Zophar. As little is to be said for the view that the chapter should be ascribed to Bildad (so Stuhlmann). Whoever may be thought to have uttered it, as it stands it renders the Divine speeches unnecessary, and it is difficult to suppose this was intended by the author. That it is worthy of the author of the book of Job is undoubted, and a number of scholars think it may be from his pen (so Dhorme; but cf. Baumgartner, *OTMS*, 1951, p. 219). But if so, it can hardly have been for its present place, and it may have been placed here later to preserve this magnificent poem composed by the author of Job. That it has affinity with his thought is clear from the fact that it would render the Divine speeches unnecessary, if it were original here.

The poem, like some psalms, has a refrain (verses 12, 20), and Duhm thinks this may have stood also originally before verse 1 (see note there). This refrain divides the chapter into three parts: there is no known road to wisdom (verses

28 'Surely there is a mine for silver,
         and a place for gold which they refine.
² Iron is taken out of the earth,
    and copper is smelted from the ore.
³ Men put an end to darkness,
    and search out to the farthest bound
    the ore in gloom and deep darkness.

1–11); no price can buy it (verses 12–19); God alone has it, and only by revelation can man possess it (verses 20–28).

THERE IS NO KNOWN ROAD TO WISDOM **28.1–11**

It cannot be discovered by man, whose skill enables him to bring out the mineral treasures which lie hidden in the earth, where no bird or beast could reach it.

1. Surely: lit. 'for'. This seems to imply that it once had a preceding context. Duhm suggested that the refrain of verses 12, 20 once preceded verse 1: 'Where shall wisdom be found? And where is the place of understanding?' This would yield a connection for 'for'. Emphasis lies on 'there is' in the Hebrew, and this is more naturally understood after the refrain.

mine: lit. 'source'. There are few references to mining in the *OT* (cf. Dt. 8.9) and few figures drawn from mining. Silver and other metals were imported from Tarshish (Jer. 10.9; Ezek. 27.12), probably Tartessus in Spain, and perhaps also from Sardinia, where the Phoenicians had mining settlements. Minerals were mined by some of Israel's neighbours (Egypt, Lebanon, Edom, Gilead, Sinai), and Nelson Glueck found evidences of a great copper refinery near the ancient Ezion-geber, where it is probable that Solomon had installations to smelt imported ores. The word 'source' is used quite widely, and it is only the context here which gives it the precision of 'mine'. It means 'place of going out'. P. Joüon (*Biblica*, XI, 1930, p. 323) thought this inappropriate, and suggested 'place of finding' (*mimṣā'* for *môṣā'*). Dahood (cf. on 23.10) finds here the root='shine', and renders M.T. 'smelter'; but this is not appropriate. The passage is thinking of the place from which silver and gold are taken.

2. copper: cf. on verse 1.

ore: Hebrew 'stone'. Dhorme takes the verb rendered **is smelted** to be an adjective='hard': 'a hard stone becomes copper', but this is less probable.

3. Men put: M.T. 'one puts'.

an end to darkness: by opening up the shaft, and by the use of lamps underground.

bound: the word used in 26.10 for the boundary between light and darkness. Here it is the limit to which the miner goes.

ore: again 'stone'.

deep darkness: cf. on 3.5.

⁴ They open shafts in a valley away from where men live;
  they are forgotten by travellers,
  they hang afar from men, they swing to and fro.
⁵ As for the earth, out of it comes bread;
  but underneath it is turned up as by fire.

---

4. Calmet declares this verse 'an enigma of which it is almost impossible to find the sense'. The ancient versions vary widely; cf. also *AV*, which is totally different from *RSV*.

They open shafts in a valley away from where men live: lit. 'one opens a valley from with (?=away from) a sojourner'. Bickell added 'light' (cf. Budde, Gray): 'away from one who sojourns in light', but this is not convincing. Ley suggested *nēr*='light' instead of *gār*='sojourner': 'away from light'. Kissane, with slight changes, secures the improbable sense ('the stone') is pierced with channels by man's agency'. With a change of vowels only, Ehrlich reads 'from a foreign people' for 'from with a sojourner', and Dhorme follows this (so Fohrer; cf. Pope) but, following Graetz, he attaches the *m*='from' to the preceding word, yielding 'A foreign people has pierced shafts'. The reference then is to foreign slaves who are set to work in the mines, the word for 'valleys' here being understood of the shafts of the mines. Of other proposals may be mentioned Driver's (*AJSL*, LII, 1935–36, p. 162) 'a strange people who have been forgotten cut shafts'; L. Waterman's (*JBL*, LXXI, 1952, pp. 167ff.) 'the people of the lamp (=miners) break open passage ways'; J. Reider (*HUCA*, XXIV, 1952–53, pp. 105f.) 'A torrent bursts forth (cf. *AV*) from chalk valleys (reading *mēʿimᵉkê gîr* for *mēʿim gār*) forgotten of the foot (of man)'. M. Tsevat (*HUCA*, XXIV, p. 14) thinks the reference to 'a strange people' is specifically to the subjugated Canaanites.

forgotten by travellers: lit. 'forgotten of the foot', i.e. of those who walk overhead. The third line is believed to refer to the hanging by a rope or swinging in a cage of the miners who are set these hazardous tasks. The thought is of the remote places from which minerals are brought to the surface and of man's skill in seeking out material treasures, in contrast to his inability to find what matters more, wisdom. By resorting to Arabic meanings for some of the words Guillaume (*Promise and Fulfilment*, ed. Bruce, 1963, pp. 117ff.) secures the meaning: 'He cuts a shaft through the covering of chalk; Those who are swept off their feet Hang suspended far from men, they swing to and fro'.

5. Here the contrast is between what takes place on the surface of the earth, and what takes place underground in the mines. For the first line cf. Ps. 104.14. Some have thought the second line refers to blasting, but this is not probable. The meaning may be that the overturning that goes on underground produces confused rubble like that caused by fire. Pope thinks that there was some idea that the ore-containing rocks had been produced by fire, and compares Ezek. 27.14,

⁶ Its stones are the place of sapphires,
   and it has dust of gold.
⁷ 'That path no bird of prey knows,
   and the falcon's eye has not seen it.
⁸ The proud beasts have not trodden it;
   the lion has not passed over it.
⁹ 'Man puts his hand to the flinty rock,
   and overturns mountains by the roots.
¹⁰ He cuts out channels in the rocks,

---

where 'stones of fire' may refer to the precious stones mentioned in the previous verse.

6. Not only metals, but precious stones reward men's search. **Sapphire** is believed to have been almost unknown before Roman imperial times, and hence it is thought that lapis lazuli is intended here (cf. *RSV* marg.). In that case **it has dust of gold** refers to the particles of iron pyrites found in lapis lazuli which glittered like gold. The alternative view that the meaning is that the earth contains dust of gold is less likely, since the metal gold has been mentioned in verse 1.

7. Editors disagree as to whether the path which is unknown to birds and beasts of prey is the path to the mines or the path to wisdom. Duhm repeats the refrain before this verse (so Fohrer) to make it clear that it is the path to wisdom, but Peake thinks it improbable that the author should leave the mines for two verses and then return to them. But it is not certain that verses 9–11 deal with the miner (see below). Peake transfers verses 7f. to follow verse 12. On the alternative view it is unnecessary to remove them. The paths trodden by the miners are remote from men and also remote from the birds and beasts that live far from men.
falcon: LXX has 'vulture' and so *AV* (so Dhorme). The same word is rendered 'kite' by *AV* and *RSV* in Dt. 14.13, and by 'kite' also in *AV* in Lev. 11.14. *RV* has 'falcon' in all cases. The precise identification of the bird is uncertain, but the reference to the keenness of its sight here favours the falcon.

8. proud beasts: lit. 'sons of pride'. The expression recurs in 41.34. *AV* renders 'lion's whelps', but it is a more general term as 41.34 shows.
lion: the word rendered 'fierce lion' in 4.10 (see note there). Dhorme again has 'leopard' here. S. Mowinckel (in *Hebrew and Semitic Studies*, ed. D. Winton Thomas, 1963, pp. 95ff.) maintains that the word here (but not in 4.10) means a mythical creature of the serpent type and that the 'sons of pride' are also mythical creatures. But mythical creatures seem out of place here after real birds of prey.

9. The poet here returns to the achievements of man, who performs remarkable engineering feats in his activities. The hardest rock has to yield before him, and he is undaunted by the mountains.

10. channels: the word is commonly used in the singular for the Nile, but

and his eye sees every precious thing.

11 He binds up the streams so that they do not trickle,
and the thing that is hid he brings forth to light.

12 'But where shall wisdom be found?
And where is the place of understanding?

13 Man does not know the way to it,
and it is not found in the land of the living.

14 The deep says, "It is not in me,"
and the sea says, "It is not with me".

15 It cannot be gotten for gold,
and silver cannot be weighed as its price.

16 It cannot be valued in the gold of Ophir,
in precious onyx or sapphire.

17 Gold and glass cannot equal it,
nor can it be exchanged for jewels of fine gold.

18 No mention shall be made of coral or of crystal;

---

here, as in Isa. 33.21, it is used more generally. It is improbable that the meaning here is of the tunnels in mines, and the reference may be to such engineering feats as the Siloam tunnel, which was made for waters to flow through.

11. **so that they do not trickle:** lit. 'from weeping'. This is thought to mean so that the water does not percolate into the mines. But the line is a poor parallel to the following line. Moreover the verb is elsewhere used especially of binding up wounds, and this is not appropriate to rivers. Vulg., Aq. and Theod. appear to have read 'search' (ḥippēś for ḥibbēś), and this was read by Houbigant and Graetz, while for 'from weeping' (mibbᵉkî) Graetz proposed niḇᵉḵê='sources' (cf. 38.16) and Hoffmann and Budde mabbᵉḵê, with the same meaning. This is followed by Ball, Dhorme, Hölscher, Kissane. The meaning then is that man has explored the sources of rivers by penetrating underground to their springs. This offers a good parallel to the following line. For Ugaritic support for this view cf. Ginsberg, *JBL*, LXII, 1943, p. 111; G. M. Landes, *BASOR*, no. 144, Dec. 1956, pp. 32f.; M. Mansoor, *RQ*, III, 1961–62, pp. 392f.; and Pope.

NO PRICE CAN BUY WISDOM 28.12–19

Man does not know in what market it is to be found, and if he could find it no wealth could equal it in value.

12. This verse is repeated with slight modification in verse 20. The terms **wisdom** and **understanding** frequently stand parallel to one another; cf. Prov. 1.2; 4.5, 7; 9.10; 16.16 (*RSV* has 'insight' for the second, save in 16.16).

13. **the way to it:** M.T. has 'its price' (so *AV*, *RV*). But most editors follow

LXX in reading 'its way' (with the change of one letter). The value of wisdom is treated in verses 15ff. But first its would-be purchaser has to locate it, and the question in verse 12 is where it can be found. Although man knows the way to the things mentioned in the preceding verses, he is ignorant of any way that can lead him to wisdom. The parallelism favours LXX.

14. The deep: this is the primeval abyss, the subterranean reservoir from which the sea is fed and the floods emerge (Gen. 7.11; 49.25). The parallelism between the deep and the sea is repeated in 38.16.

15. Not only can wisdom not be found, wherever it may be sought, but if it could be found no wealth could equal it.

gold: the word is found only here, but a slightly different form is found beside the word 'gold' in descriptions of Temple ornaments, where *RSV* has 'pure gold' (1 Kg. 6.20, etc.). Here the word 'gold' is omitted and it is construed as a noun, ='pure gold', or perhaps 'solid gold'. It comes from a root meaning 'enclose', and it may mean 'prized', but more probably it refers to gold bars. Gray renders 'sterling gold'. Note the profusion of words for gold in this passage.

16. be valued: the verb, found only here and in verse 19, is a by-form of that found in Lam. 4.2, and it appears to mean 'to be weighed against'.

gold of Ophir: cf. on 22.24, where 'Ophir' stands for 'gold of Ophir' (cf. on verse 15). The word used for 'gold' here is not that used in verse 1, but stands parallel to it in 31.24 (*RSV* 'fine gold'). It is thought to be the Egyptian name of the district from which it came, and *KB* suggests that this was Nubia. If so, its meaning must have been lost in Hebrew, since 'Nubian gold of Ophir' could scarcely be said.

onyx: the precise identification of this and other precious stones in this passage cannot be determined. Theod. has 'onyx' here, and Vulg. 'sardonyx', while Targ. and Syr. have 'beryl' (so LXX in Exod. 28.20). 'Carnelian' and 'malachite' have also been suggested. It is mentioned alongside gold in Gen. 2.11f., was found on the high priest's breastplate (Exod. 28.20) and on the ephod (Exod. 25.7; cf. also 28.9), and is mentioned in Ezek. 28.13.

sapphire: cf. on verse 6.

17. Gold: here the word used in verse 1.

glass: *AV* 'crystal'. The word is found only here. Glass was rare in the ancient world and so highly valued.

jewels of fine gold: M.T. 'a vessel of fine gold', but the versions have plural. The word for 'fine gold' is found only here in Job, but it is found elsewhere eight times (cf. Ps. 19.10 (M.T. 11); Prov. 8.19). In Ca. 5.11 it is combined with the word used in verse 16.

18. coral: the meaning of the word (found also in Ezek. 27.16) is not certain, and the versions vary. Jewish rabbinical tradition identifies with corals, but Delitzsch (also Hölscher) thought rather of pearls (so S. T. Byington, *JBL*, LXIV, 1945, pp. 340ff.).

crystal: this word is found here only (*gābîš*). The related word *'elgābîš* means 'hailstones' (Ezek. 13.11, 13; 38.22).

the price of wisdom is above pearls.

19 The topaz of Ethiopia cannot compare with it,
   nor can it be valued in pure gold.
20 'Whence then comes wisdom?
   And where is the place of understanding?
21 It is hid from the eyes of all living,
   and concealed from the birds of the air.
22 Abad'don and Death say,
   "We have heard a rumour of it with our ears".

---

price: this word is found in Ps. 126.6, where it means 'a trail of seed'. It appears to come from a root meaning 'draw'. *BDB* takes it here to mean the effort of securing, and Gray renders 'acquisition' (so A. Cohen, *AJSL*, XL, 1923–24, p. 175) and Dhorme 'extraction'. But *KB* gives it the meaning 'skin (or leather) bag', but 'a bag of wisdom' is a curious expression. Wisdom is in any case set above pearls, and the most probable sense is that wisdom is harder to come by than pearls.

pearls: *AV* and *RV* 'rubies'. Lam. 4.7 suggests that they were red, and so they have been identified with corals (so *RSV* there). In spite of this, Gray and Dhorme decide for pearls.

19. topaz: this follows Theod. and Vulg. Targ. has 'green pearl'. *KB* renders 'chrysolite'. The word is probably a foreign borrowing, and perhaps indicates the colour of the stone as yellow.

Ethiopia: according to Pliny (*H.N.* XXXVII, xxxii (108)) there was an island in the Red Sea called Topazos.

pure gold: the word for 'gold' here is the same as that found in verse 16 (see note there).

GOD ALONE HAS WISDOM, AND ONLY BY REVELATION CAN MAN POSSESS IT **28.20–28**

Hidden from the eyes of all the creatures of earth and air, and no less from the dead than the living, to the all-seeing eye of God alone is the way to it visible. He not only sees it, but also reveals it and unfolds to man its secret.

20. Repeated from verse 12, save that here we have 'whence comes?' instead of 'where shall be found?' Some editors change the text in verse 12 to bring it nearer to the text here. But Peake says if uniformity is necessary, verse 20 should be conformed to verse 12.

21. all living: here including animals and men; cf. 30.23, where it means all men.

22. Abaddon: cf. on 26.6.

Death: here personified.

we have heard with our ears: cf. Ps. 44.1 (M.T. 2).

²³ 'God understands the way to it,
   and he knows its place.
²⁴ For he looks to the ends of the earth,
   and sees everything under the heavens.
²⁵ When he gave to the wind its weight,
   and meted out the waters by measure;
²⁶ when he made a decree for the rain,
   and a way for the lightning of the thunder;
²⁷ then he saw it and declared it;

---

23. God: this is emphatic, and it means that God alone knows. Strahan says: 'To the ancient poet wisdom is more than an abstraction or an attribute, and, instead of consciously personifying an idea and playing with a rhetorical conceit, he almost, if not altogether, believes that Wisdom has an objective and independent existence.'

24. Plagued with logic, Budde and Beer delete this verse, since it appears to imply an earthly home for wisdom, while Duhm transfers it to follow verse 11. But it is unnecessary to press this meaning on the verse. All it says is that God, who sees and knows all things, knows where wisdom is to be found. The language is spatial, but the essential thought is no more spatial that if I were to say: 'I know where logic can lead a man.'

25. 'The wind is the lightest of things, and yet God determines for it a weight' (Dhorme).

26. decree: i.e. a law that should govern the rainfall. Dhorme renders 'a limit', and compares 14.5. Pope gives the word the meaning of 'groove' here (cf. 38.25, where 'channel' is used), and sees it as the path by which the rain pours down.

lightning of the thunder: in 38.25 RSV renders the same phrase 'thunderbolt', while the first word is rendered 'storm cloud' in Zech. 10.1. Dhorme holds that the meaning is 'the rumble of the thunder' (so Ben Yehuda), while Koehler (ZAW, N.F., XIV, 1937, p. 173) renders the first word 'whirlwind' and KB 'storm-cloud', whence Pope renders the whole expression 'thunder-shower', and Kissane 'thunder-storm'. In the Midrash the word means 'cumulus cloud', and in modern Hebrew 'lightning'. The precise meaning cannot be determined with certainty, but since it certainly means phenomena that accompany thunder, 'thunder-storm' seems to be the best rendering. 'Thunder' is lit. 'voices'. The thunder is regarded as the voice of God; cf. 37.4; Ps. 18.13 (M.T. 14); 29.3ff.; Isa. 30.30f.; Jer. 10.13.

27. declared it: since the reference here is to the time of Creation, when man did not exist, the meaning cannot be that he revealed it. Hence editors by re-pointing or by seeking unusual meanings for the word find the sense to be

he established it, and searched it out.
²⁸ And he said to man,
"Behold, the fear of the Lord, that is wisdom;
and to depart from evil is understanding". '

'appraised' (so Dhorme, Pope), or 'probed' (so Reider, *VT*, II, 1952, p. 127), or 'studied' (so Strahan; cf. Ball 'examined'), or 'reckoned' (so Kissane). Gray says 'our insufficient knowledge of this language (i.e. of the technical language of the wisdom school) may account for the difficulty of seizing exactly and with certainty the meaning of the verse'. The general sense of the verse is that God perfectly fathomed the nature of Wisdom.

established it: some MSS. have 'discerned it', and this is followed by some editors.

28. This verse is omitted by very many editors, on the grounds that (*a*) here only in the book of Job do we find the divine name 'Lord' (*ᵃdōnāy*) and (*b*) it is inconsistent with what precedes. As to (*a*) it is to be noted that scholars who elsewhere seek to impose rigid logic on the poet are themselves illogical here. For after declaring that this poem is an interpolation, they can hardly require the author of the poem to be governed by the practice of the author of the book. And even if it were an interpolated poem by the same author, we could not require him to be governed by the usage in a book which describes a discussion between non-Jews. As to (*b*), it is said that hitherto in the chapter the author is concerned with speculative wisdom, which he declared to be unattainable by man, whereas here he is concerned with practical wisdom which he declares to be attainable by man. But there is no declaration that man by his own searching can attain this wisdom, but only that by the divine initiative it is made available to him. Nor is the sharp distinction between two kinds of wisdom necessary. Wisdom in verses 1–27 is not necessarily to be equated with scientific or philosophical penetration into the secrets of the universe or the nature of reality. By all his restless activities Man may learn much and possess much. But wisdom, in which his truest well-being is found and in which he fulfils the deepest purpose of his being, is not attained in this way. But God in his grace reveals to him the secret, which lies in reverent submission of himself to God and in the eschewing of evil. This is fundamental to the teaching of the Bible as a whole, and it is gratuitous to deny its preception to the author of this poem. At the beginning of the book Job's greatness is expressed in terms of fearing God and eschewing evil, and whether this poem was composed by the author of the book or by another and subsequently inserted here, there is no reason why it should not have expressed the same truth that man's supreme distinction is to be found in this wisdom, and that by his unaided efforts he cannot attain it. It is a pity to rob the poem of its climax and turn it into the expression of unrelieved agnosticism.

29 And Job again took up his discourse, and said:
² 'Oh, that I were as in the months of old,
  as in the days when God watched over me;
³ when his lamp shone upon my head,
  and by his light I walked through darkness;
⁴ as I was in my autumn days,

JOB'S CONCLUDING SOLILOQUY 29-30

Job's debate with his friends is at an end, and we now have his concluding soliloquy, just as we had an opening soliloquy before the debate began. In this soliloquy Job takes no account of his friends, who are completely ignored. His speech falls into three main parts, each occupying a chapter, and each is broken up into further divisions: (*a*) Job's retrospect of his former circumstances and the position he enjoyed, subdivided into: his former happiness (29.2-10); his benevolence (verses 11-17); his serene confidence (verses 18-20); the esteem in which he was held (verses 21-25); (*b*) his present misery—subdivided into: the nobodies who now despise him (30.1-8); the indignities he suffers (verses 9-15); his present despondency (verses 16-23); the contrast between then and now (verses 24-31); (*c*) his vindication of his past life, subdivided into: his asseveration of his integrity (31.1-12); his denial of his abuse of power (verses 13-23); his declaration of his purity of heart (verses 24-34); his appeal for the charges against him to be specified (verses 35-37); his invocation of curse upon himself if his self-justification is false (verses 38-40).

JOB'S FORMER HAPPINESS 29.1-10

Leaving for a few moments the harsh realities of the present, Job lets his mind dwell on the condition he once enjoyed, when God's care was over him and he was universally respected.

1. Cf. on 27.1.

2. watched: here the thought is of God's guarding care; cf. Num. 6.24; Ps. 91.11; 121.7f. The same verb is used of God's hostile watch in 10.14; 13.27; 14.16.

3. The **lamp** and the **light** are the symbols of blessing; cf. 2 Sam. 22.29=Ps. 18.28 (M.T. 29); Ps. 36.9 (M.T. 10).

shone: Targ. has 'when he caused to shine'. Olshausen and many other editors follow this.

4. my autumn days: so M.T. *RV* has 'the ripeness of my days'. The autumn is the season of maturity, when the fruits are gathered. It is 'the time of life in which a man reaps what he has sown, a time which ought . . . to be a mellow, fruitful, happy season for the righteous man' (Strahan). *AV* has 'in the days of my youth', and so *KB* and Fohrer. This connects the word with an Arabic word meaning 'lamb', and Dhorme objects that this ought to give 'in my childhood', which would be inappropriate, as the next verse shows.

when the friendship of God was upon my tent;
⁵ when the Almighty was yet with me,
    when my children were about me;
⁶ when my steps were washed with milk,
    and the rock poured out for me streams of oil!
⁷ When I went out to the gate of the city,
    when I prepared my seat in the square,
⁸ the young men saw me and withdrew,
    and the aged rose and stood;
⁹ the princes refrained from talking,
    and laid their hand on their mouth;
¹⁰ the voice of the nobles was hushed,

---

friendship: *AV* and *RV* 'secret'. But LXX, Sym., Syr. have '(when God) protected (my tent)', and so Houbigant, Graetz, and very many editors (*k* for *d*). There is then a reference to 1.10, where the same verb is used, and the thought is of the protective hedge God set about Job. D. Winton Thomas (*JBL*, LXV, 1946, pp. 63ff.) justifies the meaning 'protected' without change of text.

5. Poignantly Job refers to the loss of his children. Strahan observes 'He would be a rash commentator who attempted to expound that'. The line is deliberately short to add to the poignancy. There is no need to add a word with Dhorme.

6. Job's prosperity and the fertility of his herds is here poetically expressed. **Milk** is the word rendered 'curds' in 21.17. *AV* and *RV* here have 'butter.'

the rock: the olive-tree thrives in a rocky soil, and the presses are cut in the rock. It is probable that there is an allusion to this here. Cf. Dt. 32.13. M. Dahood (*Biblica et Orientalia*, XVII, 1965, p. 60) renders 'and balsam' instead of 'and the rock', and transfers to the previous line.

for me: lit. 'with me'. This word overloads the line and is unnecessary to the sense. It is probably accidentally repeated from the previous verse. Dahood (loc. cit.) reads '*ᵃmûday* for '*immādî*, and renders '(Streams of oil flowed over) my legs.'

7. The city gate and the broad open space beside it formed the general meeting place for the administration of justice (Dt. 21.19) or other legal transactions (Ru. 4.1, 11), or for market (2 Kg. 7.1, 18). The prestige of Job is emphasized by the fact that he occupied a prominent seat.

8. Job's arrival was marked by the deference paid to him by young and old. The young modestly **withdrew** (*AV* and *RV* 'hid themselves'), while the old rose and remained standing respectfully until Job sat.

9. princes: here the chief magnates of the city. Respect for Job was universal, and even the highest persons in the city greeted his arrival by silence. Cf. on 21.5.

10. nobles: here the chiefs of the city next in rank to the princes.

and their tongue cleaved to the roof of their mouth.
¹¹ When the ear heard, it called me blessed,
     and when the eye saw, it approved;
¹² because I delivered the poor who cried,
     and the fatherless who had none to help him.
¹³ The blessing of him who was about to perish came upon me,
     and I caused the widow's heart to sing for joy.

---

hushed: lit. 'hidden'. This is a strange figure, but Dhorme justifies it by invoking the meaning 'be veiled'. Guillaume (*Promise and Fulfilment*, 1963, p. 119) compares the Arabic sense of the verb 'died out' (used of a fire). Siegfried and Budde change the text to read 'became dumb', but while a person might become dumb, it is unnatural to say his voice did. Duhm emended to read 'was restrained'. The parallel line shows that the meaning is as *RSV*, though it is possible that the verb is not original. The versions had some difficulties with it. Many editors transfer verses 21–25, which return to the subject of the respect shown to Job, to follow verse 10.

THE BENEVOLENCE OF JOB **29.11–17**

In his prosperity the respect in which Job was held was matched by his consideration for others. He ministered of his substance to those who were in need, and he defended those who were defenceless against the ruthless who exploited them.

11. Job's prosperity and prestige did not earn him the envy and hatred of others, because it bred no arrogance in him.

called me blessed: lit. 'pronounced me happy'; Dhorme 'congratulated me'. The verb stands also in Gen. 30.13; Prov. 31.28; Ca. 6.9. Sometimes it carries a little fuller meaning than this, as in Ps. 72.17, and we should perhaps see here the recognition that Job was not merely fortunate, but that he deserved to be, and that his happiness was due to the blessing of God.

it approved: lit. 'it bore witness to me' (cf. *AV*, *RV*). The meaning here is that men testified in support of Job, and declared their approval of him.

12. Job's declaration stands in sharp contrast to what Eliphaz had said in 22.6ff. But whereas Eliphaz had built on deduction from Job's present state, Job rested on memory which could be tested. The parallel between **the poor** and **the fatherless** as in 24.9.

cried: the verb carries the meaning 'cried for help'.

13. To evoke the blessing of those in despair by ministering to their need is a high tribute, and to make the widow sing for joy is rich satisfaction for the benevolent. The verb means 'to raise a ringing cry' of grief or of joy. The context here indicates that it is of joy.

¹⁴ I put on righteousness, and it clothed me;
   my justice was like a robe and a turban.
¹⁵ I was eyes to the blind,
   and feet to the lame.
¹⁶ I was a father to the poor,
   and I searched out the cause of him whom I did not know.
¹⁷ I broke the fangs of the unrighteous,
   and made him drop his prey from his teeth.
¹⁸ Then I thought, "I shall die in my nest,

---

14. put on righteousness: righteousness is thought of as a garment which
adorns a man. Cf. Ps. 132.9; Isa. 59.17. Similarly shame may be worn as a garment
of dishonour; cf. 8.22; Ps. 132.18.
it clothed me: lit. 'it put on me'. Cf. Jg. 6.34: 'The spirit of Yahweh clothed
itself with Gideon'. P. Joüon (*Biblica*, XI, 1930, p. 324), with a change of vowels,
renders 'it adorned me'.
robe: cf. on 1.20.
   16. a father to the poor: Strahan points out that only in one other OT
passage (Isa. 22.21) has 'father' such a wide meaning, and that Job already gives
the word a spiritual and Christian sense (cf. 1 C. 4.15). It was particularly in legal
suits that the poor needed protection, and it was here that Job gave his aid. He
not merely relieved distress, but undertook the harder task of securing legal justice
for the helpless.
him whom I did not know: this is remarkably large-hearted. Few would
undertake the case of the poor with whom they were acquainted. But to look
into the case of strangers who risked the denial of justice and to see that they were
fairly treated was still more unusual. Job used his strength and influence, not for
selfish ends, but for righteousness.
   17. broke the fangs: the language is figurative, of course. The wicked is
likened to a wild animal, whose teeth are broken so that its aggressive power is
destroyed. 'Fangs' (*AV* and *RV* wrongly 'jaws') are the 'gnawing teeth' (from a
root meaning 'gnaw') of wild animals. The word recurs in Prov. 30.14; Jl 1.6
(also with metathesis Ps. 58.6 (M.T. 7)). Job claims that he not merely rescued the
weak from the ruthless, but that he broke the power of the oppressor to injure
anyone else.
made him drop: Driver (*AJSL*, LII, 1935-36, p. 163) derives the word from
another root, and renders 'rescued'.

JOB'S FORMER SERENE CONFIDENCE 29.18-20

Honoured by God and man, gracious and benevolent, Job had felt that his continued peace and well-being were assured and that length of days would be his.
   18. in my nest: M.T. 'with my nest'. In Dt. 32.11; Isa. 16.2 'nest' stands for

and I shall multiply my days as the sand,
¹⁹ my roots spread out to the waters,
with the dew all night on my branches,
²⁰ my glory fresh with me,
and my bow ever new in my hand."

'nestlings', and it may have that meaning here. Job hoped to die with his children around him (so Gray). But Job scarcely thought he would die while his children were 'nestlings', i.e. unfledged. Driver (*PEQ*, LXXXVII, 1955, pp. 138f., and *SVT*, III, 1955, pp. 85f.) found here a cognate of an Egyptian word meaning 'strength': 'in my full strength'. Merx changed one letter to secure 'with the reed', which is then held to be a symbol of long life (so Kissane). LXX has 'my age will grow old', and Dhorme uses this to propose '(I said) to myself, (I shall die) in a ripe old age' (cf. Pope; also Saydon, *CBQ*, XXIII, 1961, p. 252). This seems the most probable view, and it has, at least, some support from LXX.

as the sand: i.e. Job's years will be as numerous as the sand, a hyperbolical expression of longevity. LXX has 'like the palm tree' and so Ball and Kissane. This involves reading *kannaḥal* for *kaḥôl* and seeing in *naḥal* a rare word for 'palm tree' (found probably in Num. 24.6), for which Arabic support can be found. For the sense then cf. Isa. 65.22. Rabbinic tradition as old as the Talmud found here a reference to the Phoenix (reading *kaḥûl*), the mythical bird which burnt itself in its nest (cf. previous line) and renewed its life from the ashes, and so was a symbol of immortality (Albright finds this bird already in Ras Shamra mythology; cf. *Festschrift Alfred Bertholet*, 1950, pp. 3f.). Many modern editors have followed this view (so Hitzig, Ewald, Budde, Duhm, Peake, Strahan, Stevenson, Weiser, Fohrer). But its origin was probably in the double meaning of the word 'phoenix' (=palm and the mythical bird), which stands in LXX (so Bochart, *Hierozoicon*, II, 1663, cols. 817ff.). The phoenix is a symbol, not merely of longevity, but of immortality, and it is improbable that Job dreamed of this. Hence the view of Dahood (*Biblica*, XLVIII, 1967, pp. 542f.) is unlikely. He renders: 'And I thought, "Though I perish like its nest, I shall multiply days like the phoenix". M.T., as represented by *RSV*, yields a satisfactory meaning.

19. Fine poetic figures for the basis of Job's confidence mark this and the following verse. For the thought of the first line cf. Ps. 1.3; Jer. 17.8; Ezek. 31.7. Cf. also Bildad's words in 8.16f.

20. glory: Hoffmann proposed to read *kîḏôn* for *kāḇôd* and to find the word found in 1 Sam. 17.6 (*RSV* 'javelin'; but cf. on 39.23), which is used parallel to 'bow' in Jer. 6.23 (*RSV* 'spear'). But parallelism is not necessarily so rigid. Very doubtful is Mansoor's rendering 'victory' or 'strength' instead of 'glory' (*RQ*, III, 1961–62, p. 388).

bow: the symbol of strength (cf. Gen. 49.24). The breaking of the bow means the reduction to impotence (cf. Ps. 46.9 (M.T. 10); Jer. 49.35; Hos. 1.5).

²¹ 'Men listened to me, and waited,
   and kept silence for my counsel.
²² After I spoke they did not speak again,
   and my word dropped upon them.
²³ They waited for me as for the rain;
   and they opened their mouths as for the spring rain.
²⁴ I smiled on them when they had no confidence;
   and the light of my countenance they did not cast down.
²⁵ I chose their way, and sat as chief,
   and I dwelt like a king among his troops,
   like one who comforts mourners.

THE ESTEEM IN WHICH JOB WAS FORMERLY HELD **29.21–25**
The thought returns here to the deference shown to Job by others. In verses 7–10
he has spoken of the respect with which his arrival was greeted, and here speaks of
the deference to his views when he spoke and of the encouragement and comfort
a word from him brought to others. Very many editors think these verses are out
of place and transfer them to follow verse 10, where they would fit excellently.

21. Men listened: if this verse is transferred to follow verse 11, the subject is
the princes and nobles, who deferred to Job on his arrival and also in council.
Dhorme transposes **waited** and **kept silence,** and so Driver (*SVT*, III, 1955, p. 86).

22. Job's wisdom was accepted like an oracle. When he had given his judgment
nothing remained to be said, and no-one ventured to question it.
dropped: this is not a very happy rendering. The meaning is that they fell drop
by drop like the rain. As Job spoke unhurriedly, all waited to receive the words
of wisdom that fell from his lips.

23. Job's opinion was received with a welcome like that accorded to the bene-
ficial rains (cf. Dt. 32.2; Prov. 16.15; Isa. 55.10f.; Hos. 6.3), and as the ground
drinks in the showers so they drank in his words.
spring rain: *AV* and *RV* 'latter rain', falling in March and April, and of the
greatest importance for the crops (cf. Jer. 3.3; Jl 2.23). If this threatened to fail
men prayed earnestly for it (Zech. 10.1).

24. The first line follows *RV* marg. Job's smile then appears as an encouragement.
Budde, Duhm and others eliminate the negative: 'and they had confidence', but
Gray pronounces this very violent and unnecessary. The verb commonly means
'they did not believe' (cf. *AV*, *RV*). Dhorme and some other editors follow this
view and find the meaning to be that when Job graciously smiled on anyone, he
could not believe his good fortune. Kissane inappropriately renders 'If I laughed
at them, they believed not', and takes this to mean that when Job laughed dis-
approvingly, everyone rejected the views at which he laughed. This is very forced,
and 'to laugh at' would require a different preposition. The second line probably
means that the despondency of others never clouded the cheerfulness of Job. He

30 'But now they make sport of me,
men who are younger than I,

---

brought encouragement and was never himself discouraged. Bickell, Budde, Duhm and others replace 'they did not cast down' by 'comforted the mourners' (transferred here from verse 25c, which is then deleted). But Gray says neither the corruption nor the subsequent changes can be thought probable. Driver (*SVT*, III, 1955, pp. 86ff.) renders 'if my face lighted up, they showed no downcast (or angry) looks'.

25. Job directed the deliberations as a king directs his army. Whenever he gave a lead, it was immediately followed.

like one who comforts mourners: this reads oddly here, and Gray and others delete. Ewald thought it provided a transition to what follows in the form of a barbed reminder to the friends that they had so miserably failed to comfort Job. This seems forced. With slight changes in the Hebrew, Herz (*ZAW*, xx, 1900, p. 163) secured the meaning 'where I led them, they were willing to go' (so Dhorme, Pope). With different changes, Ball produced 'like a captain of thousands in the camp'. This would give a good parallel, but is wholly conjectural, whereas Herz had some support in Sym. Kissane justifies the retention of the line as in M.T. by arguing that the verse is a summary of the chapter: Job's relations with the elders (25a), with the people in general (25b), and with those in trouble (25c), the last clause referring to verses 11–13.

THE NOBODIES WHO NOW DESPISE JOB **30.1–8**

From his former state Job now turns to the present, and in this chapter he sets the misery he now experiences against the honour of the past. He begins by describing the offscourings of the people who now treat him with disdain. Duhm and Peake think verses 2–8 are misplaced and belong to the description of the outcasts in 24.5ff. Peake retains verse 1, which Duhm regards as a transition to verses 2–8 (so Strahan). Budde removes only verses 3–7. Here the contempt Job shows for these outcasts is thought to be unworthy of him. Dhorme defends the retention of these verses here. Job's contempt is not because these people are miserable outcasts, but because such persons, like those Job had always treated with generosity and kindness, now turned on him and despised their quondam benefactor and treated him as beneath themselves, when the hand of fortune struck him. It is the ingratitude and arrogance of these worthless creatures which is castigated. Their moral character matches their wretched state.

1. make sport of: the verb is the same as in 29.24, but the preposition is different. Here it is vulgar mockery; there a gracious smile. Cf. 19.18, and contrast 29.8.

younger than I: reverence for one's elders was expected of all; cf. 15.10. For the

whose fathers I would have disdained
to set with the dogs of my flock.
² What could I gain from the strength of their hands,
men whose vigour is gone?
³ Through want and hard hunger
they gnaw the dry and desolate ground;

---

expression cf. 32.6. Many editors follow Merx in omitting 'than I in days' (so
M.T. lit.), but Dhorme pronounces this mere whim. It is possible that the thought
is of children's mocking cries, as in 2 Kg. 2.23f. (so Dhorme).

with the dogs: it was not merely mockery of their elders, but of their betters.
The dogs were not companions but guardians of the flocks (cf. Isa. 56.10f.),
especially by night. They were despised (cf. 1 Sam. 17.43; 2 Sam. 3.8; 16.9) as
scavengers (1 Kg. 14.11; 21.19, 23; Ps. 68.23 (M.T. 24)).

   2. This verse would seem to refer to the fathers, who were degenerate weak-
lings, unfit for honest toil.

men whose vigour is gone: *AV* 'in whom old age was perished' and *RV* 'men
in whom ripe age is perished' are meaningless. The suggestion that the meaning
is that they would not reach old age is forced. For 'old age' (*kālah*) Beer proposed
'all vigour' (*kol-ḥāyil*) and Budde 'all freshness' (*kol-lēah*), while Olshausen read
'all of it (i.e. strength)' (*kullōh*). This last is followed by Dhorme, who also reads
'*uzzāmô*='their vigour' for '*ālêmô*='upon them' (in whom). This yields 'their
vigour had wholly perished' (so also Larcher). But the word *kelah* (identical with
kālah here) is found in 5.26 (see note there), where the meaning 'firm strength' is
conjectured for it. Hence no emendation is necessary to secure the sense of *RSV*
(so Kissane).

   3. hard hunger. The word 'hunger' is rendered 'famine' in 5.22 (see note
there). 'Hard' is the word rendered 'barren' in 3.7 (see note there). It means
'stony', and here perhaps 'gaunt'. Hitzig and many others read 'they are rolled up
with hunger' but this is no improvement.

they gnaw the dry (ground): *AV* 'flee' gives an Aramaic sense to the verb (so
Theod., Targ.). The same root is found in verse 17. Ball, Hölscher, and Dhorme
add 'the roots of' (easily lost after the verb 'gnaw'): 'They gnaw the roots of the
dry ground', which greatly improves the sense. The word is again an Aramaism,
perhaps for variation on the ordinary word for 'roots' in verse 4.

and desolate ground: M.T. 'yesterday desolate and waste'. *RSV* omits two of
these words and attaches the third to the previous line. But the phrase 'desolate
and waste' is alliterative and should not be sacrificed. But 'yesterday' is strange.
Duhm proposed 'they grope' (*yemaššešû* for '*emeš*), but this implies darkness (cf.
5.14). Klostermann proposed 'their mother' ('*immām*), and so Budde, Gray,
Dhorme. But this is not convincing. Pope renders 'by night' instead of 'yesterday',

⁴ they pick mallow and the leaves of bushes,
    and to warm themselves the roots of the broom.
⁵ They are driven out from among men;
    they shout after them as after a thief.
⁶ In the gullies of the torrents they must dwell,
    in holes of the earth and of the rocks.
⁷ Among the bushes they bray;
    under the nettles they huddle together.
⁸ A senseless, a disreputable brood,

---

but this evades the difficulty. Olshausen, Siegfried and Fohrer read 'land' (*'ereṣ*): 'a desolate and waste land'. Gray pronounces this weak, but it is at least relevant.

4. mallow: cf. on 24.24. This is a saline plant (the Hebrew word is related to the word 'salt') which Bochart (*Hierozoicon*, I, 1663, cols. 874ff.) identified with the sea orach. Many editors render by 'saltwort' (so *RV*). According to Post (*DB*, I, 1900, p. 223*b*), it is a perennial shrub, with sour leaves, which grows in salt marshes.

and leaves of: M.T. 'upon'. *RSV* adds 'and' with Budde and others, and renders 'leaves of' (which is written the same as 'upon'). Only the poorest people would eat such food.

broom: the tree under which Elijah lay (1 Kg. 19.4f.). M.T. has 'the roots of the broom are their food' (cf. *AV*, *RV*). The rendering **to warm themselves** involves a change of vowels. Cf. Ps. 120.4.

5. from among men: *RV* has 'from the midst (of men)'. 'Midst' for *gēw* is an Aramaism. But there is a Phoenician word *gēw* meaning 'community' (cf. Jean-Hoftijzer, *Dictionnaire des inscriptions sémitiques de l'ouest*, p. 48), also found in Syriac. Without any ellipsis, therefore, we may translate 'from society'. Dahood (*Biblica*, XXXVIII, 1957, p. 319) suggests 'with a shout'.

as after a thief: these are not, like the people of 24.5ff., people who are forced to steal to get food, but outcasts who dare not show themselves in inhabited places for fear of being chased away.

6. It is bitter to Job to realize that people who live in such squalor and degradation feel able to taunt him, now that he is an outcast relegated to the dunghill.

and of the rocks. Guillaume (*Promise and Fulfilment*, p. 119) renders 'on the mountain tops', invoking Arabic.

7. bray: cf. on 6.5. Gray thinks it is here the cry of lust (cf. Peake), but it seems better, with Dhorme, to understand it to mean the hoarse cries of hunger.

nettles: the precise plant cannot be identified. Dhorme thinks of nettles.

huddle together: Peake finds a sexual meaning here. But there is no evidence for this. It is more probable that it is for warmth.

8. The first line is lit. 'sons of a senseless person, sons of a nameless person'.

they have been whipped out of the land.
9 'And now I have become their song,
   I am a byword to them.
10 They abhor me, they keep aloof from me;
    they do not hesitate to spit at the sight of me.
11 Because God has loosed my cord and humbled me,
    they have cast off restraint in my presence.
12 On my right hand the rabble rise,
    they drive me forth,
    they cast up against me their ways of destruction.

'Sons of' denotes the category of people to which they belong. Mentally and morally defective, they were without respectability or standing, mere nobodies and worthless creatures. W. M. W. Roth (*VT*, x, 1960, pp. 402f.) holds that for 'senseless' we should render 'outcast'.

whipped: this rendering gives to the verb *nāḵā'* (another Aramaic form) the meaning of *nāḵāh*, 'they were smitten'. *AV* 'were viler than' connects it with the adjective *neḵē'* = 'afflicted', 'dejected' (Prov. 15.13; 17.22; 18.14). Beer emends to read 'they were crushed'; Joüon (*MFO*, V, ii, 1912, p. 436) to read 'hide themselves'; Dhorme to read 'were cut off'. None of these is convincing, and no emendation is necessary. In 1 Sam. 2.14 the transitive form of *nāḵāh* means 'thrust', and we could render here 'they were thrust out of the land'.

THE INDIGNITIES JOB SUFFERS 30.9–15

Whereas he was once treated with deference by great and small, and those whom he helped blessed his name, now he is scorned and contemned and treated as one abandoned by God. On all sides he is beset until he feels like a besieged city being breached by its foes. His honour is cast to the wind and his prosperity has vanished like a cloud.

9. **their song:** this ties up with verse 1. It is the children of the wretches described in the intervening verses who make Job the butt of their taunts. The word used for 'song' here is used for the music of stringed instruments in a number of Psalm titles. It is used of drinking songs in Ps. 69.12 (M.T. 13) and of mocking songs in Lam. 3.14, as here.

byword: this is not the word used in 17.6, but is one used frequently in Job for 'word'. It is only here it has the nuance of 'byword', which the context requires.

10. **keep aloof:** cf. 19.13, 19.

spit: cf. 17.6; also Isa. 50.6.

11. **God has loosed:** M.T. 'he has loosed'. In the next line the verb is plural, **they have cast off.** Budde conforms the first line to the second 'they have loosed', i.e. Job's tormentors (so Ball, Pope). Duhm conforms the second to the

first, 'he has cast down' (so Peake, Strahan, Hölscher, Steinmann). *RSV* understands the second line to express the reaction of the scoffers to the action of God
described in the first line (so Larcher). For **my cord** (so Ḳr) Kt. has 'his cord',
and editors prefer the one or the other according to their general interpretation.
Moreover, the meaning of 'cord' is not agreed. It may mean 'bowstring' (cf.
Ps. 11.2), and in 4.21 *RSV* renders 'tent cord' (see note there). If the former is
understood and 'my cord' is read, a reference to 29.20 is found. Job is now
defenceless. Delitzsch took the 'tent cord' here to stand for the 'cord of life', but
this is most improbable. In Jg. 16.7ff. the word is used for a cord or rope to bind
a man with, and Dhorme finds this sense here, rendering: 'He who has untied his
rope now humiliates me', the rope being that with which Job is thought to have
tied him. This seems less satisfactory than *RSV*, though the text must be recognized to be obscure and uncertain.

restraint: lit. 'bridle' (cf. Isa. 30.28; Ps. 32.9).

in my presence: Dhorme, who reads the verb in the singular in this line, reads
'his' for 'my', and renders: 'as also he who has cast off the bit from his face'. This
again is not convincing, and it seems preferable to find the meaning to be that
when men saw that God had humiliated Job and robbed him of his influence and
power, they turned on him with unrestrained insolence.

12. **On my right hand:** Peake finds this puzzling, as it suggests a court of law,
where the accuser stood at the right hand, while Kissane transfers the scene to a
court of law (so Dhorme, see below). But the context is of assault. Gray thinks
the point is that a man is strongest on his right hand, but even there these outcasts
assail Job.

the rabble: this word is found only here, but is connected with a word meaning
'chicks' found in 39.30; Dt. 22.6; Ps. 84.3 (M.T. 4); hence *AV* 'youth' here. It is
probably a depreciatory term here, as we might say 'insolent puppies'. Dhorme
transfers here 'their ... destruction' from the end of the verse and reads
'witnesses' ('ēḏîm for 'ēḏām), and so brings the lawcourt directly into the verse.
But his treatment of this verse is unduly violent (see below).

they drive me forth: the verb is the same as that rendered 'cast off' in the
previous verse, and M.T. says 'they have cast off my feet' (cf. *AV*, *RV*), or perhaps
'they have sent my feet away'. This is thought to mean 'drive me from place to
place', but this is all very forced. The words are metrically superfluous, and many
editors delete them, probably rightly, as a corrupt dittograph of words in the
preceding verse. Dhorme emends the word rendered 'rabble' to read 'into the
net' and transfers it here: 'they have drawn my feet into the net'. But this introduces a quite different figure from the law court, which he has imported into the
first line. The third line of the verse he retains, with the omission of 'their ...
destruction'. Three different figures are then in the verse. It is more natural to
find a single thought, of the assaults of the tormentors against Job, now robbed
of his defence, under the figure of a besieging army. For the last line cf. 19.12.
Fohrer lightens the line metrically by striking out 'against me'. Kissane offers the
doubtful translation of the second line 'They let loose slander (against me)'. This

¹³ They break up my path,
　　they promote my calamity;
　　no one restrains them.
¹⁴ As through a wide breach they come;
　　amid the crash they roll on.
¹⁵ Terrors are turned upon me;
　　my honour is pursued as by the wind,
　　and my prosperity has passed away like a cloud.
¹⁶ 'And now my soul is poured out within me;
　　days of affliction have taken hold of me.
¹⁷ The night racks my bones,
　　and the pain that gnaws me takes no rest.

---

keeps the legal meaning in the first two lines, though by doubtful expedients, but leaves the third line incongruous with the others.

13. This verse is also difficult, and its division is abnormal for this book. It continues the figure of the previous verse, and represents the enemy as cutting off all escape from the besieged, who has no hope of relief forces coming to his aid. **break up:** this verb is found nowhere else. It is probably a variant form of that found in 19.10. The breaking-up of the path is probably to make it impassable for escape. Dhorme restores the normal rhythm by transferring to this line 'for my calamity' from the next line, and rendering 'with a view to ruining me' (cf. Kissane and Pope).

promote: AV and RV 'set forward', lit. 'profit', i.e. 'further'. Syr. has 'rejoice at', and so Graetz; but, as Gray observes, his enemies are actively adding to his troubles, not merely rejoicing at them. Bickell proposed 'they go up' (ya'ᵃlû for yōʿîlû), and so Dhorme, who notes that this is a relevant term for a military attack. Without change of text, Kissane renders 'they prevail'; but this is unjustified.

restrains: M.T. has 'helps'. But 'restrains' is the sense needed. This was proposed by Dillmann (reading 'ōṣēr for 'ōzēr), and it has been widely followed. Driver (AJSL, LII, 1935–36, p. 163) secures this meaning without change of text, arguing that the verb had polarized meanings, 'help' or 'hinder'. Guillaume (Promise and Fulfilment, p. 119) renders as an imprecation: 'May they have no helper!'

14. The figure of the attack on a besieged city is maintained. Here they breach the wall, and wave after wave of the enemy pour in.

As through: M.T. idiomatically has simply 'as', a second preposition being commonly omitted after 'as'.

breach: cf. 16.14. Perles (JQR, XVIII, 1905–06, p. 390), with a slight change, renders 'like the bursting of a flood'.

amid the crash: i.e. the crash of the falling stones of the breached wall. M.T., lit. 'under the crash', giving the suggestion that they rushed in while the stones were falling around them. Driver (*AJSL*, LII, 1935–36, pp. 163f.) takes the expression in a temporal sense 'at the moment of the crash'. Guillaume (loc. cit., pp. 119f.) explains from Arabic and secures the sense 'where the gap is made', which yields a good parallel.

they roll on: this is very expressive. The verb is a common one, meaning 'roll' (cf. Am. 5.24), but the particular form found here stands nowhere else. The noun from this root means 'wave' or 'billow'. Here the verb excellently expresses the waves of the enemy bursting through the breach.

15. Terrors: cf. 18.11, 14; 27.20.

are turned: the verb here is that which yields the noun 'overthrow', regularly used of the overthrow of Sodom and Gomorrah. It means terrors have been overturned upon him; he is overwhelmed by them.

my honour: this word is an abstract connected with the word for 'noble' or 'prince', found in 12.21; 21.28. (*AV* understood it to mean 'my noble one' and interpreted it of the soul.) The plural (='noble deeds') is found in Isa. 32.8. LXX here has 'my hope' (so Volz); Duhm proposes 'my happiness'. But there is no need for change. Job's princely dignity, once acknowledged by all, is now driven away as by (cf. on verse 14) the wind.

my prosperity: this word is commonly rendered 'salvation'. It also means 'welfare' (so *AV* and *RV*) or easy circumstances (in Arabic a cognate word means 'abundance [of means]').

like a cloud: which passes swiftly, never to return; cf. 7.9.

JOB'S PRESENT DESPONDENCY **30.16–23**

The ridicule and opposition which Job now experiences have reduced him to despair, which is aggravated by his physical sufferings and by the feeling that God has turned against him and is cruelly persecuting him and determined to end his life.

16. And now: cf. verses 1, 9. Job repeats the emphasis on the present in contrast to the past, and gives expression to his despondency. For the first line, cf. Ps. 42.4 (M.T. 5).

days of affliction: Duhm would replace 'days' by 'terrors'. But the phrase recurs in verse 27 and in Lam. 1.7, and 'night' in verse 17 may be suggested by 'days' here.

17. racks my bones: the verb means 'bore 'or'pierce'. The subject may be 'the night' personified, as *RSV*, or 'he', i.e. God (then render 'at night'). *AV* and *RV* take 'my bones' as subject and render the verb 'are pierced'. The Hebrew adds 'from upon me', and this is held to mean that his bones rot and fall away from him (cf. *RV* marg.). But the line is long, and LXX does not render 'from upon me' (*mēʿālāy*). Duhm and others omit, and so *RSV*. Dhorme omits 'ālāy as a repetition from the previous verse, but attaches the *m* to the previous word and repoints. This is then a plural, yielding the sense of *AV* and *RV* 'my bones are pierced'. The night is the time when suffering is most severe (cf. 7.3, 13f.).

the pain that gnaws me: M.T. 'my gnawers'. Some take these to be the worms

¹⁸ With violence it seizes my garment;
    it binds me about like the collar of my tunic.
¹⁹ God has cast me into the mire,
    and I have become like dust and ashes.
²⁰ I cry to thee and thou dost not answer me;
    I stand, and thou dost not heed me.
²¹ Thou hast turned cruel to me;
    with the might of thy hand thou dost persecute me.
²² Thou liftest me up on the wind, thou makest me ride on it,
    and thou tossest me about in the roar of the storm.
²³ Yea, I know that thou wilt bring me to death,
    and to the house appointed for all living.
²⁴ 'Yet does not one in a heap of ruins stretch out his hand,
    and in his disaster cry for help?

---

in his sores (7.5); others as *RSV*. LXX has 'my nerves' (cf. *AV* 'my sinews'), and Jewish tradition followed this. The cognate word in Arabic means 'veins', and Dhorme follows this. It is more probable that Job here speaks of his unceasing pain, which is especially unbearable at night.

18. it seizes my garment: M.T. has 'my garment is disguised (or disfigured)'. This is supposed to mean that his garment hangs loosely on him. LXX has 'seizes' (involving the omission of one letter). This was followed by Houbigant and many editors. But the subject is more probably God than the pain (so Dhorme). God is depicted as seizing him by his clothes and throwing him down. The verb is used of seizing the clothing in 1 Kg. 11.30. Peake approved of Duhm's double emendation and then quite unjustified translation (cf. Gray): 'By reason of great wasting, my garment is crumpled together'. Reider (*HUCA*, III, 1926, p. 114) emended to secure 'because of the great amount of phlegm my garment is disfigured'; but this is not to be commended on any ground. Guillaume (loc cit., p. 120) finds an Arabic sense 'pus' for 'violence' and renders the verb 'is saturated': 'My clothing is saturated with much suppuration'.

it binds me about: the verb means 'girdles me', which is a curious thing for the collar (lit. mouth) of a garment to do. The line suggests to us a tightly fitting collar, but the eastern garment was loose fitting. Ehrlich proposed 'it (i.e. my pain) takes hold of me (*yōʾḥᵃzēnî* for *yaʾazᵉrēnî*) by my collar'. Again it is more probable that the subject is God (so Pope). Cf. 16.12. Guillaume here renders: 'It sticks to me like my undergarment', to accord with his rendering of the previous line, but offers no justification of the translation.

19. God has cast: the Hebrew has 'he (or it) has cast', and there is no indication that the subject is other than that of the preceding verse. It is probable that in both verses it is God, whom Job supposes to be the author of his sufferings.

Cf. 9.31. The line is short, and Duhm and some others add the word 'God', while Gray would add 'Behold, God'. Duhm would also alter the verb, to read 'has made me go down', and Volz to read 'Thou hast cast me'. But neither is necessary. **like dust and ashes:** it is improbable that this is to be taken literally as a description of Job's appearance. It is rather to be taken figuratively as a symbol of Job's humiliation.

20. does not heed: this is the reading of one MS. and of Vulg. and is supported by the parallelism. All other Hebrew MSS. omit the negative. Syr. has 'Thou standest and lookest at me', and this is favoured by some editors. This is then thought to mean that God cruelly stared at Job. But this is not the natural nuance of the verb.

21. turned: the same verb as in Isa. 63.10. Cf. also 13.24; 19.11.

22. Job changes the figure. Violently thrown to the ground in verse 19, he is here lifted on the wind and borne helplessly whithersoever it would carry him. In either case he is at the mercy of forces which he can neither control nor resist. **tossest me about:** AV and RV 'dissolvest me'. The verb means 'melt' (Am. 9.5), and the form used here stands in Ps. 65.10 (M.T. 11) meaning 'soften (the earth with showers)'. The cognate root in Arabic is used of the surging of the sea, and this sense is reflected in RSV (cf. Am. 9.5, where the context speaks of rising and falling).

the roar of the storm: the Ḳr. has the word rendered 'success' in 5.12 (see note there). Duhm, who follows this, adds 'without' and renders 'without help'. But this is a meaning not found elsewhere. The Kt. has what appears to be a variant form of a word meaning 'crash' (cf. 39.7; Isa. 22.2, 'shoutings'), here probably standing for the crash of the tempest. In 36.29 it stands for the thunder. RV takes it to mean 'the storm', rather than the noise of the storm, and so Gray and Dhorme (the latter taking this as the subject: 'a storm drenches me with water'). As in every difficult text, the ingenuity of editors has provided many unconvincing emendations.

23. bring me: the Hebrew has 'bring me back'; cf. 1.21.
death: here personified, as in 28.22, and standing for Sheol.
house appointed: or 'house of meeting', i.e. meeting place, where all the dead are gathered together (cf. 3.17ff.).
all living: here living persons; cf. 28.21.

THE CONTRAST BETWEEN THEN AND NOW **30.24–31**

None pities Job today, in his bitter affliction, though in his own happier days he had ever shown sympathy to the afflicted. An outcast and unheeded, he remembers the music of the days gone by amid the tears of the present.

24. This is another difficult verse, which has given rise to many translations and interpretations. RV has 'Surely against a ruinous heap he will not put forth his hand'. The thought is then that God will not strike one so smitten as Job. RV marg. (so Davidson) finds the subject to stand for Job: 'doth not one stretch out the hand in his fall?' But this gives an unjustified meaning 'to ruin' (cf.

²⁵ Did not I weep for him whose day was hard?
    Was not my soul grieved for the poor?
²⁶ But when I looked for good, evil came;

Jer. 26.18; Ps. 79.1, where the same word occurs). *RSV* avoids this, but gives the picture of a man walking amid ruins and stretching out his hand for support. Calmet took the ruined heap to be the grave, and so *AV*. But this meaning is unsupported (cf. Rosenmüller). Dillmann proposed to read *ṭôḇēaʿ*=ʿa drowning man' for *beʿî*=in a ruin': 'doth not a drowning man stretch out a hand?' So many editors. But Beer objects that the Hebrew does not mean stretch out the hand to receive help, but rather to give help (cf. 2 Sam. 6.6, where, however, the preposition is different). Wright proposed *beʿānî*=ʿagainst the poor' for *beʿî*, and so Beer, who renders 'Have I not given a helping hand to the poor?' (reading the verb in first person with LXX). The verb is used in the same construction in Gen. 37.22 for stretching out the hand against someone, and Dhorme so takes it here: 'I did not strike the poor man with my hand'. So Kissane, save that he retains the third person: 'one doth not'. Here the view of Dhorme seems best, and it connects well with verse 25. In his prosperity Job did not strike the unfortunate, but gave him sympathy.

and in his disaster cry for help: *AV* 'though they cry in his destruction' is meaningless, and *RV* 'though it be in his destruction, one may utter a cry because of these things' is little better. Dillmann and many others emend to secure 'doth he not in his calamity cry for help?' This is followed by *RSV* (cf. also Kissane). Dhorme differently emends, claiming partial support from LXX, to get 'if in his distress he cried out for my help'. The first word commonly means 'if', but it can be a correlative interrogative. Dhorme takes it the one way, and *RSV* the other. The view of Dhorme is preferable. On the one view Job is saying 'Is it not natural for me to cry for help in my distress? I always gave sympathy when roles were reversed'. On the other he is saying 'I always gave help and sympathy to those in distress'. He expected it to be extended to him, not that he should have to appeal for it. Reider (*VT*, II, 1952, pp. 127ff.) gives to the verse the forced rendering: 'Surely he does not put forth his hand against the weak; is there advantage to him in his calamity?' and then dismisses the verse as the insertion of a pious reader, who wanted to refute Job.

25. grieved: verb found only here. With a weakened guttural an adjectival form is thought to stand in Isa. 19.10. With various changes Driver (*AJSL*, LII, 1935–36, pp. 164f.) rendered verses 24f.: 'Surely no beggar would put out his hand, if he had found no relief in his plight, without my having wept for one hardly treated by life, and my soul being grieved for the needy'. This is very ingenious, but not convincing.

26. While Job disputes the view of the friends that virtue leads to happiness, he shares with them the view that it ought to. His generous sympathy gave him

and when I waited for light, darkness came.
27 My heart is in turmoil, and is never still;
   days of affliction come to meet me.
28 I go about blackened, but not by the sun;
   I stand up in the assembly, and cry for help.
29 I am a brother of jackals,
   and a companion of ostriches.
30 My skin turns black and falls from me,
   and my bones burn with heat.
31 My lyre is turned to mourning,
   and my pipe to the voice of those who weep.

---

the assurance that his prosperity would continue. But it did not.

27. My heart: lit. 'bowels' (*AV, RV*), the seat of emotion; cf. Jer. 4.19 (*RSV* 'my anguish'); Isa. 16.11 (*RSV* 'my soul').

is in turmoil: lit. 'boils' (cf. 41.31 (M.T. 23); Ezek. 24.5).

28. blackened: the word sometimes means 'dark coloured', but here blackened by disease (so Hitzig, Duhm). The word also developed the meaning 'sad', 'mourning' (cf. 5.11; Ps. 38.6 (M.T. 7)). Gray takes it here to mean squalid and dark in attire (so Budde), but this is less probable than the thought of his disease. **but not by the sun:** *AV* and *RV* '(mourning) without the sun'. This is strange. Duhm emended to secure '(mourning) without comfort' (so Peake, Strahan, Gray). Kissane, with a change of vowels, reads '(mourning), but not with butter' (cf. 29.6, 'milk'), which is then held to mean 'not in affluence'. But this is not convincing. The word used for 'sun' here refers to its heat (cf. Ps. 19.6 (M.T. 7), where it is rendered 'heat').

and cry for help: Duhm emends to read '(in the assembly) of jackals', which Peake commends as brilliant (so also Strahan). But Dhorme rightly rejects it, as the word for 'assembly' would not be used of jackals.

29. jackals: not the word Duhm emends into verse 28. They lived in the desert, and were known for their plaintive cry. Probably the thought here is that Job's cries were like theirs. They are mentioned alongside the ostrich in Mic. 1.8. The ostrich also is known for its cry.

30. black: not the root found in verse 28, but that which describes the Shulammite in Ca. 1.5.

and falls from me: lit. 'from upon me'. Ball would read 'by reason of disease', but this is without support.

burn: in Ezek. 24.10 this verb is used of the burning of bones with fire. Here, as in Ps. 102.4 (cf. Isa. 24.6), metaphorically.

31. The glad music of Job's former life (cf. 21.12, where he is describing the lot of the wicked) has given place to weeping and lamentation.

31 'I have made a covenant with my eyes;
        how then could I look upon a virgin?
² What would be my portion from God above,
    and my heritage from the Almighty on high?
³ Does not calamity befall the unrighteous,
    and disaster the workers of iniquity?

JOB'S ASSEVERATION OF HIS INTEGRITY 31.1–12

Job solemnly declares that his piety had banished all lust from his heart, and invokes curse upon himself if he has been guilty of deceit or adultery. Strahan observes that the picture Job here presents of himself is 'extraordinarily like that of the citizen of God's Kingdom, as etched by Christ in his Sermon on the Mount'. He goes behind act to thought, and beneath conduct to the heart.

1. made a covenant: lit. 'cut a covenant'; cf. Gen. 15.10; Jer. 34.18.
with mine eyes: the Hebrew preposition here is 'to', and editors say that this means that Job imposed the terms of the covenant upon his eyes, since this preposition implies that the parties are not equal. This is forced, since, as Dhorme points out, the same preposition is found in 2 Chr. 29.10, where we can hardly suppose that Hezekiah thought of himself as imposing a covenant on Yahweh.
how then?: Duhm emends this to read 'from looking', or 'not to look'. The word 'how?' can also mean 'not', and without emending Dhorme renders 'I would not look'. But, as Gray notes, this is not the content of the covenant, but an illustration of its effect.
a virgin: many editors think this is out of place here, since sexual matters are dealt with below. Hence Peake (so Pope) emended this word to 'folly' (*neḇālāh* for *beṯûlāh*), and Kissane to 'calamity' (*behālāh*). The former is more appropriate than the latter, but there is no need for either. Job's covenant with his eyes is by implication to refrain from sinning by desire, and the example he selects is the one most easily experienced, especially by the owner of slaves. Below Job repudiates the act of adultery; here he rejects the desire for what Hebrew law regarded as a different and lighter form of sin. Cf. Mt. 5.28.
2. In verse 1 Job is clearly thinking of his behaviour in the days of his prosperity. So here he describes his expectation at that time. Editors accuse Job of here accepting the views of the friends on desert and experience. But Job all along takes it for granted that piety ought to be rewarded by blessing, and the whole burden of his complaint is that in practice he now sees that it is not.
3. This is the principle on which Job thought he could count.

⁴ Does not he see my ways,
   and number all my steps?
⁵ 'If I have walked with falsehood,
   and my foot has hastened to deceit;
⁶ (Let me be weighed in a just balance,
   and let God know my integrity!)
⁷ if my step has turned aside from the way,
   and my heart has gone after my eyes,
   and if any spot has cleaved to my hands;
⁸ then let me sow, and another eat;

---

workers of iniquity: a common expression in the Psalter. The view of Mowinckel, that it there denotes those who were believed to have put a spell on the psalmist, is excluded here. It is not because he refrained from sorcery that Job felt secure, but because he eschewed even the thought of sin.

4. It is possible that Job is here still thinking back to the old days and the confidence he then had that God was watching him and numbering his steps in friendship (cf. 14.16). It is more probable that he is here asking in bewilderment how it is that he suffers his present miseries. Does God not see his life, or is he indifferent to Job's piety and purity?

5. If I have walked: *RV* and *RSV* take this verse as a protasis, resumed in verse 7 after a parenthesis. *AV* takes verse 6 as the apodosis, and verse 7 as a new protasis. Dhorme takes verse 5 as an independent question, and verse 6 as an independent wish.

falsehood: here personified, as a companion.

6. a just balance: cf. Lev. 19.36; Ezek. 45.10. For the condemnation of false balances, cf. Am. 8.5; Prov. 11.1; 20.23. For the weighing of a man in the balance for the assessing of his character cf. Dan. 5.27.

integrity: God had borne witness to Job's integrity in 2.3, where the same word is used as here. Job's conscience is in harmony with the judgment of God, though he could not know it. M. Dahood (*Hebräische Wortforschung*, Baumgartner Festschrift, 1967, p. 47) here renders 'my full weight', instead of 'my integrity', adducing Ugaritic evidence, but the meaning would still have to be 'my moral weight', and this is indistinguishable from the integrity.

7. It is here made clear that Job's covenant with his eyes was wider than the example in verse 1. They had never led him to stray from the path of rectitude or to covet what was another's.

my hands: sin is frequently pictured as staining the hands (cf. 11.14; 16.17; Isa. 1.15), and clean hands are a symbol of righteousness (cf. 22.30; Ps. 24.4).

8. Job here invokes curse upon himself, if he has sinned in thought or deed in the ways indicated. Cf. 5.5; 27.16f.; Dt. 28.30; Isa. 65.22; Mic. 6.15.

and let what grows for me be rooted out.
⁹ 'If my heart has been enticed to a woman,
    and I have lain in wait at my neighbour's door;
¹⁰ then let my wife grind for another,
    and let others bow down upon her.
¹¹ For that would be a heinous crime;
    that would be an iniquity to be punished by the judges;
¹² for that would be a fire which consumes unto Abad'don,
    and it would burn to the root all my increase.
¹³ 'If I have rejected the cause of my manservant or my
        maidservant,
    when they brought a complaint against me;
¹⁴ what then shall I do when God rises up?
    When he makes inquiry, what shall I answer him?
¹⁵ Did not he who made me in the womb make him?
    And did not one fashion us in the womb?
¹⁶ 'If I have withheld anything that the poor desired,
    or have caused the eyes of the widow to fail,
¹⁷ or have eaten my morsel alone,
    and the fatherless has not eaten of it

---

what grows for me: the word here may be used of human offspring (so *AV* here; also Kissane and Pope) or of the produce of the earth (so *RV*, *RSV*, Gray, Dhorme and many editors). The latter seems more relevant here (cf. note on 5.25).

9. The sin of adultery is here repudiated. **A woman** here means a married woman, as the parallel makes plain.

lain in wait: in Prov. 7.12 it is the adulteress (cf. verse 19) who lies in wait for her victim; here the thought is of the adulterer who watches for his opportunity, which would be found particularly at dusk (24.15).

10. grind: This was the work of the slave (cf. Exod. 11.5; Isa. 47.2). To this work Samson was reduced by the Philistines (Jg. 16.21). In the second line Job invokes the principle of the *lex talionis*. His hypothetical adultery would in Hebrew eyes be an offence against her husband, and so another's adultery with his wife would be a similar offence against him. In Hebrew law adultery always involved a married woman. The marital state of the man was immaterial.

11. Dhorme omits this verse as a gloss, since it is the only reference to a human tribunal in the chapter, and the verse is short. The following verse refers to the punishment adultery incurs in Sheol. Others find no difficulty in the thought that adultery is punished by the law of man and by the law of God.

a heinous crime: the word is used especially of sexual offences (cf. Lev. 18.17; 20.14; Jg. 20.6).

an iniquity to be punished by the judges: the expression is grammatically irregular, but the omission of one letter yields the expression found in verse 28. The word used here for judges recurs only in Exod. 21.22; Dt. 32.31.

12. Abaddon: cf. 26.6. For the first line cf. Dt. 32.33; also Prov. 6.27ff. Yellin (*JPOS*, I, 1920–21, p. 11) improbably renders 'Abaddon' as 'for ever' here, taking it as an accusative of time.

burn to the root: M.T. 'root out' (so *AV*, *RV*). But this is not appropriate to 'fire'. Hence Wright suggested changing one letter to yield 'burn' and very many editors follow. Driver (*SVT*, III, 1955, pp. 88f.), with the transposition of two letters, justifies the rendering, 'scorch up'.

JOB'S DENIAL OF HIS ABUSE OF POWER **31.13–23**

Though his position gave him great power and influence, Job denies that he had ever wronged his servants, or failed to help the poor, or let the weak suffer injustice at his hand, and again calls down curse on himself if this is not so.

13. manservant: i.e. slave. The rights of slaves were few (Exod. 21.1–11), though the lot of the slave was better in Israel than elsewhere in the ancient world. But Job recognized his slaves as fellow creatures (verse 15), who had rights even though they were not enforceable at law, and he was ready to listen to their complaints. In 19.15f. we see how his slaves requited him in his misfortunes.

14. Job felt himself answerable to God for his treatment even of his slaves, for to him they were persons and not chattels.

rises up: i.e. to judge; cf. Ps. 76.9 (M.T. 10).

makes inquiry: this verb means 'visit' (7.18), 'inspect' (5.24), or 'punish' (35.15). Though his slave might not appeal to a human tribunal, Job is conscious that his appeal to God might lead to its investigation by God, with its consequences in Divine punishment.

15. In 10.8ff. Job had spoken of the care God had lavished upon him in the process of birth. Now he acknowledges that the same care had been lavished upon the meanest slave. He and the slave were creatures of the same God, so that the person of the slave was no less sacred than his own. Cf. Eph. 6.9. The lofty ethical character of this passage is very remarkable in the setting of the ancient world.

16. How far from the truth Eliphaz was in 22.7ff. Job now makes plain. In mercy he had not failed any more than in justice. To the poor, the widow, and the fatherless, all so easily exploited, he had ministered in their need, and never had they looked to him in vain for aid.

eyes . . . to fail: for the phrase cf. 11.20; Ps. 69.3 (M.T. 4).

17. eaten my morsel alone: not an open house for his friends, but the sharing of his plenty with the destitute is Job's noble claim. His haunting word still lives in the conscience of many. Cf. Isa. 58.7.

¹⁸ (for from his youth I reared him as a father,
       and from his mother's womb I guided him);
¹⁹ if I have seen any one perish for lack of clothing,
       or a poor man without covering;
²⁰ if his loins have not blessed me,
       and if he was not warmed with the fleece of my sheep;
²¹ if I have raised my hand against the fatherless,
       because I saw help in the gate;
²² then let my shoulder blade fall from my shoulder,
       and let my arm be broken from its socket.
²³ For I was in terror of calamity from God,
       and I could not have faced his majesty.
²⁴ 'If I have made gold my trust,

---

18. This verse is read as a parenthesis by *EVV*, since it breaks the protasis which leads up to verse 22. Here Job claims that he went far beyond mere charity to the needy, and gave them fatherly care.

from his youth: M.T. 'from my youth'. Many editors retain M.T., but with a variety of interpretations.

I reared him: M.T. 'he grew up with me' (cf. *AV*, *RV*). Graetz proposed the change to 'I reared him', and so Budde, Dhorme, Pope. If with this 'from my youth' is retained, Job is hyperbolically saying that far back in his life he displayed this benevolence. Merx, Duhm, and others read 'he reared me' (a change of vowels only), and then understand the subject to be God. On this view it was because God had so cared for him that Job cared for others. But this involves the change of the second line to agree with it. Stevenson comments that this involves a quite arbitrary intrusion of God's activity.

as a father: if M.T. is retained, this must mean 'as with a father' (a second preposition after 'as' being idiomatically omitted). With the emended text, either Job is a father to the fatherless, or God is a father to him.

from his mother's womb: M.T. 'from my mother's womb', which is again hyperbolical.

I guided him: M.T. 'I guided her'. Those who make God the subject in the previous line change this to 'he guided me'. If Job is made the subject of the previous line, there is no need to alter M.T. The 'her' refers to the widow. Job is saying that he was father to the orphan, and guide to the widow. Editors prosaically ask how Job could have cared for the widow from his infancy, and the orphan from his youth. In common speech today men often say 'All my life I have done so-and-so', when in literal truth they have not. Surely a poet may be allowed as much licence.

19. perish: cf. 29.13, where the one perishing is mentioned with the poor, the fatherless, and the widow.

clothing . . . covering: cf. 24.7 for the same parallelism. Cf. also Mt. 25.36ff.

20. loins: part of the body is used for the whole, here the part which especially is protected from the cold. Cf. Ps. 35.10, where the bones are credited with speech. Driver (*AJSL*, LII, 1935–36, pp. 164f.) renders 'without his loins having blessed me', taking 'if . . . not' as an Aramaism, 'except'.

21. raised my hand: lit. 'waved' or 'shaken' (cf. Isa. 11.15; 19.16; Zech. 2.9 (M.T. 13)); here in threat. Job could easily have exploited his power to secure a verdict against the weak in the court (cf. on 29.7), but had never stooped to this. **against the fatherless:** Graetz wished to avoid the further mention of the fatherless, and proposed 'against the perfect' (so Duhm, Budde, Strahan, Gray, Stevenson, Fohrer). But the upright man is not necessarily weak, whereas the orphan is, and the latter is therefore the more relevant here.

22. Here follows the imprecation pronounced by Job against himself, if he had done any of these things. It is related especially to verse 21. If he has raised his hand in threat against the weak, may his arm fall helpless and broken. Cf. Ps. 137.5.

socket: lit. 'reed'. Only here is this word used in the present sense. Gray thinks the meaning 'socket' developed from the hollow tube of the 'reed'. Kissane takes 'socket' to mean the elbow joint. Dhorme renders 'humerus', and thinks the meaning developed from the beam of the balance, for which 'reed' is sometimes used (Isa. 46.6). Pope thinks the meaning is the 'upper arm', while 'arm' means the 'lower arm'. But 'arm' cannot be limited to the lower arm, since it is sometimes used for the 'shoulder' of an animal (Num. 6.19; Dt. 18.3), or the upper arm of a man (2 Kg. 9.24).

23. What restrained Job from exploiting his power over others was his dread of the power of God, who was ever present to his thought. The first line is lit. 'For a terror unto me was calamity from God'. LXX and Syr. have 'For the terror of God restrained (LXX, or terrified Syr.) me'. On the basis of this Duhm, Budde, Dhorme, Kissane, and Fohrer read 'For the terror of God came upon me' (Gray, Beer, Stevenson follow LXX 'restrained'). Driver kept closer to M.T. to secure 'The fear of God was burdensome (an Arabic root) to me', while I. Eitan (*JBL*, XLII, 1923, pp. 22ff.) rendered 'The terror of God was mighty (another Arabic root) upon me'. There is no need to emend the text, which yields a clear meaning. Job feared that God would send calamity upon him. In the second line *RSV* renders freely; lit. 'By reason of his majesty I was powerless'. Bickell needlessly transferred this verse to follow verse 14 and Duhm to follow verse 18.

JOB'S DECLARATION OF HIS PURITY OF HEART 31.24–34

Turning now to further sins in the heart, Job repudiates any secret love of wealth, any worship of the heavenly bodies, any pleasure at the misfortune of his foes, any meanness or hypocrisy.

24. Cf. Ps. 49.6f. (M.T. 7f.); 52.7 (M.T. 9); 62.10 (M.T. 11); Prov. 11.28;

or called fine gold my confidence;
²⁵ if I have rejoiced because my wealth was great,
   or because my hand had gotten much;
²⁶ if I have looked at the sun when it shone,
   or the moon moving in splendour,
²⁷ and my heart has been secretly enticed,
   and my mouth has kissed my hand;
²⁸ this also would be an iniquity to be punished by the judges,
   for I should have been false to God above.
²⁹ 'If I have rejoiced at the ruin of him that hated me,
   or exulted when evil overtook him

Sir. 5.1. On **fine gold** cf. on 28.16. Job is repudiating the charge which Eliphaz had made against him in 22.24ff.

26. the sun: lit. 'the light'. The parallelism shows that the meaning here is as *RSV*.

in splendour: lit. 'as a precious thing' (cf. 28.10, 16, where the same word is used). The word is used especially of gems, and Budde renders 'as a jewel'.

27. Job denies that he had ever been so impressed with sun or moon that he had ever been tempted into worshiping it. He had never mistaken the creation for the Creator. Under Assyrian influence the worship of the heavenly bodies became widespread in Israel (2 Kg. 21.3ff.). For condemnations of such worship cf. Dt. 4.19; 17.2ff.; Jer. 8.1f.; and cf. 2 Kg. 23.5.

my mouth has kissed my hand: the Hebrew says 'my hand has kissed my mouth'. The thought is of throwing kisses to the moon, a practice not again alluded to in *OT*, but known elsewhere. While it is the mouth which kisses, it is the hand which is placed on the mouth in adoration and which is active in throwing the kisses.

28. judges: cf. on verse 11. In the law worship of the heavenly bodies was a capital offence (cf. Dt. 17.2ff.).

been false to: *AV* 'denied'; *RV* 'lied to'. The root meaning is 'grow lean', 'disappoint', 'deceive'. Here it appears to mean 'fail'. In worshipping the heavenly bodies, even in his heart, Job would have been guilty of disloyalty to God, who alone is the true object of worship. Despite the variety of Divine names used in the book (see p. 24), it is clear that Job is presented as an uncompromising monotheist.

29. The Law enjoins help to one's enemy (Exod. 23.4f.), and the same spirit is commended in Prov. 20.22; 24.17f.; 25.21f. Psalmists often fall below this spirit and show fierce hatred of their enemies (58.10 (M.T. 11); 109.6ff.; 118.10ff.; 137.8f.), or exult over their misfortunes (54.7; 59.10 (M.T. 11); 92.11 (M.T. 12);

30 (I have not let my mouth sin
   by asking for his life with a curse);
31 if the men of my tent have not said,
   "Who is there that has not been filled with his meat?"
32 (the sojourner has not lodged in the street;
   I have opened my doors to the wayfarer);
33 if I have concealed my transgressions from men,
   by hiding my iniquity in my bosom,

118.7). Job declares that he has never even in his heart found pleasure in the ruin of his enemies. Duhm observes: 'If chapter 31 is the crown of all the ethical development of the O.T., verse 29 is the jewel of that crown'. 'His heart would have burned within him', says Strahan, 'if he could have listened to Mt. 5.43ff.'

30. The protasis is again interrupted by a verse which carries on the thought of the preceding verse. Not only has Job not rejoiced over his enemies' troubles; he has never in his heart wished them harm.

my mouth: lit. 'my palate', implying that the cursing of one's enemies was a dainty morsel, which Job never suffered himself to taste.

31. Job's spirit of hospitality has been shared by his servants, who eagerly desired that others might be found to whom it might be extended.

the men of my tent: i.e. Job's household.

Who is there?: the expression is the same as in verse 35: 'Oh, that there were one!', lit. 'Who will give?' Duhm omits 'will give', to yield the sense of *RSV*.

his meat: i.e. the meat at his table. Tur-Sinai gives to the phrase an uglier meaning, taking 'to be sated with his flesh' to mean 'to abuse him sexually'. Such a desire to abuse a guest (cf. the story of the angels at Sodom) had never crossed the minds of Job's servants. So also Pope. It is as unlikely that it crossed the author's mind here.

32. This verse again interrupts the protasis to continue the thought of the preceding verse. Job has offered bed as well as board freely to strangers and wayfarers.

wayfarer: this follows the versions in the change of a vowel in the Hebrew, which says 'to the way'. It is accepted by almost all editors, and is supported by the parallel.

33. from men: *AV* 'as Adam' (cf. *RV*). Some editors (Ewald, Davidson, Dhorme, Kissane) take it to mean 'like ordinary men'. Graetz proposed to read 'from men', and so Budde, Fohrer and others. Job here repudiates the sin of hypocrisy.

in my bosom: this word is found only here in *OT*, but is known in Aramaic. Pope, who renders 'like Adam' in the previous line, takes this word from another root, and renders 'in a covert', finding the reference to be to the Paradise story.

34 because I stood in great fear of the multitude,
    and the contempt of families terrified me,
    so that I kept silence, and did not go out of doors—
35 Oh, that I had one to hear me!
    (Here is my signature! let the Almighty answer me!)
    Oh, that I had the indictment written by my adversary!

This is less likely. Adam hid himself, and not merely his sin, from God. What Job repudiates is the idea that he had concealed his sin from men, cherishing it in secret and appearing before men as virtuous.

34. This verse explains why Job might have been hypocritical, if he had had any sin to hide: for fear of the contempt of men.

I stood in fear: lit. 'I was terrified' (cf. on 13.25).

the multitude: AV and RV have 'the great multitude', and so Budde, Gray, Fohrer and others, with a slight change of the Hebrew. Ehrlich takes the word rendered 'great' adverbially (so RSV): 'greatly'. Chajes (GSAI, xx, 1907, p. 307), with the change of a vowel, read 'the hubbub of the city', i.e. the idle tongues of men (so also Dhorme). The third line of the verse describes how the hypocrite may avoid others, as much as possible, lest his hypocrisy, despite his hiding of his sin in his bosom, may yet become known. (Pope emends the line to read 'I brought no man out the door', and so reads sexual abuse into the text.) Here the avowal breaks off, without the imprecation to which the sustained protasis had been building up. Duhm and Dhorme transfer verses 38–40b to follow verse 32, and so provide the imprecation in verse 40. But then the new protasis, which begins in verse 33 is left uncompleted. Strahan thinks Job broke off here, feeling that it was useless to say any more. Instead he turns from men to God. But verses 38–40b certainly seem out of place, with their return to imprecation after the appeal to God. Pope transfers them to follow verse 8, Budde to follow verse 12, and Gray and Fohrer to follow verse 34. They seem most in place after verse 8, in which case we are left here in verse 34 with a despairing break in the asseveration of integrity.

JOB'S APPEAL FOR THE CHARGES AGAINST HIMSELF TO BE SPECIFIED 31.35–37

Every accused person is entitled to have the charges against him specified. Job in thought appends his signature to the avowal of his character and asks that God would in turn present him with the accusation against him. Proudly would he carry the document to which he could give so confident an answer.

35. one to hear me: Peake thinks Job means a sympathetic human ear. But most think he means God. Again and again Job has longed to come face to face with God to present his case or to hear God's case against him. Gray and Ball avoid the repetition of 'to me' in M.T. by reading 'Oh, that God would hear me!'

36 Surely I would carry it on my shoulder;
  I would bind it on me as a crown;
37 I would give him an account of all my steps;
  like a prince I would approach him.
38 'If my land has cried out against me,
  and its furrows have wept together;

---

my signature: Hebrew 'my *Taw*'. *Taw* is the last letter of the Hebrew alphabet. Hence Bickell thought the meaning was 'Here is my last word' (so Kissane). The letter was in the form of a cross, and most take it here to mean 'my mark', or 'my signature', authenticating a document (in Ezek. 9.4, 6 marked on the forehead). Job is then in thought appending his signature to what he has been avowing. He has, so to speak, deposited his defence with the court. But he has not yet learned the charge against him. The next line refers to this. Here he asks that God should overturn his defence, if he can. Sutcliffe (*Biblica*, xxx, 1949, pp. 71f.) argues for the meaning 'desire' instead of 'signature': 'This is my desire, that God would answer me' (so Driver, *AJSL*, LII, 1935–36, p. 166; Saydon, *CBQ*, XXIII, 1961, p. 252). The last line is very cryptic: 'A scroll (which) my adversary at law has written.' *RSV* takes it as dependent on 'Oh, that I had', which it repeats. Kissane takes it as following 'Here is', in which case the scroll is Job's indictment against God (hence he reads 'his adversary'). The former is to be preferred, unless, with Duhm, we suppose that a line which would give the connection for this line has fallen out. Many unconvincing emendations have been proposed.

36. on my shoulder: cf. Isa. 22.22. Job means that he would carry it proudly and conspicuously.
bind it: this verb is found elsewhere only in Prov. 6.21.
as a crown: Hebrew plural, 'crowns', perhaps referring to the tiers of a crown. Peake comments: 'He would bind God's accusations to him, transfiguring the shame into glory by the radiant glow of conscious innocence. Never had his independence of all approval save that of his own conscience reached a height more sublime.'
37. Job is prepared to defend his integrity to God, and to submit his life to the fullest examination. Not as a criminal would he appear before God, but as an innocent man with head held high as a prince.

JOB'S INVOCATION OF CURSE UPON HIMSELF IF HIS SELF-JUSTIFICATION IS FALSE **31.38–40**

If Job's estates should cry out against him because they had witnessed anything that contradicted his claim, he invokes the curse of weeds instead of grain upon it. These verses are probably out of place; see on verse 34.

38. cried out: Duhm supposed that the meaning is that the land should testify that Job has not observed the year of release (Dt. 15.1ff.), or the law against

39 if I have eaten its yield without payment,
    and caused the death of its owners;
40 let thorns grow instead of wheat,
    and foul weeds instead of barley.'
  The words of Job are ended.

---

sowing two kinds of grain (Lev. 19.19). This involved him in the necessity of deleting verse 39. But verse 39 well follows verse 38 and indicates that the land was conceived of as protesting because Job had oppressively acquired it without payment and by causing the death of its rightful owner, presumably by a false capital charge (cf. the story of Naboth's vineyard). Note the personification of the land, which is thought of as identified with its rightful owner.

39. yield: lit. 'strength' (cf. Gen. 4.12).

caused the death: the versions rendered 'grieved'; *EVV* and most modern interpreters render as *RSV*. The verb means 'breathe'. In Mal 1.13 the verb means 'sniff (in contempt)'. But in 11.20, with 'soul', as here, it refers to death, and in Jer. 15.9 (also with 'soul') it is used of a mother on the point of death. It is probable that it has this meaning here, though in view of the ancient versions we cannot rule out the possibility that it meant caused suffering to the dispossessed rightful owner (M.T. 'owners'). Larcher thought the distress was caused to the labourers (so Steinmann), rather than owners, and emended accordingly, and Dahood (*Gregorianum*, XLIII, 1962, p. 75; *Biblica*, XLI, 1960, p. 303; XLIII, 1962, p. 362) argues for this meaning without change of text.

40. The imprecation fits the hypothetical crime. If Job has wrongfully acquired the fruits of the land, let it cease to bear fruit. Instead of useful grains, wheat and barley, let it yield thorns and rank-smelling weeds.

The words of Job are ended: generally held to be an editorial note; cf. Ps. 72.20; Jer. 51.64. They mark the end of the debate between Job and his friends with its introduction and conclusion in soliloquies by Job.

THE SPEECHES OF ELIHU 32–37

Elihu now appears and makes four speeches, to none of which does Job give any answer. Nowhere outside these speeches is Elihu referred to in the book. It has been sometimes thought that he was one of the bystanders, listening to the debate, who now interposed. But this would not explain why he is not referred to in the speeches of Yahweh or in the Epilogue. His speeches could be omitted from the book without requiring any modification outside them. On the other hand, they show a knowledge of the preceding debate. It is therefore widely accepted that they are a later addition to the book (see pp. 12f.). Budde and Cornill (*Introduction to the Canonical Books of the O.T.*, Eng. trans. by Box, 1907, pp. 426ff.) accepted their originality and found in them the climax of the book, where alone a solution to the problem of suffering is offered. But it is a solution which is excluded by the Prologue. For Elihu's solution is that suffering is disciplinary, to cleanse the sufferer of sin (cf. already Eliphaz in 5.17ff.). But in the Prologue we are told that Job was not suffering for his sin, but to vindicate God's confidence in him against the slander of the Satan. Self-righteousness can be found in Job's speeches, indeed, but it was not for this that he was suffering. Hence, whatever may be said of the contribution of the Elihu speeches to the problem of suffering, they are irrelevant to the book of Job.

ELIHU'S FIRST SPEECH 32–33

The first speech is introduced by a prose section, which is repetitious and diffuse. No less than four times are we informed that Elihu was angry. His professed modesty is belied by his self-importance and pomposity. Unable to contain his feelings any longer, he breaks into the debate to rebuke the friends for their failure to answer Job, and to supply the deficiency. After the introduction (32.1–5), the speech falls into the following sections: Elihu's youth is wiser than the friends' age (verses 6–14); the collapse of the friends moves him to intervene (verses 15–22); Elihu invites the attention of Job (33.1–7); Job's affirmation of innocence and unjust treatment is false (verses 8–13); Job's complaint that God does not answer is belied by experience (verses 14–28); Elihu's final appeal to Job (verses 29–33).

PROSE INTRODUCTION 32.1–5

Although in prose, these verses are supplied with the Hebrew poetical accentuation. Elihu is angered by Job's assumption that he is more righteous than God, and by the drying up of the friends' arguments. Owing to his youth, he had refrained from intervening hitherto.

1. men: in 2.11; 19.21; 42.10 'friends'. This is probably one indication of a change of author.

because he was righteous: the friends are said to give up the debate as useless because of Job's incorrigible self-righteousness. In fact three rounds of the debate were probably originally given and the intervention of Yahweh followed Job's final appeal to God to answer him, which stood at the end of Job's concluding soliloquy. There was no giving up the debate, but a complete artistry in the plan of the book.

in his own eyes: LXX, Sym., Syr. have 'in their eyes' (so Dhorme, Kissane). But there is no indication anywhere that the friends had changed their attitude to Job.

2. Elihu: meaning 'he is my God'; found elsewhere in 1 Sam. 1.1 (Samuel's great-grandfather); 1 Chr. 27.18 (a brother of David); 1 Chr. 12.21 (a Manassite); 1 Chr. 26.7 (a Korahite).

son of Barachel: we are not told the name of Job's father, or of the fathers of the three friends. Barachel means 'God has blessed'.

the Buzite: of the clan of Buz, the brother of Uz (Gen. 22.21), and so closely related to Job (cf. 1.1). In Jer. 25.23 and Arabian Buz is mentioned.

Ram: again we have a detail not given for the three friends. The name means

32 So these three men ceased to answer Job, because he was righteous in his own eyes. ² Then Eli'hu the son of Bar'achel the Buzite, of the family of Ram, became angry. He was angry at Job because he justified himself rather than God; ³ he was angry also at Job's three friends because they had found no answer although they had declared Job to be in the wrong. ⁴ Now Eli'hu had waited to speak to Job because they were older than he. ⁵ And when Eli'hu saw that there was no answer in the mouth of these three men, he became angry.

⁶ And Eli'hu the son of Bar'achel the Buzite answered:
'I am young in years,
    and you are aged;

'lofty', 'exalted'. It occurs elsewhere as an ancestor of David, and therefore a Judahite (Ru. 4.19), or as a Jerahmeelite (1 Chr. 2.9f., 25), whereas Buz is an Aramaean name.

rather than God: LXX and Vulg. have 'before God', and so Dhorme and others. But Job not only was prepared to vindicate himself before God; he was prepared to bring an indictment against God.

3. friends: cf. verses 1, 5.

declared Job: Jewish tradition says this was one of the eighteen 'corrections of the scribes', and that the original text read 'declared God (in the wrong)'. The thought then is that in abandoning the debate they were conceding the verdict to Job and thereby condemning God. This is followed by Duhm, Strahan, Ball, Dhorme, Kissane, Steinmann, Larcher, Fohrer, Pope. But, as Tur-Sinai says, no such condemnation of God is implied by their failure to answer Job. With M.T. we might render 'and so (i.e. by finding an answer) shown Job to be in the wrong'. This is preferable to *RSV* **although**.

4. to speak to Job: lit. 'for Job with words'. Many follow Wright in reading as *RSV*, with a change of vowels (some rendering 'while they were speaking to Job', or omitting 'to Job' as an intrusion from the preceding verse).

older than he: Elihu's modesty about his youth is equalled by the assurance with which he will speak.

5. The prolixity of the introduction matches the style of Elihu himself.

men: cf. on verse 1.

ELIHU'S YOUTH IS WISER THAN THE FRIENDS' AGE 32.6–14

Elihu denies that wisdom is reserved for the aged, though he had given his elders a chance to vanquish Job in argument before he ventured to speak.

therefore I was timid and afraid
    to declare my opinion to you.
⁷ I said, "Let days speak,
    and many years teach wisdom."
⁸ But it is the spirit in a man,
    the breath of the Almighty, that makes him understand.
⁹ It is not the old that are wise,
    nor the aged that understand what is right.
¹⁰ Therefore I say, "Listen to me;
    let me also declare my opinion."
¹¹ 'Behold, I waited for your words,
    I listened for your wise sayings,
    while you searched out what to say.
¹² I gave you my attention,

---

6. was timid: this verb is found here only in OT, but it is found in the
Aramaic inscription of Zakir of Hamath (9th cent. B.C.), and its cognate is found
in later Aramaic (cf. Dan. 5.19; 6.26 (M.T. 27)).
opinion: lit. 'knowledge'. It is more than an opinion to which Elihu gives
expression. He is assured that it is knowledge. For he has the omniscience of youth.

8. it is the spirit: Houbigant read 'the spirit of God' to balance the following
line (so Budde and others). But this is needless. Elihu is right in saying that years
alone do not give wisdom, and that it belongs to the spirit rather than the age.
But this does not justify his immodest assertions that he has it in its completeness.

9. the old: M.T. has 'the great' or 'many'. The versions understood 'the old',
and this is supported by the parallelism. Many editors emend to make this clearer,
but Dhorme defends without change, citing Gen. 25.23, where the singular of
the same word means 'the elder'. Driver (*Textus*, IV, 1964, p. 91) postulates a
wrongly expanded abbreviation. In his youth Elihu denies wisdom to the aged.
In old age he might less readily agree that he had lost the wisdom of which he
now boasts.

10. Listen: in most MSS. this is singular, addressed to Job. The versions and
2 Hebrew MSS. have plural, and it is probable that Elihu was addressing the
friends as well as Job.
opinion: cf. on verse 6.

11. Pompously Elihu repeats in other words what he has just said.
wise sayings: lit. 'understandings' or 'insights'.
searched out: Elihu suggests that all their laborious efforts to comfort Job have
been less successful than his inspired genius will prove.

12. Though Elihu had followed the debate closely, he had failed to find any

and, behold, there was none that confuted Job,
or that answered his words, among you.
13 Beware lest you say, "We have found wisdom;
God may vanquish him, not man".
14 He has not directed his words against me,
and I will not answer him with your speeches.
15 'They are discomfited, they answer no more;
they have not a word to say.

---

cogency in their arguments. With this Job would fully agree. What cogency he might have found in Elihu's we are not told. For Job makes no reply to him.

13. We have found wisdom: this is thought to mean that the friends have found in Job a wisdom which only God can refute. They recognise that Job is too clever for them. But confident Elihu declares that there is no need for God. He is equal to the occasion himself. On this view, as Peake says, this is a direct polemic against the poet for his inclusion of the Divine speeches. Another view is that the friends have found that their own wisdom lay in leaving Job to be dealt with by God.

God may vanquish him: Dhorme (cf. Steinmann and Larcher) emends the text to read 'It is God who instructs us'. Elihu then attributes to the friends the claim that they were wise and that their wisdom rested on divine teaching, and warns them that he will not listen to such a claim.

14. directed: or 'marshalled'. This is held to mean that Job had not yet tried conclusions with Elihu, who has heavier artillery than the friends had used. When he has finished with Job there will be no need to call in God. As Gray points out, the promise is not fulfilled. Elihu's arguments do not go beyond what the friends have said. Gray emended the text to read 'I will not set forth such words as these' and so Dhorme, Hölscher, Steinmann, Larcher. The evidence for this reading is very weak, and while it imposes precise synonymous parallelism on the two lines of the verse, it loses not a little of the force of M.T.

THE COLLAPSE OF THE FRIENDS MOVES ELIHU TO INTERVENE 32.15–22

Turning to Job, Elihu caustically comments on the discomfiture of the friends, and declares that he can no longer contain himself, but must express himself to set everyone right. Before delivering himself of his views, he gives himself a certificate of impartiality. It is hard to escape the feeling that whoever added the Elihu speeches to the book intended him to look somewhat ridiculous, or he would not have made him so wordy, so self-important, and so unoriginal.

15. discomfited: lit. 'dismayed'. P. Joüon (*MFO*, V, II, 1912, pp. 428f.) argued for the meaning 'be speechless'.

they have not a word to say: lit. 'words have moved away from them'. The

¹⁶ And shall I wait, because they do not speak,
  because they stand there, and answer no more?
¹⁷ I also will give my answer;
  I also will declare my opinion.
¹⁸ For I am full of words,
  the spirit within me constrains me.
¹⁹ Behold, my heart is like wine that has no vent;
  like new wineskins, it is ready to burst.
²⁰ I must speak, that I may find relief;
  I must open my lips and answer.
²¹ I will not show partiality to any person
  or use flattery toward any man.

---

same verb is used in 9.5 of removing mountains, and in Gen. 12.8; 26.22 of moving
to another locality. Here it is a picturesque way of expressing the speechlessness
to which the friends are reduced. Apparently Elihu is here addressing the
bystanders.

  16. Elihu once more emphasizes the patience he has shown.

  17. Further repetition to build up expectation of the momentous words he is
about to speak.

  18. full of words: none would dispute this.

the spirit within me: lit. 'the spirit of my belly'. For the belly as the source of
speech, cf. 15.2 (see note there).

  19. my heart: lit. 'my belly'.

new wineskins: only here does the word for 'wineskins' have this meaning.
Elsewhere it is always associated with necromancy. In Mt. 9.17 it is said that new
wine must be put into new wineskins. Hence Delitzsch and Gray take the
expression to mean 'new skins of wine', i.e. skins filled with new wine. But this
is not a very natural rendering. What Elihu appears to mean is that he is bursting
to speak, and that his pent up feeling is so intense that it is like the force of
fermentation that would burst even new wineskins. LXX read 'smiths' for 'new',
and Tur-Sinai follows this and renders 'like smiths' bellows'. A. Guillaume
(*PEQ*, xciii, 1961, pp. 147ff.) has challenged the rendering 'wineskins', holding
that the word ('ōḇôt) is connected with Arabic *wa'b*, which means a wide vessel,
shaped like a cup or bowl. He cites evidence from Gibeon, dating probably from
the sixth century B.C., of wine-jar handles and stoppers, and maintains that the
reference here is to earthen vessels.

  21. Elihu gives himself another certificate, this time for impartiality. He is
doubtless deadly sincere, for he takes himself so seriously.

use flattery: the verb means 'to give an honorific title' (Isa. 44.5; 45.4, *RSV*

²² For I do not know how to flatter,
    else would my Maker soon put an end to me.

33 'But now, hear my speech, O Job,
    and listen to all my words.
² Behold, I open my mouth;
    the tongue in my mouth speaks.
³ My words declare the uprightness of my heart,
    and what my lips know they speak sincerely.
⁴ The spirit of God has made me,
    and the breath of the Almighty gives me life.

'surname'). Here it means that Elihu will not treat anyone with special respect. He proposes to lay about him with impartial vigour.

22. Not only is Elihu a stranger to anything that savours of partiality. He would be afraid of immediate divine vengeance if he gave way to it.

ELIHU INVITES THE ATTENTION OF JOB **33.1–7**

Now that everyone is assured of the wisdom and impartiality of Elihu, and of his competence for his task, he addresses himself directly to Job, giving him some further assurance of his own integrity and inspiration, but modestly adding that, like Job, he is only human.

1. O Job: none of the other speakers had addressed Job by name, as Elihu does (cf. 34.5, 7, 35f.; 35.16). With interminable prolixity he repeats himself (cf. 32.10).

2. The self-importance of Elihu is boundless, and he is the master of banality. Peake observes that 'it would show a strange lack of literary tact to credit the great genius to whom we owe the poem with such bathos as this'. But whoever wrote the Elihu speeches probably deliberately put such banal lines into his mouth, since his purpose was rather to expose this type of character than to exalt it.

3. declare: not in the Hebrew. The first line is without a verb. For **the uprightness of my heart** Duhm proposed 'my heart overflows' (*yāšîq* (cf. Jl 2.24) for *yōšer*), Beer 'my heart is astir' (*rāhaš*, cf. Ps. 45.1 (M.T. 2)), Dhorme 'my heart will repeat' (*yāšûr*, a doubtful meaning), and Hölscher 'my heart affirms' (*yāšēr*, a Syriac sense; cf. Kissane 'shall reveal', an Arabic sense). The second line says: 'and the knowledge of my lips they speak purely'. But there is a want of balance in the two lines, and many editors transfer the first word to the previous line (with omission of 'and'), leaving 'my lips will speak purely (or sincerely)'. For the first line Kissane's slight change of vowels yields the most suitable meaning 'my heart will reveal words of knowledge'. Elihu is once more giving assurance of his own brilliance.

4. Peake and Dhorme transfer this verse to follow verse 6, and Kissane to

⁵ Answer me, if you can;
   set your words in order before me; take your stand.
⁶ Behold, I am toward God as you are;
   I too was formed from a piece of clay.
⁷ Behold, no fear of me need terrify you;
   my pressure will not be heavy upon you.
⁸ 'Surely, you have spoken in my hearing,
   and I have heard the sound of your words.
⁹ You say, "I am clean, without transgression;

---

follow 32.13; but Gray defends its present position. Budde and Duhm omit the
verse. Elihu is not here saying that he is like all men in having the breath of God
in him (cf. Gen. 2.7), but that he in particular is inspired by God, so that his words
are not alone sincere, but of special value.

5. set your words in order: 'words' is not in the Hebrew. The verb means
'arrange', 'set in order', and it can be used of marshalling arguments (cf. 32.14),
or of arranging troops in battle array (6.4; cf. 1 Sam. 17.8). Dhorme takes it in
the latter sense here: prepare to do battle with me.
before me: should better be taken with what follows.

6. toward God: i.e. in relation to God. Elihu, like Job, is human. He and
Job stand on the same footing, so that Elihu will have no advantage over Job in
this respect. At the same time, he is persuaded that Job will stand but a poor
chance against his superior armoury.
formed: lit. 'nipped off', as a potter breaks off a piece of clay before moulding it.

7. Cf. 9.34; 13.21. Editors find here renewed implied criticism of the poet for
introducing the Divine speeches. Peake observes: 'One can imagine how the
poet's scorn would have crushed this presumptuous meddler'.
my pressure: this noun is found only here, but the verb stands in Prov. 16.26.
LXX has 'my hand' (with the omission of a letter), and so many editors. But it is
a pity to get rid of a rare word which makes good sense here.

JOB'S AFFIRMATION OF INNOCENCE AND UNJUST TREATMENT IS FALSE 33.8-13

To Elihu it is inconceivable that God should persecute an innocent man. He is
too great to be guilty of such unworthy conduct.

8. At last Elihu gets down to his self-appointed and much advertised task. He
is going to take Job's arguments to pieces, and he begins by recalling the
positions Job has taken up.

9. Cf. 9.21; 10.7; 16.17; 23.7, 10ff.; 27.4ff.; chapter 31.
without transgression: Job had not claimed sinlessness; cf. 7.21; 13.26. What
he had consistently maintained was that he had not sinned so heinously as to
explain his terrible sufferings.

I am pure, and there is no iniquity in me.

¹⁰ Behold, he finds occasions against me,
    he counts me as his enemy;

¹¹ He puts my feet in the stocks,
    and watches all my paths".

¹² 'Behold, in this you are not right. I will answer you.
    God is greater than man.

¹³ Why do you contend against him,
    saying, "He will answer none of my words?"

¹⁴ For God speaks in one way,
    and in two, though man does not perceive it.

¹⁵ In a dream, in a vision of the night,
    when deep sleep falls upon men,
    while they slumber on their beds,

¹⁶ then he opens the ears of men,
    and terrifies them with warnings,

¹⁷ that he may turn man aside from his deed,
    and cut off pride from man;

---

pure: only here, from a root meaning 'wash', or 'cleanse' (especially the head).
   10. For the first line cf. 10.13ff.; 19.6ff.; for the second line cf. 13.24.
occasions: the Hebrew has 'frustrations', or 'oppositions' (cf. Num. 14.34, RSV 'displeasure'). Rashi suggested reading, with metathesis, the word found in Jg. 14.4: 'pretexts', 'occasions'; so very many editors (Syr. renders in this sense). But Fohrer finds this unnecessary.
   11. Cf. 13.27.
   12. right: or 'justified'. Duhm emends the line to yield a further citation of the views of Job: 'if I cry, he does not answer'. But this is unnecessary, and with no adequate basis.
God is greater than man: LXX has 'He that is above men is eternal', which Duhm uses to reconstruct 'He hideth himself from men'. This is less satisfactory than M.T. The meaning of the verse is variously taken to be that God is too great to be called to account by men, as Job has sought to call him, or that God is above the petty feelings that Job has attributed to him. The latter is the more probable, since in what has preceded Elihu has not referred to any calling God to account. That he comes to in verse 13.
   13. contend: i.e. 'Why do you make it a ground of complaint against him that he does not answer?'
saying: not in the Hebrew; better 'that'.

my words: M.T. has 'his words', perhaps referring to 'man' in the previous verse. Hitzig and many others substitute 'thy words', for which Vulg. support is claimed (against this cf. Dhorme), while Bickell, Duhm, and others read as *RSV*, claiming the support of LXX (against this also cf. Dhorme). Kissane wrongly says Syr. has 'my words'.

JOB'S COMPLAINT THAT GOD DOES NOT ANSWER IS BELIED BY EXPERIENCE **33.14–28**

Against this Elihu maintains that God answers by dreams, and by sickness which chastens his spirit and leads him to accept instruction from a ministering angel, by whose mediation he is then restored.

14. though man does not perceive it: it would be better to render with Kissane 'though one perceiveth him not'. The meaning then is that, though God is not visible to the eye, he does speak to men. Syr. and Vulg. render 'and he does not repeat it' (i.e. he gives man two warnings but no more). Houbigant proposed to omit two letters to secure this meaning, and so Beer. Dhorme proposed to find this meaning without change of the text, by assuming the existence of another Hebrew verb *šûr* with this meaning. But this is very doubtful (cf. L. Dennefeld, *RB*, XLVIII, 1939, p. 175). Peake desiderated this sense, and Houbigant's proposal is the most satisfactory way of providing it.

15. Cf. 4.12ff., which probably inspired this passage.

16. opens the ears: this expression sometimes means 'inform' (cf. Ru. 4.4; 1 Sam. 20.2, 12, 13). When God is the subject it means 'make a revelation' (cf. 36.10, 15; 1 Sam. 9.15; 2 Sam. 7.27).

and terrifies them with warnings: M.T. has 'and seals their bond'. This is not lucid. Dahood (*Biblica*, XXXVIII, 1957, p. 311) retains 'their bond', which he interprets as 'their body', and repoints the verb to yield 'he snatches them'. This is then held to mean that men are carried out of the body and sleep to receive revelation. But this is very forced. Aq., Vulg., Syr. and Targ. have 'their correction' for 'their bond', and this is reflected in *AV* and *RV*, which is then held to mean 'confirms their moral education', or 'imparts instruction under the seal of secrecy'. But LXX, Aq., and Syr. instead of 'seals' have 'terrifies them' (a difference of pointing only), and this is widely followed and is reflected in *RSV*. But again LXX has 'appearances of fear' instead of 'their bond' (*mōsārām*), and this led Dhorme to propose *mare'îm*='apparitions' (so Dennefeld (*RB*, XLVIII, 1939, p. 176), Steinmann, Larcher, Pope), and Duhm *môrā'îm*='terrors' (so Hölscher). H. H. Nichols (*AJSL*, XXVII, 1910–11, p. 156) kept closer to LXX in reading *mare'ê môrāyîm*='appearances of terrors'. The general sense would seem to be well represented by *RSV*. By terrifying dreams God awakens men to the error of their ways.

17. from his deed: M.T. simply 'deed'. But by haplography the two needed letters could easily have fallen out. On the basis of LXX Bickell proposed 'from his iniquity' (*mē'awlāh* for *ma'ăśeh*), and so Duhm, Strahan, Pope.

cut off pride from man: M.T. 'pride from man he covers', which *AV* and *RV* interpreted to mean 'hide pride from man'. Reiske, followed by many others,

¹⁸ he keeps back his soul from the Pit,
   his life from perishing by the sword.
¹⁹ 'Man is also chastened with pain upon his bed,
   and with continual strife in his bones;
²⁰ so that his life loathes bread,
   and his appetite dainty food.

---

read *yᵉḵassēaḥ*='cuts away' instead of *yᵉḵasseh*='covers'; while Dillmann proposed *yᵉḵalleh*='puts an end to'. Dhorme prefers to transpose two words and read *m* for *w* to secure 'to turn away man from pride he (i.e. God) hides from man his action'. This does not seem convincing, and it seems best to follow Dillmann. The purpose of God's warning dreams is to turn man from his deeds and to humble him.

18. In all this God's action is beneficent, in that it is designed to save him from a worse fate.

the Pit: cf. on 17.14.

perishing by the sword: this is highly doubtful. The verb more naturally means 'to pass through', and though the noun sometimes means 'a weapon', this is not very relevant here, where we expect something parallel to 'pit'. Duhm proposed 'from going down to Sheol' (*šᵉ'ōlāh* for *šālaḥ*), and has been followed by Strahan, Hölscher, Steinmann. Dhorme sees in the word *šelaḥ* (here written *šālaḥ* in pause) the vertical Canal by which souls descended to the Underworld through the pit, or grave (so Larcher). M. Tsevat (*VT*, IV, 1954, p. 43) thought Dhorme was on the right track, but held *šelaḥ* to be the horizontal river of the Underworld, and rendered the phrase 'passing the river of the Underworld' (cf. Svi Rin, *BZ*, N.F., VII, 1963, p. 25, where *šelaḥ* is identified with the Underworld itself). Cf. also Pope. This general idea of crossing the river of death seems most suitable here. A. Guillaume (*ALUOS*, Supplement ii, 1968, p. 118) thinks *šlḥ* is by metathesis for *ḥlš*, which he connects with an Arabic root and then renders 'by a fatal seizure'.

19. Elihu now passes to a second channel of divine communication in warning.

and with continual strife in his bones: the Kt. has 'the strife of his bones is perennial'; the Kr. 'the multitude of his bones are firm'. The latter is unsuitable. Peake takes the former to mean that his bones are wrenched by pain as if two parties were at strife over them, but this is forced. Dhorme (so Steinmann, Larcher) adduces Akkadian evidence for the rendering 'shaking', which is not strong enough for this context. Pope renders 'agony', which is the sense required, but which is not really a justified rendering of *rîb*.

20. life: here and in 38.39 means 'appetite'. It is parallel to 'soul' (here rendered 'appetite', which it means elsewhere; cf. Ps. 107.9).

loathes: a verb found only here, but probably to be restored in 6.7 (see note there).

dainty food: lit. 'food of desire'.

²¹ His flesh is so wasted away that it cannot be seen;
    and his bones which were not seen stick out.
²² His soul draws near the Pit,
    and his life to those who bring death.
²³ If there be for him an angel,
    a mediator, one of the thousand,

---

21. Sickness destroys appetite, and lack of food leads to the wasting away of the body, and the projection of the bones once well covered with flesh. The meaning of the verse is clear and unexceptional. Editors who think poetry should be scientifically exact prosaically point out that a sick man's flesh does not disappear from view, and his bones are not actually visible. Reconstructions as far from probability as the following are attempted: 'So his flesh ceases to be polluted, and his bones are purified, no more unclean' (Tur-Sinai); 'His flesh consumeth with sickness, and his bones are dried up for lack of moisture' (Ball).

that it cannot be seen: lit. 'from sight'. Duhm and Budde propose 'through leanness' (cf. Isa. 24.16 for Duhm's; Isa. 10.16 for Budde's). Both are needless.

which were not seen: Duhm regards these words as a variant of 'from sight' and deletes them, leaving the line short. Budde emends them to read 'they were not beautiful' (Richter comments 'a remarkable litotes').

stick out: the Kt. is a noun meaning 'bare height' (cf. Jer. 3.2, 21); the Ḳr. is a verb, which may mean 'are laid bare', if from the same root as the noun. Dhorme derives it from a different root, meaning 'be thin', and renders 'are emaciated' (cf. Hölscher). But do bones become emaciated? It is preferable to follow the meaning 'are laid bare', as a hyperbolical way of saying there is little flesh left to cover them, so that they protrude.

22. to those who bring death: here commentators see death-bringing demons, unmentioned elsewhere in OT. But the line is short. Hoffmann and Budde read 'to the dead' (dividing M.T. into two words). It is better, with Dhorme, to add three letters which could easily have fallen out and read 'to the abode of the dead' (so Hölscher), restoring the rhythm and providing a good parallel to 'the pit'. Driver (*Textus*, IV, 1964, p. 91) postulates an abbreviation in the text, for 'the place of the dead'. Pope proposes 'to the waters of death' with enclitic -*m* (a King Charles's head to some Ugaritic enthusiasts).

23. When reduced by illness until he is at death's door God seeks again to reclaim him, this time by sending an angel to him. The angel is a 'messenger' of God, who may be human or super-human, here probably the former.

mediator: the word means an 'interpreter' (cf. Gen. 42.23) or a mediator (cf. on 16.20). The term is applied to the prophets (Isa. 43.27), who interpret the will of God to men or mediate between God and men.

one of the thousand: 'No sick man need fear that there are not enough angels

to declare to man what is right for him;
²⁴ and he is gracious to him, and says,
   "Deliver him from going down into the Pit,
   I have found a ransom;
²⁵ let his flesh become fresh with youth;
   let him return to the days of his youthful vigour;"
²⁶ then man prays to God, and he accepts him,

---

deputed for this service to serve all needs' (Gray). The heavenly court is a large one; cf. 1. Kg. 22.19ff.; Dan. 7.10; Rev. 5.11.

what is right for him: lit. 'his uprightness', i.e. wherein his uprightness lay, hence 'his duty'. LXX has 'his fault', whence Duhm emends to 'his discipline', i.e. the reason for his illness. But the rendering of LXX here is widely different from M.T., and it is not to be relied on for this word. The purpose of the angelic visitation is not to justify the sickness, but to recall to rectitude.

24. he is gracious: Budde and Steuernagel introduce the word 'God' as the subject. But it is more probably the angel, who after his implied success in reclaiming the sick man, turns to intercede for him. Some think the appeal is to God to release him from imminent death, and some to the angel of death.

a ransom: Bickell, Budde and others complete the line by adding 'of his soul', which could easily have fallen out. The ransom is not specified. Dillmann thought it was the implied repentance of the sick man (so Kissane), but a ransom should be provided by another. It would appear to be provided by the mediator as the expression of his graciousness, after reclaiming the sufferer, to buy him an extension of life.

25. The sick man is now restored to health, and his flesh once more clothes his bones.

become fresh: M.T. has a word found nowhere else and of unusual form. Many editors follow Siegfried in changing one letter to secure 'become plump'. Dhorme (so Steinmann, Larcher) proposes *yirṭab*='become fresh' (cf. 8.16; 24.8, where this root, in the sense of moist or sappy, is found). H. H. Nichols (*AJSL*, XXVII, 1910–11, p. 158) deviates farther from M.T. in reading *yēraḵ*='become tender'.

26. After the successful mediation of the angel the restored man's prayers are accepted, and he is admitted to the presence of God. Cf. 22.27.

comes into his presence: commentators think this means in the Temple. But there is no reason to think that the author of the Elihu speeches any more than the author of the rest of the book set the scene in Israel. It is better to take it to mean in worship, without limiting this to a particular shrine.

with joy: this is here the cultic cry (cf. on 8.21). It can also mean the battle-cry, but that is not in place here.

> he comes into his presence with joy.
> He recounts to men his salvation,
> ²⁷ and he sings before men, and says:
> "I sinned, and perverted what was right,
> and it was not requited to me.
> ²⁸ He has redeemed my soul from going down into the Pit,
> and my life shall see the light".

He recounts . . . his salvation: M.T. 'he restores . . . his righteousness'. This is out of place here, since the sick man has already been accepted as righteous again when his health was restored. Hence many editors follow Duhm and Beer in reading the verb as *RSV* and in rendering the noun 'salvation'. It normally means 'righteousness', but can mean 'victory' or 'salvation'. On this view the restored man publishes abroad the mercy shown to him in his recovery. Dhorme transfers the line to follow verse 23, where it fits without any emendation. Both verses are tristichs, and the transfer restores the normal rhythm as well as giving a good parallel to verse 23*c*. The mediator then recalls the sick man to the path of duty and brings him back to righteousness.

27. he sings: *AV* 'he looketh'. The verb is generally rendered as *RV* and *RSV*, being either regarded as an unusual poetic form for the usual form, or amended to the usual form. Dhorme sees here again the verb 'repeat' which he has already found in verses 3, 14. But this is a very doubtful root, and it is better to follow the more usual view. The restored man sings for joy as he tells of his recovery. J. Reider (*ZAW*, N.F., xxiv, 1953, p. 275) reads *yāšēr* (for *yāšōr*), and connects with an Arabic root to secure the meaning 'he confesses'. Guillaume (*Promise and Fulfilment*, p. 122) renders 'he says joyfully', finding an Arabic sense.

it was not requited to me: the line is short, and the verb is nowhere else found in this sense. Elsewhere it means 'to be equal', but 'it was not equal to me' yields little sense. Many editors point here 'make equal', but there is no evidence that this meant 'requite'. Budde suggested making this meaning explicit by reading *šillēm* instead of *šāwāh* (so Fohrer). To fill out the line Budde adds as subject 'God', while Duhm added at the end 'according to my iniquity' and Bickell 'according to my sin'.

28. going down into the Pit: the phrase is used nowhere else, and the verb means 'passing through'. Dhorme finds it to be equivalent to verse 28*b*, where the same verbal idiom is used (cf. note there).

shall see: this is the idiom used elsewhere for looking with satisfaction on something. When used of enemies it means 'gloat over' (cf. Ps. 22.17 (M.T. 18)). Here it means looking with relief and joy on the light, instead of going down to Sheol.

²⁹ 'Behold, God does all these things,
   twice, three times, with a man,
³⁰ to bring back his soul from the Pit,
   that he may see the light of life.
³¹ Give heed, O Job, listen to me;
   be silent, and I will speak.
³² If you have anything to say, answer me;
   speak, for I desire to justify you.
³³ If not, listen to me;
   be silent, and I will teach you wisdom.'

ELIHU'S FINAL APPEAL TO JOB **33.29–33**

Elihu repeats that this is God's way with men, and asks if Job has anything to say in response, and if not to listen while Elihu further enlightens him. As Job makes no reply to any of Elihu's speeches we are left to infer that he was reduced to silence and that after a pause to give him an opportunity, Elihu resumed. It is hard to think that the author of Job's speeches in the rest of the book would have been at a loss for an answer here. For Elihu is no less doctrinaire than the rest of the friends, and nowhere comes to grips with Job's problem.

29. twice, three times: repeatedly.

30. Cf. verse 28. Elihu likes to repeat himself 'twice, three times'.

that he may see. M.T. 'that he may be enlightened with'. Duhm reads 'to enlighten him with' (so Pope), while Budde, on the basis of Syr., reads as *RSV* (so Gray, Hölscher, and others). The idiom is then the same as in verse 28 'see with satisfaction'.

31. Cf. 32.10; 33.1. Filled with sense of his own importance, Elihu frequently demands attention.

32. After telling Job to be silent and listen, Elihu tells him to speak if he has anything to say. But Elihu cannot imagine anyone having any answer to make to him.

I desire to justify you: of this Elihu has given little indication.

33. LXX, perhaps tired of the verbosity of Elihu, omitted verses 31b–33.

ELIHU'S SECOND SPEECH 34

Elihu now turns to defend the character of God against the charges Job has made. Continuing to ignore the particular situation of Job he deals in generalities, and while Job had argued from the particular to the general, from his own case to the character of God, then confirmed by other injustices around him, Elihu deals with the general concept of his theology, and concludes from it the sin of Job. Elihu's speech falls into the following parts: he declares Job to be essentially irreligious (verses 2–9); he replies to Job's charge that God is unjust (verses 10–15); he

34 Then Eli'hu said:
² 'Hear my words, you wise men,
   and give ear to me, you who know;
³ for the ear tests words
   as the palate tastes food.
⁴ Let us choose what is right;
   let us determine among ourselves what is good.
⁵ For Job has said, "I am innocent,
   and God has taken away my right;
⁶ in spite of my right I am counted a liar;

---

defends the impartiality and omniscience of God (verses 16–30); he exposes Job's folly and rebellion against God (verses 31–37).

ELIHU DECLARES JOB TO BE ESSENTIALLY IRRELIGIOUS 34.2–9

After calling on his audience once more to pay attention to him, he recalls Job's accusation of injustice against God and assertion that piety is unprofitable, and declares that this shows Job to be a scoffer and a sinner.

2. you wise men: these can hardly be the three friends, after what Elihu has said of them in 32.11ff. It may be to a presumed audience of bystanders, from among whom Elihu himself had emerged, that Elihu here addresses himself, or it may be to readers that the interpolator makes Elihu appeal.

3. Cf. 12.11.

4. choose: better 'discriminate'. What Elihu means is 'choose after careful examination'.

what is right: AV 'judgment', a meaning the word often has. But it has a variety of meanings in different contexts, and here it refers to the result of the process of discrimination. Hence the whole phrase means 'let us reach a sound conclusion'.

5. Cf. 27.2. Elihu here in part cites what Job has said and in part summarizes Job's position. His method here, as in the previous speech, was to take Job's views to pieces.

6. I am counted a liar: M.T. 'I lie'; cf. RV marg.: 'should I lie (against my right)?', i.e. 'should I confess guilt when I am innocent?' Duhm repoints to get 'I am deceived' (cf. 41.9 (M.T. 1)), but this could be rendered 'I am made a liar' (cf. Prov. 30.6), which would yield the sense of RSV. Ehrlich proposed to read 'ek'āb='I am in pain' (instead of 'aḵazzeḇ), and this is followed by Nichols (AJSL, XXVII, 1910–11, p. 176) and Gray. LXX has 'he (i.e. God) lies', and this is followed by Barton (JBL, XLIII, 1924, p. 228), Dhorme, Hölscher, Steinmann, Pope. The reading 'aḵzar is followed by Kissane and Larcher, with the further change of 'al mišpāṭî ('in spite of my right') to 'ālay mešōpᵉṭî, giving 'Against me my judge is cruel'. Ball had already rejected 'cruel', and favoured 'Against me my judge lies'. M.T., rendered as RV marg., yields an appropriate sense, and any change is needless.

my wound is incurable, though I am without transgression".
7 What man is like Job,
      who drinks up scoffing like water,
8 who goes in company with evildoers
      and walks with wicked men?
9 For he has said, "It profits a man nothing
      that he should take delight in God".
10 'Therefore, hear me, you men of understanding,
      far be it from God that he should do wickedness,
      and from the Almighty that he should do wrong.
11 For according to the work of a man he will requite him,
      and according to his ways he will make it befall him.
12 Of a truth, God will not do wickedly,
      and the Almighty will not pervert justice.
13 Who gave him charge over the earth
      and who laid on him the whole world?
14 If he should take back his spirit to himself,
      and gather to himself his breath,
15 all flesh would perish together,

Job has repeatedly affirmed that despite his innocence he is made to appear in the wrong, but that he will never compromise his integrity by admitting this.

my wound: Hebrew 'my arrow'. Many editors follow Duhm in adding a letter to yield 'my wound'. This is preferable to the forced interpretation of 'arrow' as the wound caused by an arrow. The line fairly summarizes what Job has maintained. I. Eitan (*JQR*, N.S., xiv, 1923–24, pp. 41f.) thinks the word rendered 'arrows' here has the meaning 'lot' or 'luck' and so renders 'my bad luck is incurable'. This is not to be preferred.

7. Cf. 15.16; here with the substitution of **scoffing** for 'iniquity'. Job had spoken of God scoffing at the calamity of the innocent (9.23), Zophar of Job scoffing at sound doctrine (11.3), and Eliphaz of the innocent scoffing in delight at the misfortunes of the wicked (22.19). Here Job is regarded as a public menace, scoffing at religion and thereby subverting morals. Sympathy had no place in the heart of Elihu, any more than in the heart of the friends.

8. goes: lit. 'takes the path'; cf. 22.15.
evil-doers: cf. on 31.3. For the thought of the verse cf. Ps. 1.1.

9. In 9.22ff. Job had said that calamity falls on good and bad alike, and in 21.7ff. had spoken of the uninterrupted prosperity of the wicked. Hence Elihu argues that Job maintained that virtue is useless (cf. Mal. 3.14). Yet Job had never regretted his integrity, but had clung to it for its own sake, and not for what it had brought him.

ELIHU REPLIES TO JOB'S CHARGE THAT GOD IS UNJUST 34.10–15

Repudiating such a charge, Elihu maintains that exact justice is meted out to men by God. None of whom he might stand in awe is over him, who is the sovereign Lord of all men, so that he is subject to no pressures to be unjust.

10. Cf. 8.3.

men of understanding: lit. 'men of heart'; so also in verse 34.

11. Elihu, like all the friends and like every wise theologian, is persuaded that God is not unjust. Where they err is in tracing all human experience to the working of this one principle, and refusing to consider anything that might imperil it. A theology that must wear blinkers is inadequate. From the story of Cain and Abel onwards, the Bible recognizes that desert and fortune are not precisely matched. Any bland assurance that they are can never satisfy men of Job's honesty. Some-times the right question is not 'Why does God not prevent injustice?' but 'Why do men perpetrate injustice?' In the case of Job, though none could know it, the cruel injustice was Satanic and not divine, and it was permitted by God as the expression of his confidence in Job and willingness to stake himself on Job's integrity, and therefore of God's supreme honour of Job. At the beginning of the book God calls Job 'my servant', and Job served God most of all in his suffering. **will make it befall him:** lit. 'will cause it to find him'.

12. Elihu cannot forbear to repeat what he has said in verse 10.

13. The thought of Elihu seems to be that because God is supreme and answer-able to no one, therefore he can do no wrong. He can have no possible motive for so doing. Job had already said that God is answerable to no one (9.12), but had wrongly concluded that all the injustice in the world is to be laid at his door (9.24). **on him:** this is not expressed in this line, but the force of the corresponding word in the first line can be carried over to this.

14. In M.T. the verse reads 'If he should set his heart upon him (i.e. upon man), or should gather to himself his spirit and his breath' (cf. *AV*, *RV*). This is then given the forced interpretation 'If God thought alone of himself and ceased to think of all creatures with a benevolent consideration, giving them life and up-holding by his spirit, all flesh would perish' (Davidson). The Oriental Kt., sup-ported by LXX and Syr., has 'If he should take back unto himself (i.e. to God)', and as this is supported by the parallel, almost all editors follow. As 'heart' is then unsuitable, and as the verse is overloaded, this word is then omitted, and the verse divided at 'spirit' to yield the rendering of *RSV*. At the creation God breathed into man the breath of life (Gen. 2.7; cf. Job 33.4). When he withdraws it, he dies (Ps. 104.29; Ec. 12.7). The thought seems to be that since all men are alike and equally dependent on God, there can be no reason why he should favour one more than another.

15. all flesh: in 12.10; 28.21 we had 'all living' for 'every living creature'.

and man would return to dust.

16 'If you have understanding, hear this;
  listen to what I say.

17 Shall one who hates justice govern?
  Will you condemn him who is righteous and mighty,

18 who says to a king, "Worthless one,"

Here we have 'all flesh' to indicate that when the 'breath' is withdrawn, only the lifeless flesh is left.

ELIHU DEFENDS THE IMPARTIALITY AND OMNISCIENCE OF GOD 34.16–30

Since God is omnipotent, none can influence him, and as the Ruler over all he must be impartial (cf. Gen. 18.25; Rom. 3.5f.). Since God is omniscient, he must be infallible. When he punishes, it is because he has observed iniquity and has heard the cry of its victims.

16. you have: not expressed in M.T., which has 'if understanding'. Budde and others slightly change the text to secure the verbal form. Elihu in this verse turns to the singular and invites Job's attention.

17. Editors point out that Elihu begs the question at issue. The suggestion that the fact of government guarantees justice is not cogent, when this is precisely what Job challenges. And when Elihu asks if Job would condemn the righteous and mighty, again the righteousness of God is not established by affirmation when this is the issue debated, and omnipotence is not necessarily the proof of impartiality. **govern:** lit. 'bind up' (Hos. 6.1; Isa. 1.6, of wounds; Exod. 29.9, of headgear). Here only does it have the sense of keeping a kingdom under control; but cf. Isa. 3.7. Sutcliffe (*Biblica*, xxx, 1949, pp. 73ff.) maintains the medical associations of the verb here and renders 'Can he (i.e. God) restore to health a hater of justice?'

18. who says: *AV* and *RV* have 'Is it fit to say?' That none would denounce a king to his face is evidence of power and not of righteousness. To rebuke Job for daring to accuse God, who is mightier than any king, could be understood as an appeal to prudence. But this is not what Elihu is doing. He is making the unblushing appeal to the principle that might is right. But LXX, Vulg., Syr. presuppose a different pointing, represented in *RSV*, and so many editors (but not Pope). The meaning then is that God is so mighty that kings and nobles can be rebuked by him with impunity, and he treats high and low with the same impartiality. This is just as completely begging the question.
Worthless one: Hebrew 'Belial'. Usually we find 'son of Belial' or 'man of Belial'. Here we have ellipsis (cf. 2 Sam. 23.6). The word is commonly thought to be a compound word meaning 'not profitable'. D. Winton Thomas (*Biblical and Patristic Studies*, ed. Birdsall and Thomson, 1963, pp. 1ff.), after a survey of

and to nobles, "Wicked man";
¹⁹ who shows no partiality to princes,
    nor regards the rich more than the poor,
    for they are all the work of his hands?
²⁰ In a moment they die;
    at midnight the people are shaken and pass away,
    and the mighty are taken away by no human hand.
²¹ 'For his eyes are upon the ways of a man,

---

other derivations, argues that it comes from a root meaning 'swallow' and that it means one who engulfs a man and brings him to the underworld. In later writings it became a synonym for Satan.

19. The reason why God can treat all impartially is that all are the creatures of his hand.

the rich. This is a rare word which is found parallel to 'noble' in Isa. 32.5, and here parallel to 'princes' but in contrast to 'poor'. Joüon (*Biblica*, xviii, 1937, pp. 207f.) regards it as a term of social distinction.

20. The proof of God's impartiality is in the swift destruction he sends on the mighty.

at midnight. In M.T. this stands awkwardly at the end of the first line 'and at midnight'. Dhorme transposes two words, and this brings 'and pass away' into the first line, and allows the second line to begin with 'and at midnight'. This indicates the swiftness and unexpectedness of the blow that falls on them (cf. Lk. 12.20; 1 Th. 5.2). Sutcliffe (*Biblica*, xxx, 1949, pp. 75ff.) leaves 'they pass away' where it is and adds 'they expire' after 'at midnight'.

the people. This reads oddly. Budde suggested that the last two letters of the previous word should be repeated, they having fallen out by haplography, and we then have the plural of 'the rich' of the previous verse. This has been widely followed, though not by Dhorme or Weiser.

are shaken: this verb means 'are violently agitated'. Of the emendations proposed mention may be made of 'expire' (*yigweʿû* for *yeḡōʿašû*), so Ball, Hölscher, Steinmann, Larcher, Fohrer; and 'are smitten' (*yenuggeʿû*), so Gray; 'he smites' (*yiggaʿ*) suggested by Budde but rejected, accepted by Beer and Kissane (also Sutcliffe, loc. cit.). Dhorme and Pope retain M.T. As Gray says, this is not very strong as a parallel to the previous line, and of the suggestions made 'expire' would seem the most relevant.

by no human hand: this emphasizes the effortlessness of God's removal of the wicked.

21. Cf. 24.23; 31.4. Elihu means that because God is omniscient, when disaster falls it is the evidence that he has seen wickedness. Job believed that God is omniscient, and therefore that he must know Job is innocent (10.7). The Prologue

and he sees all his steps.
²² There is no gloom or deep darkness
where evildoers may hide themselves.
²³ For he has not appointed a time for any man
to go before God in judgment.
²⁴ He shatters the mighty without investigation,
and sets others in their place.
²⁵ Thus, knowing their works,
he overturns them in the night, and they are crushed.
²⁶ He strikes them for their wickedness
in the sight of men,

---

shows that Job is right on this issue. Where he goes wrong is in concluding that God is indifferent to moral issues.

22. God's all-seeing eye can penetrate the deepest darkness, and no act of man is concealed from him; cf. Ps. 139.11f.; Jer. 23.24.

deep darkness: cf. on 3.5.

evildoers: cf. on 31.3.

23. Job has lamented that he could not go to law with God (9.32), though he has also recognized that God would be not only adversary but Judge (10.2). Elihu says that God does not need to go through the process of the court to establish guilt. Because he knows all, his just sentence can be pronounced and executed at any time without summoning a man to the tribunal.

a time. M.T. has 'yet' (*'ôḏ*). Reiske and Wright proposed 'a set time' (*mô'ēḏ*, the *m* having fallen out by haplography), and this has been widely followed.

24. without inquiry: lit. 'no investigation'. A similar phrase means 'unsearchable' in 5.9; 9.10. *RV* 'in ways past finding out', i.e. 'unsearchable', is less suitable here. The point here is not that God is so arbitrary that he brushes investigation aside, but that he does not need it. Moreover, his power matches his will, and he can execute justice as well as pronounce it.

25. This verse is transferred to follow verse 22 by Dhorme, Kissane, Fohrer, and it would seem to fit better there. F. Zimmermann (*JBL*, LV, 1936, pp. 306f.) invokes Arabic and Syriac meanings for the verb of the first line, to yield a better parallel to the second: 'Therefore he repudiates their works'. But if the verse is transferred this is unnecessary, and the ordinary sense is appropriate.

26. There is a want of balance in the verse, which editors have sought to redress. M.T. has 'under wicked men', which *AV* and *RV* understood to mean 'as wicked men'. J. C. Greenfield (*ZAW*, N.F., XXXII, 1961, p. 227) shows that in Ugaritic the preposition can mean 'among' as well as 'under'. We might render here 'among wicked men'. The preposition can mean 'instead of' and *RSV*, reading 'their

²⁷ because they turned aside from following him,
   and had no regard for any of his ways,
²⁸ so that they caused the cry of the poor to come to him,
   and he heard the cry of the afflicted—
²⁹ When he is quiet, who can condemn?

---

wickedness' with Syr. for 'wicked men', understands it to mean 'in return for'.
Bickell and Budde pointed differently (*tāḥēṭ* for *taḥaṭ*) and added a word as subject
to secure 'his wrath breaks the wicked'. If this is accepted the verb 'he strikes them'
would be read with the second line, which is short. But the introduction of 'his
wrath' is less good than the retention of God as the subject, as in the preceding
verse. Kissane, reading the same verb as Bickell but with different vowels, and
transposing 'therefore' from verse 27, secures 'Therefore hath he smitten the
wicked', leaving 'he hath stricken' for the second line. This is the most suitable of
the many suggestions. An alternative way of filling out the second line, lit. 'in
the place of seers', which is held to mean 'publicly', is Dhorme's transfer of the
first word of verse 27 (translated there 'because'), which overloads the line there,
to verse 26, after 'place': 'in the place where there are spectators', but this is not
very satisfactory. Reiske, Wright and Ball read 'Shades' instead of 'seers', but this
is improbable. Despite the difficulties of the verse, it seems to say that God makes
a public example of the wicked by his condign punishment of their iniquities.

   27. Because: the Hebrew consists of three words, of which Dhorme transfers
the first to the previous verse and Kissane the other two. Bickell omits these two.
Beer omits the third word and transposes the other two. The translation is in all
cases left unchanged.

   28. so that they caused: the verb here is infinitive and it could be rendered
by singular or plural. Davidson preferred the singular, and took the meaning to
be that by destroying the wicked God brought the cry of the oppressed to himself.
But Peake rightly objected that this would be the cause rather than the consequence
of their punishment. Hence the plural is to be preferred.

   29. *RSV* takes this verse as a parenthesis, and this and the following verses are
generally recognized to be very cryptic. The most probable sense seems to be that
if God remains quiet (cf. Isa. 7.4 for the same verb) and does not intervene to
punish the wicked, no one has any right to condemn him. The verb may, however,
be transitive, as in *AV* and *RV* (cf. Ps. 94.13), and the interpretation then offered
is that as God gives respite from tyrannical rule, he is not to be condemned for
injustice. *AV* gives a further turn to the verse by rendering the second verb 'who
can make trouble?' The meaning then is that when God intervenes none can with-
stand him. Hitzig transposed two letters of the second verb to yield 'who can stir
up (or cause disquiet)?', and this has secured some following, including Dhorme.
A. S. Yahuda (*JQR*, xv, 1902–03, p. 713) rendered the first verb 'casts down', and

When he hides his face, who can behold him,
    whether it be a nation or a man?—
³⁰ that a godless man should not reign,
    that he should not ensnare the people.
³¹ 'For has any one said to God,
    "I have borne chastisement; I will not offend any more;
³² teach me what I do not see;
    if I have done iniquity, I will do it no more"?
³³ Will he then make requital to suit you,
    because you reject it?

Ehrlich emended the second to 'who can be saved?' Guillaume (*Promise and Fulfilment*, p. 122) transposes two consonants of the first verb to secure: 'If he declares a man just, who can condemn?' The first of these interpretations seems the most probable, though Elihu is giving his case away, and in any case this has nothing to do with Job's fundamental problem, which is not 'Why does not God punish the wicked?' but 'Why does he torment the innocent?'

who can behold him? Budde proposed 'who can correct him', which Peake approves. This would yield a good parallel, but is unnecessary.

whether it be a nation or a man: M.T. 'upon a nation or upon a man together'. The word 'together' is odd here, and many emendations have been proposed: 'he visits' (*yipḳōḏ* for *yaḥaḏ*, so Beer); 'he watches over' (*yā'ūr*, so Duhm; or *yāḥaz*, so Ehrlich, Dhorme, Hölscher, Steinmann); 'he is compassionate' (*yāḥōn*, so Kissane and Larcher). Ball changes this and the preceding word ('man') to secure 'his wrath is kindled'. Fohrer strikes out the line altogether. Some editors take the line with verse 30. So, e.g. Dhorme, who thinks the meaning is that God watches over men and nations to see that no wicked man should reign. But Peake says this line can only be connected with verse 30 by violence. *RSV* keeps this line in the parenthesis, connecting verse 30 with verse 28. If we follow the reading of Ehrlich, we have the meaning that though God hides his face so that no man may see him, he is yet watching over men and nations with unceasing vigilance.

30. By emendation Kissane secures for verse 29c and this verse: 'With a nation or with a man he is compassionate, delivering a miscreant from the snares of affliction'. This is not convincing. Dhorme transfers 'godless' to the next verse to reduce this verse to the parallel to verse 29c: 'that no one of those who ensnare the people should reign'. But it is still long for a half verse. It is more probable that a word has been lost, and we should perhaps read *miṭṭᵉmōn mōḳᵉšê* for *mimmōḳᵉšê* ('from the snares of'), giving 'and should not hide snares for the people' (cf. Ps. 64.5 (M.T. 6)). *RSV* **that he should not ensnare** is an unjustified rendering, since it implies that the construction is similar to that of the first line, whereas the Hebrew has 'from snares of the people'. *RSV* rightly connects the verse with verse 28. When God hears the cry of the afflicted he intervenes to remove the godless ruler.

ELIHU EXPOSES JOB'S FOLLY AND REBELLION AGAINST GOD 34.31–37

These verses are among the most obscure and difficult in the book. They appear to say that if any man should repent and confess his sin under divine correction, ought God not to spare him without first consulting Job? This question is squarely put to Job, and an answer is demanded, and Elihu appears to think he has Job on the horns of a dilemma. Job will be bound to agree that God should pardon the penitent, and from this Elihu goes on to conclude that Job cannot be penitent, and he therefore adds stubbornness to his sin, and so his punishment must go on to the end.

31. has any one said to God: 'to God' is emphatic, as is 'to you' in verse 33. If confession is made to God, why should he have to get Job's permission before accepting it? Is Job setting himself above God? For 'any one' Dhorme has 'a godless man', imported from verse 30 (see above). He also redivides two words to secure 'said to Eloah', instead of 'to El shall one say?'

I have borne chastisement: the Hebrew simply says 'I have borne'. Ball proposed to change the vowels to secure 'I have been led astray' (so Dhorme, Hölscher, Kissane, Fohrer, Pope). The thought then is that he is pleading that he is not fundamentally bad, but has been beguiled into evil ways. This is probably correct. G. R. Driver (*SVT*, I, 1953, pp. 39f.) thought the ellipsis should be completed 'I have lifted up (my head)', i.e. 'I have presumed'.

I will not offend any more: this involves adding 'any more' ('*ôḍ*) to the line. The consonants are part of the first word of the next verse, and Dhorme and others think they accidentally fell out here. A less satisfactory way of understanding M.T. is as a circumstantial clause: '(I have borne chastisement) although I did no wrong'. The verse is then a declaration of innocence, rather than a confession of sin. But the next verse is against this. Kissane understands the verse to say 'I only committed a sin of inadvertence; I did not sin with a high hand'. But the tenses are against this.

32. Teach me what I do not see: the Hebrew for 'what I do not see' is lit. 'apart from (that which) I see'. Dhorme deletes the first two consonants as a dittograph of the end of the previous verse, and then renders 'until I see'. But this is unnecessary. This verse is clearly a confession and a promise of obedience to God, and there is no reason to iron this out of the previous verse. Driver (loc. cit.) deletes 'apart from' and reads the first verb in an Arabic sense= 'I am vile, (teach me)'.

33. to suit you: lit. 'from with thee'. The meaning probably is 'according to thy judgment', which is reflected in *RSV*. Must God go on punishing to satisfy Job, or is he free to pardon?

because you reject it: the line is short and no object is expressed. Dhorme suggests that some such word as 'my doctrine' has fallen out, and Kissane 'If you

For you must choose, and not I;
    therefore declare what you know.
³⁴ Men of understanding will say to me,
    and the wise man who hears me will say:
³⁵ "Job speaks without knowledge,
    his words are without insight."
³⁶ Would that Job were tried to the end,
    because he answers like wicked men.
³⁷ For he adds rebellion to his sin;
    he claps his hands among us,
    and multiplies his words against God.'

---

reject (his decision, must he smite?)', transferring the bracketed words from verse 37 and emending to secure this sense.

and not I: Peake prefers to read 'and not God', reading into the words Elihu's scornful suggestion that Job is claiming that the final word rests with him and not God. But this is unnecessary. Elihu is simply challenging Job to answer his question. Job has expressed his dissatisfaction with the way God rules the world. Is he really asking that he should direct it?

34. Possibly we should suppose that Elihu paused to give Job a chance to reply, but it is improbable that it seriously occurred to Elihu that anyone should think of replying to the cogent arguments he thought he was using.

36. Would that: the natural meaning of the Hebrew is 'my father' (so Vulg.), which gives no sense. *AV* has 'my desire is that', taking the word as from the root meaning 'desire'. Others explain from an Arabic root used in the Hauran, meaning 'entreat', and render 'I pray', 'would that!' LXX read 'but' and Syr. 'truly', whence Dhorme with the change of a letter reads 'but'. The meaning is not then a wish that Job's trial might be continued, but the reason why Elihu must still further expose his errors. Most editors understand as *RSV* and think it better expresses the hardness of Elihu's vain spirit.

37. he claps his hands among us: Duhm (so Hölscher, Steinmann, Fohrer) deletes these words (Kissane transfers to verse 33; see above); 'his hands' is not in M.T. and has to be supplied. Hence Budde added these words to fill out the line. Ehrlich emended 'among us' to 'our face'; 'he slaps our face'. Dhorme repointed the word for 'he claps', and understood it in an Aramaic sense: 'In our midst he casts doubt upon' and then brought 'his transgression' (*RSV* 'rebellion') from the previous line to provide an object (Bickell and Duhm delete it there). The first line then reads simply 'he adds to his sin' (so Pope). If we retain M.T. and add 'his hands', the line castigates Job for the contempt he has shown for God and what Elihu regards as sound doctrine.

35   And Eli'hu said:

    ² 'Do you think this to be just?
    Do you say, "It is my right before God,"
³ that you ask, "What advantage have I?
    How am I better off than if I had sinned?"
⁴ I will answer you
    and your friends with you.

ELIHU'S THIRD SPEECH 35

Elihu now proceeds to deal with Job's declaration that virtue is of no avail, and argues that neither virtue nor sin can affect God, but that both affect man. When men cry to God in vain for help, it is because they do not cry to him aright. The speech falls into two parts: Job's claim that virtue avails nothing refuted (2–8); when the cry of the afflicted goes unanswered, they have not learned their lesson (9–16).

JOB'S CLAIM THAT VIRTUE AVAILS NOTHING REFUTED 35.2–8

As before Elihu first states the position of Job that he is going to deal with. He then points to the greatness of God, who can neither be profited nor injured by anything that man does. It is only man who can be affected by man's act.

2. this: refers to what follows, in verse 3.

my right: the versions add one letter to give 'I am righteous'. So Olshausen and Kissane. This is unnecessary. In either case Elihu is quoting Job's claim to be in the right.

before God: AV and RV have 'more than God's'. But Job has not claimed that he is more righteous than God (so AV, RV), but only that he is in the right as against God, or in his presence (cf. on 4.17).

3. have I: M.T. 'to thee'. Dhorme understands this to mean 'to God' (so Kissane). Most understand as RSV.

than if I had sinned: M.T. has '(How am I profited) from my sin'. But Job had not admitted his sin as the cause of his suffering. The Hebrew could also be rendered 'rather than my sin', which is then held to mean' more than if I had sinned'. The translation is strained, but is probably to be accepted. It can also be rendered '(What do I profit) without sin?' (so Hölscher, Steinmann, Weiser, Fohrer). On the basis of LXX Ehrlich suggested reading: 'What do I do if I sin?' (so Dhorme, Kissane, Larcher).

4. your friends: Elihu is prepared to instruct Job and his friends, for whom Elihu has already expressed contempt. Dhorme thinks the onlookers are included, and Elihu in his vanity would be ready to include them. Peake observes 'That Elihu proceeds to appropriate the thoughts of the friends is no proof that he cannot be professing to instruct them; such conduct would be quite characteristic of him'.

⁵ Look at the heavens, and see;
    and behold the clouds, which are higher than you.
⁶ If you have sinned, what do you accomplish against him?
    And if your transgressions are multiplied, what do you do
       to him?
⁷ If you are righteous, what do you give to him;
    or what does he receive from your hand?
⁸ Your wickedness concerns a man like yourself,
    and your righteousness a son of man.
⁹ 'Because of the multitude of oppressions people cry out;
    they call for help because of the arm of the mighty.

---

5. Cf. 22.12 (Eliphaz); also 11.7ff. (Zophar). Job too had acknowledged that God controlled the heavens (9.8ff.). The thought here is that the God who is so far above us is beyond the reach of our actions.

6. Elihu here appropriates the thought of Job (cf. 7.20).

7. Cf. 22.3 (Eliphaz).

8. Elihu does not mean that a man's righteousness or wickedness only profits or injures himself, but another man like himself. In 22.2 Eliphaz had said that a man's righteousness only profited himself. Elihu is more perceptive than that. Strahan finely observes: 'Elihu exalts God's greatness at the cost of his grace, his transcendence at the expense of his immanence. He sets up a material instead of a spiritual stand of profit and loss. He does not realise that God does gain what He desires most by the goodness of men, and loses what He most loves by their evil.'

WHEN THE CRY OF THE AFFLICTED GOES UNANSWERED, THEY HAVE NOT LEARNED THEIR LESSON 35.9-16

Elihu now proceeds to deal with the case where oppressed people, presumably recognized to be innocent, cry to God for help and are not delivered. He says they are more interested in themselves than in God, and have not let their pride be chastened by suffering.

9. Job had raised the question of the oppressed who cry to God for help and are not heard (24.12). Elihu can deal easily and superficially with this, as with any other question.

the multitude of oppressions: the noun is really an abstract noun, of the same formation as the words for 'youth', 'virginity'. It is found again in Am. 3.9; Ec. 4.1. The expression means 'the excess of oppression'. There is no need to change it to 'oppressors', with the versions.

arm: cf. on 22.8. The arm is the instrument of oppression.

¹⁰ But none says, "Where is God my Maker,
   who gives songs in the night,
¹¹ who teaches us more than the beasts of the earth,
   and makes us wiser than the birds of the air?"
¹² There they cry out, but he does not answer,
   because of the pride of evil men.
¹³ Surely God does not hear an empty cry,
   nor does the Almighty regard it.

---

10. They merely cry out against their oppressors. They are not driven by their sorrows to seek God.

who gives songs in the night: Peake observes: 'If the author could only have kept at this height!' Cf. Ps. 42.8 (M.T. 9). Peake also cites Ac. 16.25. Kissane renders 'who gives succour in the night', connecting the word rendered 'songs' with a root meaning 'be strong', with which some connect the similar word found in Exod. 15.2; Isa. 12.2; Ps. 118.14 (so also Pope). Dhorme thinks the songs in the night are the crashes of thunder. Ehrlich altered the text to read 'lights' and Wright to read 'constellations'. It is a pity to rob Elihu of a poetic line when he creates one.

11. Cf. 12.7, where Job had said that the beasts and the birds could instruct his friends. Dhorme thinks it is too commonplace to say that God has given man more understanding than the beasts and the birds, and so gives the alternative rendering, of which the Hebrew is patient, that God instructs us by the beasts and birds. But while Elihu is always ready to pick up ideas from the earlier part of the book and put them forward as his own, he is equally able to descend to the commonplace.

12. This verse is commonly held to resume verse 9. Kissane transfers it to follow verse 9, where it would have a good connection. On the other hand it connects with what follows. This is not the only place where Elihu goes back to something he has already said.

because of the pride of evil men: it is not clear whether this goes with the opening of the verse, giving the reason for their cry, or whether it gives the reason why they are not heard. Against the second view is urged that the oppressed are usually the innocent and not **evil men.** But in Elihu's view they are godless men, who do not really turn to God even in their sufferings. They are therefore suffering for their discipline, though they do not recognize it.

13. God does not hear an empty cry: the cry is not really addressed to God, but to the void. Therefore God does not hear it. The Hebrew order is 'Only vanity God does not hear'. Dhorme takes the first two words as an exclamation: 'It is a pure waste of words! God does not hear'.

¹⁴ How much less when you say that you do not see him,
   that the case is before him, and you are waiting for him!
¹⁵ And now, because his anger does not punish,
   and he does not greatly heed transgression,
¹⁶ Job opens his mouth in empty talk,
   he multiplies words without knowledge.'

---

14. If God does not listen to those who do not turn to him, how much less will he listen to Job who complains against him. Job's cry is not only not to God, says Elihu, but is directed against him. In the previous verses Elihu has been dealing with those who cry out against their oppressors. But Job is not crying out against men at all. He is thoroughly impious. Others do not look to God, but Job professes that he is looking for him but cannot see him. Insolently he claims that his case against God has been presented and he is waiting for God to answer the charge. How can he expect that God will come to his aid and deliver him from his sufferings? In the second line Perles and Duhm read 'Be silent before him!' instead of 'the case is before him', and Budde, Beer, Pope, and Fohrer 'wait for him!' instead of 'you are waiting for him'. To this Driver (*SVT*, III, 1955, p. 89) adds the suggestion of reading 'the cause' as a verb, and rendering the line 'be lowly in his presence and wait anxiously upon him'. The line then becomes an exhortation to Job to have patience. But Elihu is stronger in polemic than in exhortation. Kissane reads 'he was silent before him and waited for him', which is no more convincing.

15. This verse is very obscure, and Davidson observes that *AV* 'competes worthily with the original in darkness'. In 21.14ff. Job had declared that the wicked go unpunished. It is probably to this that Elihu is referring. Such blasphemy sufficiently explains why Job is still suffering, since it calls for punishment from a God who visits their iniquity upon men.

his anger does not punish: to secure this meaning the order and pointing of the Hebrew words must be changed, and this is done by Gray, Fohrer and others. Dhorme retains M.T. and renders 'his anger does not punish anything', lit. 'nothing his anger punishes'. Kissane by a slight change of the word 'nothing' secures 'iniquity his anger is punishing', i.e. Job's iniquity.

transgression: *AV* 'extremity', *RV* 'arrogance'. The latter follows Delitzsch in deriving the M.T. *paš*, found only here, from an Arabic root meaning 'belch', 'utter calumnies', with an assumed primary meaning 'overflow'. This is very doubtful. *BDB* renders 'folly', and derives from an Arabic root meaning 'be weak (in mind or body)'. Houbigant on the basis of Theod., Sym., Vulg., proposed *pešaʿ* = 'transgression', and this is widely followed. Kissane deviates more widely from M.T. to secure 'he (i.e. God) hath not held back his (i.e. Job's) soul from calamity'. *RSV* is to be preferred, though **greatly heed** conceals the difficulty of the Hebrew, which has 'greatly know', where we should expect 'does not

36

And Eli'hu continued, and said:
² 'Bear with me a little, and I will show you,
  for I have yet something to say on God's behalf.
³ I will fetch my knowledge from afar,
  and ascribe righteousness to my Maker.
⁴ For truly my words are not false;
  one who is perfect in knowledge is with you.

---

know at all'. This difficulty Hölscher met by transposing the letters of the word rendered 'greatly', yielding 'the transgression of man' (so Larcher). Hoffmann (*ZAW*, N.F., VIII, 1931, p. 271) instead of 'transgression' read '*epeś*='nothing at all', but 'greatly' then reads oddly.

16. This verse is apparently addressed to the friends or the bystanders.

ELIHU'S FOURTH SPEECH 36–37

Elihu now sets out to instruct Job in wisdom and to expound to him the meaning of affliction and the greatness and unfathomableness of God, before whom he should bow in humility and awe. This is the most impressive of Elihu's speeches, and in some respects it anticipates the Divine speeches in its description of the marvellous works of God. But, as Strahan says, 'while there are striking phrases and memorable sentences in this poem, it cannot for a moment be compared in power with the divine speech which follows it'. The speech falls into the following parts: (*a*) the discipline of suffering (36.2–25), dealing with the meaning and purpose of suffering (verses 2–15); the application of this to Job (verses 16–25); (*b*) the work and wisdom of God (36.26–37.24), dealing with God's work in nature (36.26–37.13), and the majesty and unsearchableness of God (verses 14–24).

THE MEANING AND PURPOSE OF SUFFERING 36.2–15

In his defence of the righteousness of God, Elihu now develops his thought on the disciplinary meaning of suffering. God is great, but he does not despise men. The incorrigibly wicked he does not preserve, but in mercy he afflicts the righteous that they may be cleansed of all sin and pride.

2. Bear with me: elsewhere in *OT* this verb means 'surround' (cf. Jg. 20.43 (*RSV* here follows LXX); Ps. 22.12 (M.T. 13); Hab. 1.4). Here it has the meaning 'wait' which is common in Syriac. Several other words in this verse are Aramaisms.

3. from afar: what Elihu means is that he will display the range of his knowledge, and this he does in the second part of his speech, where he considers the wonders of God's works in the world.

4. Elihu is a stranger to modesty, and frequently finds it necessary to certify his own genius. **Perfect** means 'complete', as in God's testimony to the wholeness of Job's character (2.3).

⁵ 'Behold, God is mighty, and does not despise any;
   he is mighty in strength of understanding.
⁶ He does not keep the wicked alive,
   but gives the afflicted their right.
⁷ He does not withdraw his eyes from the righteous,
   but with kings upon the throne
   he sets them for ever, and they are exalted.
⁸ And if they are bound in fetters
   and caught in the cords of affliction,
⁹ then he declares to them their work
   and their transgressions, that they are behaving arrogantly.
¹⁰ He opens their ears to instruction,
   and commands that they return from iniquity.
¹¹ If they hearken and serve him,
   they complete their days in prosperity,
   and their years in pleasantness.
¹² But if they do not hearken, they perish by the sword,
   and die without knowledge.
¹³ 'The godless in heart cherish anger;
   they do not cry for help when he binds them.
¹⁴ They die in youth,
   and their life ends in shame.

---

5. In this verse the repetition of **mighty,** the lack of an object for the verb **despise** (*RSV* **any** is not in M.T.), and the expression 'strength of heart (understanding)' arouse suspicion. Duhm reduces the verse to 'See, God despises the stubborn of heart' (so Beer, Strahan), while Gray reduces it to 'God does not reject (or despise) the perfect' (so Steinmann). It is improbable that we should import 'the perfect' here, where it might seem to refer to Elihu himself, in view of verse 4. Fohrer reduces the verse to 'Lo, God rejects the mighty'. Nichols (*AJSL*, XXVII, 1910–11, p. 162) transferred 'strength' to the first line and for the second 'mighty' (*kabbîr*) read 'pure' (*bar*), rendering 'Lo, God is mighty in strength, and rejecteth (or despiseth) not the pure of heart' (so Dhorme, Pope). With this cf. Kissane, who reduces the whole verse to 'Lo, God rejecteth not the pure of heart', transferring 'mighty in strength' to verse 6 (so Larcher). All of these, save Nichols, deal violently with the text. For his substitution of *bar* for *kabbîr* (2°) Syr. offers support, and this slight reconstruction of the text eliminates all the difficulties and is to be preferred. The thought of the verse is then akin to that of Isa. 57.15.

6. Job had asked why the wicked are allowed to live. Elihu here replies to him that they do not. God destroys the wicked and rights the wrongs suffered by those who are reduced to poverty by their oppression. Kissane transfers 'mighty in strength' to the beginning of this verse (see on verse 5).

7. withdraw his eyes: for 'his eyes' Bickell suggested reading 'his right' (*dînô* for *'ênāw*), and so Budde, Beer, Peake, Dhorme, Steinmann and Larcher. There is no reason to change M.T. To say that God does not rob the righteous of their rights is inferior to saying he has them ever in his watchful care.

with kings: many editors who accept this reading, omit the 'and' before 'he sets them' (so *RSV*). Perles suggested reading 'he places' (*šāt*) for 'with' (*'et*), and so Dhorme, Hölscher, and Steinmann, while Larcher reads *biśe'ēt*='while he elevates'. On this view there is a break in the sense in the middle of this verse, and the righteous are now left while Elihu turns to kings as a separate class. In M.T. it is the righteous, who are not merely protected from their oppressors, but exalted to the seats of the mighty. This seems more suited to the context, and verse 8 continues with the thought of the righteous rather than the kings.

8. if they: i.e. the righteous. When the righteous suffer, before God has delivered them from their wicked oppressors, it is because he is seeking through discipline to refine them. Dhorme thinks the verse continues to deal with the kings, who may be reduced to captivity for their discipline. But it is unlikely that Elihu thought all kings were righteous, and here the discipline is for those who are fundamentally good, though not without moral faults.

9. The purpose of their affliction is to bring home to them their sins, and to awaken them to a recognition that their exaltation has bred pride in them.

10. opens their ears: cf. 33.16.

instruction: or 'discipline' as *AV*.

to return: the verb frequently used for 'repent' in *OT*.

11. and serve him: Kissane changes a letter and renders 'they shall pass' and then transfers some words from verse 16 to complete the thought, rendering 'from the mouth of distress, freedom unrestrained shall be instead thereof'.

complete: some MSS. have the reading 'wear out'.

and their years in pleasantness: Duhm and others delete these words for metrical reasons. Metre alone is rarely an adequate ground for emendation.

12. they perish by the sword: cf. on 33.18. If they will not learn from their discipline, final doom overtakes them.

13. cherish anger: the Hebrew says 'put anger'. This has been understood by some interpreters to mean 'lay up (God's) anger' (cf. Rom. 2.5). More commonly it is thought to mean 'nourish anger' in their hearts, instead of realizing that their deserved chastisement is for their profit. Dhorme would make this meaning more explicit by reading 'keep their anger' (cf. Am. 1.11; also Jer. 3.5), reading *yišmerû* for *yāśîmû*.

14. in shame: lit. 'among the male prostitutes'. Duhm thought the point here to be that these persons, attached to the shrines for infamous purposes, commonly died early. Dhorme preferred to find an abstract noun here, 'in adolescence',

15 He delivers the afflicted by their affliction,
   and opens their ear by adversity.
16 He also allured you out of distress
   into a broad place where there was no cramping,
   and what was set on your table was full of fatness.
17 'But you are full of the judgment on the wicked;
   judgment and justice seize you.

---

because it was the young who were used for these purposes. This seems less likely. Elihu is no less sure than the friends of the certainty and untimeliness of the death of the wicked, who do not repent.

15. Those who profit by their discipline are delivered. Here Elihu restates his view of the meaning of discipline to lead on to his application of the principle to the case of Job.

opens their ear: cf. verse 10; also 33.16.

ELIHU APPLIES HIS PRINCIPLE TO JOB **36.16–25**

He accuses Job of having been led by his prosperity into injustice and corruption and so bringing his misfortunes on himself. Instead of crying out against God, he should be taking to heart what God is seeking to teach him. In part this is the message of the Divine speeches, which rebuke Job for passing judgment on what is beyond his knowledge. But whereas the advice of Elihu is to learn his lessons that his prosperity may be restored, the effect of the Divine speeches is to make Job realize that he may have the Divine fellowship in his sufferings, and not merely when he has been delivered from them. The restoration of his fortunes in the Epilogue was not the result of his confession that he was suffering for his sin, but the necessary consequence of the end of the trial.

16. This and the following verses are extremely difficult to understand, and scarcely any two interpreters are agreed as to their meaning. The ancient versions differ widely, and the Confraternity Version gives them up in despair (so also Ehrlich).

allured you: the tense is uncertain. *AV* and *RV* render 'would have removed (led)', and this is a possible rendering. Peake says it is possible to render 'allures', indicating what God is doing. Others render 'has allured' or 'allured'. Dhorme and Steinmann render 'he will remove'. The subject is uncertain. It may be God, as in verse 15, or the word rendered 'a broad place', which is found only here and 38.18, where it is rendered 'expanse'. The verb is generally used of enticing to evil, and Gray thinks it is unlikely to be used of God. Ewald rendered 'the wide place hath led thee astray'. Similarly Duhm 'freedom has led thee astray'. Gray thinks the subject of the verb may be lost, but interprets the text to mean that Job's ample life had been his undoing. Kissane, who transfers part of this verse to verse 11 (see note there), makes the word rendered 'what was set', but rendered 'comfort', the subject.

out of distress: lit. 'from the mouth of distress'. Beer suggested reading *miprāṣ* for *mippî ṣār*, and connected the noun with the verb rendered 'grow rich' in Gen. 30.43. It could then be rendered 'wealth'.

a broad place: this word is variously rendered 'amplitude' (Gray), 'abundance' (Dhorme), 'freedom' (Duhm and Kissane), 'expanse' (Pope). Cf. 38.18.

where there was no cramping: or 'unrestricted', 'unconfined'. The Hebrew says 'beneath it' or 'instead of it', but this is not clearly indicated in *EVV*. Duhm alters this to 'frightens you' (see below). Vulg. has 'beneath thee' and so Dillmann and Budde.

what was set: this connects it with the verb meaning 'rest', but in Isa. 30.15 it means 'quietness' or 'resting'. Some render 'comfort' (cf. Kissane, above). Budde omits the word altogether as a corrupt dittograph of the preceding word, and so Dhorme, who renders the whole verse: 'He will remove you from the jaws of trouble; instead of it, you will enjoy unrestricted abundance, and your table will be filled with fatness'. Duhm effects various transpositions in the verse and renders: 'Freedom has led thee astray and rest from the mouth of distress; no trouble which terrifies thee, and thy table full of fatness'. This is too violent to be convincing, and it offers no clear sense. From this welter of problems and solutions the following translation may be essayed: 'Wealth hath enticed thee, unlimited abundance beneath thee (in our idiom, behind thee), thy table loaded with rich food'. This involves the omission of 'what was set', and two slight changes, one of which is supported by Vulg. The sense of the verse is then that Job's great wealth and prosperity had drawn him away from God and so brought his misfortunes upon him.

17. This verse again has caused much trouble, and it is hard to suppose that Elihu was accusing Job of being full of the judgment on the wicked, when Job has maintained that there is no moral government of the world and the wicked often escape punishment. Some suggest that the meaning is that Job joins the wicked in their judgment of God when he punishes them. But it is hard to extract this from the verse, and the meaning of the verb would be unparalleled. The words of the first part of the verse may be redivided to yield the sense 'The judgment of the wicked (plural) thou didst not judge' (so Kissane). This avoids the repetition of the word 'full' of the previous verse (which Dhorme omits here), and also the repetition of the noun 'judgment' in this verse (the use of the verb with the cognate noun is found elsewhere). Then Elihu is condemning Job because in his position of power he did not execute justice, and so called down on himself his sufferings.

and justice seize you: this is insufficient for a line, and Dhorme, who also takes the second 'judgment' into the first line and reads it as a verb supplies 'your hands' as the subject of 'seize justice'. Again the view of Kissane is preferable. He redivides and slightly changes the word rendered 'seize' ('you' is unexpressed in M.T.) and the first word of the following verse (unrepresented in *RSV*, and omitted by many editors), to secure 'and the right of the orphan was taken away'.

¹⁸ Beware lest wrath entice you into scoffing;
 and let not the greatness of the ransom turn you aside.
¹⁹ Will your cry avail to keep you from distress,
 or all the force of your strength?
²⁰ Do not long for the night,
 when peoples are cut off in their place.
²¹ Take heed, do not turn to iniquity,
 for this you have chosen rather than affliction.

Job is here charged with what he had strenuously denied in 31.16ff. This is preferable to the proposal of Guillaume (*Promise and Fulfilment*, p. 122), who retains M.T. and finds two different senses for the word rendered 'judgment', translating the first line: 'Thou art full of a wicked man's food'. More recently (*ALUOS*, Supplement ii, 1968, p. 124) he modifies this to secure of 'a rich man's food', connecting the word rendered 'wicked' with a different Arabic word, meaning 'rich'.

18. Beware lest wrath entice you: M.T. 'for wrath lest it entice you' (note that the word 'entice' here means 'entice to evil'). *RV* understood the wrath to be God's; *RV* marg. and *RSV* understand it to be Job's. But there is no indication of anything that would arouse Job's wrath. Moreover, the two halves of the verse have nothing in common. The word rendered **scoffing** is rendered 'sufficiency' in 20.22 (so *RV* here). For the meaning 'scoffing' resort must be had to the verb rendered 'clap' (written with *s* there, *ś* here in most mss.) in 27.23 (cf. *AV* 'his [i.e. God's] stroke' here). Beer read the word rendered 'wrath' as *ḥᵃmēh* instead of *ḥēmāh*. This is an Aramaism (many are found in the Elihu speeches) meaning 'beware' (which *EVV* supply in addition to 'wrath'). Dhorme, Kissane, and Pope follow, and then take the word 'sufficiency' to mean 'generosity' or the like. The line is then an excellent parallel to what follows: 'Beware lest one entice you by a generous gift'. The whole verse is then a warning against the corruption of justice.

19. This and the following verse are extraordinarily difficult. Dhorme rejects them as a gloss. The word rendered **your cry** is not found elsewhere in this meaning (elsewhere *šāw‘āh*, not *šûa‘*), and it may have this meaning, or be connected with the word for 'rich' (*šôa‘*) in 34.19 (hence *AV* and *RV* 'riches' here). Similarly the word for **from distress** (*bᵉṣār*) could be pointed *beṣer*='gold' (22.24), and so *AV* here. Reconstructions and renderings too numerous and too varied to be recorded have been offered. The verb rendered **avail** means 'set in order (shewbread, battle lines, words)', 'compare' (Isa. 40.18), whence 'be equal to' and then 'avail for' as extensions of this. Gray renders 'Will thy riches be equal to it without affliction?'; Dhorme 'Can one compare your crying out to him (reading *lô* for *lō'*) in distress?'; Pope 'Will your opulence avail with him (reading *lô*) in trouble?' Kissane redivides the words with slight changes to secure 'Arraign the rich as well as the penniless (lit. with no gold)' or 'Treat alike the rich and the penniless'. The interpretations vary with the translations and the general understanding of the context. If the previous verse is a warning against corruption, this is a warning against being influenced by the status of the parties. This seems the most satisfactory view. Alternatively the verse is held to mean Job's cry (or his wealth) would be of no avail to him to escape his troubles, brought on by his own wickedness.

or all the force of your strength: the word rendered 'force' (actually a plural form) is found only here. We find the adjective with 'strength' in 9.4; Isa. 40.26. Pope takes the 'strength' here to be wealth, and the meaning to be as in the previous line that Job could not buy immunity from trouble. Gray takes it to mean 'exertions of strength'. Dhorme's '(Can one compare your crying out to him in distress) with all the energies of might?' is not very lucid. Kissane substitutes *d* for *k* and adds *w* to secure 'and the weak and the mighty in strength'. This then accords perfectly with his view of the preceding line, but with chiasmus: 'Treat alike the rich and the penniless, the weak and the powerful'.

20. Gray says this is 'perhaps the most unintelligible of all these verses'. Kissane describes the Hebrew as nonsense. It is supposed that Job is warned not to long for the night of calamity when nations are swiftly cut off ('in their place' could be rendered 'on the spot'). But why should Job long for such a thing? And what relevance has this to the context? Budde thinks Elihu is warning Job not to long for death, as he has done more than once. But in Elihu's view death is the supreme punishment of the wicked, and not the relief from the present miseries which Job considered it. On Elihu's view Job by his insolence towards God was deserving death rather than longing for it. Duhm reconstructs the verse to yield 'Do not let folly deceive you to exalt yourself with him who thinks himself wise'; Ball to yield 'Prolong not the night over wine, till the rising of day in its place'. These will convince whom they will. The verb rendered **long for** may have this meaning (5.5), or it may mean 'trample on', 'crush' (Am. 8.4). Kissane takes it in this sense here, and then instead of **the night** (*laylāh*) he reads 'not belonging to thee' (*bᵉlî lāk*), and 'thy people' (*'ammᵉkā*) for 'peoples' (*'ammîm*). This gives 'Oppress not them that belong not to thee, that thy kinsmen may mount up in their place'. This is now again lucid and relevant to the context, condemning the letting of kinship influence the judgment. In view of the extreme difficulty of finding sense in M.T., this may be accepted as the most promising suggestion yet offered.

21. for this: the construction is unusual, and the Hebrew would more naturally be rendered 'on account of this'. Budde and some others read '*awlāh* for '*al zeh*, rendering 'unrighteousness (you have chosen)'. But Syr. understood the verb in its Aramaic sense of 'test' and rendered 'you have been tested'. This is followed by Wright, Dhorme, and others, yielding 'because of this you have been tested by affliction'. This is more appropriate to the context than *RSV*. Job is not being rebuked because he did not choose affliction. The affliction of which he complains is rather being traced to his iniquity, as described in the preceding verses.

²² Behold, God is exalted in his power;
   who is a teacher like him?
²³ Who has prescribed for him his way,
   or who can say, "Thou hast done wrong"?
²⁴ 'Remember to extol his work,
   of which men have sung.
²⁵ All men have looked on it;
   man beholds it from afar.
²⁶ Behold, God is great, and we know him not;
   the number of his years is unsearchable.
²⁷ For he draws up the drops of water,
   he distils his mist in rain
²⁸ which the skies pour down,
   and drop upon man abundantly.
²⁹ Can any one understand the spreading of the clouds,
   the thunderings of his pavilion?
³⁰ Behold, he scatters his lightning about him,

---

22. Elihu now turns to the purpose of the suffering which Job's iniquity has entailed, and in accordance with what he has said above, he declares that God is teaching him by it.

23. God is supreme, and there is none over him, to assign his duty to him, and he is subject to the judgment of no one. The implication of this is that Job should cease to criticize God for his sufferings, but instead should seek to learn what his Teacher is seeking to make plain to him.

prescribed for him: Kissane understands the verb in the sense of punishing, or calling to account, and finds this supported by the parallelism. Either is a possible rendering. But Job has nowhere claimed the right to punish God. He has claimed that he knows what God ought to do, and has complained because God does not conform to the standards he lays down. There is no need to attach the Ugaritic meaning of 'power' to **his way**, as does Dahood (*Biblica*, XXXVIII, 1957, p. 320).

24. Wiser than criticism would be the humble recognition of the greatness of God's work, of which psalmists and others have sung.

25. looked on it: with satisfaction and delight; cf. on 33.28.

from afar: cf. 26.14. Man cannot see the work of God close at hand, and therefore cannot understand it completely.

GOD'S WORK IN NATURE **36.26–37.13**

Elihu now turns to unfold to Job the greatness of God as revealed in his control of the universe and of the forces of nature.

26. Cf. 37.5 and Ps. 102.27 (M.T. 28).

27. Duhm concluded from this verse that the author of the Elihu speeches lived some two centuries later than the author of the Divine speeches, since the latter did not know the source of the clouds, but thought they were kept in God's treasuries. He thought the author of this verse had derived his knowledge through some Greek channel. Pope describes this as fanciful.

he draws up: another form of the verb used in verse 7. Rosenmüller connected it with an Arabic root, meaning 'swallow (in gulps)', but this is not very convincing.

drops of water: Duhm changed the text to read 'drops from the sea', and so some editors. But this is needless.

he distils: the verb used in 28.1 ('refine'). M.T. says 'they distil'. The subject would appear to be the 'drops of water', which is inappropriate. The verb is transitive, meaning 'filter' or 'refine'. Hoffmann read the passive 'they are distilled', while Duhm read the singular as *RSV* (so many editors), and Steuernagel 'he distils them'. Dhorme renders 'he volatilises the rain into mist', but this is quite inappropriate. It is the condensation of the moisture into rain which falls on men (verse 28) which is in mind.

his mist: cf. Gen. 2.6. Albright (*JBL*, LVIII, 1939, pp. 102f.) argues that in Gen. 2.6 this word means 'the subterranean source of fresh water', and Pope maintains that here it means the subterranean cosmic reservoir and he translates 'the flood'. The passage is then translated 'he draws the waterdrops that distil rain from the flood, that trickle from the clouds'. This is not lucidly expressed, and the conception is not very convincing. Cf. P. Reymond, *SVT*, VI, 1958, pp. 205f. Dahood (*EThL*, XLIV, 1968, pp. 48f.) needlessly eliminates 'his mist' (*'ēḏô*) and reads (*'āḏô*), which he takes as an unusual form for '(from) his hand', for which he claims Ugaritic evidence; but why the usual form should not have been used, if that were the meaning, is hard to understand.

28. abundantly: most scholars take this word (*rab*) as an adjective, and render 'upon many men', or the like. Wright took it as the equivalent of *rebîbîm* ='showers' (Dt. 32.2), yielding 'fall upon man as showers' (so Beer, Pope). This gives an excellent meaning, and may be right.

29. Can any one? Syr. reads 'Who can?', and so many editors.

spreadings: from the root found in 26.9.

thunderings: cf. 30.22 (see note there). Tur-Sinai suggested reading *tašwît*='bed', for *tešu'ôt* (cf. *KB*), and the Confraternity Version renders 'carpet'. But Tur-Sinai later proposed rendering 'heights'. These are not to be preferred to *RSV*.

pavilion: rendered 'canopy' in Ps. 18.11 (M.T. 12), where the clouds are described as the pavilion of God.

30. scatters: the root from which 'spreadings' (verse 29) comes. We should probably render here 'spreads'.

lightning: M.T. has 'light'. In verse 32 it means 'lightning', but most scholars here follow Theod. in reading 'mist' (cf. verse 27), i.e. *'ēḏô* for *'ôrô*. This is more appropriate to the verb and to the context. Pope changes **about him** (*'ālāw*) to '*āliy* and finds here a divine name, 'Aliy, for which Ugaritic support is adduced, and finds here the subject of the verb. It is highly improbable that a further divine

and covers the roots of the sea.

³¹ For by these he judges peoples;
   he gives food in abundance.

³² He covers his hands with the lightning,
   and commands it to strike the mark.

³³ Its crashing declares concerning him,
   who is jealous with anger against iniquity.

---

name should be added to those on which the changes are rung in the rest of the book.

the roots of the sea: this should mean the deepest parts of the sea. Dhorme conceals the difficulty by rendering 'he veils the depths of the sea' and takes the reference to be to the dense fogs. Duhm emended to read 'the tops of the mountains' (so many others) but the change is violent. Kissane with a much slighter change secured 'the sun by day'. The storm clouds certainly obscure the sun, but can hardly be said to cover the roots of the sea. Marshall proposed to read 'his throne' (*kise'ô*) for 'covers' (*kissāh*) and Pope follows this: 'The roots of the sea are his throne.' But this is not relevant to the context, which speaks of celestial phenomena.

31. This verse would read more naturally after verse 28, and Dhorme and other editors transfer it there. It certainly breaks the connection between verse 30 and verse 32. Verses 27f. describe the formation of the clouds and the falling of the rains, which are a source of blessing, while verses 30, 32f. describe the terrifying storms. As verse 31 stands, the two halves are not parallel. The first speaks of judgment and the second of blessing. For 'judges' (*yādîn*) Houbigant proposed 'nourishes' (*yāzûn*), and this has been widely accepted by editors, including Gray, Dhorme, Kissane, Pope, Fohrer. Guillaume (*Promise and Fulfilment*, p. 123) secures this meaning without change of text by appealing to an Arabic dialectal form. This seems very questionable. Driver (*SVT*, III, 1955, pp. 88ff.) retains M.T., but gives the meaning of 'enriches' for the verb.

32. Rosenmüller observed that scarcely any two interpreters of this verse were in agreement. Fresh interpretations have been advanced since his time, and there is still considerable disagreement.

He covers his hands with the lightning: *AV* 'with clouds he covereth the light', the clouds being thought of under the figure of hands (cf. 1 Kg. 18.44). 'Light' is here for 'lightning' (cf. 37.3, 11). The line has been thought to mean that God seizes handfuls of light and hurls it as lightning. But this is not well expressed by the verb 'covers'. Dhorme proposed *nissāh*='lifts' for *kissāh* ='covers' and so secured the thought of God taking the lightning and directing it to its target (so Hölscher, Steinmann, Larcher, Fohrer). Less satisfactory is Pope's reading *nassāh*, to which he gives the questionable meaning 'prances': 'On his palms the lightning prances'.

37 ¹'At this also my heart trembles,
       and leaps out of its place.
² Hearken to the thunder of his voice
   and the rumbling that comes from his mouth.

---

and commands it to strike the mark: Driver (*SVT*, III, 1955, pp. 88ff.) for *yᵉṣaw ʿālêhā*='commands it' proposed *yaṣlîʿōh*, which he renders 'discharges it'.

33. Peake knew of more than thirty explanations of this verse. Others have since been propounded. The versions are in disagreement as to the meaning of vital words in the verse, and the word rendered in *RSV* **its crashing** could be rendered 'his companion', or 'his purpose'. *AV* has 'The noise thereof sheweth concerning it, the cattle also concerning the vapour'; *RV* 'The noise thereof telleth concerning him, the cattle also concerning the storm that cometh up'. Literally rendered M.T. says 'He declares his purpose (or his shout) concerning it; cattle also concerning what rises'. A few modern renderings may be cited, without giving the emendations on which they are based: 'The flock which sniffs the coming storm has warned its shepherd' (Dhorme); 'Its shout of triumph declares to him, stirring up wrath against iniquity' (Hölscher); 'The thunder declareth concerning him (i.e. God), as he exciteth wrath against iniquity' (Kissane); 'It cuts down the shepherds; it makes the flock a holocaust' (Sutcliffe, *Biblica*, xxx, 1949, p. 89); 'In his anger he creates the storm and by his thunder announces its coming' (Driver, *SVT*, III, 1955, pp. 88ff.); ' *ʿAliy* speaks with his thunder, venting his wrath against evil' (Pope); 'The thunder declareth his indignation, and the storm proclaimeth his anger' (Gray). Of these Gray's seems most relevant to the context, but the changes are too great to inspire confidence. It sees the violent storm as the instrument of the Divine anger. *RSV* carries the same thought, but with slighter change of the text. For 'its crashing' (*rēʿô*) we should perhaps read 'its thunder' (*raʿmô*, with Budde, Kissane, Fohrer) or 'the thunder' (*raʿam* with Gray). For the second line, *RSV* agrees with Hölscher, Kissane, Pope and Fohrer in reading *mᵉḳanneh* (or *maḳneh*, or *maḳnî*) for *miḳneh*='cattle', and *ʿawlāh* (so Theod., Aq., Hitzig and many others) for *ʿal ʿôleh*='concerning what rises'. It also understands *ʾap* in the sense of 'anger' instead of 'also'.

37.1. this: the thunderstorm.

my heart: LXX has 'thy heart' and so Bickell and Duhm. But Budde notes that Job is not addressed until verse 14. In verse 2 the verb is plural.

leaps: a verb found only here and Lev. 11.21; Hab. 3.6 (a transitive form, *RSV* 'shook').

2. thunder: the word rendered 'troubling' in 3.17. In Arabic this root in some forms denotes the booming of the sea and the rumbling of the thunder. For thunder as the voice of God, cf. on 28.26.

rumbling: elsewhere only in Ezek. 2.10 (*RSV* 'mourning'); Ps. 90.9 (*RSV* 'sigh').

³ Under the whole heaven he lets it go,
   and his lightning to the corners of the earth.
⁴ After it his voice roars;
   he thunders with his majestic voice
   and he does not restrain the lightnings when his voice is heard.
⁵ God thunders wondrously with his voice;
   he does great things which we cannot comprehend.
⁶ For to the snow he says, "Fall on the earth";
   and to the shower and the rain, "Be strong".
⁷ He seals up the hand of every man,
   that all men may know his work.
⁸ Then the beasts go into their lairs,
   and remain in their dens.
⁹ From its chamber comes the whirlwind,
   and cold from the scattering winds.

In Isa. 31.4 the verb is used of the growling of the lion.

3. Under the whole heaven ... to the corners of the earth: cf. the parallelism in 28.24.

he lets it go: the 'it' refers to the lightning mentioned in the second line. The verb is an Aramaism, meaning 'loose', 'release'.

lightning: lit. 'light' (cf. on 36.32).

corners: lit. 'wings', then the loose ends of a garment, or 'skirt', then 'extremity' (cf. Isa. 24.16).

4. voice: cf. on 28.26. M.T. has 'a voice', save in two MSS., which have 'his voice' (so Budde, Duhm, and others).

roars: especially of the roaring of the lion (Jg. 14.5; Am. 3.4, 8; Ps. 104.21); used of the roaring of God in the thunder in Am. 1.2; Jer. 25.30; Jl 3.16.

the lightnings: M.T. has 'restrain them' ($ye^{\prime}akkeb\bar{e}m$). Budde proposed $ye^{\prime}akk\bar{e}b$ $ber\bar{a}k\hat{i}m$ (=RSV), and so many editors. Pope prefers to find the favourite enclitic m at the end and to give the verb an intransitive sense, for which no evidence is given, and to render 'one does not stay'. This is to make the thought conform to a passage in Ugaritic. The verb '$\bar{a}kab$ means 'hold by the heel' (Hos. 12.3 (M.T. 4)), and hence 'hold back'. But 'to hold oneself by the heel' is an improbable figure.

5. God thunders wondrously with his voice: Duhm read 'shows us' ($yar^{\prime}\bar{e}n\hat{u}$) for 'thunders' ($yar^{\prime}\bar{e}m$) and suppressed 'with his voice' and rendered 'wondrous things' instead of 'wondrously' (so Strahan, Hölscher, Fohrer). Budde also sought to take thunder out of this verse and violently emended to yield 'he does wondrous things past finding out, great things which we cannot comprehend' (so Gray). Even Dhorme was dissatisfied with the thunder here and read 'God by his voice works (ya'ᵃmōl) wonders'. But no change is needed. That there is some repetition is not surprising in Elihu, and the verse provides the transition from the thunderstorm to the winter frosts.

6. Fall: the verb 'to be' is found here in its Aramaic form, but with the meaning 'fall', known in Arabic (here only in OT in this meaning). AV has 'be'. Graetz and others change to 'saturate', but it is a pity to change a rare expression to a common one.

the shower and the rain: M.T. 'shower of rain and shower of rains'. Syr. omits the second of these expressions, which are probably variant readings. Three MSS. omit the first, and so Olshausen and many editors. RSV adds 'and' between the two words retained (so Duhm and Fohrer).

Be strong: M.T. 'of his strength' (so AV); cf. RV 'of his mighty rain'. Hoffmann proposed to change the vowels, to yield the sense of RSV, and so many editors.

7. This verse describes the suspension of agricultural operations while the winter rains and snow prevail.

the hand of every man: Hitzig and many editors read the preposition beʿaḏ instead of beyaḏ='the hand of', and so secure the idiom found in Gen. 7.16: 'he seals up every man'.

that all men may know: this rendering, found also in AV, involves an emendation of the text. M.T. has 'that all men whom he has made (lit. of his work) may know' (cf. RV). Olshausen suggested reading 'ᵃnāšîm='men' for 'anšê (the final m lost by haplography) and most editors follow this or read the singular 'enôš. D. Winton Thomas (JTS, N.S., v, 1954, pp. 56f.) finds the verb here to mean, not 'know', but 'rest' (a meaning found in Arabic) and reads 'enôš and supplies m before 'his work' (lost by haplography), to secure the excellently relevant sense 'that every man might rest from his work (in the fields)'.

8. Here the hibernation of animals for the winter is indicated.

lairs: the noun is found only here and in 38.40 with this meaning. The verb means 'lie in wait (or in ambush)'.

dens: this word is used of the dwelling of God (Ps. 76.2 (M.T. 3)) or of men (Jer. 21.13), and also of the lairs of wild beasts (38.40; Am. 3.4; Nah. 2.12 (M.T. 13); Ps. 104.22).

9. its chamber: M.T. 'the chamber'. In 9.9 there is a reference to 'the chambers of the south' and AV and RV so understood the text here. But 'of the south' is not in the Hebrew (Duhm adds it there). But it is more probable that the meaning is general here (cf. Ps. 135.7).

the scattering winds: lit. 'from the scatterers'. In the Qur'an the name 'scatterers' is given to the north winds which bring the rain, and Dhorme renders 'the north' here (so AV, RV). It is doubtful if we should give the word a geographical reference here. Budde, Gray, Kissane emend the word to 'storehouses' or 'granaries', found in Ps. 144.13, but Dhorme objects that the reading is not certain there and so rejects it (so Hölscher). Hoffmann improbably finds the name of a constellation here.

¹⁰ By the breath of God ice is given.
   and the broad waters are frozen fast.
¹¹ He loads the thick cloud with moisture;
   the clouds scatter his lightning.
¹² They turn round and round by his guidance,
   to accomplish all that he commands them
   on the face of the habitable world.
¹³ Whether for correction, or for his land,
   or for love, he causes it to happen.
¹⁴ 'Hear this, O Job;
   stop and consider the wondrous works of God.
¹⁵ Do you know how God lays his command upon them,
   and causes the lightning of his cloud to shine?
¹⁶ Do you know the balancings of the clouds,
   the wondrous works of him who is perfect in knowledge,
¹⁷ you whose garments are hot

---

   10. Frost and ice are poetically thought of as the result of the cold blast of the breath of God.

the broad waters: lit. 'the breadth of the waters'. The word is closely connected with that used in 36.16 (see note there), and here we may render 'the expanse of the waters'.

frozen fast: or 'become a solid mass'; cf. on 11.15. AV and RV (and so Gray) 'straitened' ('narrowed'), but Peake rightly prefers RV marg. 'congealed'.

   11. loads: cf. the noun 'burden' (Isa. 1.14) from this root. Dhorme connects the verb with another root, found in Arabic, 'fling', 'hurl' (so Pope); but see next note.

moisture: this takes the word ($r\hat{\imath}$) as a contraction for $r^e w\hat{\imath}$. Duhm proposed reading $b\bar{a}r\bar{a}\underline{d}$='hail' for $b^e r\hat{\imath}$='with moisture'. Beer suggested $b\bar{a}r\bar{a}\underline{k}$='lightning' (so Budde, Gray, Dhorme, Pope). Dhorme had earlier (*JPOS*, II, 1922, pp. 66ff.) held $b^e r\hat{\imath}$ to be an Aryan loan-word=Boreas, the North wind, but retracted this. O. Komlós (*VT*, x, 1960, pp. 75ff.) reads $b\hat{o}r\bar{e}$'='creator' for $b^e r\hat{\imath}$, and renders '*ap* (untranslated in *RSV*; *AV* 'also', *RV* 'yea') by 'nose', giving 'the nose of the Creator hurls the cloud'. But there is no need to change M.T., which is quite satisfactory (hence there is no need to render 'hurl'). *AV* has the bizarre rendering 'by watering he wearieth the cloud'.

lightning: M.T. 'light'; cf. on 36.30. *AV* (cf. *RV*) has 'his bright cloud' (lit. 'his cloud of light'). But most scholars by the change of a vowel make 'cloud' the subject (as *RSV*). The word is singular in M.T., but *RSV* treats as a collective.

12. Here <u>Elihu emphasizes the thought that all these natural forces obey the</u> <u>will of God and fulfil his purposes.</u> Budde added *yithallēk*='goes to and fro' before *mithappēk*='wheeling about', and Duhm and Dhorme after it, since there is no main verb in M.T. The meaning then is 'it (the cloud) goes round in circles, wheeling about according to his plans'. The word *mithappēk* stands in Gen. 3.24, where it describes the turning around of the flaming sword.

by his guidance: better 'plans' or 'purposes'; cf. Prov. 12.5 (*RSV* 'counsels').

13. Elihu closes this section of his speech by <u>ascribing God's control of natural</u> <u>forces as sometimes in wrath for punishment, and sometimes in mercy for</u> <u>blessing, thus summarizing what he has been saying.</u>

for correction: lit. 'for the rod'.

or for his land: this reads oddly. Hoffmann for *le'arṣô* proposed *lerāṣô*='for favour', and Dahood (*The Bible in Current Catholic Thought*, ed. McKenzie, 1962, p. 72), while retaining M.T., defended this meaning, suggesting that a prosthetic *'āleph* had been added (so Pope). Duhm read *lime'ērāh*='for a curse' (so Gray). But 'correction' and 'love' already balance, and neither needs a supporting term. What is wanted is a verb in the first half. Hence Dhorme redivides the two words rendered 'or for his land', and with slight changes secures 'he accomplishes his will'.

love: cf. on 10.12.

THE MAJESTY AND UNSEARCHABLENESS OF GOD **37.14–24**

<u>Rising in his eloquence Elihu now exhorts Job to consider the greatness of God</u> <u>that he may be awed into humility.</u> Clothed in majesty and beyond man's reach, God is just and righteous, and has no regard even to the wisest of men.

14. <u>Elihu now returns to address Job in particular.</u>

15. Do you know?: Elihu here imitates the ironic questions of the Divine speeches, which belonged to the book before Elihu's were added.

lays his command: M.T. does not express 'his command'.

upon them: the clouds (verse 12). G. R. Driver (*SVT*, XVI, 1967, pp. 61f.) reads *'allêhem* for *'alêhem* and renders 'assigns them their tasks'.

causes . . . to shine: lightning, like other natural phenomena, was a mystery that could only be ascribed to the direct activity of God, who by his specific intervention caused the clouds to send forth the flashes.

16. balancings: in 36.29 we had 'the spreading (of the clouds)' where the word differed from the word here by one letter (*r* for *l*). Similarly **wondrous works** here differs by one letter from that in verse 14. Budde conforms here to those others. It is a pity to rob Elihu of stylistic variation. 'The idea of the clouds laden with moisture being poised in the sky is more picturesque' (Gray). The word 'balancings' is from the same root as 'balance' in Prov. 16.11; Isa. 40.12 (*RSV* 'scales'). Duhm reconstructs the second line to read 'making a deluge to pour down at the thunder'. This is not to be preferred.

17. whose garments are hot: Davidson cites Thomson: '<u>This sensation of</u> <u>dry hot clothes is only experienced during the siroccos</u>'.

> when the earth is still because of the south wind?
> ¹⁸ Can you, like him, spread out the skies,
>   hard as a molten mirror?
> ¹⁹ Teach us what we shall say to him;
>   we cannot draw up our case because of darkness.
> ²⁰ Shall it be told him that I would speak?
>   Did a man ever wish that he would be swallowed up?
> ²¹ 'And now men cannot look on the light
>   when it is bright in the skies,
>   when the wind has passed and cleared them.
> ²² Out of the north comes golden splendour;
>   God is clothed with terrible majesty.
> ²³ The Almighty—we cannot find him;
>   he is great in power and justice,
>   and abundant righteousness he will not violate.

---

is still: 'the very air is too weak and languid to stir the pendent leaves even of the tall poplars' (Thomson). At such a time what is most desired is cloud, with the promise of cooling rain.

the south wind: only here of the south wind; elsewhere simply 'south'. Cf. Lk. 12.55. Elsewhere the sirocco is called the east wind.

18. spread out: the verb means 'beat out', 'flatten', and from it the noun 'firmament' is derived.

hard: the word used for 'solid mass' in verse 10. The verb means 'pour out', 'cast (metals)', and from this derives the sense 'hard', 'firm'.

mirror: a word found only here and in Sir. 12.11. Ancient mirrors were made of molten metal.

19. With biting sarcasm Elihu asks Job to instruct him how he should approach God, since he himself would not dare to approach him. The reference to drawing up a case is doubtless an allusion to Job's expressed desire to meet God in a court of law. The term here used for drawing up a case is the verb used for setting in order (words, battle line); cf. 13.18.

because of darkness: the darkness of our minds and the darkness in which God himself is concealed from us.

20. Elihu shrinks from the very idea of such an encounter with God, which would simply be to court destruction.

be swallowed up: Dhorme derives this word from another root, and renders 'When a man has spoken, is he informed?' (so Fohrer). It is unnecessary to depart from the frequently occurring root, which yields a more effective sense here.

21f. The return to natural phenomena here is curious. Kissane transfers these

verses to follow verse 8, but they do not seem in place there. Pope transfers
verse 21 to follow verse 18.

21. The meaning appears to be that when the wind has blown away the clouds
the sky is too bright for the eyes. The point then is that if the clear sky is too
bright for human eyes, the dazzling brightness of God's presence would be even
more unbearable. *RV* 'And now men see not the light which is bright in the
skies, but the wind passeth, and cleanseth them' (cf. *AV*) offers quite another
sense. Here it is suggested that the clouds which now hide God will soon be
swept away. But this is quite alien to Elihu's thought. The word rendered **bright**
is found only here, though a related word is found in Lev. 13f. of a bright spot
on the skin. In Aramaic and Arabic the root means 'shine', 'be clear', but in
Syriac it means 'be dark', 'be obscure'. This meaning was suggested here by
Delitzsch, and it has been followed by some editors, including Gray and Dhorme.
The sense then found is: 'And now men saw not the light, it was obscure in the
skies (Dhorme: it was darkened by the clouds), but a wind passed and cleansed
them (Dhorme: swept them away)'; so Gray. But this does not seem to be
relevant to any moral Elihu is drawing.

22. The interpretation of this verse is difficult. 'Out of the north comes gold'
(so M.T.) might refer to the north as the source of gold in the ancient world,
but it does not seem relevant to anything Elihu is saying. Graetz substituted
'brightness' (*zōhar*) for 'gold' (*zāhāḇ*), and so many editors. *AV* surprisingly
renders 'fair weather', while *RV* and *RSV* import into the term what is not in
the text when they render **golden splendour.** Dhorme defends this and himself
renders 'rays of gold'. Gray, who follows the reading of Graetz, suggests that the
reference is to the Aurora Borealis. Pope finds some allusion to the mythological
associations of the north here (cf. on 26.7), and refers to the myth of the building
of a splendid palace of gold and lapis lazuli for Baal on Mt. Zaphon. But no
reference to gold as a metal is relevant here. Some bright light is needed to suggest
the majesty with which God is clothed. This is best secured by Graetz's very
slight emendation. If there is any reference to golden rays or splendour from the
north, it can hardly be to the rays of the sun, and the Aurora Borealis would seem
to be the most probable reference. This mysterious radiance, illuminating the
night sky, might well suggest the splendour of God. Guillaume (*Promise and
Fulfilment*, ed. by F. F. Bruce, 1963, p. 109) retains M.T. and explains by the
cognate Arabic *ḍihbah*='light rain (shot through by the rays of the sun)'. He then
translates 'Out of the north comes golden splendour' (*ALUOS* Supplement ii,
1968, p. 129).

23. Elihu reasserts the unsearchableness of God and his conviction of the
righteousness of God, who can never violate justice, as Job has so consistently
maintained that he does.

abundant righteousness: lit. 'greatness of righteousness'. A slight change of
vowel gives 'great in righteousness', and so most editors.

he will not violate: M.T. could be rendered 'he will not afflict' (so *AV*, *RV*), or
'he will not oppress' (so Dhorme, Kissane, Pope). Gray emends to 'pervert',

24 Therefore men fear him;
    he does not regard any who are wise in their own conceit.'

---

while Fohrer omits the whole line as a gloss. No change is necessary here, but the
rendering 'violate' is less suitable than 'oppress': 'great in righteousness, he will
not oppress'. God is too inflexibly just to maltreat any man.

24. Men reverence God because he is so great and good. He is high above men
and even the wisest of them are utterly beneath his notice.

wise in their own conceit: there is no justification for this nuance, though it is
found in Vulg. The Hebrew says 'the wise of heart', a phrase found in 9.4 with
no pejorative connotation.

THE FIRST DIVINE SPEECH 38-39

We now return to the original author of the book, 'a welcome change, more
than ever to be enthralled by the spell of his genius' (Peake). Cf. Strahan: 'It is in
the divine speech that the author of Job proves himself one of the supreme poets
of nature, a writer gifted with descriptive powers almost without a parallel'.
S. R. Driver (*LOT*, p. 427) says: 'The first speech of Jehovah transcends all other
descriptions of the wonders of creation or the greatness of the Creator, which are
to be found either in the Bible or elsewhere.' Job has successfully borne his trial.
During the trial he has made grave charges against God and has adopted an
attitude towards God which the friends have rightly condemned. But nowhere
has he renounced God, as the Satan had predicted he would. Nowhere has he
regretted his integrity, and amid all his complaints against the God of his present
experience, as he conceived him, he has clung to the God he has known. Both he
and his friends were unaware of the real reason for his sufferings, and that cannot
be revealed to him, or the book would lose its meaning for others who must
suffer in the dark. But clearly the trial must be brought to an end. To that end
God now intervenes. He does so, not to solve the intellectual problem, which
had been the subject of the debate between Job and his friends, but to resolve the
spiritual problem which lay behind the arguments on both sides. The friends
were persuaded that Job had sinned and therefore was abandoned by God. Job
maintained that his sufferings were not the result of his sin, but he had yet been
abandoned by God. The common ground between Job and his friends was that
he was cut off from God, and that his suffering was the evidence of this. The effect
of the Divine speeches was to make Job conscious that this was not so, and that
in his suffering, even though he could not know its cause, he might yet have the
presence of God. While therefore the Divine speeches rebuke him for things he
had said under his trial, their burden is that he cannot have the knowledge on
which judgment should rest, and that he is wiser to bow humbly before God
than to judge him. The first speech falls into the following parts: the opening
challenge (38.1–3); a survey of the mysteries of earth and sky that surpassed Job's
understanding (verses 4–38); a survey of the mysteries of animal and bird life
that surpassed his understanding (38.39–39.30).

38 Then the LORD answered Job out of the whirlwind:
² 'Who is this that darkens counsel
    by words without knowledge?'
³ Gird up your loins like a man,
    I will question you, and you shall declare to me.
⁴ 'Where were you when I laid the foundation of the earth?

THE LORD'S OPENING CHALLENGE 38.1-3

Job, who had so often demanded to face God, is now summoned to gird himself for the contest he had invited. But it was not to be the contest Job had longed for. It was not to be about his sufferings and their cause, but about the limits of his knowledge. Job had recognized that God would overwhelm him if he ever designed to meet him, and in this he proved abundantly right.

1. **the LORD:** the divine name, Yahweh, is used here as in the Prologue and Epilogue and in 40.1, 3, 6; 42.1, but not in the Dialogue, or the Elihu speeches. **ob:** Elihu is ignored.
whirlwind: the storm is elsewhere described as the fitting accompaniment of a theophany; cf. Ezek. 1.4; Nah. 1.3; Zech. 9.14. It is not here the storm described by Elihu.
2. **this.** If the Elihu speeches were integral to the book, the reference here should be to him. Yet it is plainly to Job (cf. 40.4f.; 42.2-6).
counsel. The reference is not to the discussion between Job and his friends, but to the purposes of God, which were obscured and misrepresented by Job. For this meaning of the word cf. Ps. 33.10 (where it is parallel to 'plan'); Prov. 19.21; Isa. 19.17. Hence Dhorme renders here 'Providence'.
words without knowledge: cf. 35.16.
3. Cf. 40.7. The girding of the loins is the preparation for a hard task (Jer. 1.17), or for battle (Isa. 5.27), or for running (1 Kg. 18.46). C. H. Gordon (*HUCA*, XXIII, Part 1, 1950-51, p. 136) thinks it possible, though not demonstrable, that belt-wrestling was a Hebrew court procedure, and that it is referred to here.

A SURVEY OF THE MYSTERIES OF EARTH AND SKY THAT SURPASSED JOB'S UNDERSTANDING 38.4-38

By a series of swift ironical questions Job is challenged to prove his omniscience. The wonders of creation, of the ordering of nature, of the movements of the stars, are successively indicated, and Job is asked whether he comprehends all their mysteries.
4. Cf. 15.17. In this and the following verses the work of creation is conceived in terms of the erection of a building, with foundation stones and supporting pillars set in sockets, and with the use of a measuring line.

> Tell me, if you have understanding.
> 5 Who determined its measurements—surely you know!
>   Or who stretched the line upon it?
> 6 On what were its bases sunk,
>   or who laid its cornerstone,
> 7 when the morning stars sang together,
>   and all the sons of God shouted for joy?
> 8 'Or who shut in the sea with doors,
>   when it burst forth from the womb;
> 9 when I made clouds its garment,
>   and thick darkness its swaddling band,
> 10 and prescribed bounds for it,

---

5. its measurements: as though builder's plans had been drawn up beforehand. Joüon (*MFO*, VI, 1913, p. 209) needlessly suggesting changing to 'its foundations'.

surely: or 'since', or 'if'.

6. bases: the earth was conceived of as standing upon pillars (cf. 9.6), which needed pedestals or bases on which to rest. In 26.7 the earth was thought of as suspended from above, and resting on nothing; in Ps. 24.2 as resting on the sea. **sunk:** *AV* and *RV* 'fastened'. The same verb is used of the mountains being sunk into the ground in Prov. 8.25.

7. When the foundation of the Second Temple was laid, there was music and song (Ezr. 3.10, 11). So here the laying of the foundation of the world is represented as accompanied by song. But since man was not yet created, it was the stars and the angels who sang. In Gen. 1.16 the stars are represented as created after the earth.

sons of God: cf. on 1.6.

8. Or who shut?: M.T. 'and he shut'. Vulg. reads 'Who?', and so Merx, Wright, Dhorme, Fohrer, and others. We pass here to the origin of the sea. The verb is the same as that of 1.10; 3.23. Gray proposed to read 'Where were you when the sea was born?' to secure a more close parallel with the second line. But this is without support.

burst forth: the turbulent sea is likened to a child breaking out of the womb. Two figures are used, therefore, in this verse: the sea as a child bursting from the womb, and as an unruly flood needing to be securely controlled.

9. Here the figure of birth is carried on. As the child is wrapped in swaddling clothes, so the sea was wrapped in the clouds.

swaddling band: this noun is found only here, but the verb is found in Ezek. 16.4, and a related word is used for a bandage for a broken arm in Ezek. 30.21.

10. prescribed: this follows *RV* marg., but the rendering is unjustified. M.T.

and set bars and doors,
11 and said, "Thus far shall you come, and no farther,
    and here shall your proud waves be stayed"?
12 'Have you commanded the morning since your days began,
    and caused the dawn to know its place,
13 that it might take hold of the skirts of the earth,
    and the wicked be shaken out of it?
14 It is changed like clay under the seal,

---

says 'broke', and the verb cannot mean 'prescribe'. LXX and Vulg. represent this meaning, for which we should read 'āšît, with Merx, Wright, Gray, and others, for M.T. 'ešbōr. Dhorme transposes the two verbs in the verse, and thinks that after the divine imposition of bounds, the doors of verse 8 were no longer needed, and were therefore broken. But the versions give no support to this idea. Fohrer reads 'esgōr='I shut (it within its (so Dillmann, Duhm and others) bound).' Guillaume (*Promise and Fulfilment*, p. 123) retains M.T. and finds an Arabism, giving the improbable meaning 'measured it by span by my decree'. God would scarcely have issued a decree to himself.

11. The second line in M.T. means 'here he will put on the pride of thy waves.' This makes sense only if 'a limit' is supplied as the object of the verb. LXX has 'shall be broken' and Merx and Wright so read (exchanging the word in verse 11 (see note there) with the word here; cf. also Ewald). Bickell proposed 'will cease' (so Budde and others), Gray 'will be stayed'; Dhorme 'will be destroyed'; Kissane 'will be turned back'. All of these agree in finding the second line, like the first, to declare God's control of the sea.

12. With this verse we come to the succession of night and day, which must be carefully regulated if the world is to be ordered. Cf. Ps. 104.19ff.
since your days began: lit. 'from your days', idiomatic for 'since you were born'.

13. In this finely poetic conception night is depicted as covering the earth like a garment, which the dawn takes hold of by the finger tips of its rays and shakes out. The wicked, whose works are carried on under the cover of darkness (cf. 24.13ff.), are shaken out of the garment. It was usual to use the cloak as a coverlet at night, and this was why the pledged garment should be returned at nightfall (cf. on 22.6).
skirts: *AV* and *RV* 'ends'; cf. on 37.3 ('corners').

14. As the formless surface of the clay takes meaningful shape under the impress of the seal, so the landscape, which under the cover of night is shapeless, stands out in the morning light. Another very poetic figure. Dhorme thought the reference here was to 'sealed clay', or *terra sigillata*, reddish clay used in ancient medicine, mentioned here for its colour, which suggested the pink hues of the earth at sunrise.

and it is dyed like a garment.
15 From the wicked their light is withheld,
    and their uplifted arm is broken.
16 'Have you entered into the springs of the sea,
    or walked in the recesses of the deep?
17 Have the gates of death been revealed to you,
    or have you seen the gates of deep darkness?
18 Have you comprehended the expanse of the earth?
    Declare, if you know all this.
19 'Where is the way to the dwelling of light,
    and where is the place of darkness,
20 that you may take to its territory
    and that you may discern the paths to its home?
21 You know, for you were born then,
    and the number of your days is great!
22 'Have you entered the storehouses of the snow,
    or have you seen the storehouses of the hail,
23 which I have reserved for the time of trouble,
    for the day of battle and war?
24 What is the way to the place where the light is distributed,
    or where the east wind is scattered upon the earth?
25 'Who has cleft a channel for the torrents of rain,
    and a way for the thunderbolt,
26 to bring rain on a land where no man is,

---

it is dyed: M.T. 'they stand forth' (cf. *AV*, *RV*). This goes oddly with 'like a garment', and Hoffmann suggested reading 'in shame' (*lāḇōš*) for 'a garment' (*leḇûš*). The reference would then be to the wicked who are exposed in their ignominy by the light of day. Ehrlich suggested reading *tiṣṣāḇaʿ* = 'it is dyed' for *yityaṣṣeḇû*, and so many editors. The reference then is to the colours which the landscape takes on under the light of day.

15. their light: the light of the wicked is darkness (cf. 24.17). With the coming of the day darkness is banished. G. R. Driver (*JTS*, N.S., IV, 1953, pp. 209ff.) argues that **the wicked** means the Dog-stars, Canis major and Canis minor, whose light is cut off.

arm is broken: the arm of violence which is active in the darkness is paralysed in the daytime. Driver (loc. cit.) maintains that the **uplifted arm** is the Navigator's Line, i.e. the line of stars extending like a bent arm across the sky from the horizon to the zenith, passing through Sirius, Procyon, Castor and Pollux. The arm is broken as one star after another fades before the oncoming light.

16. Job is challenged to show his knowledge, not only of the origins of things, but of the range and extent of things not visible to the human eye.

springs: found only here; but cf. on 28.11. The springs of the sea are the subterranean depths from which its waters were thought to be replenished.

recesses: *AV* 'search'. The word denotes what is to be sought out; cf. 11.7 ('the deep things').

17. gates of death: giving access to Sheol; cf. Ps. 9.13 (M.T. 14); 107.18; Isa. 38.10.

gates (2°). Guillaume (*Promise and Fulfilment*, pp. 123f.) finds here a different word from 1°, and renders 'boundaries'.

deep darkness: cf. on 3.5. The parallel shows that the reference here is to the darkness of Sheol (cf. 10.21f.).

18. expanse: this word is found only here and in 36.16 (cf. note there). Here it stands in the plural, intensifying the idea 'the vast expanse'.

19. Light and darkness are personified as two separate beings, each with its own abode, from which it comes daily forth and to which it returns.

20. it . . . its: though the pronouns are singular, the reference must be to the light and darkness of verse 19.

discern: Hoffmann, by the addition of two letters, produced the reading 'bring it into', and so many editors. But Dhorme compares 28.23, and retains the text here.

21. Yahweh is represented as a master of sarcasm.

22f. Snow and hail are thought of as being kept in store by God, ready to be brought out as required, in times of crisis (cf. Sir. 39.29), and especially of battle. For hail in battle cf. Jos. 10.11; cf. also Exod. 9.22ff.; Isa. 28.17; Ezek. 13.13. For the thought of hail as a weapon of God, cf. Isa. 30.30; and for its use in theophanies, cf. Ps. 18.12f. (M.T. 13f.); Isa. 30.30f.

22. storehouses (2°): Guillaume (loc. cit., p. 124) again finds a different word from 1°, and renders 'large rocks', the 'large rocks of the hail' being huge hailstones.

24. light: light has been dealt with in verse 19, and the author does not repeat himself like Elihu. Moreover, the parallel between 'light' and 'east wind' is not very good. Hence Hoffmann proposed to read *'ed*='mist', instead of *'ôr*='light' and this has been widely followed. Wind and weather are a closer parallel than wind and light. Other proposals instead of 'light' are *ruaḥ*='wind' (Ewald, Merx and others); *kepōr*='hoar frost' (Siegfried); *ḳîṭôr*='smoke' (Beer). These are all farther from M.T. G. R. Driver (*AJSL*, LII, 1935–36, p. 166) argues for the meaning 'parching heat' (cf. *SVT*, III, 1955, pp. 91f.), and so Guillaume (loc. cit.).

25. The second line is identical with 28.26*b* (see note there), though *RSV* translates differently. In 28.26 the parallel is 'rain', here 'downpour' or 'torrential flood.' **channel:** a word elsewhere used for 'conduit' (Isa. 7.3), or 'trench' (1 Kg. 18.32).

26. God's providence extends to more than man. His rain falls on lands where

on the desert in which there is no man;
²⁷ to satisfy the waste and desolate land,
and to make the ground put forth grass?
²⁸ 'Has the rain a father,
or who has begotten the drops of dew?
²⁹ From whose womb did the ice come forth,
and who has given birth to the hoarfrost of heaven?
³⁰ The waters become hard like stone,
and the face of the deep is frozen.
³¹ 'Can you bind the chains of the Plei'ades,
or loose the cords of Ori'on?
³² Can you lead forth the Maz'zaroth in their season,
or can you guide the Bear with its children?
³³ Do you know the ordinances of the heavens?
Can you establish their rule on the earth?
³⁴ 'Can you lift up your voice to the clouds,
that a flood of waters may cover you?
³⁵ Can you send forth lightnings, that they may go
and say to you, "Here we are"?
³⁶ Who has put wisdom in the clouds,
or given understanding to the mists?

---

no human beings are found. 'It is not merely Job's ignorance of things he could not know, it is his narrow outlook . . . for which Yahweh rebukes him' (Peake). The repeated **no man . . . no man** is less inelegant in the Hebrew, since two different words for 'man' are used.

27. waste and desolate land: the same expression, differently translated, as in 30.3. The second line is lit. 'to cause to sprout a source of vegetation'. 'Source' is the word rendered 'mine' in 28.1. For this word (*mōṣā'*) Wright and others read *ṣāmē'*='the thirsty (land)', and Beer and others *miṣṣiyyāh*='from the steppe'. Either improves the sense, but the former, which involves only the transposition of two letters, is nearer M.T. I. Eitan (*HUCA*, XIV, 1939, pp. 3f.) connects the verb with a different root, and with very slight changes secures the meaning 'to cause shoots to spring up from the waste'. But the personification of M.T. is much finer.

grass: rendered 'vegetation' in Gen. 1.11.

28. Bickell and Duhm omit this verse, and so some others. But it is closely linked to verse 29 (cf. 'father' and 'from whose womb', i.e. mother; also 'begotten' and 'given birth to'), and Gray pronounces it a beautiful verse.

drops of dew: the word rendered 'drops' is found only here, but its meaning is beyond doubt.

29. ice: as in 6.16; 37.10. In Gen. 31.40; Jer. 36.30, it means 'frost'.

30. become hard: AV and RV connected this verb with the root 'hide', but Hitzig and many others take the verb to be a dialectal form of another verb meaning 'coagulate', whence the rendering of RSV. But the argument for this is very weak. Merx, Budde and Gray preferred to transpose the two verbs of this verse, giving 'the face of the deep is hidden'. This is more satisfactory than guessing at the meaning.

is frozen: lit. 'takes'. Dhorme compares the similar French idiom 'La rivière a pris' ('The river has become frozen').

31. chains. This word is found elsewhere only in 1 Sam. 15.32 (AV and RV 'delicately'; RSV 'cheerfully'). It is possible that here there has been a metathesis of two letters, and the word is derived from the root which stands in 31.36 ('bind'). AV has 'sweet influences', but this is certainly to be rejected. RV has 'cluster', which Driver (JTS, N.S., VII, 1956, p. 3) justifies without change of consonants by reference to Ugaritic and Arabic.

Pleiades: cf. on 9.9.

cords: a word found only here, but from a well-known root. The reference is perhaps to Orion's belt (cf. Driver, loc. cit., p. 4).

Orion: cf. on 9.9.

32. Mazzaroth: this has been equated by some with the word *mazzālôt* (2 Kg. 23.5, RSV 'constellations'), which is variously understood to mean the planets, or the signs of the Zodiac, and by others connected with the word for 'crown' and interpreted as *Corona Borealis*, or the Northern and Southern Crowns (so Ewald, Dhorme). Driver (loc. cit., pp. 5ff.) thinks the word is for *ma'azārôt*= 'girdling stars', i.e. the Zodiacal circle.

the Bear and its children: cf. on 9.9.

33. ordinances of the heavens: the laws which govern the movements of the various heavenly bodies.

rule: a word found only here, from a root elsewhere only associated with scribal activity. Dhorme takes it to mean 'what is written' in the heavens. The line rests on the idea that the conjunctions of the heavenly bodies determine events on earth, and Job is asked if he can direct their influence in any way.

34. In the same way, Job is asked if he can interfere with the weather which the elements bring upon earth. The second line is identical with 22.11b. For **cover you** LXX has 'answer you', which some editors prefer. But M.T. is more expressive.

35. lightnings: the servants of God (cf. 36.32; 37.11f.), not of man.

36. Two uncertain words make the meaning of this verse difficult to determine. These are the words rendered **clouds** and **mists.** AV has 'heart' and 'clouds'; RV 'inward parts' and 'mind'. The first word recurs in Ps. 51.6 (M.T. 8), where RSV has 'inward being', but where the meaning is not necessarily the same as here, though Vulg. and Targ. represent this meaning. Targ. has a double rendering of

³⁷ Who can number the clouds by wisdom?
    Or who can tilt the waterskins of the heavens,
³⁸ when the dust runs into a mass
    and the clods cleave fast together?
³⁹ 'Can you hunt the prey for the lion,
    or satisfy the appetite of the young lions,
⁴⁰ when they crouch in their dens,
    or lie in wait in their covert?
⁴¹ Who provides for the raven its prey,
    when its young ones cry to God,
    and wander about for lack of food?

---

the second word, the first of these being 'heart', and so some rabbinical commentators. But the context deals with phenomena of nature, and hence both of these terms must be differently rendered. Both terms have been connected with the clouds (so Peake), while Duhm connected the first with clouds and the second with comets, meteors, or the Aurora Borealis. *RV* marg. rendered the second term 'meteors'. Hoffmann saw in the first term a transliteration of the Egyptian god, Thot, and proposed Mercury for the second, depending on a Coptic cognate, and Pope follows this view. But these do not seem to be in place among natural phenomena. Cheyne (*JBL*, XVII, 1898, pp. 104f.) identified the first with the star Procyon and the second with Sirius. Dhorme started from the second word, for which Vulg. and the second rendering in the Targ. have 'cock', which has support in Jewish tradition. He then suggested for the first word the bird sacred to Thot, or the 'ibis'. He has been followed by Hölscher, Steinmann, Larcher and Fohrer. But Weiser rightly objects that this is alien to the context. Later in the speech various animals and birds will be spoken of, but none is in place here. While there can be no certainty of the meaning, *RSV* gives the most probable sense. For this sense the root meaning 'wander' is relied on, and it was this which also gave the meaning 'meteors'. The second word is connected with a root meaning 'look' and so assigned the meaning '(celestial) appearance'. Neither of these is really convincing. Driver (*AJSL*, LII, 1935-36, p. 167) renders 'Who put wisdom in dark mysteries, or who made understanding an object of hope?' This is too unrelated to the context to be convincing. Kissane emended the second word to give 'my covert' or 'pavilion' and cited 36.29, where the clouds are spoken of as God's pavilion. The ascription of wisdom and understanding to the clouds is in line with much else in the speech.

37. number. Ehrlich connected the verb with an Arabic root meaning 'chase away', and so Driver (*SVT*, III, 1955, p. 92), the thought being then of the clouds scudding across the sky.

tilt: lit. 'cause to lie down'.

38. When the rain descends the particles of dust are joined together to form a single mass again.

runs into a mass: the verb and noun are cognate, the latter standing also in 37.10. The verb means 'flow' or 'cast (of metals)', and hence the noun could develop the meaning 'hard', as of cast metal. But this is not appropriate here, where the reference is to the fusing of the dust into mud, like molten metal.

A SURVEY OF THE MYSTERIES OF ANIMAL AND BIRD LIFE THAT SURPASSED JOB'S UNDER-STANDING 38.39–39.30

The second part of the speech now begins. Here the author passes in review in brilliant verse a number of animals and birds, and asks if Job knows the secrets of their life and behaviour. Most famous and brilliant of them all is the unrivalled description of the horse.

39f. This section begins with the king of beasts. Does Job provide the lion with its prey, while it waits in its den? The lion is more capable of securing its own prey than any man could be on its behalf, and no man would be interested in serving it in this way. Yet God cares for it and has given it its strength and cunning in stalking its prey, and causes its prey to come into its vicinity. Cf. Ps. 104.21.

lion: in 4.11 'lioness', and so *RV* here. Cf. Bochart, *Hierozoicon*, I, 1663, col. 719.
appetite: cf. on 33.20 ('life').

40. covert: the word rendered 'lairs' in 37.8.

41. The position of the raven between the lion and other wild animals has seemed suspect to some. Wright read 'ereḇ='evening', for 'ōrēḇ='raven': 'Who provides its (i.e. the lion's) prey in the evening' (so Duhm, Beer). We should then have to go back to verse 39a for the reference in 'its'. Most retain the text as it is.

its prey: this is not the word used in verse 39. *AV* and *RV* here render 'his food'. The word may be derived from either of two roots, and may mean 'what is taken in hunting' (Gen. 25.28; 27.3), or 'food', 'provisions' (Jos. 9.14; Ps. 132.15). Hence either rendering may be justified. Cf. Ps. 147.9. The raven is black (Ca. 5.11) and it is found in ravines (1 Kg. 17.4, 6) and in the wilderness (Isa. 34.11). It picks out the eyes of its victim (Prov. 30.17).

and wander: this can scarcely refer to the nestlings which cry out for food, and Bickell and Budde read the singular, making the parent bird the subject. Beer proposed to change one letter and read 'they cry' (cf. Isa. 42.14, *RSV* 'cry out'), but there is no evidence that this verb was used of the cry of birds. Driver (*AJSL*, LII, 1935–36, pp. 167f.) connected the verb with an Arabic root meaning 'guffawed', 'burst into laughter'. But this does not appear to be used of birds, and it would be surprising to burst into laughter for lack of food. It is more probable that the verse originally had four lines, and that the third, which would have made clear the subject of this verb, has been lost.

39 'Do you know when the mountain goats bring forth?
       Do you observe the calving of the hinds?
2 Can you number the months that they fulfil,
       and do you know the time when they bring forth,
3 when they crouch, bring forth their offspring,
       and are delivered of their young?
4 Their young ones become strong, they grow up in the open;
       they go forth, and do not return to them.
5 'Who has let the wild ass go free?
       Who has loosed the bonds of the swift ass,
6 to whom I have given the steppe for his home,
       and the salt land for his dwelling place?
7 He scorns the tumult of the city;
       he hears not the shouts of the driver.
8 He ranges the mountains as his pasture,
       and he searches after every green thing.
9 'Is the wild ox willing to serve you?
       Will he spend the night at your crib?
10 Can you bind him in the furrow with ropes,

39.1. mountain goats: or 'ibex', found on high mountains (Ps. 104.18).
From 1 Sam. 24.2, it is clear that they were in the neighbourhood of En-gedi.
They have long and imposing horns, but are very shy. The word is masc., though
it must stand here for the fem. The first line of this verse is long, and Bickell
suggested omitting the word **when,** which repeats the last two consonants of the
preceding verse (so Steuernagel, Dhorme and others). The line then means 'Do
you know the parturition of the ibex?' This improves the parallel with the following line, and removes the duplication with the following verse.

2. The first line concerns the period of pregnancy, and the second the season of
foaling. There is no need to change the verb of the second line to 'appoint', with
Duhm and others.

3. crouch: used of a woman in childbirth in 1 Sam. 4.19. It is commonly thought that this line refers to the ease with which the ibex bears, but
rabbinical commentators understood it of the difficulty of their bearing, doubtless owing to the common meaning of the word rendered 'their young' (see
below).

bring forth. The verb means 'cleave' (16.13; Ps. 141.7), which is commonly
held to be inappropriate here, since 'their offspring' is the object. Olshausen
suggested reading *ṭ* for *ḥ*, giving the verb used in 21.10 (*RSV* 'calves'), and this is

widely followed. But Driver (*SVT*, III, 1955, pp. 92f.) defends M.T., and says the verb is idiomatic for 'breach the womb'.

their young: *AV* and *RV* 'their sorrows'. The word usually means 'birth pangs' (cf. Isa. 13.8), but here it must stand for what causes the pangs. A cognate noun in Arabic means 'foetus'. Dahood (*The Bible in Current Catholic Thought*, 1962, p. 73) renders 'their flocks'. Pope transfers 'in the open' from verse 4 to the end of this verse.

4. The rapid maturity and independence of parental care of these mountain creatures is next emphasized. The ease with which they are born is matched by the swiftness with which they become capable of fending for themselves.

in the open: an Aramaism, found only here, meaning the open countryside. *AV* 'with the corn' confuses the word with a homonym, meaning 'grain' (Am. 5.11, and 12 other passages).

5ff. The wild ass, roaming the steppes, is here conceived of as really a domestic ass, that patient drudge, released from bondage. The fine description perhaps reflects the sympathy of the author with this untamable creature.

wild ass: cf. 6.5; 11.12; 24.5.

swift ass: an Aramaic word, found only here in *OT*, for the same animal. The wild ass is so swift that only the fleetest horses can equal its speed.

6. the steppe: cf. 24.5, where the wild ass's home is described as the desert, a different term being used. Both of these terms and **the salt land** are mentioned together in Jer. 17.6. Salty soil was infertile (cf. Ps. 107.34), and we read of land being sown with salt to make it so (Jg. 9.45).

7. scorns: lit. 'laughs at'. The freedom of the open country is more exciting to the wild ass than all the hubbub of the city.

shouts: cf. on 30.22.

driver: the word used sometimes for the overseer of forced labour; here only of the driver of an animal (but cf. Isa. 9.3, where deliverance from oppression is described in figures drawn from the labour of beasts).

8. In the desert pasturage is scarce, and the wild ass must roam far and wide in search of it. Davidson records that Arab poets 'compare a deep ravine or abyss to the "belly" of the wild ass, which is often lank and empty from want of food (Jer. 14.6)'. It pays the price of its freedom.

9ff. The domestic ass and ox are often mentioned together (e.g. Exod. 21.33; Isa. 1.3); so here the wild ox follows the wild ass. Like the wild ass, it is untamable, and its great strength cannot be harnessed to the service of man.

wild ox: *AV* 'unicorn'. This animal is mentioned nine times in *OT*. It certainly had two horns (cf. Dt. 33.17), and it was thought to be some kind of ox (cf. Ps. 29.6; Isa. 34.7, where the parallelism implies this). It was very powerful, and the frequent references to its horns suggest that they were very dangerous (cf. Num. 23.22; 24.8; Ps. 22.21 (M.T. 22)). It was hunted by the Assyrians, and is probably to be identified with the aurochs.

crib: elsewhere only in Prov. 14.4; Isa. 1.3.

10. him: M.T. repeats 'the wild ox', but as this overloads the line and is need-

or will he harrow the valleys after you?
11 Will you depend on him because his strength is great,
and will you leave to him your labour?
12 Do you have faith in him that he will return,
and bring your grain to your threshing floor?
13 'The wings of the ostrich wave proudly;

---

less after verse 9, it is generally deleted. Siegfried proposed for the first line 'Can you bind them (Budde him) to the furrow with ropes (Budde his rope)'. But Dhorme rightly objects that this is odd. Duhm transposed to obtain 'by his furrow rope', which is also odd. Beer transposed the words for 'furrow' and 'valleys' and for the latter read *'ᵃnāḳô* for *'ᵃmāḳîm,* and secured the meaning 'Can you bind a rope about his neck? Will he harrow the furrows behind you?' Dhorme and Larcher follow this, but Gray thinks it is too violent. With a much slighter change Kissane secures the same sense, rendering the first line 'Wilt thou bind him with a halter of cord?', and retaining M.T. in the second line. This involves a very slight consonantal change, and the reading of a noun cognate with the verb found in Ps. 32.9 (*RSV* 'curb'). This yields a more natural picture than binding an animal to the furrow with ropes.

11. The wild ox has great strength which might be useful to man if he could harness it. But his inability to do this is matched by the unreliability of the wild ox, which could not be trusted to do what was wanted.

12. Though the wild ox were sent to bring home the harvest, no one would trust him to come back with it.

to your threshing floor: M.T. reads 'bring back (your grain) and gather your threshing floor'. The slight change of reading and the different division of the verse improve it.

13ff. LXX lacked the whole of the section on the ostrich, and many editors omit it as an interpolation. It is to be noted that the series of rhetorical questions is broken by this section, and that God is referred to in the third person in verse 17. To many editors these considerations are not decisive, and the passage is felt to be worthy of the author and an enrichment of the speech. It is possible that it once stood in a different place, as it now separates sections dealing with animals, and is itself separated from the bird sections. Kissane restores an interrogative at the beginning, and as the second line begins with a word which is often used as a correlative interrogative this may be right.

ostrich: *AV* 'peacocks'. The Hebrew word is used nowhere else, and it means 'shrill cries'. Hoffmann, Budde, and others read the word for 'ostrich', found in Lam. 4.3. If M.T. is correct here, we have a poetic name for the ostrich, drawn from its characteristic cry. That the ostrich is meant is beyond doubt.

wave proudly. Innumerable proposals to secure a suitable meaning have been

but are they the pinions and plumage of love?
¹⁴ For she leaves her eggs to the earth,
    and lets them be warmed on the ground,

---

made. *RV* 'rejoiceth' is not very appropriate; nor is *RSV*. Dhorme renders 'is gay', which again is not convincing. Kissane, who turns the verse into a question, renders '(Can the wing of the ostrich) be compared (with the pinions of the stork and falcon)'; on the second line, see below. The point then is that the ostrich cannot fly with her wings, whereas the other birds mentioned can. The verb of M.T. means 'exult', and Strahan's 'flap joyously', while a very free rendering of this, yields perhaps the most appropriate sense. Guillaume (loc. cit., p. 125) gives to the verb an Arabic sense and renders: 'Is the wing of the ostrich weak, Or is it strong like that of the stork and hawk?' It does not seem likely that the first line invited the answer 'Yes' and the second the answer 'No'. For other objections to this rendering cf. D. F. Payne, *ASTI*, v, 1967, pp. 50, 58, 64f.

are they the pinions and plumage of love? A few of the innumerable renderings of this line will give some impression of its difficulties: 'Or (gavest thou) wings and feathers unto the ostrich?' (*AV*); 'But are her pinions and feathers kindly?' (*RV*); 'Or is it strong on the wing like the hawk and the falcon?' (Wright); 'Or (dost thou) love her that lacketh counsel?' (Ball); 'She possesses a gracious plumage and pinions' (Dhorme); 'Though her pinions lack feathers' (Pope); 'Is it the pinion and plumage of the heron?' (Fohrer). For Kissane's rendering see above. To examine all of these, to say nothing of others, and the textual changes they imply, is impossible here. Of the three words in the line the first means 'pinion' in Dt. 32.11; Ps. 91.4. The third means 'plumage' in Ezek. 17.3. The second may be either (*a*) a feminine adjective, meaning 'kindly', or 'pious' (very common), or (*b*) 'stork' (Lev. 11.19; Ps. 104.17; Jer. 8.7). The latter is rendered by the Greek versions and Vulg. 'heron' (cf. Fohrer, above). Both stork and heron are known for their parental affection, and this is reflected in the name. On the other hand the ostrich is popularly supposed to be lacking in parental care (cf. verses 14ff.) and the choice of the second word here, whichever meaning it is held to carry, may be intended to bring this out. For the third word, Kissane substitutes *nēṣ*, which means 'hawk' or 'falcon' in verse 26, for *nōṣāh*='plumage'. It is improbable that the hawk or falcon would be anticipated here. Pope's rendering follows an emendation of Hoffmann's, and is strangely contradicted by his note, which says: 'The ostrich's wings, though absurdly small, are beautifully plumed'. The most likely meaning is 'Or are they the pinions and plumage of the stork (or heron)?' The meaning of the whole verse then is that while the ostrich can flap its wings about, it cannot fly with them as the stork can.

14. leaves: or 'forsakes': Masterman (Hastings's one-volume *DB*, 1909, p. 671a) says: 'During the day the heat of the sun is a sufficient incubator, but at night the birds take turns in keeping the eggs warm. A few scattered eggs, said to be used

¹⁵ forgetting that a foot may crush them.
    and that the wild beasts may trample them.
¹⁶ She deals cruelly with her young, as if they were not hers;
    though her labour be in vain, yet she has no fear;
¹⁷ because God has made her forget wisdom,
    and given her no share in understanding.
¹⁸ When she rouses herself to flee,
    she laughs at the horse and his rider.
¹⁹ 'Do you give the horse his might?
    Do you clothe his neck with strength?

---

for food for the young chicks, are laid after the nest is closed, and these have given rise to the popular view'. M. Dahood (*JBL*, LXXVIII, 1959, pp. 307f.) defends the reputation of the ostrich and says the parents display great solicitude for their young. He maintains that the author was aware of this, and so argues for the meaning 'places (or arranges)', instead of 'leaves' here. Others emend to secure this meaning. In view of verses 15f., it is hard to escape the view that the author shared the popular view.

   16. deals cruelly: this verb recurs in Isa. 63.17, where it is used of hardening the heart. For the thought, cf. Lam. 4.3.
no fear: i.e. no concern. Dahood (*The Bible in Current Catholic Thought*, p. 74) proposes to render 'without a flock'.
   17. Cf. the Arabian proverb 'more stupid than an ostrich'.
   18. rouses herself to flee: the verb is found only here. *AV* and *RV* 'lifteth up herself on high'. Some have thought that 'on high' implies flying through the air, but Gray rejects any need for emendation. Dhorme takes the meaning to be 'rears herself up'. But in Arabic the verb means 'whip (a horse)', and the reference here may be to the flapping of the wings against the body when in flight, which resembles the whipping of a horse. Gray renders 'spurs herself', and so Kissane. J. Boehmer (*ZAW*, N.F., XII, 1935, p. 290) reads 'when she runs fast', but the emendation is violent.
laugheth at the horse: the ostrich is said to attain a speed of 26 miles an hour.
   19. The mention of the horse leads on to the superb verses on the horse, and especially the war horse.
strength: *AV* 'thunder'; *RV* 'the quivering mane'. The word is found only here. It is connected with the verb 'thunder' (37.4f.) and the noun 'thunder' (26.14). The rendering of *RV* rests on the conjectured root meaning of the verb 'to quiver' (cf. Ezek. 27.35, where *RSV* has 'be convulsed'), and many editors have adopted it (so among recent commentators Dhorme, Hölscher, Kissane, Steinmann, Larcher, Weiser, Fohrer, Pope). Davidson thought the meaning was the quivering of the neck, and not the mane alone. Gray objects that noise rather than movement

²⁰ Do you make him leap like the locust?
    His majestic snorting is terrible.
²¹ He paws in the valley, and exults in his strength;
    he goes out to meet the weapons.
²² He laughs at fear, and is not dismayed;
    he does not turn back from the sword.
²³ Upon him rattle the quiver,
    the flashing spear and the javelin.

---

is fundamental to the root (cf. Ps. 96.11; 98.7, 'roar'; in Ezek. 27.35 he disputes
the reading). He desiderates a word parallel to 'strength', such as 'might'. This is
followed by *RSV*. Hontheim emended to secure this meaning, but Gray thought
it precarious to assume a different reading, but offered no defence of it without
emendation. The rendering of *RV* seems to be the most probable, and it is still the
most widely accepted. Dahood (*Biblica*, L, 1959, p. 58) follows *AV* rendering.

20. leap: the verb means 'quiver' or 'shake', and Gray renders 'cause him to
quiver like a locust'. But this does not seem very appropriate. In Jl 2.4 the locust
is compared to a horse in its running, and it would seem probable that the same
comparison is made in reverse here. The reference is probably to the galloping of
the horse. *AV* is wholly inappropriate in rendering 'makest him afraid as a grass-
hopper'.

snorting: the word is a variant form of the word found in Jer. 8.16 (*RSV*
'snorting'). It comes from a root meaning 'blow' (Jer. 6.29), and from it the word
'nostrils' (41.20 (M.T. 12)) comes.

21. He paws: the verb normally means 'dig' and here only in *OT* means 'paw'.
A noun from the cognate Arabic root means 'hoof'. M.T. has 'they paw', but
LXX, Vulg., Syr. read the singular.

in the valley: armies were drawn up for battle in valleys; cf. Gen. 14.8; Jg. 7.1.
But in Ugaritic *'mk* means both 'force' (also in Akkadian; cf. *Chicago Assyrian
Dictionary*, IV, 1958, pp. 157ff.) and 'valley' (cf. Gordon, *Ugaritic Manual*, 1955,
p. 305) and the former sense would fit well here, parallel to 'in strength' (so
Albright, *SVT*, III, 1955, p. 14, and Dahood, *Biblica*, XL, 1959, p. 166). Hence
render 'He paws vigorously'. Impatience to go into the battle is indicated. It is
now clear that the war horse is especially in mind.

23. rattle: this verb is found only here, and it is probably a by-form of the
verb which means 'raise a ringing cry' (in Arabic used of the twanging of the
bow). Here it is used of the rattling of the arrows in the quiver of the rider.
flashing: 'flame of'.
javelin: more probably a scimitar; cf. A. Dupont-Sommer, *RHR*, CXLVIII, 1955,
p. 143n.; K. G. Kuhn, *ThLZ*, LXXXI, 1956, cols. 29f.; G. Molin, *JSS*, I, 1956,
pp. 334ff.

24 With fierceness and rage he swallows the ground;
  he cannot stand still at the sound of the trumpet.
25 When the trumpet sounds, he says "Aha!"
  He smells the battle from afar.
  the thunder of the captains, and the shouting.
26 'Is it by your wisdom that the hawk soars,

---

24. With fierceness and rage. In Ps. 77.18 (M.T. 19); Isa. 14.16 the verbs from which these nouns come are rendered 'shake' and 'tremble'. Both nouns, therefore, indicate excitement rather than anger. Hence Gray renders 'quivering and excited he dashes into the fray'.

swallows the ground. The same idiom is found in Arabic, where a swift horse is called a 'swallower'.

cannot stand still: AV and RV 'neither believeth he'. This was supposed to mean that the horse could hardly believe his own ears for excitement and joy when the attack was sounded on the trumpet. But the root meaning of the verb 'believe' is 'be firm', and from this many editors derive the extended meaning 'stand still'. This is far from sure, and the more usual and well established meaning is more expressive. His pawing the ground has already been mentioned.

25. Kissane transfers the first line to follow the first line of verse 20, where it fits no better than here.

When: or 'as often as'. But there is no verb in M.T., which means lit. 'in the sufficiency of'. I. Eitan (JQR, N.S., XIV, 1923-24, pp. 36ff.) connected the word with an Arabic word meaning 'noise', 'roar': 'At the sound of the trumpet' (so also S. I. Feigin, AJSL, L, 1933-34, p. 219). Pope along quite different lines connects the word with an Ugaritic verb meaning 'sing', and renders 'at the call of the trumpet'.

Aha!: a cry of satisfaction; cf. Ps. 35.21, 25; 40.15 (M.T. 16); Isa. 44.16; Ezek. 25.3; 26.2; 36.2.

smells: by zeugma the verb has three objects, of which it strictly fits but the nearest. P. A. H. de Boer (Words and Meanings, edited by P. R. Ackroyd and B. Lindars, 1968, pp. 29ff.) argues that the verb means 'smells of', or 'recalls', 'suggests'.

shouting: cf. on 8.21.

26ff. Does Job inspire the migration of the hawk, or direct the eagle to build its nest on the lofty crag—so unlike the ostrich (verse 14). They are joined together here since both are birds of prey.

hawk: some eighteen species of hawks exist in Palestine.

soars: this verb, found only here, is connected with the word rendered 'pinions' in verse 13. Dhorme concludes that the verb means 'grow feathers', but most more naturally take it to mean 'use the wings', or 'soar'.

and spreads his wings toward the south?
27 Is it at your command that the eagle mounts up
    and makes his nest on high?
28 On the rock he dwells and makes his home
    in the fastness of the rocky crag.
29 Thence he spies out the prey;
    his eyes behold it afar off.
30 His young ones suck up blood;
    and where the slain are, there is he.'

40 And the LORD said to Job:
    2 'Shall a faultfinder contend with the Almighty?

---

towards the south: this refers to the migratory instinct of many of the smaller species of hawks. Duhm thought the meaning was 'against the south wind', indicating the strength and courage of the hawk. But this would be expressed differently in Hebrew.

27. eagle: cf. on 9.26. Some render 'vulture' here, but 'eagle' better carries in English the associations of this passage. LXX has 'vulture'; Vulg. 'eagle'. Four species of vultures and eight of eagles are found in Palestine.

nest on high: the eagle sometimes, the vulture always, nests in inaccessible places.

28. Cf. Jer. 49.16.

rocky crag: lit. 'tooth of rock'; the same expression in 1 Sam. 14.4.

29. Testimonies to the keen-sightedness of the eagle are cited by Strahan and Dhorme. On the swiftness of the eagle to descend on the prey, cf. Dt. 28.49; Jer. 48.40; 49.22.

30. Cf. Mt. 24.28; Lk. 17.37.

suck up. The verb which stands here is otherwise unknown. With the addition of a letter or the omission of a letter it can be connected with the Aramaic equivalent of the verb used in 1 Kg. 21.19 (*RSV* 'lick up').

JOB'S ANSWER TO THE DIVINE CHALLENGE 40.1–5

Summarily Yahweh calls on Job to answer the speech he has just listened to, and Job in abasement confesses that he is reduced to silence. If the second Divine speech is secondary, Job's speech is continued in 42.2–6 (see p. 341).

40.1. This verse was lacking in LXX, and many editors omit it, on the ground that it separates the last verses of the first Divine speech (see below) from the rest of the speech. Alternatively we may suppose that Yahweh paused at the end of the speech and then asked Job if he had no reply to make.

2. a faultfinder: *RV* 'he that cavilleth'. The word is found only here, but from

He who argues with God, let him answer it.'
³ Then Job answered the LORD:
⁴ 'Behold, I am of small account; what shall I answer thee?
   I lay my hand on my mouth.
⁵ I have spoken once, and I will not answer;
   twice, but I will proceed no further."
⁶ Then the LORD answered Job out of the whirlwind:
⁷ 'Gird up your loins like a man;
   I will question you, and you declare to me.
⁸ Will you even put me in the wrong?
   Will you condemn me that you may be justified?
⁹ Have you an arm like God,
   and can you thunder with a voice like his?
¹⁰ 'Deck yourself with majesty and dignity;
   clothe yourself with glory and splendour.
¹¹ Pour forth the overflowings of your anger,
   and look on every one that is proud, and abase him.
¹² Look on every one that is proud, and bring him low;

---

a common root, meaning 'correct', 'reprove'. Ehrlich read a finite verb *yāsûr* =
'depart', 'come to an end' (cf. Isa. 11.13) for *yissôr*, and for **contend** read 'contention'. Dhorme similarly read *yāsûr*, but with the meaning 'turn aside' 'yield'.
For 'contend' he read the participle 'contender'; 'Will he who argues with Shaddai
yield?' (so Pope). K. Fullerton (*AJSL*, XLIX, 1932–33, pp. 197–211) defends M.T.
(cf. F. Zimmermann, ibid., LI, 1934–35, pp. 46f.). Either Job must show his competence to criticize God by answering the questions that have been put to him or
he must forfeit his right to criticize.

4. Job at once admits that he cannot face the challenge, and confesses his
insignificance.

of small account. The verb means 'be swift', 'be light', and then 'be contemptible'
(cf. Gen. 16.4f.; 1 Sam. 2.30; Nah. 1.14).

hand on my mouth: cf. 21.5; 29.9.

5. I will not answer. Hitzig with the change of one letter read 'I will not
repeat it', and many editors have followed this as yielding a closer parallel to the
second line. But the change is unnecessary. He is challenged to answer and he
declines to answer, having already said all he would say.

THE SECOND DIVINE SPEECH 40.7–41.34

After Job has confessed and submitted, a second Divine speech comes, as Peake says, perilously near nagging. It is probable that the parts of this speech dealing with Behemoth and Leviathan are secondary (see below). We should then be left with but a few verses (40.7–14) for this second speech. In that case it is probable that these verses should be joined to the first speech, and Job's words of submission in 40.4f. be joined to 42.2–6 to form a single speech of Job's. The first Divine speech had been directed against Job's venturing to confront a God whose ways were so far beyond his fathoming. Now it turns to Job's complaint that God is unrighteous. He is therefore with new irony invited to assume the control of the world and show how it should better be run. After this comes the passages on Behemoth and Leviathan, which have nothing to do with this, and which would better have stood with the animal passages in the first speech. As it stands then the speech falls into three parts: Job invited to assume the throne of the universe (40.7–14); the description of Behemoth (verses 15–24); the description of Leviathan (41.1–34).

JOB IS INVITED TO ASSUME THE THRONE OF THE UNIVERSE 40.7–14

If Job's condemnation of the injustice which marks God's rule is justified, then he ought to be able to show God how it should be governed. He is therefore invited to show that he has not merely the moral integrity but the power to govern it better.

7. Cf. 38.3.

8. put me in the wrong: lit. 'break (or render ineffectual) my judgment'. Had Job only defended his own integrity, he would have been wholly justified, as the Prologue makes clear. But beyond this he had impugned the righteousness of God, and had declared God to be in the wrong and had challenged God's moral right to be in charge of the world.

9. Even if Job thought he had the wisdom and integrity to rule the world, has he the power? Such rule requires not only skill but resources. Unless he has these resources, criticism is idle.

arm: cf. on 22.8.

thunder: cf. 37.2ff. The governance of the world involves the power to terrify and to keep under restraint the wicked. It is no task for the armchair critic, such as Job has proved himself, and an academic idea of the sort of rule the world needs has to be matched with the might to implement it before it is of any value.

10. Job is invited to adorn himself with the attributes of power.

clothe yourself with glory and splendour: cf. Ps. 104.1, where the same terms are used. The expression 'glory and splendour' recurs in Ps. 21.5 (M.T. 6); 96.6; 111.3 (though there are variations of rendering in *RSV*).

11. Pour forth: the term used in 37.11 of 'scattering' the lightning. Here Job is invited to exercise power. He had supposed that the moral government of the world required the swift punishment of the wicked, and he is invited to effect it.

12. The first line is identical with verse 11*b*, save that the verb **bring him low** is a synonym of 'abase him'. Duhm proposed the change of a letter in the word for **proud** in this verse, giving 'lofty', and so Dhorme and Kissane. But Fohrer

and tread down the wicked where they stand.
13 Hide them all in the dust together;
    bind their faces in the world below.
14 Then will I also acknowledge to you,
    that your own right hand can give you victory.
15 Behold, Be'hemoth,

---

and others find no reason to change. Some editors strike out verse 12*a* altogether.

13. in the dust: probably meaning 'in the grave'. The cutting off of the wicked had been affirmed as a fact of experience by the friends, but demanded by Job, who had denied that this happened in experience. He is now ironically invited to effect it.

bind: used of binding something on the head in Exod. 29.9. In 34.17 used in the sense of governing a kingdom. Dhorme finds here the meaning 'imprison', found in Arabic, and then understands 'their faces' to stand for 'their persons'.

in the world below: M.T. 'in the hidden (place)'. This probably means in the dark recesses of Sheol.

14. If Job is able to assume the authority and to exercise this government of the world, God will acknowledge his power. God is one whose power is equal to his purposes (cf. Ps. 98.1; Isa. 59.16; 63.5). Let Job show that his power is equal to the purposes he would impose upon God.

THE DESCRIPTION OF BEHEMOTH 40.15–24

This seems out of place in this speech. It is irrelevant to the theme of the preceding verses. Its ten verses are more than were devoted to any of the creatures in the first speech, though less than Leviathan gets. They give a description of the bodily form of Behemoth, more suitable for a text-book than the brilliant sketches of the first speech, and are generally recognized to be of inferior poetic quality. Moreover, if Behemoth and Leviathan are real creatures (see below), they are probably Egyptian creatures, and almost certainly not Palestinian (but see below), whereas all the creatures of the first speech were such as could be found in Palestine. Some scholars, including Dhorme, defend the retention of this and the Leviathan passage (see pp. 14f), but the view that they are an addition seems more probable.

15. Behemoth: the view that Behemoth and Leviathan are mythological creatures and not real animals has been maintained by Gunkel (*Schöpfung und Chaos*, 1895, pp. 41ff.) and Cheyne (*EB*, 1, 1899, cols. 519ff.), Pope, and some others. But most regard them as real creatures, though it is agreed that not all details are accurate and that either the writer deliberately exaggerated, or was not perfectly acquainted with the animals he depicted. By most Behemoth is identified with the hippopotamus, but G. R. Driver (*Studi orientalistici* (Levi della Vida Festschrift), 1, 1956, pp. 234ff.) identified it with the crocodile.

which I made as I made you;
he eats grass like an ox.
16 Behold, his strength in his loins,
   and his power in the muscles of his belly.
17 He makes his tail stiff like a cedar;
   the sinews of his thighs are knit together.
18 His bones are tubes of bronze,
   his limbs like bars of iron.
19 'He is the first of the works of God;
   let him who made him bring near his sword!

Behemoth, which I made as I made you: Driver (loc. cit., p. 235) emends to secure 'the chief of the beasts, the crocodile'.

he eats grass: the hippopotamus eats mainly grass and aquatic plants, and makes heavy inroads on growing crops by night. Driver (loc. cit., p. 236) renders 'he eats cattle like grass'.

16. **in his loins:** Gray notes that this is not very distinctive, since the loins were proverbially the seat of strength (cf. Nah. 2.1 (M.T. 2); Ps. 69.23 (M.T. 24); Dt. 33.11).

muscles of his belly: these are said to be particularly strong in the hippopotamus.

17. **makes . . . stiff.** This verb is found only here, and its meaning is uncertain. *AV* and *RV* have 'moveth'. *BDB* and *KB* render 'bends' (so Gray and Fohrer), after the meaning of an Arabic cognate, and supported by Targ. Pope renders 'arches'. LXX and Syr. render 'erects' and Vulg. *stringit*, whence Ball invokes another Arabic root to yield the meaning '(his tail) is rigid' (cf. Wetzstein in Delitzsch, Budde, Duhm), and Dhorme renders 'stiffens' (so Strahan, Szczygiel, Buttenwieser, Hölscher, Steinmann, Larcher). This seems more appropriate, since the tail of the hippopotamus, which is very short, would be oddly compared to a cedar. If the point of the comparison is its rigidity it would be less odd, though still somewhat incongruous.

18. **bones . . . limbs:** these words are really synonymous, the one being Hebrew and the other Aramaic (cf. on 39.5).

19. **first:** better than *AV* and *RV* 'chief'. The reference is perhaps to Gen. 1.24, where the first of the animal creation is said to be 'cattle', i.e. *behēmāh*.

ways: here='works' (LXX renders by 'moulding'; in 34.21; 36.23 LXX has 'works'). In Ugaritic the corresponding word may mean 'power', and this meaning has been proposed here (cf. H. Zirker, *BZ*, N.F., II, 1958, p. 293), but there is no need to find this meaning (cf. also on 36.23).

God: cf. 39.17.

let the one who made him bring near his sword: this is a literal rendering of M.T., but it conveys little clear meaning. *RV* marg. 'He that made him hath

²⁰ For the mountains yield food for him
    where all the wild beasts play.
²¹ Under the lotus plants he lies,
    in the covert of the reeds and in the marsh.

---

furnished him with his sword' would be more intelligible; but it is a doubtful translation, though it was much favoured by older commentators (e.g. Delitzsch, Zöckler). The sword is supposed to be a reference to the teeth or tusks of the hippopotamus, which shear vegetation like a scythe or sword. It is hard to think of the teeth as a sword, or of a sword as an instrument of mowing. It would rather suggest a weapon to be used against an enemy, and Pope finds a reference to the slaying of Behemoth by God, and adduces rabbinical fancies about the slaying of Behemoth and Leviathan (cf. also Larcher, 'his Maker threatened him with the sword'). LXX has 'made to be played with by my angels'(cf. Ps. 104.26). Hoffmann proposed to read 'who was made to draw near to his desert' and Gunkel 'who was made to dominate the desert'. But these are inappropriate, since the hippopotamus is a creature of the marsh and not of the desert. Giesebrecht (*GGA*, 1895, p. 595; so Driver, loc. cit., p. 237) suggested 'who was made to dominate his companions' reading *he‘āśû* with LXX for *hā‘ōśô*='the one who made him', and *yiggōś ḥaberāw* for *yaggēś ḥarbô*='let him bring near his sword'). This was followed by Duhm with the slight change of *yiggōś* to *nōgēś*, without change of meaning, and this is accepted by Strahan, Dhorme, Hölscher, Weiser, Steinmann, Fohrer (cf. Gray 'may be right'). Kissane transfers an emended 41.17 to precede this verse and regards this verse as the prayer that God would destroy Behemoth. Terrien declares the line corrupt beyond recognition. It is improbable that the sword is God's sword, and equally that the sword is for the obtaining of food. More likely is it that the sword is Behemoth's, and that it is for use against his enemies. It is then probable that the reference is to the sharp, chisel-edged tusks with which the hippopotamus attacks its enemies when aroused. If the rendering of *RV* marg. could be accepted with confidence it would yield the best sense.

20. food: Ball equates this word (*bûl*), found only here (in Isa. 44.19='block (of wood)') with Akkadian *bûlu*='beasts', and renders 'the cattle of the hills gaze (*yišta’û* for *yiśe’û*) at him (in wonder)'. Most take the word to be for *y^ebûl*= 'produce of the soil'. Dhorme connects the word with Akkadian *biltu*='tribute' and renders 'the mountains bring him tribute' (in Ezr. 4.13, 20; 7.24 *biltu* appears as *b^elô*). Instead of **yield** (plural), Duhm reads singular: 'he takes to himself the produce of the mountains'. On this view or that of *RSV* the thought is of the vegetable diet of the hippopotamus. Driver (loc. cit., p. 237), who sees the crocodile here, follows Duhm in the verb and Ball in the noun, and so secures: 'he takes the cattle of the hills for himself'. Of other proposals mention may be made of 'Niles' (Wright) or 'rivers' (Siegfried) for 'mountains', and 'are at ease' (Pope)

²² For his shade the lotus trees cover him;
   the willows of the brook surround him.
²³ Behold, if the river is turbulent he is not frightened;
   he is confident though Jordan rushes against his mouth.
²⁴ Can one take him with hooks,
   or pierce his nose with a snare?

---

for 'yield . . . for him' (following Ball for the noun: 'the beasts of the steppe
relax'). The rendering of RSV is preferable to any of the others. Against it is the
consideration that in Egypt mountains are at some distance from the Nile and are
bare. But lower hills could also be called 'mountains', and the hippopotamus can
climb steep slopes in search of food despite its clumsy appearance. In the upper
valley of the Nile vegetation on the hills is more abundant.

21. lotus plants: the same word as in verse 22. Why RSV calls them 'plants'
here and 'trees' there is not clear. The *Zizyphus Lotus*, a thorny tree found in
Syria and the whole of Africa, and which likes hot and damp valleys (so Wetzstein
in Delitzsch), and not *Nymphaea Lotus*, the water lily, is intended. In Syria it is
seldom more than 24 ft. high, but in Egypt it is 'far stronger and taller' (Wetzstein).
The word is found in OT only here and in verse 22, but the cognate name is
known in Arabic. P. Humbert (*ZAW*, N.F., xxi, 1949-50, p. 206) connects the
word rather with a Coptic word, and renders 'branches'.
marsh: cf. on 8.11.

22. the brook: or 'wady'. This is more suggestive of Palestine than of Egypt.
G. Haas (*BASOR*, no. 132, 1953, pp. 30ff.) offers evidence that the hippopotamus
was found in the coastal area of Palestine in the Iron Age.

23. is turbulent: the verb ordinarily means 'oppress', which is unsuitable here.
Hence various emendations have been proposed: 'overflows' (Beer); 'sinks'
(Gunkel, Budde); 'gushes' (Duhm). But Dhorme derives the meaning 'swells
violently' from a fundamental meaning 'be strong'. Guillaume (*Promise and
Fulfilment*, p. 126) gives to the verb an Arabic sense: 'rises and falls'.
is confident: Driver (*Studies in Old Testament Prophecy*, ed. H. H. Rowley, 1950,
p. 60) argues for the meaning 'lies flat'; cf. Guillaume, loc. cit.
Jordan: this does not imply a Palestinian scene for the habitat of Behemoth, but
is merely an illustration of a swift running current. The name of the Jordan means
'descender', and some reaches of the river show a rapid descent.
against his mouth: the picture is that of the hippopotamus submerged save for
his muzzle, with a fast stream running against him, but in no way disturbed.
Dhorme refers to buffaloes on the edges of Lake Huleh in this position, and Pope
thinks the poet has drawn on memories of the buffalo in his description of the
imaginary Behemoth.

24. Can one? No interrogative is expressed (though this is often left to be
understood), and the line is short. Hence many editors add at the beginning 'Who

41   'Can you draw out Levi'athan with a fishhook,
         or press down his tongue with a cord?
2 Can you put a rope in his nose,
   or pierce his jaw with a hook?
3 Will he make many supplications to you?
   Will he speak to you soft words?
4 Will he make a covenant with you
   to take him for your servant for ever?
5 Will you play with him as with a bird,
   or will you put him on leash for your maidens?
6 Will your traders bargain over him?

---

indeed?' (*mî-hû'*, which could easily have fallen out after *pîhû* = 'his mouth' at the end of verse 23).

with hooks: M.T. 'with his eyes', which *RV* understands to mean 'when he is on the watch'. Ehrlich thought of the hunter's eyes ensnaring Behemoth by staring at him. But the parallel suggests that it is the animal's eyes. Some have thought the meaning is 'take him by the eyes', i.e. by attacking his eyes and blinding him. Dhorme refers to a technique mentioned by Herodotus, which consisted in stuffing the eyes of the animal with clay. Others have resorted to emendation 'by his teeth' (Reiske); 'in his lair' (Kissane); 'with fish hooks' (Ball); 'by blinding its eyes' (Driver, loc. cit.), reading *ḥaḇeʾappēl ʿênāw* for *beʿênāw*. Of these the proposal of Ball would give the most appropriate sense, and the reference is then to the difficulty of hunting the hippopotamus. This reading seems to be followed by *RSV*.

with a snare: this is an odd thing to pierce a nose with. With a slight metathesis of the consonants Ehrlich read 'with thorns (or barbs)' and this is followed by Dhorme, Driver (loc. cit.), and Pope.

THE DESCRIPTION OF LEVIATHAN 41.1–34 (M.T. 40.25–41.26)

The thirty-four verses devoted to Leviathan are even more out of balance than the verses devoted to Behemoth, and again we have in much of the passage a minute description quite unlike the passages in the first speech. Hence this passage, like the Behemoth passage, is generally rejected as secondary (see above, on 40.15–24). B. D. Eerdmans (*Studies in Job*, 1939, pp. 27ff.) held that the Leviathan passage consisted only of verses 1–8, after which the description reverted to the hippopotamus, while Driver (loc. cit. on 40.15), similarly limited the passage devoted to Leviathan.

1. **Leviathan:** that Leviathan was a mythological creature is beyond question (cf. on 3.8), and some editors so understand the name here (cf. on 40.15), and Gunkel (loc. cit.) identifies Leviathan with Tiamat. Pope cites passages from Ras Shamra texts showing beyond doubt the mythological character of Leviathan,

which was generally recognized before those texts were known. But this does not prove that a mythological creature is being described here. When Egypt is called Rahab (Isa. 30.7) a mythological name is applied to a real nation, and most scholars hold the view that here the crocodile is described under a mythological name. B. D. Eerdmans (loc. cit.) argued for the dolphin, while S. Spinner (*BZ*, XXIII, 1935-36, p. 148) identified Leviathan with the tunny fish, and Driver (loc. cit. on 40.15) sees in Leviathan the whale. There is evidence that the crocodile was found in Palestine in both ancient and modern times (cf. Gray and Kissane), but it seems probable that the author was thinking principally of the crocodile as an Egyptian creature.

fish hook: a word found only here and in Isa. 19.8; Hab. 1.15. The author clearly thought it was impossible to capture a crocodile by this method. But Herodotus (II.70) tells how one was caught in this way.

press down: lit. 'cause to sink', if this is the root found in Am. 8.8; 9.5. But Sam. uses this root in Lev. 8.13 in the sense 'bind', and Dhorme finds this sense here. Those who follow *RSV* rendering suggest that when the line was drawn tightly, it pressed the tongue down. But Herodotus (II.68) records the popular idea that the crocodile has no tongue. In fact it has an immobile tongue, attached to the lower jaw. Gray supposes that the author would have shared the erroneous view. But of this we cannot be sure. Hoffmann substituted 'to his teeth' for **his tongue.** But this is generally rejected. Peake thought the meaning was 'Can you put a rope round his tongue and lower jaw when you have caught him?' This would be more natural if we render 'bind'.

2. rope: lit. 'reed' (cf. Isa. 9.14 (M.T. 13); 19.15; 58.5); here a rope made of reeds. The figure is that of the treatment of prisoners, which is well attested of the Assyrians. Dhorme cites an inscription of Ashurbanipal in which he declares that he pierced a prisoner's jaw and put a rope through his chin (cf. Isa. 37.29).

3. Leviathan is here treated as though he were a human prisoner. Will he plead for mercy as such a prisoner might? Commentators fancifully suppose there may be an allusion here to crocodile tears.

4. Here the impossibility of domesticating Leviathan is indicated. Ironically the question is asked whether he could be induced to make an agreement to enter into service (cf. Exod. 21.5f.).

a servant for ever: cf. Dt. 15.17; 1 Sam. 27.12.

5. Can he be made a children's plaything, like a captive bird? Such playthings are still found in the east.

put him on leash for your maidens: D. Winton Thomas (*VT*, XIV, 1964, pp. 114ff.) renders 'tie him with a string like a young sparrow', adducing an Arabic cognate. Cf. also R. Gordis, ibid., pp. 491ff.

6. traders: better 'associates', or 'partners'. Fishermen commonly work in companies, and divide the catch when it is landed (cf. Lk. 5.10); and this involves bargaining with one another.

bargain over: cf. on 6.27.

> Will they divide him up among the merchants?
> 7 Can you fill his skin with harpoons,
>   or his head with fishing spears?
> 8 Lay hands on him;
>   think of the battle; you will not do it again!
> 9 Behold, the hope of a man is disappointed;
>   he is laid low even at the sight of him.

---

divide him up: the catch has to be sold, and Leviathan is too big to be sold to a single merchant. He must be cut up into pieces.

merchants: lit. 'Canaanites', but this name is elsewhere used for 'merchants' since the Canaanites were the merchants *par excellence* in the world in which Israel lived (so Prov. 31.24; Isa. 23.8; Zeph. 1.11).

7. harpoons . . . fishing spears: both words occur only here. The former is connected with a word for thorns (cf. Num. 33.55), and the second comes from a root meaning 'whirr'. One of the words for 'locust' (Dt. 28.42) and the word for 'cymbals' come from this root. Both words clearly represented barbed implements, and the second would seem to have been thrown from a distance and to have whizzed through the air. Neither could make any impression on the hard skin of Leviathan.

8. By the vivid imperatives effective advice is given. Before you come to close quarters with Leviathan realize what you are doing! No one lives to repeat his folly.

9. With this verse chapter 41 begins in M.T. Some editors hold that from this point the description of Behemoth is resumed (see above on verses 1–34). Duhm transfers verses 9–12 to form the termination of the Behemoth section. Merx and Bickell transfer verses 9–12 to precede 38.1, making them, after rewriting the verses, a divine soliloquy.

the hope of a man: M.T. 'his hope'. If the text is retained, the meaning must be the hope of any assailant, but this is not how we should expect it to be expressed. Budde reads 'thy hope', and so Steuernagel, Hölscher, Kissane, Larcher, Steinmann, Fohrer. This has the insignificant support of 1 MS. As there is no antecedent for the pronoun, Dhorme transposes this and the following verse, and so Driver (loc. cit., p. 237). This is probably to be followed.

he is laid low even at the sight of him: M.T. has an interrogative particle at the beginning of this line, but this is omitted by Gray, Dhorme and others. Budde reads 'thou art laid low' (so Steuernagel, Hölscher, Steinmann). Kissane changes the vowels and secures 'even a mighty man is flung down at the sight of him'. Gunkel (op. cit., pp. 55f.) read 'his appearance casts down even a god', and Cheyne (*JQR*, IX, 1896–97, p. 579) 'even divine beings the fear of him brings low'. This is closely followed by Pope ('were not the gods cast down at the sight

¹⁰ No one is so fierce that he dares to stir him up.
   Who then is he that can stand before me?
¹¹ Who has given to me, that I should repay him?
   Whatever is under the whole heaven is mine.

---

of him?'), who adduces mythological material from Mesopotamia and Ugarit. There seems no need to bring mythological material to a text which is intelligible as it stands. Any man who would lay hands on Leviathan is warned not to, or he will have bitter reason to regret it, since he will collapse as soon as he sees him.

10. **No one is so fierce:** it is probable that the word 'fierce' (lit. 'cruel') characterizes Leviathan rather than his awakener. Hence Gray: 'is he not too fierce for one to stir him up?'; Dhorme: 'Is he not cruel, as soon as he is awakened?'; Kissane: 'is he not fierce if one rouse him up?' (so Steinmann, Pope; cf. Driver (loc. cit.), Larcher). All of these agree substantially in finding the verse to be a warning against the folly of arousing Leviathan. *RSV* (so Hölscher) is in fundamental agreement, but is less good.

before me: if this reading is correct, the meaning is that if it is madness to arouse Leviathan, it is much more foolish to challenge God, as Job has done. But many mss. and Targ. read 'before him', keeping the thought on Leviathan, and this is more natural (so Dhorme, Hölscher, Driver (loc. cit.), Pope and others).

11. **Who has given to me that I should repay him?:** the Hebrew says 'who has confronted me?' (cf. *AV* 'prevented me', i.e. come to meet me). Nowhere else does the verb carry the idea of making a gift. Moreover the sense thus obtained is alien to the context. It would mean that no one has any claim on God, but this could have nothing to do with Leviathan. If M.T. is retained in verse 10 it would mean that to challenge God is more dangerous than to rouse Leviathan. But no one would rouse Leviathan because he had made him a gift and now had a claim on him. To turn this in verse 11 to the pressing of a claim on God would be to get right away from Leviathan. LXX has 'who will confront me and remain (i.e. be safe)?' This involves reading *wayyišlām* for *wa'ašallēm*, and it is followed by Merx and very many editors. It is much more appropriate to M.T. of verse 10, and it keeps to the normal meaning of the verb 'confront'. It emphasizes that if one cannot rouse Leviathan with impunity, still less can one challenge God with impunity. But it is probable that we should here again read 'who has confronted him and remained safe?' (cf. verse 10) and keep the thought entirely to Leviathan (so Gunkel (loc. cit.), Cheyne (loc. cit.), and very many editors).

Whatever is under the whole heaven is mine: this again has nothing to do with Leviathan, but is held to mean that none can have a claim against God since he is the owner of all that is. But the context is not about the legal invalidity of challenging Leviathan, but of the physical inequality of the conflict. By very

¹² 'I will not keep silence concerning his limbs,
      or his mighty strength, or his goodly frame.
¹³ Who can strip off his outer garment?
      Who can penetrate his double coat of mail?
¹⁴ Who can open the doors of his face?
      Round about his teeth is terror.
¹⁵ His back is made of rows of shields,

---

slight changes in the words *lî hû'* = 'is mine' we get *lō' hû'* or *lō' 'eḥād* = 'there is no one', or *mî hû'* = 'who indeed?' Very many editors follow one or other of these readings. The meaning of the line then is 'There is no one under the whole heaven who could face Leviathan and survive'.

12. The thought now turns to the detailed description of Leviathan.

limbs: cf. on 18.13. Duhm connected the word with 'boastings' (11.3) and, with the change of a letter in the verb rendered 'keep silence', secured 'he would not renew his boastings', keeping the thought on the challenger of Leviathan. But there is no need to depart from *RSV*. The line is the introduction to the new section of the passage.

or his mighty strength, or his goodly frame: lit. 'and the word of might and the grace of his arrangement'. One would scarcely associate grace with the crocodile. With slight changes Dhorme reads 'and I will tell (*wā'ₐdabbēr* for *ûdebar* = 'and the word of') of his incomparable might (*geḇūrāṯô 'ên 'ereḵ* for *geḇūrôṯ weḥîn 'erkô*)'. This is very attractive (cf. Driver, *AJSL*, LII, 1935–36, p. 168). It follows Houbigant for the first part and Ehrlich for the second. Less convincing is Pope's rendering 'Did I not silence his boasting by the powerful word Hayyin prepared?', where Hayyin is an epithet of an Ugaritic deity, here thought to stand for the master enchanter who prepared spells before a military encounter. But why import an encounter between Yahweh and Leviathan into a context where nothing suggests it?

13. **his outer garment:** lit. 'the face of his garment'. This is thought by many to indicate the scales of the crocodile. Dhorme takes it to mean the front of his garment as opposed to the back.

his double coat of mail: M.T. 'his double bridle' (so *AV* and *RV*). This is held to mean his upper and lower jaws, but these could scarcely be described as a bridle, and moreover they are referred to in the next verse. LXX read *siryôn* = 'armour', 'coat of mail' (Jer. 46.4; 51.3) instead of *resen* = 'bridle', and so most editors.

14. The formidable teeth of the crocodile inspire terror. In the upper jaw there are thirty-six, and in the lower thirty.

of his face: Syr. has 'of his mouth', and some editors needlessly follow.

15. **His back:** M.T. '(his) pride'. But LXX, Aq., Vulg. read 'his back' (*gēwōh*)

shut up closely as with a seal.

16 One is so near to another
    that no air can come between them.
17 They are joined one to another;
    they clasp each other and cannot be separated.
18 His sneezings flash forth light,
    and his eyes are like the eyelids of the dawn.
19 Out of his mouth go flaming torches;
    sparks of fire leap forth.
20 Out of his nostrils comes forth smoke,

---

instead of 'his pride' (ga'ᵃwāh), and almost all editors follow. The reference is to
the rows of hard scales which cover the crocodile.

shut up closely as with a seal: this may mean that the scales are tightly packed
together, and that they are as alike as a row of seal impressions. But instead
of 'closely' (ṣār) LXX read 'stone' or 'flint' (ṣōr) and so some editors. The
thought then is of the hardness of the rock-like seal with which the scales are
compared.

16f. It is here that the tightly packed character of the scales is mentioned. Not
even air can get between them.

18. sneezings: *AV* and *RV* have the obsolete 'neesings'. The vapour or spray
that issued from the nostrils of the crocodile flashed in the sunlight. Pope, who
interprets Leviathan as a mythological creature, finds here the breathing out of
flames of fire.

like the eyelids of the dawn: cf. 3.9. The reference is to the reddish eyes of the
crocodile. In Egyptian hieroglyphs the eyes of the crocodile are said to symbolise
the dawn. Delitzsch says: 'The eyes of the crocodile alone by themselves are no
hieroglyph: how could they have been represented by themselves as *crocodile's
eyes*? But in the Ramesseum and elsewhere the crocodile appears with a head
pointing upwards . . ., and the *eyes* of the crocodile are rendered specially
prominent. . . . The crocodile's eyes are, notwithstanding, a figure of the light
shining forth from the darkness'. Pope again rejects the reference to the crocodile,
and interprets of fire issuing from the eyes. But the eyelids of the dawn emit rays
of light, not flashes of fire.

19ff. When the crocodile issues from the water, it expels its pent-up breath
together with water in a hot stream from its mouth, and this looks like a stream
of fire in the sunshine. Peake observes that the author may have embroidered his
picture with reminiscences of stories of fire-breathing dragons, while Pope
represents this whole passage as just such a story.

20. nostrils: a word found only here, from the root which occurs in 39.20.

as from a boiling pot and burning rushes.
21 His breath kindles coals,
and a flame comes forth from his mouth.
22 In his neck abides strength,
and terror dances before him.
23 The folds of his flesh cleave together,
firmly cast upon him and immovable.
24 His heart is as hard as a stone,
hard as the nether millstone.
25 When he raises himself up the mighty are afraid;
at the crashing they are beside themselves.
26 Though the sword reaches him, it does not avail;
nor the spear, the dart, or the javelin.
27 He counts iron as straw,
and bronze as rotten wood.
28 The arrow cannot make him flee;
for him slingstones are turned to stubble.
29 Clubs are counted as stubble;
he laughs at the rattle of javelins.

a boiling pot and burning rushes: the word 'burning' is not expressed in M.T. 'Rushes' is the word found in verse 2 (M.T. 40.26), there rendered 'rope'. *AV* here has 'caldron'. This rests on the Arabic rendering of Saʿadia, but is without philological justification. Syr. and Vulg. have 'a seething and boiling pot' (reading *ʾōḡēm* for *ʾaḡmôn*), and this was proposed by Bickell and is generally followed.

21. Cf. verse 19. Strahan observes that a certain plausibility is given to the mythological theory by the hyperbolical language.

22. neck: this is not prominent in the crocodile. The neck is elsewhere thought of as the seat of strength (cf. on 15.26; also Ps. 75.5 (M.T. 6)).

terror: better 'dismay'. The word is found only here, and it comes from a root meaning 'languish' (cf. Ps. 88.9 (M.T. 10); Jer. 31.12, 25). Here it represents the dismay which the crocodile inspires, a dismay which is said to dance before him, where the dancing is transferred from the panic-stricken victims to the dismay itself. F. M. Cross (*VT*, II, 1952, p. 163) with the metathesis of two letters reads 'strength' instead of 'terror', and justifies by reference to an Ugaritic passage, but M.T. yields a satisfactory meaning.

23. folds: lit. 'fallings'.

firmly cast: cf. on 37.10. Dhorme derives from a different root, meaning 'press', and renders 'if pressed, it does not yield'. In either case it is the hardness of the flesh of the crocodile that is indicated.

24. hard: the same word as that found in verse 23 ('firmly cast'). The triple repetition of this word is perhaps deliberate to emphasize the effect. Many editors regard it as an inelegance of style, and Duhm rejects the end of verse 23 and the whole of verse 24. The hardness of the heart here indicates fearlessness and cruelty. **nether millstone:** this was harder and heavier than the upper millstone for obvious reasons.

25. Kissane transfers this verse to follow 40.18, but the transfer is arbitrary. The verse is difficult, and it has occasioned much discussion. **When he raises himself up** could be so rendered, or 'at his majesty', which Dhorme prefers. **The mighty** could be so rendered (cf. Ezek. 31.11; 32.21), or 'the gods'. Aq., Sym., Targ., Syr. support the former (Vulg. 'angels'); Pope follows the latter, and claims that this is proof of the mythological character of the passage, adducing evidence of the cowering of the gods in Mesopotamian and Ugaritic texts. Beer, Budde, Steuernagel, Ehrlich, Dhorme, and Hölscher change one letter to secure 'the billows'. **At the crashing** (lit. 'at the breakings'; cf. AV) could be rendered 'by reason of consternation' (so RV) or 'breakers (of the sea)'. Reiske and many others divide the word to yield 'the breakers of the sea'. **Are beside themselves** (lit. 'lose themselves') is rendered by Dhorme 'retire' and by AV 'purify themselves' (as in Num. 8.21). With so many possibilities it is not surprising that translations are numerous. Suggested emendations offer yet other possibilities. Dhorme's rendering 'The billows are afraid of his majesty; the waves of the sea draw back' does not seem relevant to this context, where it is a question of the formidable defence of Leviathan against any weapons that can be brought against him. RSV rendering of the first line seems quite satisfactory, but 'at the crashing' yields little clear meaning. In Isa. 65.14 this word is rendered 'anguish (of spirit)'. Just as 'lowly' (Ps. 138.6) and 'lowly of spirit' (Isa. 57.15) are synonymous, so 'anguish' (here in the intensive plural) may be used in the sense of 'anguish of spirit', and the second line be rendered, after RV 'in their dire consternation they are beside themselves'. P. Joüon (MFO, V, ii, 1912, p. 432) emended to secure a parallel to the first line: 'and strong men are terrified'. But rhythmically this is inferior to M.T.

26ff. Every kind of weapon is useless to bring against Leviathan. His natural defences render him impervious to them all.

it does not avail: lit. 'it does not stand', i.e. it does not penetrate, but glances off. **the dart or the javelin:** these words are found only here, the first probably from a root meaning 'throw' and the second the equivalent of an Arabic word meaning 'a short arrow'.

28. arrow: lit. 'son of the bow'; cf. Lam. 3.13 ('sons of his quiver').

29. Clubs: another word found only here. An Arabic cognate yields the meaning 'club'. **javelins:** not the same word as in verse 26, but the word found in 39.23 (see note there).

30 His underparts are like sharp potsherds;
  he spreads himself like a threshing sledge on the mire.
31 He makes the deep boil like a pot;
  he makes the sea like a pot of ointment.
32 Behind him he leaves a shining wake;
  one would think the deep to be hoary.
33 Upon earth there is not his like,
  a creature without fear.
34 He beholds everything that is high;

---

30. His underparts: so *RV*; or 'under him' (so *AV*).
like sharp potsherds: lit. 'the sharp points of potsherds'. Commentators cite a passage from Aelian (*De natura animalium*, x. 24) in which the same comparison of the scales of the crocodile, but of the back, with potsherds is made.
threshing sledge: The word means 'sharp' and in Isa. 41.15 it stands with 'threshing sledge' to describe it, while in Isa. 28.27 and Am. 1.3 it stands alone, as here, to denote the threshing sledge. This consisted of two boards studded on the underside with sharp pieces of stone. Here it is said that when the crocodile has lain on the ground it leaves marks similar to those left by the threshing sledge. Guillaume (loc. cit., p. 126) renders the verb 'leaves imprints', adducing an Arabic cognate. Davidson says that the belly scales of the crocodile, though smoother than those on the back, are still sharp, especially under the tail. Duhm objects that the underside is smooth, and emends the line to read 'a goad and a pickaxe against him are as mud'. M.T. is to be preferred!
31f. We now have the evidences of Leviathan's motion in the water, which he churns up to a foam.
boil: the word used in 30.27.
pot: an ordinary household utensil, the word used in Jer. 1.13.
pot of ointment: the point of the comparison is differently understood by commentators. It is thought to be the foam on the top of the boiling ingredients of the unguent, or the foam created as the perfumer beats the ingredients together. Many commentators refer to the musk-like smell of the crocodile as having suggested the comparison.
32. he leaves a shining wake: lit. 'he lights a path'. The white foam he leaves behind him as he swiftly goes through the water has the appearance of a path. M. Dahood (*EThL*, XLIV, 1968, p. 36) connects *'aḥᵃrāyw* ('behind him') with the root *nḥr* and renders 'with his snout he lights up his path', but this does not seem a sufficiently notable improvement to warrant the creation of a new Hebrew word out of a common one.
33f. Peerless and without fear, Leviathan is the king of beasts and feared by all.
34. He beholds: with very slight changes many scholars read '(everything

he is king over all the sons of pride.'

42 Then Job answered the LORD:
² 'I know that thou canst do all things,
and that no purpose of thine can be thwarted.

. . .) fears him', which provides a better contrast to the previous line. He knows
no fear, but he inspires it.
sons of pride: i.e. the proud beasts; cf. 28.8 where the same phrase occurs.

JOB'S ANSWER TO THE DIVINE CHALLENGE CONTINUED 42.1-6

With the removal of the second speech of Yahweh as secondary these verses
connect with 40.4f. and continue Job's response to Yahweh in submission and
surrender. He has not only realized his folly in passing judgment on things that
were beyond his understanding. He has found the answer to his problem. For at
bottom this was not a problem of theodicy, but a problem of fellowship. He has
not learned the cause of his sufferings or the explanation of the apparent injustices
in the world, but he has found God again. For hitherto he, no less than his
friends, had believed that his sufferings meant that God had cast him off and that
he was isolated from him who had been his friend in days gone by. But now God
had come to him and spoken to him, and he knew that he could have fellowship
with God even in his sufferings. Therefore Job declares that he has found a new
understanding of God, compared with which his former knowledge was but as
the knowledge of rumour compared with sight. This is the climax of the book,
as we should expect to find at the end of the poetic portion, for which the
Prologue and Epilogue are but the setting.

42.2. purpose: cf. on 17.11. *AV* 'no thought can be withholden from thee' is
unsatisfactory. The meaning is that the realization of no purpose of God can be
withheld from him (cf. Gen. 17.11, where the same verb is used). Job recognizes
that the power of God matches his will. This would seem to go no further than
he had acknowledged all along. For his complaint had been against the will rather
than the power of God. The injustice of God, which he had affirmed, had not
been traced to God's inability to execute justice, but to his indifference to moral
issues. Yet there is perhaps implied the recognition that Job did not fathom all
the purposes of God, and the acknowledgement of the inscrutability of the
wisdom as well as the omnipotence of God. Davidson says: 'His confession
corresponds to the Almighty's address to him. That address did not insist on any
one Divine attribute, but rather presented God in the whole circle of His attributes, power and wisdom but also goodness, for He refreshes the thirsty ground
where no man is, He feeds the ravens, and presides over the birth-pangs of the
goats of the rock; and His omnipotence goes hand in hand with His moral rule.

³ "Who is this that hides counsel without knowledge?"
  Therefore I have uttered what I did not understand,
    things too wonderful for me, which I did not know.
⁴ "Hear, and I will speak;
    I will question you, and you declare to me."
⁵ I had heard of thee by the hearing of the ear,
    but now my eye sees thee;
⁶ therefore I despise myself,
    and repent in dust and ashes.'

The Divine nature is not a segment but a circle. Any one Divine attribute implies all others. Omnipotence cannot exist apart from righteousness.'

3. The first line is a variant of 38.2, which most editors regard as a marginal note here, though S. R. Driver thought it might be original, being cited for the purpose of admitting the justice of its implied rebuke (cf. also Delitzsch and Zöckler); similarly Kissane.

4. This verse repeats with slight variations 33.31 and 38.3; 40.7. Again most editors delete as a marginal gloss. It cannot, in any case, be regarded as what Job is now saying to God, but at best as reminiscence of what God has said to him.

5f. These verses terminate the main part of the book, devoted to discussion, and they give the conclusions of the matter. Job is no longer tortured with doubts and blasphemous complaints, but lifted to a new plane of peace. His intellectual problem is unsolved, for he has transcended it. He does not simply resign himself passively to the impossibility of a solution, but yields himself in active reverence to find peace in the living presence of the God he thought he had lost. His restless spirit found rest when he rested in God.

my eye sees thee: no physical vision is implied, but an experience of God that was real and personal. The hope of 19.27 has been realized, but not after death. Instead it has come in an experience which can continue in suffering or in prosperity, bringing the truest bliss because it brings God. 'This mystical solution', says Peake, 'is the most precious thing the book has to offer us'. Theodicy is transcended in religion.

6. Job's repentance is not of any sin which had brought his suffering on him, such as the friends had called for. It was of the things he had said in his ignorance in the course of the debate.

despise myself: the object 'myself' is not expressed, and some editors supply 'what I have said' or the like. Pope observes that the object need not be expressed when it is to be found in the context and compares 7.16 where the same verb has no object in the Hebrew. Whether Job is despising himself for the things he has said or recanting the things he has said (so L. J. Kuyper, *VT*, IX, 1959, pp. 91ff.) does not need to be decided, since the one would involve the other. Hoffmann

⁷ After the LORD had spoken these words to Job, the LORD said to Eli′phaz the Te′manite: 'My wrath is kindled against you and

---

would derive the word from another root and renders 'I despair', but this is not the mood of Job now that he has found God anew.

EPILOGUE 42.7–17

The Epilogue has been held by many to mar the book, since it is said to give the case away to the friends. Here Job's prosperity is restored, and righteousness finds its reward in happiness, as the friends had said it always did, and as Job had maintained it should. But this seems to miss the point completely. Job's sufferings, as we are told in the Prologue, though Job could not know it and is never told, were to see if his righteousness rested on more than self-interest. Job had come through that test successfully, and the Satan's test has proved him entirely wrong on the issue that was being tried. In the Epilogue God's verdict is clearly expressed, and the discredited Satan has betaken himself from the scene. The trial is concluded when the verdict is given, and since the form of the trial was the sufferings of Job, those sufferings must cease. The Epilogue is demanded by the artistry of the book, and without it the work would be seriously incomplete. The restoration of Job's prosperity was not the reward of his piety, but the indication that the trial was over. Any judge who left a defendant to languish in prison after he had been declared innocent would be condemned as iniquitous, and if Job's trials had continued after he was acquitted it would have been similarly iniquitous. The author recognized that the cause of human suffering cannot be deduced by man, and in the case of Job says that it was to vindicate God's trust in him. But if the sufferings were now continued, they would no longer be for that purpose, but would merely be the expression of God's arbitrary malice, which the author was less interested to maintain than some of his critics. Hence the *status quo* had to be restored. Job's children could not be restored to him, but others were given to take their place. This was not to suggest that the loss could really be so lightly made good, but the best that could be done in the conditions created by the setting of the trial. Material prosperity could be restored, and was restored as the fitting end of the story. Job is prosperous at the end, not because he is righteous, but because he was prosperous at the beginning. The Epilogue falls into two parts: The Lord's censure of the friends and vindication of Job (verses 7–9); Job's fortunes restored (verses 10–17).

THE LORD'S CENSURE OF THE FRIENDS AND VINDICATION OF JOB 42.7–9

The friends are rebuked and bidden to offer a sacrifice and ask Job to intercede for them. Because Job is righteous his intercession will avail.

7. to Eliphaz: Eliphaz, as probably the oldest of the friends, is addressed, but the message is for all the friends (cf. verse 9).

against your two friends; for you have not spoken of me what is right, as my servant Job has. ⁸ Now therefore take seven bulls and seven rams, and go to my servant Job, and offer up for yourselves a burnt offering; and my servant Job shall pray for you, for I will accept his prayer not to deal with you according to your folly; for you have not spoken of me what is right, as my servant Job has.' ⁹ So Eli'phaz the Te'manite and Bildad the Shuhite and Zophar the Na'amathite went and did what the LORD had told them; and the LORD accepted Job's prayer.

---

of me what is right: God is concerned only with what has been said about him. The friends had said many true things about God, and Job had said many wrong things, for which he had been condemned in the Divine speech. Had Job not just repented of things he had said, and confessed that they were wrong? But the friends had maintained that merit and experience were invariably and manifestly matched, while Job had declared that they certainly were not. In this Job was right, though he had drawn wrong deductions from it; but the friends were certainly wrong, as the *OT* again and again makes clear. Abel was killed by his brother and Naboth judicially murdered at Jezebel's instigation, in neither case as the just penalty for their wickedness. Prophets no less than Job declaimed against the injustice they saw in human affairs. More particularly the friends had declared that Job's sufferings proved that he had offended against God to bring them on himself, and this was not a right thing to say about God. On the other hand Job had consistently maintained that he had not by sin called down this punishment from God, and this was a right thing to say about God. Since the Epilogue was demanded by the Prologue, so its focal point should be the subject of the trial, and on that the friends had spoken wrongly and Job rightly.

my servant Job: cf. 1.8; 2.3.

8. burnt offering: cf. on 1.5. The sacrifice was a large one; cf. Num. 23.1ff. **Job shall pray for you:** the value of intercessory prayer is often recognized in the Bible; cf. Gen. 18.23ff.; 20.7; Exod. 8.30; 32.11ff., 32; Num. 14.13ff.; 21.7; Dt. 9.20; 1 Sam. 7.5, 8f.; 12.19, 23; Isa. 53.12; Jer. 37.3; Am. 7.2f., 5f.

9. Elihu is unmentioned.

JOB'S FORTUNES RESTORED 42.10–17

His possessions are doubled, and his friends bring presents to him. Children equal in number to those he had lost are born to him, and he dies in a happy old age. Curiously, nothing is said of his physical restoration of health, though this is to be inferred.

10 And the LORD restored the fortunes of Job, when he had prayed for his friends; and the LORD gave Job twice as much as he had before. 11 Then came to him all his brothers and sisters and all who had known him before, and ate bread with him in his house; and they showed him sympathy and comforted him for all the evil that the LORD had brought upon him; and each of them gave him a piece of money and a ring of gold. 12And the LORD blessed the latter days of Job more than his beginning; and he had fourteen thousand sheep, six thousand camels, a thousand yoke of oxen, and a thousand she-asses. 13 He had also seven sons and three daughters. 14And he called the name of the first Jemi'mah; and the name of the second Kezi'ah; and the name of the third Ker'en-hap'puch. 15And in all

---

10. **restored the fortunes:** *AV* and *RV* 'turned the captivity'. This much discussed phrase, elsewhere used of the nation cannot well have anything to do with 'captivity' or 'exile' here, and its meaning must be as *RSV*. For discussions of the form and meaning of the words cf. E. Preussen, *ZAW*, xv, 1895, pp. 1ff.; A. Kuenen, *ThT*, vii, 1873, pp. 519ff.; E. L. Dietrich, *BZAW*, xl, 1925; E. Baumann, *ZAW*, N.F., vi, 1929, pp. 17ff.; N. Schlögl, *WZKM*, xxxviii, 1932, pp. 68ff.; R. Borger, *ZAW*, N.F., xxv, 1954, pp. 315f.

11. **that the LORD had brought upon him:** Batten (*AThR*, xv, 1933, p. 127) observes that this 'ignores and probably excludes the Satan stories of the prologue'. But how could Job's friends, any more than Job himself, know anything of the scene in heaven? The author is more self-consistent than his critics would have him be.

a piece of money: Heb. *ḳeśîṭāh*. This was a piece of uncoined silver, mentioned in Gen. 33.19; Jos. 24.32, and therefore appropriately used in a story set in the patriarchal age. Coined money was not made until the sixth century B.C.

a ring of gold: worn by ladies in the nose (cf. Gen. 24.47; Isa. 3.21; cf. also Prov. 11.22), and by men and women in the ears (Gen. 35.4; Exod. 32.2f.; Jg. 8.24ff.). Abraham's servant carried a ring as a gift when he went to seek a wife for Isaac (Gen. 24.22).

12. Cf. 1.3. The numbers here are precisely double.

13. **seven sons:** the form of the word for 'seven' is unusual, and as Targ. has 'fourteen' (so also Rashi) it has been thought that the unusual form meant 'twice seven' (so Ehrlich, Dhorme, Robin, Steinmann). But Peake well observes that it is a fine trait that the number of children remains the same.

14. **Jemimah** = 'dove'; **Keziah** = 'cassia' (Ps. 45.8 (M.T. 9)); **Keren-happuch** = 'horn of eye-paint' (i.e. a dark mineral powder used on the edges of eyelids to mark them out conspicuously; cf. 2 Kg. 9.30 (Jezebel)).

the land there were no women so fair as Job's daughters; and their father gave them inheritance among their brothers. ¹⁶ And after this Job lived a hundred and forty years, and saw his sons and his sons' sons, four generations. ¹⁷ And Job died, an old man, and full of days.

---

15. gave them inheritance: according to Israelite law daughters were entitled to inherit when there was no male heir (Num. 27.1ff.). This does not necessarily mean that a father could not will part of his property to his daughters, or present it to them during his lifetime. It is clearly mentioned as something unusual here, marking Job's daughters as remarkable not only in their fairness but also in their fortune.

16. a hundred and forty years: cf. Gen. 50.22f.
four generations: something appears to have fallen out of the text, since only three are mentioned.

17. LXX adds at the end of the verse a note saying that Job will share in the resurrection of the dead, and a long additional note, on the authority of 'the Syriac book', giving some purported traditional information about Job and his kindred.

Index

Abaddon, 217, 255
Abel, 18, 279, 344
Abraham, 40, 345
Adam, 39, 53, 123, 259f.
Aelian, 340
Aeschylus, 5
Africa, 198, 331
Afterlife, 21, 46, 70, 129, 171, 174
Akkadian, 40, 54, 74, 120, 137, 144,
    158, 163, 171f., 177, 181f., 187,
    189, 211, 218, 272, 323, 330
Alalakh, 47
Albright, W. F., 40, 44, 86, 92, 219,
    239, 299, 323
Aldebaran, 92
Alfrink, B., 192
'Aliy, 299, 301
Almighty; see Shaddai
Alt, A., 61
Anacrusis, 24, 114, 120
Angels, 31, 55, 57, 90, 136, 215
Anthropomorphism, 83, 85
Apocrypha, 6
Apollyon, 217
'Aqaba, 73
Aquila, 92, 117, 130, 230, 271, 301,
    336, 339
Arabia, 28, 40, 198, 202, 207, 228
Arabic, Arabisms, 23, 26, 29, 36, 46,
    49, 60, 69, 78, 81f., 85, 91, 98,
    101, 105, 108, 111f., 114, 117,
    119f., 122, 129f., 135f., 137, 139f.,
    144, 146, 148, 152f., 157f., 159,
    161f., 166f., 170f., 177, 180, 185,
    189, 197, 199, 235, 237, 239, 243,
    247f., 249, 257, 267f., 272, 275,
    282, 285f., 290, 296, 299f., 301,
    303f., 307, 311, 315f., 317, 319,
    321f., 323f., 328f., 331, 333, 339f.
Arabic Version of Sa'adia, 68, 87, 141,
    338

Aram, 28, 34
Aramaic, Aramaisms, 22f., 59, 65, 69,
    83, 86f., 108, 118, 123, 135, 150,
    171, 189, 208, 242f., 244, 257,
    259, 265, 286, 291, 296f., 302f.,
    307, 319, 325, 329
Arcturus, 92
Aryan, 304
Ascending enumeration, 64
Ashurbanipal, 333
Assyria, 258, 319, 333
Assyrian texts, 47
Atlas, 219
Atonement, Day of, 36
Augustine, 39
Aurochs, 319
Aurora Borealis, 307, 316
Autumn, 235
Avenger of blood, 172
Azariah, 48

Baal, 92, 179, 218, 307
Babylon, 79f., 93
Babylonian Wisdom, 6
Ball, C. J., 38, 41, 44, 46, 48, 51f., 54,
    56f., 58f., 60f., 62f., 65, 68f., 70f.,
    74f., 76f., 78f., 80f., 82, 84f., 87f.,
    90f., 93f., 96, 99f., 101f., 103f.,
    105, 107f., 109, 112, 115f., 117,
    119, 123, 125f., 127f., 130f., 132,
    135f., 137f., 139f., 142, 152, 155,
    157f., 159, 161f., 163f., 165f.,
    168, 171, 173, 175, 185, 191f.,
    196, 199, 200f., 206f., 212f., 215,
    221, 230, 234, 239, 241f., 244,
    251, 260, 264, 273, 277, 281,
    283f., 285, 297, 321, 329f.
Bar-Hebraeus, 92
Barachel, 263
Barton, G. A., 204, 221, 277
Batten, L. W., 17, 345